DEPENDENCY THEORY AFTER FIFTY YEARS

Studies in Critical Social Sciences Book Series

Haymarket Books is proud to be working with Brill Academic Publishers (www.brill.nl) to republish the *Studies in Critical Social Sciences* book series in paperback editions. This peer-reviewed book series offers insights into our current reality by exploring the content and consequences of power relationships under capitalism, and by considering the spaces of opposition and resistance to these changes that have been defining our new age. Our full catalog of *SCSS* volumes can be viewed at https://www.haymarketbooks .org/series_collections/4-studies-in-critical-social-sciences.

DEPENDENCY THEORY AFTER FIFTY YEARS

The Continuing Relevance of Latin American Critical Thought

CLAUDIO KATZ

TRANSLATED BY
STANLEY MALINOWITZ

Haymarket Books
Chicago, IL

First published in 2022 by Brill Academic Publishers, The Netherlands
© 2022 Koninklijke Brill NV, Leiden, The Netherlands

Published in paperback in 2023 by
Haymarket Books
P.O. Box 180165
Chicago, IL 60618
773-583-7884
www.haymarketbooks.org

ISBN: 978-1-64259-813-1

Distributed to the trade in the US through Consortium Book Sales and
Distribution (www.cbsd.com) and internationally through Ingram Publisher
Services International (www.ingramcontent.com).

This book was published with the generous support of Lannan Foundation and
Wallace Action Fund.

Special discounts are available for bulk purchases by organizations and
institutions. Please call 773-583-7884 or email info@haymarketbooks.org for more
information.

Cover design by Jamie Kerry and Ragina Johnson.

Printed in the United States.

10 9 8 7 6 5 4 3 2 1

Library of Congress Cataloging-in-Publication data is available.

Contents

Prologue   XI

PART 1
Background

1   **Marx and the Periphery**   3
    1   Cosmopolitan Socialism   3
    2   Rebellions and Rethinking   4
    3   Slavery and Oppression   5
    4   Democracies and Communes   6
    5   A New Paradigm   7
    6   Convergence and Cleavages   8
    7   Exogenous and Endogenous Causes   10
    8   Liberal Interpretations   12
    9   Varieties of Eurocentrism   13
    10   People without History   14
    11   Nations and Nationalism   16
    12   State and Progress   18
    13   Legacies   19

2   **Underdevelopment in the Classical Marxists**   21
    1   Justifications for Colonialism   22
    2   The Revolutionary Position   23
    3   Rights to Self-Determination   24
    4   Pillars of Anti-Imperialism   26
    5   Uneven Development   27
    6   Stages and Imperialism   29
    7   The Function of the Periphery   30
    8   Accumulation by Dispossession   33
    9   Uneven and Combined Development   34
    10   Challenges and Extensions   36
    11   Enduring Concepts   37

3   **Center and Periphery in Postwar Marxism**   38
    1   Deindustrialization and Surplus   38
    2   Stagnation and Domination   39
    3   Polemics with Liberalism   40

4   Amin's Five Theses   42
5   World Value and Polarization   43
6   Unequal Exchange   45
7   Dependency and Socialism   46
8   Collective Imperialism   48
9   Mandel's Perspective   49
10   Bifurcations and Neutralizations   51
11   Imbalances and Fluctuations   52
12   Socialist Convergences   54

PART 2
Development

4   **The Rise of Dependency Theories**   59
1   Socialism and Liberalism   59
2   Developmentalism and Marxism   60
3   The New Categories   62
4   Subimperialism and the National Bourgeoisie   64
5   Theories and Particularities   65
6   The Metropolis-Satellite Perspective   66
7   Two Different Approaches   68
8   Development and Dependency   70
9   Theoretical Confusion   71
10   An Illuminating Debate   72
11   Socio-liberal Regression   73

5   **Critiques and Convergences**   76
1   Functionalism without Subjects   76
2   Mechanical Exogenism   77
3   Problems of Pan-Capitalism   78
4   Methodological Singularity?   80
5   Perspectives on 'Popular Unity' in Chile   81
6   Endogenism: Traditional and Transformed   82
7   Agreement against Post-Marxism   84
8   Return to Dependency   85
9   The Opposite Path   86
10   Theoretical Synthesis   87
11   Methodological Convergence   88
12   Assessments and Declines   90

6   **Dependency and World-System Theory**   93
     1   Cycles and Hegemonies   93
     2   Orders and Hierarchies   94
     3   Relationship to Dependency Theory   96
     4   Convergences and Separations   97
     5   Convergent Concepts   98
     6   Systems or Modes of Production?   100
     7   Terminal Crises and Social Subjects   102
     8   Two Views on Long Cycles   103
     9   Discrepancies on Socialism   104
     10   Anti-imperialism and National Traditions   105
     11   Only Now Is It Possible?   107
     12   Political Strategies   108

7   **Three Stages of the Metropolis-Satellite Perspective**   110
     1   Variety of Approaches   110
     2   Controversies over Colonization   111
     3   More Elaborate Answers   112
     4   Commercial Capitalism   113
     5   Political Simplifications   115
     6   The Turn toward World-System Theory   116
     7   Debates over the Proletariat   117
     8   Long Transitions   118
     9   The Missing Subject   119
     10   Debates over the East   121
     11   Problems with 'Asia-Centrism'   122
     12   Misunderstanding Capitalism   123
     13   Contemporary Influences   124
     14   No Response to Dependency   125

8   **Anti-dependency Arguments**   127
     1   Reformulating the Same Approach   127
     2   Interdependence?   128
     3   Simplified Comparisons   129
     4   Stagnationism?   131
     5   Monopolies and the Law of Value   132
     6   Underdevelopment as a Simple Fact   133
     7   Classifications and Examples   134
     8   Argentina as a Developed Country?   135
     9   Political Challenges   137

10   Marx, Lenin, Luxemburg   139
11   Mythical Proletariat   141
12   Globalist Socialism   143

PART 3
Concepts

9   **Subimperialism I**
      Review of a Concept   149
      1   Foundations and Objections   149
      2   Evaluation of a Concept   150
      3   Another Context   152
      4   Economic Interpretations   153
      5   Reformulation of a Status   154
      6   Controversial Extensions   156
      7   Misunderstanding a Category   157
      8   Comparison with Semi-Colony   158
      9   Dogmatic Inconsistencies   160

10   **Subimperialism II**
      Current Application   163
      1   The Main Prototype   163
      2   An Adventurous Experiment   164
      3   An Uncertain Reconstitution   166
      4   Co-imperial Appendages   167
      5   Contrasting Situations   168
      6   Peculiarities of Another Power   170
      7   Empire in Formation   171
      8   Another Variant in Formation   172
      9   Is Brazil Subimperial Today?   174
      10   Comparisons with Other Cases   176
      11   Controversies over Application   177
      12   Reconsideration and Usefulness   178

11   **Insights and Problems of the Super-exploitation Concept**   180
      1   Logic and Interpretation   180
      2   Compatible Objections   181
      3   Low Value of Labor Power   182
      4   Statistical Irresolution   183
      5   The Centrality of Transfers   185

6   Dependency without Super-Exploitation   186
7   Variety of Uses   187
8   Super-exploitation with and without Marx   188
9   Absence of Fordism   189
10   Where Is Exploitation Greater?   190
11   Current Applications   191
12   A Tentative Model   193
13   Controversies over the Extension of Super-Exploitation   195

12   **Similarities and Differences with the Age of Marini**   198
1   Productive Globalization   198
2   Exploitation and Industrial Remodeling   199
3   The Crisis of Capitalism   200
4   Imperial Reformulations   202
5   The Collapse of the USSR and the Rise of China   203
6   Polarities and Neutralizations   204
7   Diverse Inequalities   205
8   Internationalization without a Political Counterpart   206
9   Problems of Transnationalism   207
10   Semi-peripheral Reordering   208
11   Extent of Subimperialism   210
12   Global South?   211
13   Renewing Dependency Theory   213

13   **The Dependent Cycle Forty Years Later**   214
1   Tensions and Crises   214
2   Industrial Regression, Obstruction to Consumption   215
3   Effects of Extractivism   217
4   Cycle and Crisis   218
5   The Contrast with Korea   219
6   Other Interpretations   221
7   Other Comparisons   223
8   Relation with China   224
9   Geopolitics, Classes, Governments   226
10   Determinants of Dependency   228
11   Reasons for Reconsideration   229

14   **Dependency and the Theory of Value**   232
1   Causes of Unequal Exchange   232
2   The Extent of Globalization   233
3   Productive Globalization   234

4   The Meaning of Intensified Labor   236
5   Monopoly and the Duality of Value   237
6   Misunderstanding Underdevelopment   239
7   Raw Material Cycles   240
8   The Reintroduction of Rent   241
9   Imperialist Rents   243
10   International Rent   244
11   Forced Incompatibilities   245
12   The Contrast with Venezuela   247
13   Totalizing Visions   248

Epilogue   249

References   253
Index   275

Prologue

This book[1] proposes a reconsideration of dependency theory, which achieved great prestige in the 1970s, then faced a decline, and began to reemerge in the current period. Taking stock of this approach requires clarification of, above all, its internal divisions. At its origin, its spectrum included the three main schools of Latin American economic thought. In the radicalized climate of the times, different types of Marxism, liberalism, and developmentalism shared the same self-denomination, creating an ephemeral kinship between opposing approaches.

Only the Marxist variant endured and developed a school of thought consistent with the pillars of dependency theory. Ruy Mauro Marini, Theotônio Dos Santos, and Vania Bambirra were its main exponents. They first reformulated old interpretations of underdevelopment focused on imperialist confiscation of the resources of the periphery, then combined this legacy with certain peculiarities of Latin America to explain dependent economic reproduction and the subordinate international insertion of the region.

A completely opposite trajectory was followed by the variant inspired by Fernando Henrique Cardoso. It began with a Weberian view and conceived of dependency in restrictive political terms. After depicting the different levels of autonomy of regions and countries in Latin America, it rejected the basic conflict between dependency and development. Cardoso posited a path to development associated with transnational corporations, and later incorporated all the dogmas of neoliberalism. His earlier affinity for modernization theories helps to understand the right-wing profile he adopted as head of state of Brazil – there was continuity of thought, not just improvisation, in the man who burned all his writings in order to occupy the presidential palace.

The third variant of dependentism was the godchild of ECLAC (U.N. Economic Commission for Latin America and the Caribbean), and represented the most radicalized stage of developmentalism in Latin America. This variant had many exponents, but few unifying figures. It promoted a combination of dependentism and industrialism, promoted state regulation of the economy, and supported agrarian reform proposals. However, like its liberal adversaries, it later dropped its dependentist conceptual framework, which has been completely associated with Marxism since the 1980s.

---

1 Based on, and an update of, the original: Claudio Katz, 2018, *La teoría de la dependencia, 50 años después*, Buenos Aires: Batalla de Ideas Ediciones.

Some commentators claim that dependency theory lost influence because of its adherence to 'deterministic Marxism', but its main exponents reasoned in the Marxist tradition of ascribing to the economy only a fundamental and conditioning role in relation to social struggles and political outcomes. Marini and Dos Santos even downplayed their status as economists, and were more committed to political militancy than to university teaching.

Political action motivated, oriented, and defined the profile of dependentist ideas in close harmony with the Cuban revolution, without which the theory would not have existed in the form that it did. What determined the rise and fall of its tenets was the course of the revolution and of the project of forging socialism in Latin America. Dependency theory conceptualized that aspiration and promoted an anti-capitalist program. Along those lines, an explanation must be sought for the paradoxical retreat of the theory at a time when its postulates were more relevant than ever. While Latin America is more affected by dependency than forty years ago, the approach that most clarifies those bonds carries less weight than in the past. The reasons are to be found in developments on the political level.

Three major events ended the cycle that began with the Cuban revolution: first, the defeat of the guerrilla movements that sought to extend the Cuban transformation to the entire region; second, the dramatic end to the Popular Unity government in Chile; and finally, the revolutionary rebirth in Nicaragua being cut short with the electoral defeat of the Sandinistas. These developments allowed the expansion of neoliberalism, which was barely contained by the progressive cycle of the last decade. The new progressive governments were not enough of an obstacle to halt the conservative restoration in progress. The dependentist tradition reappeared at various times and under various circumstances in this period, but the regional context was mostly unfavorable to that project.

When these political factors are omitted, assessments of dependency theory incur in all kinds of arbitrariness. One example of these errors is to assume that dependentism declined because of its inability to foresee the takeoff of Southeast Asia. A number of analysts espouse this diagnosis based on failures of prediction. But the industrialization of the East was not anticipated by any school of thought. The sad omission of dependentism would also be valid for neoclassical and heterodox thinkers. In these cases, the failure has been even greater, since they didn't even provide a basic explanation of growth rooted in the exploitation of wage-earners. Dependentism at least described how large corporations began to shift to Southeast Asia in order to profit from the low cost and discipline of the labor force, also demonstrating that dependentism did not share any version of the stagnation hypothesis.

Our book is focused on the path followed by Marxist authors. It first examines the observations on the topic by the author of *Capital* himself, analyzing why Marx moved from his youthful cosmopolitan views to direct criticism of colonialism and a significant reevaluation of the national struggle. It also examines the views of Lenin, Trotsky, and Rosa Luxembourg on the impact of primitive accumulation and of unequal and combined development in the periphery. The theories of Paul Sweezy, Ernest Mandel, and the postwar Marxists with regard to of the drainage of resources from the less-developed countries are reviewed.

Marxist dependency theory transformed this conceptual baggage into a systematic approach, oriented toward elucidating the functioning of the underdeveloped economies. Debates over the scope of this focus included methodological controversies about the status of the proposed laws. But the status of the theory itself was later reformulated in terms of paradigm, perspective, or research program. In any of these senses, it formed a school of thought with a solid foundation for interpreting the economic backwardness of Latin America.

We also analyze the fruitful encounter of dependency theory with Immanuel Wallerstein's world-system theory, which broadened the horizons of both approaches and made it possible to explore new notions of the semi-periphery in studying intermediate formations. There were also areas of discrepancies between the two approaches. Marini and Dos Santos were classical Marxists whose reasoning did not include a predetermined end to capitalism.

In another section, we evaluate the trajectory followed by André Gunder Frank, whose initial consecration as a great propagator of dependency theory lost weight with his early abandonment of that focus. He first counterposed certain world-system ideas to the dependency approach and later stressed the distance between them, postulating a controversial theory of millennial capitalism centered on China. In the text, we analyze the connections between that evolution and his metropolis-satellite model.

We examine in more detail the figure of Agustín Cueva, who, after launching criticisms, converged with dependentism. This convergence produced a substantial enrichment of the paradigm. Cueva questioned the exaggeratedly exogenous interpretations of underdevelopment as an effect exclusively of dependency. Marini objected, on the other hand, to the inverse unilateralism of the solely endogenous explanations. They debated the causes of regional backwardness, highlighting the effects of the *latifundio* and of imperial extraction. The complementarity of the two postures became clear in their mutual confrontation with Cardoso.

This convergence coincided with changes on the political stage. Cueva and Marini disagreed on socialist strategy, maintaining opposing affinities for projects of gradual transitions to socialism on the one hand, and uninterrupted processes of radicalization on the other. But in the 1980s, this disagreement took a back seat to the mutual battle against the social-democratic adaptation to the neoliberal turn. That new context modified all the dividing lines on the dependentist spectrum. Cueva not only stayed closer to that approach than Frank, but also contributed more accurate historiographic conceptions on the origins of capitalism in Latin America.

Cueva's complementarity with Marini also derives from the types of problems they studied. He focused his analysis on countries like Ecuador, Bolivia, and Peru that were still dominated by questions of the peasantry and the *latifundio*. Marini examined the change of course of a society like that of Brazil, already marked by the imbalances of industrialization. They evaluated the two different contexts with the same logic of dependency. Their convergence made it possible to reconsider that theory while going beyond simple description or ritual vindications. The synthesis of Cueva with Marini provides solid foundations for an approach that is comprehensive and that challenges liberalism and developmentalism. Around this foundation, the great theoretical divergences of the past and present are resolved.

Dependency theory went beyond Latin America and was enriched by significant extra-regional writings. The work of Samir Amin constitutes the most outstanding contribution, dealing with the same topics from the viewpoint of Europe, Asia, and Africa and with a more global outlook. He examined the problems of the old Eastern societies subjected to colonialism, rather than the New World captured by this form of domination. Thus, his analysis of tributary formations is very different from the classical controversy over feudalism and colonial capitalism. Like his Latin American colleagues, Amin combined historical and economic approaches, with great attention to leftist political sources. His thinking was especially motivated by the convergence of revolutionary nationalism with socialism in different parts of the Third World.

In this book, we analyze the economic categories of dependency theory more closely than the political ones. We plan to address this second level in a study of Latin American Marxism, which is why Marini occupies a more prominent role in this book than some other figures, such as the recently deceased Dos Santos. Theotônio worked within a tradition of approaches closer to Lenin than to the abstract models of *Capital*. Thus, he entered into detailed reflections on the state, the ruling classes, and the bureaucracy, which in his later work took on controversial connotations.

The economic categories of dependentism are reviewed in this text in light of contemporary reality. Thus, the analysis of super-exploitation includes the reconsideration that Marini faced in highlighting how the globalization of capitalism altered the singularity of the concept in referring exclusively to the periphery. This reformulation opens up a debate between those of us who rethink the dynamics of this principle and the authors who defend the traditional formulation.

Our review of the dependent cycle provokes less polemics, but generates more questions about its current forms. It is evident that it does not operate the same way in South Korea as in Brazil. In the text, we propose some hypotheses regarding these differences, which radically bifurcate the trajectories of the ascending and descending intermediate economies.

Since this divergence is not determined exclusively be economic conditions, we reevaluate the concept of subimperialism, which has reappeared in recent debates about the BRICS. It is our understanding that the category has more geopolitical than economic significance, and that it clarifies the role of intermediate powers with the capacity for military action. It conforms to the profile adopted by Turkey and India more than to Brazil or South Africa. These characterizations lead us to also debate the current meaning of imperialism, in its traditional, collective, and emergent forms.

Finally, we address the complex relationship between dependentism and the theory of value. Interest in this relationship is rooted in a reconsideration of the debates on unequal exchange in light of the current globalization of production. We draw especially upon research on how surplus value is transferred to corporations located at the top of the value chain. The intuition of dependentism about the *maquilas* is now corroborated by the phenomenon of global manufacturing networks. As the meaning of rent has also been reconsidered, we analyze a way of integrating this category into dependency theory.

This book was prepared with readings and presentations complemented by intense discussions with followers and opponents of dependentism. The passion of those debates has provided a good thermometer of the reactions this theory provokes. I want to express my appreciation to all the participants in these debates, but especially to Gabriela Roffinelli, Julio Fabris, Adrián Piva, Leandro Morgenfield, and Facundo Lastra, who commented on the first versions of each chapter. Our revision of super-exploitation has already generated replies and arguments. In these discussions we should be careful not to repeat the extreme clashes between followers of the same approach.

Dependency theory is not a museum piece. It contributes a key foundation for understanding the underdevelopment of the periphery. However, its original formulation is insufficient to reach this understanding. It requires renovation to reconstitute itself as an explanatory thesis of dependent capitalism. The objective of this book is to suggest pathways toward this reinvention.

PART 1

Background

∴

CHAPTER 1

Marx and the Periphery

It is known that Marx modified his views on underdeveloped countries. Initially, he conceived of a passive connection of these nations to the rise and fall of world capitalism. Later, he highlighted resistance to colonialism. This shift was discussed intensely in the 1970s by scholars of Marx's writings. The backdrop to this interest was enthusiasm for socialist revolutions in the periphery.

Marxists assessed the continuing gap between advanced and backward economies in the light of the intuitions expressed by the author of *Capital*. Nationalist authors criticized Marx's hostility (or indifference) toward the colonial world, while neoliberals disputed or demonized his writings. How did Marx deal with the problem of the periphery?[1]

1 Cosmopolitan Socialism

In his initial view, Marx believed the periphery would repeat the industrialization of the center as capitalism expanded to a world scale, creating un interdependent system that would facilitate accelerated routes to socialism. He thought that the dispossession of artisans and peasants would lead to a final expropriation of the expropriators. *The Communist Manifesto* presents this view. Capitalism is portrayed as a regime that tears down walls and expands its dominion from the center out to the periphery (Marx, 1967).

China is described as a barbaric society that will be modernized by colonial penetration, and India as a country stagnated by the preeminence of rural communities, mystical beliefs, and parasitical despots. It was thought that these structures would be demolished with the installation of railroads and the importation of British textiles (Marx, 1964: 30–58, 104–111). Yet unlike his contemporaries, Marx combined that analysis with strong denunciations. He pointed to the destruction of archaic economic forms while at the same time denouncing the atrocities of colonialism, and emphasizing the modernizing function of capital while objecting to the massacres perpetrated by the invaders.

---

1 In this book we do not include the debates about Marx and Bolívar, which will be addressed elsewhere.

Within this parameter he evaluated free trade. His praise of trade – which broke the isolation of old societies – was complemented by criticisms of the dramatic consequences of that expansion. This tension between praise and rejection was compatible with an expectation of rapid victories of socialism. Marx assumed that the generalization of capitalism would, in a few decades, accelerate the eradication of that system, and also expected a rapid spread of that outcome from the European center to the rest of the world.

This cosmopolitan conception of socialism presupposed an accelerated sequence of global industrialization, weakening of nations, and elimination of colonialism. It was a vision close to the proletarian internationalism of the age, which built upon the universalist utopias developed during the Enlightenment. Marx shared the humanist project of immediately transcending the nation by means of communities without borders. Unlike the radical cosmopolitanism that was a legacy of the French Revolution, it called for social equality together with universal citizenship (Lowy, 1998: 11–21).

By emphasizing that "capital has no nationality," the German revolutionary saw the globalization of bourgeois rule as a step toward the joint dissolution of nations and classes. This goal of global fraternity was highly regarded among the geographically mobile craftsmen who formed an important part of the First International (Anderson, P., 2002).

2   Rebellions and Rethinking

The Taiping Rebellion in China (1850–1864), which ended only after millions of deaths, had a big impact on Marx. He denounced British colonialism and saw that tragedy as a destructive process devoid of alternatives. He was also moved by the revolt of the sepoys in India (1857–58), which the British brutally crushed. At that point, he began to pay more attention to how the expansion of capitalism unleashed great forms of resistance among the oppressed (Marx, 1964: 139–143, 161–181).

Those uprisings changed his view. He no longer undervalued what was happening in the colonies, nor would he any more repeat that Asiatic societies were destined to copy the European pattern. The missing actor in *The Communist Manifesto* began to take form. Marx was one of the first Western thinkers to support the independence of India. But the biggest change came from the uprisings in Ireland. There he confirmed that colonial plunder destroys societies without facilitating their internal development. Marx compared England's devastation of its neighbor to the depredations by the Mongols. He saw that the rural reorganization imposed on the island was a caricature of what had been done in England – far from increasing agrarian productivity, it reinforced territorial aristocracy, expulsion of the peasants, and concentration of property.

The author of *Capital* also noticed how the English bourgeoisie blocked the rise of Irish manufacturers in order to guarantee the dominance of its own exports. In addition, capitalists took advantage of cheap labor there in order to limit the improvements of British wage-earners. Having observed the pillaging of Ireland, Marx abandoned his earlier expectation about capitalist expansion. He perceived how primitive accumulation is not the immediate prelude to processes of industrialization in a country subjected to plunder (Marx, 1964: 74–80). From this point on, he transformed his sympathy for the resistance in India and China into explicit praise for the national struggle. He extolled the Irish rebellion which, returning to old communal traditions, forced the British to militarize the island.

Marx participated intensely in campaigns to gain the adhesion of the English workers to that struggle. He understood the need to counteract the division encouraged by the capitalists between wage-workers of the two nations. He claimed that the Irish struggle contributed to reducing those tensions, and adopted the famous slogan in favor of the Fenian resistance: "A people that oppresses another cannot be free" (Barker, 2010).

The writings of 1869–70 illustrate this maturing of his thought. Marx no longer conceived of Irish independence as a result of proletarian victories in England; he now favored an inverse sequence and even considered that the elimination of national oppression was a condition for social emancipation. He highlighted the close interaction between the two processes, and recalled how, in the past, the crushing of Ireland had contributed to the failures of the revolutions against the English monarchy (Marx and Engels, 1979).

3   Slavery and Oppression

Marx's new understanding of the convergences between the European proletariat and the dispossessed of the rest of the world motivated his support for the North in the Civil War in the United States (1860–65). He took up the cause of abolitionism as the British industrialists applied great pressure in favor of the South. The capitalists were supplied by cotton that was harvested by slaves, and they called on the English textile workers to preserve their employment by avoiding any participation in the American conflict. Marx denounced that blackmail and ratified the need for joint actions on both sides of the Atlantic to defeat the partnership of British exploiters with Southern planters.

That campaign also aimed to counteract the racial division within the nascent working class in the United States. Immigrant wage-workers viewed the slave as a competitor who flattened their wages. Marx encouraged pronouncements by the First International to create ties between the white workers and the oppressed Afro-Americans. The Civil War took place in a country perceived as a potential democracy of great importance. Marx believed that the liberation of the slaves and the defeat of the plantation owners would provide a tremendous example of revolutionary achievement. For those reasons, he criticized the initial timidity of Lincoln, who rejected the arming of the Blacks promoted by the radical abolitionists. These vacillations put the victory of the North in danger, even as it was superior to the Confederacy economically and militarily (Marx and Engels, 1973: 27–74, 83–171).

In this new stage, Marx celebrated rebellious processes in different parts of the world. He never doubted European primacy in the passage to the socialist future, but he emphasized the protagonism of other subjects. He praised the establishment of the radical juntas in Cádiz following the Napoleonic invasion, and portrayed the rebellions against Anglo-French colonialism in the West Indies with great sympathy.

But of greatest significance was his support of Mexico. He denounced Maximillian's expedition that occupied the country to collect debts, and supported the major democratic reforms introduced by Benito Juárez. With this conviction, he left behind his earlier justification for the appropriation of Texas by the Anglo-American colonizers (Marx and Engels, 1972: 217–292). Marx abandoned his previous view of the external liberation of the periphery, no longer assuming that changes in the world would move more rapidly than the internal maturation of non-European societies. His vision of the post-capitalist future began to include rebellions in the periphery converging with the European proletariat.

4   Democracies and Communes

This new perspective enriched Marx's approach to the democratic struggles on the Old Continent, which included demands for national self-determination for peoples subjected to the imperial monarchies of Russia and Austria. The communist theoretician was an active participant in those confrontations, and supported the unifications of Germany and Italy that the autocracies resisted. Marx encouraged the socialist radicalization of those struggles. He proclaimed the lack of nationality of the proletariat and imagined processes of popular convergence that would cross borders, but he also favored the national insurrections that weakened czarism and the Habsburgs (Munck, 2010).

Marx put the spotlight on who was resisting and how each battle arose, reasoning in terms of the actions and protagonists of the major struggles. Thus, he defended the resistance of the Hungarians against the occupying Austrians, and the bellicosity of the Poles against the Russian oppressors. He especially viewed the combat in Poland as a 'thermometer' of the European revolution. That country had lost its independence with partition between Russia, Prussia, and Austria, and was the epicenter of recurrent uprisings (1794, 1830, 1843, 1846).

Marx adopted this national aspiration as a permanent cause. He not only expressed the spontaneous solidarity that arose across the continent; he also argued with the anarchist tendencies that rejected that resistance, for both its connection to the nobility and its distance from workers' demands. When he proclaimed that "Poland must be freed in England," Marx argued against an approach that anaesthetized the internationalist conscience of the workers (Healy, 2010). The German revolutionary ascribed great weight to the independence of that country for the battle against czarism. Since he prioritized the defeat of that conservative force, he took sides against Russia in the Crimean War against the Ottoman Empire. He rejected neutralism and prioritized triumphs over the main enemy.

Based on what he observed in India, China, Ireland, and Mexico, Marx incorporated a new hypothesis about the transformational forces inside the Russian empire. He reconsidered the role of old communal forms in agriculture, which he had previously seen as simple remnants of the past. He felt they could play a progressive role, and he considered the possibility of a direct route to socialism from these collective formations (Marx and Engels, 1980: 21–65). Marx's new view of the periphery influenced his acceptance of a direct leap to post-capitalist stages, modifying his previous rejection of this possibility. What he had dismissed in 1844 as a naïve form of 'crude communism' became, thirty years later, a feasible alternative. For that reason, he extended his study of communes to other cases (India, Indonesia, Algeria).

5   A New Paradigm

In his earlier stage, Marx emphasized the objective dynamics of capitalist development as a process of absorption of previous forms of production, focusing on the role of the productive forces as the paramount determinants of the course of history. As a result, he assumed that as capitalism developed it would incorporate the periphery into the mainstream of civilization.

In his second period, Marx abandoned the idea of a passive molding of the colonial world into capitalist transformation. He considered skipping stages and pointed to active forces that could accelerate the introduction of socialism in the periphery. Kohan (1998) interprets this conceptual turn as a change in paradigm: a unilinear philosophy based on the behavior of the forces of production was replaced by a multilinear view that highlighted the transformative role of subjects. Marx's rethinking of the national-colonial question precipitated the shift.

This characterization contrasts with the traditional dichotomy between the young Marx and the mature Marx that was introduced by Althusser, which distinguishes the young 'humanist', focused on philosophical questions of alienation, from the old 'scientist' absorbed in detecting the laws of capitalism. In his treatment of the periphery, this sequence is reversed. The young thinker of the *Manifesto* paid more attention to objective processes of capitalist expansion, while the mature author of *Capital* emphasized the subjective effects of the national and social struggle. Kevin Anderson underscores this same change of direction. The rigid chronology of the absorption of the periphery to the modernization of the center was replaced by a view of open and multiple paths of historical development.

Anderson also argues that the singularities of the periphery led Marx to leave behind the strict model of adaptation of the superstructures (political, ideological, or social) to the economic base. The idea of the social context (relations of production) being shaped by economic growth (forces of production) was replaced by a view of processes that were codetermined and without preestablished direction (Anderson, 2010: 2–3, 9–10, 237–238, 244–245). Other authors claim that this pivot by Marx did not alter his original model (Sutcliffe, 2008), but the tenor of the changes would indicate substantial modifications. In 1850 Marx saw the democratic movements of China and India as simple allies of the European workers. By 1870 he already saw the independence of Ireland as a driver of the revolution in England. In 1880 he went further, as he considered that Russia shared with Europe a key place in the inauguration of socialism.

6   Convergence and Cleavages

The rudimentary viewpoint expressed by the first Marx was in tune with the immaturity of his economic thought. Thus, the Manifesto foresaw a vertiginous process of globalization that occurred only in the last century. Together with *The Poverty of Philosophy* and *Wage-Labor and Capital*, the *Manifesto* is located halfway through Marx's work. He had already developed his critique of private property, discovered the centrality of labor, modified his anthropological analysis of alienation, and grasped the utility of the materialist conception of history.

However, he had not yet gone beyond Ricardo in reformulating the theory of value with the concept of surplus value. The same qualitative corrections that Marx introduced in his views on China, Ireland, or Russia were incorporated into his economic views. In the *Manifesto*, Marx made analogies between the worker and the slave that still resembled Ricardo's 'subsistence wage'. He did not yet characterize the value of labor power as a social-historical parameter, subject to the contradictory impacts of accumulation. There were references to 'increasing misery' that would be replaced by a focus on the *relative* decline of wages. Crises were presented as effects of underconsumption, without connecting the tightening of purchasing power with the tendency for the rate of profit to fall (Katz, 1999).

These insufficiencies help us to understand the errors Marx committed in his first characterizations on Asia and Latin America. As his research on capitalism advanced, he replaced his presentation of the generic tendencies of the world market with specific analyses of accumulation on a national scale. In preparing *Capital*, Marx analyzed the English economy in detail. He studied tariffs, wages, prices, profits, interest rates, and rents, and he could perceive contrasts between development and underdevelopment. For example, he analyzed the connections between Irish backwardness and British industrial expansion, pointing out how the comparability between the central economies coexisted with increasing gaps with the rest of the world.

Marx's era (1830–1870) was marked by the emergence of several centers of accumulation (Western Europe, North America, Japan) together with a second variety of colonialism. That is why there was protectionism in the emerging economies and free trade on a world scale. In his second stage, Marx began to perceive varieties of evolution in the periphery, based on the diversity of events in the center. The British debut with industrialization, undertaken for commercial and agricultural benefits, was followed by the expansion of French manufacturing with a large role for the banks. Russia expanded its industrial structure with military means while preserving serfdom, and the United States followed an opposite model of pure capitalist takeoff.

When Marx stated that "The country that is more developed industrially only shows, to the less developed, the image of its own future," he was alluding to these types of equivalent economies. He did not extend this leveling to the periphery; he was referring to an evolution between peers or a movement toward that leveling. At this stage of his maturation, Marx not only distinguished classical industrialization with open economies (England) from late industrialization with protected structures (Germany). He also distinguished this group from the countries subordinated to the imperatives of foreign capital (China).

This characterization anticipated the later division between rising semi-peripheries and relegated peripheries. In the first group were only the economies that took part in industrialization, who created internal markets and absorbed the agricultural revolution (Bairoch, 1973: Chapters 1–2). Germany and the United States also sprouted right under the noses of England and France, as the colonial powers were not able to slow down their rivals. The periphery was explicitly excluded from these convergences. The Irish case illustrates how the colonial authorities levied high taxes on all local manufacturing activity in order to ensure the entry of English imports.

Marx matured his approach, and some researchers hold that he distinguished two types of economies: those that assimilated capitalist expansion from an inferior position ('backwards') and those that did not prosper because of their subjection to colonialism ('transplants') (Galba de Paula, 2014: 101–108, 141–143).

7   Exogenous and Endogenous Causes

Marx grasped that capitalism creates segmentations between the center and the periphery, but he did not lay out the causes of this polarization. He suggested several exogenous determinants in his critique of colonialism, and specified endogenous causes in his analysis of pre-capitalist structures, but he did not specify which of those components most impacted the global cleavage. He only noted the widening of that gap in the origin and development of capitalism.

Marx analyzed the first of these impacts in his study of the pillage carried out during primitive accumulation. He described the transfers of resources taken to generate the initial stock of money required by the system, and related how the metals taken from the colonies laid the foundation for the unfolding of European capitalism. This line of analysis was continued with studies of forced deindustrialization in Ireland and the confiscations endured by China and India (Marx, 1973: 607–650).

Marx also described enlargements of the center-periphery gap under already formed capitalism. His observations on unequal exchange illustrate that treatment. He affirmed that in the world market, the more productive labor received a higher remuneration than the less productive, reinforcing the supremacy of the economies operating with advanced techniques. However, in other equally numerous commentaries, Marx attributed the backwardness of the periphery to pre-capitalist hindrances that impede the massification of wage-labor, preserve serfdom, or broaden the use of slavery. He indicated that these archaic forms of exploitation were recreated to satisfy international demand for raw materials, increasing the rents captured by capitalist (*latifundio*), feudal (*hacienda*), and slave (plantation) landowners in Africa, Asia, and Latin America.

Marx did not specify the primacy of the colonial-exogenous or rentier-endogenous origin of underdevelopment. He merely seemed to point to a changing balance at different moments of capitalist history. Many Marxist and systems historians have emphasized one or another component. The exogeneity theorists demonstrate how Europe was fueled by the "primitive dis-accumulation" imposed on the Americas and the holocaust of slavery imposed on Africa (Amin, 2001a: 15–29). They highlight how colonialism managed to separate Europe from societies that had reached a similar level of development (Middle East, North Africa, Meso-America) and conferred primacy to Great Britain over her competitors, arguing that under comparable agricultural, state, and industrial conditions, England took the lead because of its overseas advantages (Wallerstein, 1984: 102–174; Blaut, 1994).

On the other hand, endogeneity theorists explain the underdevelopment of the periphery by the absence of agrarian transformations. They believe that colonial plunder was not relevant to the consolidation of central capitalism. They maintain that the maritime powers (Portugal, Spain, France, Holland) were weakened in this period, that the winner (England) was a late entrant, and that several successful contenders (Belgium, Switzerland, Germany, Scandinavia, Austria, Italy) avoided external battles (O'Brien, 2007). They also point out that Europe progressed by taking advantage of its self-sufficiency in raw materials, and they maintain that colonialism had adverse effects on the entrepreneurial spirit. They attribute England's advantages to a tripartite model of agrarian revolution (landowners, tenants, and wage-workers) that laid the groundwork for the manufacturing boom through demographic expansion and rural industries (Bairoch, 1999: 87–137; Meiksins Wood, 2002: 94–102).

But Marx's approach also inspired intermediate positions that illustrate how colonialism affected the origin of capitalism more than its consolidation. They claim that the initial importance of resources taken from the colonies was replaced by the supremacy of surplus profits obtained by internal processes of accumulation. This hypothesis is consistent with the shifting primacy of internal and external determinants suggested by Marx (Mandel, 1978: Chapter 2).

8   Liberal Interpretations

Liberal authors ignore Marx's dual view of the national-colonial question. They only take note of the first period, paying particular attention to his characterizations of India and omitting his later attention to Ireland. With this omission, they place the socialist theoretician in the 'expansionist' tradition that emphasizes capitalist progress and expansion. Bill Warren was the main exponent of this view, which ascribes to the initial approach in the *Manifesto* the status of a theory of development. He claims that Marx defended British colonialism in Asia for its role in dissolving its vegetative life. He also interprets Marx as approving of the economic achievements of Western colonization, contrasting these advancements with prior conditions in the periphery. But Marx never espoused these exaltations of empire, nor did he make use of linear historical counterpoints. What must be explained is the contrasting effects of capitalist expansion in Europe and the colonies, and why it generated accumulation at one pole and dis-accumulation at the other. Liberals simply do not recognize this cleavage.

The liberals claim that Marx avoided moral judgments, shied away from romanticism, and valued individualism. They believe that he especially approved of the humanist culture of industrial modernization (Warren, 1980: 7–18). Yet Marx's whole life's work was a denunciation, not a celebration, of capitalism. His horrifying descriptions of primitive accumulation, child labor, and industrial exploitation illustrate this rejection. Indeed, his initial concessions to bourgeois personalism were tempered in his later embrace of the commune. The social improvements that liberals attribute to capitalism were seen by Marx as outcomes of worker resistance. It is absurd to affirm that the communist theoretician endorsed the crimes committed by England to facilitate the establishment of capitalism in non-European societies (Warren, 1980: 39–44, 116). If Marx had been a Cecil Rhodes, insensitive to colonial suffering, he would not have promoted campaigns of solidarity with the victims of imperial plunder.

Other authors, fascinated by the market, agree with the portrayal of Marx as an enthusiastic supporter of the British occupation of India. They consider this support to be consistent with the idea of the installation of a more advanced mode of production (Sebreli, 1992: 324–327). However, this positivist reasoning ignores the human suffering that Marx recorded with close attention. He was committed to popular struggle and was not indifferent to the dramatic social consequences of capitalist development.

The liberals put their fanatical celebration of the bourgeoisie in Marx's mouth. They claim that the German revolutionary represented the ascent of that social class as being of the highest advantage for all of society (Sebreli, 1992: 24). But even in his earliest stage, Marx emphasized the other side of this process – the appearance of a proletariat that must bury the bourgeoisie to make possible the eradication of exploitation. Sebreli detaches Marx's observations on the colonial question from that anti-capitalist foundation, and therefore does not recognize how social indignation motivated Marx's research. That attitude distinguished him from his contemporaries and explains his rejection of imperial interventions. The mature Marx also objected to the illusions of free trade. Thus, instead of encouraging the internationalization of markets, he promoted cooperative association between peoples.

9   Varieties of Eurocentrism

Some nationalist authors agree with their liberal adversaries on the portrayal of Marx as an apologist for Western capitalism, and object in virulent terms to this position. They claim that this attitude led him to "look down on the non-Western peoples" and justify the use of violence for their subjection (Chavolla, 2005: 13–14, 255–261). This characterization inverts reality. A fierce opponent of capitalism is presented as a champion of the status quo, while his internationalism is identified with submission to Queen Victoria. This approach presents the pro-Ireland writings as proof of his approval of colonialism, and attributes this position to Marx's extreme Eurocentrism (Chavolla, 2005: 16, 265–269).

But Marx was in the opposing trenches to imperial figures like Kipling; he was a fighter for liberation through communist projects contrary to imperial oppression. The erroneous cosmopolitan aspirations of his youth expressed that humanistic hope for a rapid development of a world without exploiters. It makes no sense to classify this approach with imperial Eurocentrism.

Other authors claim that Marx ignored the oppression of the periphery because of his 'class reductionism'. They assume that he only inquired into social tensions, with no interest in national and racial subjection (Lvovich, 1997). But they forget that the second Marx treated class relations in a hierarchical manner, incorporating race, nationality, and ethnicity in a simultaneous questioning of exploitation and domination. This synthesis explains his defense of Ireland and Poland and his commitment to the anti-slavery cause in the U.S. Civil War.

The disparaging Eurocentrism that nationalists attribute to Marx is completely imaginary. However, another sense of that concept can be considered, as a synonym for commitment to a model of universal diffusion of the values forged on the Old Continent. This second approach assumes that Europe offered the face of the future by developing a civilization superior to that which it inherited from classical antiquity. This conception influenced the positivist profile adopted by traditional social sciences (Wallerstein, 2004: Chapter 23).

Does this more benevolent characterization of Eurocentrism apply to the Marx of the *Manifesto*? The answer is no, if we remember that the flowering of Europe includes the capitalism forged in that region. Marx was the most important critic of the system that the 'Europeanizers' idolatrized. These approaches also universalize a particular form of development, highlighting the intrinsic supremacy of Europe over all other cultures. On the contrary, the socialism that Marx promoted aimed to forge egalitarian and cooperative development among all the peoples of the world.

Certainly, the author of *Capital* was German, lived in Europe, and was imbued with Western culture, but he developed a theory that went beyond this origin. In contrast to many thinkers, he did not reason by counterposing the virtues of one civilization over another. He explained the general logic of social evolution in terms of economic (forces of production) and social (class struggle) contradictions.

Eurocentrism is a term that is also used by several Marxist authors to characterize a theoretical defect of the early Marx. In this case, the classification does not imply rejection. It indicates an error in the initial conception, conferring absolute protagonism to the European proletariat in the liberation of all the oppressed. The same classification of Eurocentrism has been used in very different senses to evaluate Marx's trajectory. Identifying his youthful mistakes is different from claiming his acceptance of colonialism. This last interpretation is unacceptable.

10   People without History

The allusions of Engels to 'people without history' are seen by nationalist critics as another confirmation of the Marxist lack of consideration for the periphery. This approach would treat all forces outside of the Western proletariat as irrelevant and stagnant masses (Chavolla, 2005: 188, 255–269). It is true that Engels resorted to this controversial notion to refer to masses of people incapable of leading their own self-liberation. He took this category from Hegel, who used it to characterize the peoples without sufficient attributes to create national structures.

Marx did not use this concept. However, he spoke strongly against the southern Slavs in their passionate political battle against imperial autocracies. Since the czar and the Habsburgs had managed to include these peoples in their counterrevolutionary campaigns, his reaction included a rejection of the national rights of those groups (Lowy and Traverso, 1990). The socialist militant assumed, in addition, that many demands of this type would not come to fruition. He felt that the small nations would be absorbed by the vertiginous waves of international transformations before reaching the threshold required for creating their own states.

Marx expected an external liberation for many peoples without a clear national identity. He thought the fall of the monarchical regimes would lead to that outcome. In his early stage, Marx did not recognize the existence of significant historical forces that could constitute differentiated states in different parts of Asia and Eastern Europe. Without a doubt the thesis of 'people without history' was mistaken, and it has been forcefully refuted by Marxist theorists, who showed how political alignments of one period were transformed into invariable facts of national trajectories. If the Russian empire had managed to coopt the Ukrainian, Romanian, Slovakian, Serbian, or Croatian peasants, it was because of the oppression they suffered at the hands of the Polish and Hungarian nobility.

This tripolar situation has been verified on numerous occasions – peoples who had been subjugated by intermediate oppressors were pushed into playing a reactionary role. But what happened with the Irish illustrated the variable historical character of those alignments. They played a counterrevolutionary role in the Cromwell period, and afterward led the national struggle (Rosdolsky, 1981).

In his second stage, Marx distanced himself from any variety of the 'people without history'. Some authors think that Engels also reevaluated that controversial concept in his characterization of the peasant wars in Germany (Harman, 1992). It is equally wrong to present this problem as proof of Marx's pro-colonial Eurocentrism. The nations he initially defended (Polish, Hungarian), initially rejected (southern Slavs), or first dismissed and later approved of (Irish) were all European. If belonging to the Old Continent were his criterion for deciding who enters into history, he would not have made these distinctions. The critics also claim that he supported the Poles and the Irish but rejected the southern Slavs, Scandinavians, Mexicans, Chinese, and North Africans (Nimni, 1989). But this geographical argument is inconsistent.

The disqualified peoples are not located only in Asia, Africa, or Latin America, but also in Europe.

Perhaps it could be said that the Eurocentric sin is found in his fascination with Western Europe. But Marx did not at first recognize the revolutionary vigor of a country in that region (Ireland), and attached great importance to another in the eastern part (Poland). The objectors also suggest that his Eurocentrism consisted most of all of a cultural dimension of idolatry of the West, which is why Marx got involved in the non-European conflict of the American Civil War. But they are missing the obvious. The Confederacy was more like Europe, and Marx supported the Yankees, who fought for the liberation of the slaves of African origin. He was not guided by criteria of ancestry, but by objectives of social liberation.

11   Nations and Nationalism

The critics consider the thesis of 'people without history' to be an aberration derived from characterizing the nation in purely objective terms. They feel that Marx committed this error in recognizing only the communities that form traditional states, dismissing the remaining cases (Chavolla, 2005: 117, 153–155). This criterion was very common in the 19th century, when the formation of the liberal state presupposed certain conditions of markets, territory, historical cohesion, and language. It was a conception also adopted by the Marxist currents that classified the nation based on its economic, linguistic, and territorial components (Kautsky), and adding psychological or cultural components (Stalin).

But Marx's view did not fit into this scheme, since he attached great importance to political action as a defining element of national configuration. He was guided more by the process of struggle than by *a priori* considerations. Thus, he supported the national aspirations of the Irish, but not the Welsh absorbed by Great Britain or the Bretons incorporated into the French state. The objectors ignore this attitude and accuse Marx of dogmatic reasoning. But his behavior was exactly the opposite, as proved by his support for a nation like Poland, which did not meet the market or territorial conditions for state formation.

The rigid criteria attributed to Marx were devised by objectivist successors who dismissed the centrality of subjects, which kept them from recognizing the great variety of national configurations. In opposition to this approach, a subjectivist (Austro-Marxist) current defined the nation as a 'community of character' associated with culture and common experience (Lowy, 1998: 49–54).

Marx provided clues for how to combine the two ideas, and stressed both identities and objective determinants. He suggested that economic, linguistic, or geographical intertwining give rise to a memory of a common past. But the critics ignore those contributions and see in Marx an 'undervaluing of nationalism'. They claim he made that mistake because he subordinated the struggle against national oppression to class considerations (Chavolla, 2005: 95). With this criticism, they in fact postulate an inverse hierarchy, leaving out the continuity of exploitation and inequality under any national state. In contrast, Marx promoted socialism to eradicate these ailments.

The objectors disconnect Marx from his times (Saludian and Dias Carcanholo, 2013). They assume that he did not recognize the legitimacy of nationalisms, which in fact had only recently arisen. In the mid-19th century, states were in the process of formation, overcoming the fragmented sovereignties and porous borders of the feudal dynasties. The classical French (or English) model of national formation based on the state had been consolidated through the delimitation of territories, administration of laws, identification of loyalty to the homeland, and construction of a school system that instilled attachment to the flag. But the opposite German (or Italian) model of passage from the nation to the state, based on prior cultures and languages, had only recently come into being. Nationalism as an ideology that extolled the virtues of public-military obligations of the citizenry had not yet emerged.

Marx did not undervalue nationalism, since he acted within a setting previous to the development of that doctrine. In that context, he had the merit of suggesting a distinction between progressive (Ireland, Poland) and regressive (Russia, England) varieties of the national ideal. He established that difference in accordance with the role it would play in speeding up or slowing down the socialist objective (Hobsbawm, 1983). Marx clarified his positions with this compass. On the one hand, he emphasized the common internationalist goals of the workers, rejected the supremacy of one nation over another, combatted the rivalries between countries, and did not accept the existence of virtuous peoples. On the other hand, he valued cases of national resistance against imperial oppression as a step toward the post-capitalist future.

Marx laid the foundations for evaluating nationalisms and defined the nation with objective-subjective criteria. His view contrasted with romantic approaches that harkened back to historical, ethnic, or religious myths to glorify different countries. This glorification tends to evade corroboration of the foundations it espouses. Nationalism imagines remote and continuous origins of each national identity, ignoring the enormous mutations of the communities that intermixed in each territory. It appeals to assumptions of ethnic cohesion that clash with the great variety of ancestries formed over the populational cycles. It assumes that religion facilitated the constitution of certain nations, forgetting that transnational ecclesiastic structures also obstructed that formation (Hobsbawm, 2000: Chapter 2). It forgets, too, that language did not contribute a definitive connection to the nation. An enormous variety of languages coexisted, got diluted, or were reinvented when the time came to standardize state activity around a predominant lexicon. From 8,000 languages, only 2,000 states arose (Gellner, 1991: Chapter 4; Anderson, B., 1993: Chapter 7).

Marx did not undervalue nations, but rather he contributed to demystifying beliefs in their millennial, unique, or superior origin. He provided the pillars for dismantling the fantasies transmitted by nationalism. His initial cosmopolitanism distanced him from those mythologies, and his revolutionary sensitivity allowed him to grasp the legitimacy of national struggles against colonialism.

12   State and Progress

The nationalist critics also object to Marx's views on the state, claiming he idealized conventional bourgeois forms over of other ethno-cultural modes arising from popular origins. This challenge is quite strange, if we remember that Marx was a communist theorist who supported the dissolution of all states as class distinctions were extinguished. It does not make much sense to attribute to him an enthusiasm for traditional varieties of the state.

The institution of the state is exalted by nationalists, who see it as the natural level for achieving the welfare of multi-class communities. Marx rejected that as way of perpetuating exploitation, and only favored the transitory emergence of states formed in the struggle against autocracy. As a fighter for socialism, Marx encouraged action from below rather than institutionalization from above – an opposite position to what his critics supposed. The image of a statist Marx who did not value popular constructions makes no sense.

Marx could not know how important the existence of autonomous national states would turn out to be in determining the place occupied by each country in the global hierarchy, as this was not clear until after his death. But his defense of that sovereignty anticipated a key feature of the center-periphery relation. The communities that did not win political independence suffered the consequences of underdevelopment more harshly. The contrast between Japan and India, or between Germany and Poland, illustrate this bifurcation.

The objectors do not value the intuitions of the great socialist thinker, and they attribute to him a 'theory of progress' that condemns the backward nations to follow the path of the advanced nations (Nimni, 1989). This portrayal might fit the Social Democrats of the Second International, but does not square with the second Marx. In this stage, no remnant is found of the teleological view of history, which the critics ascribe to his closeness to Hegel.

The author of *Capital* did not assume that the development of humanity followed a predetermined path unconnected to the will of its subjects. He felt that under certain conditions, within the range of human intervention, individuals grouped together into social classes are active builders of their future. This view is reflected in the multilinear model of multiple alternatives. But even his early unilinear reasoning was very different from Adam Smith's sketch of four successive stages; Marx did not postulate automatic or inevitable transitions from primitive modes of subsistence to the commercial phase, nor did he share the mythology of progress (Davidson, 2006).

His theoretical evolution was antagonistic to the positivist portrait painted by his critics. He perceived that capitalism did not expand by universalizing advanced forms, but by combining development with retrograde forms (Rao, 2010). His final studies on Russia illustrate the extent to which Marx had moved toward ideas of unequal development and skipping historical stages. These hypotheses are diametrically opposed to objectivist fatalism (Di Meglio and Masina, 2013). The objectors do not grasp the flexibility of a form of reasoning based on socialist aspirations. They forget that theories of progress presuppose an eternal capitalism, closer to nationalist conceptions than to Marx's thought.

13   Legacies

In his analytical trajectory from India to Ireland, Marx laid the foundation for explaining how capitalism creates underdevelopment. This is the main contribution of his writings on the periphery. He did not formulate a theory of colonialism, nor did he present a theory of the center-periphery relation, but he left a seed in his observations about global polarization and the recreation of backwardness. Marx's considerations on the positive impact of national struggles on the consciousness of workers in the center provided foundations for contemporary anti-imperialism. They pointed to the opposition between oppressing powers and oppressed nations, and formulated a principle of convergence between national and social struggles. These ideas inspired later strategies of alliances between workers in the center and the dispossessed of the periphery. They also anticipated the increasing protagonism of the non-European peoples in the battle against capitalism.

Marx's writings on the periphery were not minor works, nor were they simple descriptions or journalistic commentaries. They contributed to his analysis of central capitalism and motivated methodological changes of great importance.

Underdevelopment in the Classical Marxists

Lenin, Luxemburg, and Trotsky acted in a context of crises, wars, and revolutions. In the early 20th century, the great powers competed for the conquest of territories and to ensure the provision of raw materials. They put surpluses in markets that operated on a world scale, while trade grew more rapidly than production and the modernization of transportation connected all corners of the planet. England was able to neutralize its old rival France, but faced new competition from Germany and was increasingly losing ground to the United States. The biggest disputes involved aggressive Japanese power and the declining Ottoman, Austro-Hungarian, and Russian empires. Conflicts grew in the disputed regions, and the resources committed to the conflicts went beyond anything known in the past.

The rivals propagated imperial ideology. They glorified armed incursions, massacres of natives, and appropriation of lands, and they portrayed the installation of colonizers and racial denigration as normal acts of civilization, as they silenced the humanist traditions forged in the rejection of slavery. In the years preceding the outbreak of the First World War, the metropolis subjected the underdeveloped economies to the priorities of accumulation. They forced the predominance of their manufactures, taking advantage of the cheapening of the means of communication and the high profitability of foreign investment. In a more interconnected and polarized international economy, the gap between advanced and backward countries quickly widened.

The three leaders of revolutionary Marxism participated in socialist parties in two of the countries that were involved in imperial confrontations. German capitalism had arrived late to colonial repartition and needed markets to continue its industrial growth. The old nobility and the new bourgeoisie worked out an autocratic system eroded by great social conquests. The Czarist empire confronted similar contradictions. It combined industrial vigor with agrarian underdevelopment, and border expansion with subordination to the major powers. The monarchy faltered in the face of the revolutionary effervescence of the workers, peasants, and intellectuals.

1   Justifications for Colonialism

Luxemburg led the left flank of German socialism in dispute with the right (Bernstein) and center (Kautsky) tendencies. The most conservative sector considered capitalism to be perfectible through improvements achieved with greater parliamentary representation. They extolled free trade and supported outward expansion (Bernstein, 1982: 95–127, 142–183). This tendency encouraged the integration of the underdeveloped peoples to Western civilization, and stressed the advantages of colonialism for "educating the inferior cultures." Some leaders (Van Kol) justified the tutelage of the natives, claiming that "the weak and ignorant cannot govern themselves." Others (David) promoted a "socialist colonial policy."

These positions had severe political consequences. With regard to the imperial massacres in Turkey, Bernstein argued that "the savages must be subjugated and made to conform to the rules of higher civilization." He also approved of the crimes of England in India, and his colleague Vandervelde supported the annexation of the Congo to Belgium (Kohan, 2011: 303–309).

The social-democratic right felt that social progress would be achieved in each country when the workers won over the citizenry. To apply this principle, they reintroduced nationalism, in contrast to the cosmopolitan traditions of the First International. Bernstein made a distinction between sociological nationalism in the civilized regions and ethnic nationalism in the colonies. He praised the first variant while rejecting the second group's demands for sovereignty, returning to theories of the "people without history." This erosion of internationalism also had a social basis in the changes happening within the Second International. The new workers arriving from the provinces were more susceptible to nationalist propaganda than the old migrant craftworkers.

The centrist socialist tendencies initially rejected these proposals. They objected to the atrocities of colonialism, denounced militarism, and refuted the aristocratic idea of the superiority of one people over another. But with the passage of time, they moderated those objections and developed an intermediate conception combining critique and acceptance of colonialism (Kautsky, 2011a). Kautsky stressed the advantages of replacing imperial policies with coexistence strategies. He urged the ruling classes to consider the negative economic effects of expansionism, and proposed another business direction for capital accumulation. With this message, he divorced colonial policy from its competitive foundation and imagined forms of capitalism without rivalries for profit-making.

The leader of the centrist tendency postulated the existence of regressive and benevolent forms of imperialism, and differentiated the negative colonial forms from acceptable varieties. He denounced the inefficiency and corruption of England and Germany in their African possessions, but praised modern colonization in the temperate regions (United States, Australia), ignoring the fact that these varieties were achieved by means of the genocide of the local populations (Howard and King, 1989: 67–68, 92–103).

Kautsky promoted forms of collaboration between dominators and dominated. He encouraged aid from the central countries to the colonies. Thus, he at first interpreted India's incorporation into the British empire as favorable to both nations; later, he accepted the struggle of India for its sovereignty, but without supporting that resistance. Like the early Marx, he assumed that the liberation of the colonies would be the result of socialist advances in the center. However, he conceived of this goal as an evolutionary unfolding, and ruled out the participation of the periphery in this process. This objectivist naturalism had dramatic consequences in 1914–17 (Kautsky, 1978).

2 The Revolutionary Position

Luxemburg initially agreed with Kautsky on his criticisms of colonial paternalism but defended the popular resistance of the colonies and called for active support for the rebellions in Persia, India, and Africa (Luxemburg, 2011). Trotsky and Lenin shared this attitude. They went back to the legacy of the second Marx, describing the devastating effect of colonialism and stressing the double function of the anti-imperial struggle. They argued that that resistance confronted the main enemy and promoted a socialist consciousness among the metropolitan workers. The left also objected to the idealization of free trade as a reaction to growing protectionism, and rejected the primacy given to legal parameters in evaluating foreign policy. They emphasized the capitalist interests at stake (Day and Gaido, 2011).

The rupture was set off with the outbreak of the First World War. The right attached itself to the imperial cause, and the center accepted this capitulation. The old argument defending the German democratic process in the face of foreign aggression was unsustainable; Germany was now acting as a power and openly exhibited its colonial ambitions. Kautsky sought to avoid conflict, promoting disarmament while advocating in favor of the investments affected by the war. When his arguments went unheeded, he resigned himself to accepting the conflict.

Luxemburg's critique was devastating. For years she had warned of the ingenuity of the pacifist argument in light of the evidence of a coming war (Luxemburg, 2008: 258–265). Lenin adopted this same attitude, recognizing the international association between bourgeoisies and the pernicious character of the military business that Kautsky described and rejecting illusions about the buildup to the immanent conflagration. Trotsky also agreed with this analysis, arguing that the tightness of the national economies in a globalized capitalism was leading to war.

The inter-imperialist war precipitated a division between revolutionaries and reformists that was consolidated with the Russian Revolution. This event shook the socialist world. For years, Marxists had debated the form post-Czarist democratization would adopt. The tendency close to Bernstein (Tugan, Bulgakov) promoted liberal reforms complemented by economic-unionist demands from the workers. The tendency close to Kautsky (Plekhanov, Mensheviks) proposed alliances with the bourgeoisie in order to develop capitalism. They considered this maturation of the productive forces as a condition for any further evolution, and assumed that social subjects would passively adapt to the demands of the economy.

In contrast, Lenin espoused agrarian Jacobinism by means of nationalization of property in the land, in order to bring the peasants into a democratic revolution led by the workers. He envisioned a radical political process while the conditions for advancing toward socialism emerged (Lenin, 1973: 20–99). Trotsky shared this position, but he noted the great protagonism of the proletariat and their new organizations (soviets) in the revolution of 1905, and argued that this preeminence blocked all spaces for the expansion of capitalism (Trotsky, 1975).

When Czarism finally collapsed during the First World War and the soviets reappeared, Lenin radicalized his approach, united with Trotsky, and led the Bolshevik revolution. With some tactical objections, Luxemburg joined their initiative, leading to the creation of the Communist Parties and the Third International. The debut of socialism outside of Western Europe shook up theories of colonial paternalism, protagonism of the developed countries, and subordination of the backward regions to the rhythms of the West. The new revolutionary model shattered all the assumptions about the center-periphery relation.

3   Rights to Self-Determination

In Lenin's time, sovereignty was the main political demand of the peripheral nations. In Eastern Europe this demand clashed with Czarism, which had made a prison of border towns, and with the Austro-Hungarian Empire, which contained a complex variety of dominant, intermediate, and subjugated nations

(Germans, Hungarians, Ukrainians). The demand grew for creating institutions in the East similar to the already constituted states in Western Europe.

However, this desire coexisted with another variety of chauvinist nationalism, encouraged by the major powers to justify their conquests. This ideology used arguments drawn from national mythologies that resembled those of the subjected peoples. With these theories, the empires claimed rights of domination and the oppressed demanded their liberation (Hobsbawm, 2000: Chapter 4). In this confusion, Lenin proposed the right of each nation to create its own state. His goal was to encourage convergences of subjugated peoples with the working class. He sought to reduce the national, ethnic, and religious tensions promoted by the foreign and local oppressors to consolidate their hegemony (Lenin, 1974a: 7–14, 15–25).

The Bolshevik leader wanted to link resistance to national and social oppression. He promoted self-determination, noting the positive (and peaceful) way that the separation of the Norwegians from Sweden was resolved (Lenin, 1974b: 99–120). He also noted how national and social consciousness reinforced each other through immediate complaints and demands for sovereignty. In contrast to the nationalists, he did not place self-determination on a higher level of priority than social demands. He delimited its range, and stressed the undesirability of organizing separately from the socialist workers of different nationalities in the countries that had such diversity. He promoted unified groupings to encourage an internationalist culture among the proletariat.

The right to self-determination that Lenin espoused was not a blanket approval. He indicated that the appropriateness of secession should be determined in each case, taking into account the risks of coinciding with imperial strategies. Thus, he proposed carefully evaluating the forces acting in each case. With this approach, the communist leader provided a compass for deciding the progressive or regressive character of each nationalist movement. It should respond to whichever movement or action favored the socialist goal.

The Soviet leader developed his ideas in contention with the social-democratic tendencies of the Austro-Hungarian Empire that were opposed to self-determination, and instead proposed cultural autonomy for each conglomerate in a federal framework, stressing the historical durability of nations in the socialist future. The Austro-Marxists rejected the cosmopolitan tradition of the first Marx and his expectation of the post-capitalist dissolution of nations. They supported the association of workers in separate sections and emphasized the subjective dimension of the nation (Lowy, 1998: 49–50).

Lenin also engaged in a polemic with Luxemburg's pure internationalism, which questioned all forms of separatism. She considered the subjected countries (Poland) to be economically integrated with the dominant powers (Russia) and lacking the space for autonomous development. She believed that in this dependent framework, sovereignty was an illusion (Luxemburg, 1977: 27–176).

The viability or unviability of autonomous economic paths were for Lenin an unforeseeable possibility. He objected to speculation on the topic and demanded a case-by-case resolution of whether or not a people had a right to define its national future, stressing the primacy of this political definition. Luxemburg also argued that the right of national self-determination affected the unity of the workers and the priority of their class interests. But Lenin responded by emphasizing the existence of multiple forms of oppression (national, racial) that should converge with the social struggle, and that this convergence required affirming that no nation has the right to subjugate another.

4   Pillars of Anti-Imperialism

The politics of self-determination inspired an anti-imperialist strategy when the national question shifted to the East, following the frustrated initial attempt to repeat the Soviet model with revolutionary experiments (Germany, Hungary) on the Old Continent. The meager results of that experiment and the irruption of great uprisings in Asia induced the communist turn toward colonial revolution. In the First (1920) and Fourth (1922) Congresses of the Third International, policies were established for national liberation, to confront classical (England, France) and newer (Japan, United States) imperialism.

The distinction between regressive and progressive nationalism was again put forth in opposition to interventionist theories that purported to protect communities belonging to the same ethnic, cultural, or linguistic line. Lenin highlighted the opposite process of dispossession carried out by foreign occupiers and objected to all the abstract debates over legitimacies and rights in dispute. The Russian revolutionary proposed establishing who were the dominators and the dominated in each conflict. Rather than inquiring into the French, Chinese, or Malaysian identity of each individual, he emphasized the objective role of the powerful countries and the semi-colonies. He specified the roles of the different nationalisms according to their stabilizing or defiant function with regard to the imperial order, returning to the ideas developed in the debates on Eastern Europe.

Lenin sought to build bridges between communism and the anti-imperialist nationalism of China, India, and the Arab world. He returned to the critique of the proletarian puritanism of those who objected to the national struggle (Pyatakov), which revived the naive cosmopolitanism of the 19th century ("down with borders"). He distanced himself from all speculations about the economic autonomy of India or Egypt, and focused on popular demands for sovereignty (Lenin, 1974b: 120–122).

The key innovation in communist strategy in this period was the distinction between conservative ('bourgeois-democratic') and radical ('revolutionary nationalist') tendencies of the anti-colonial movements. The first group was the expression of the dominant classes of the periphery, and the latter of the impoverished sectors. The conservative conduct of the nascent bourgeoisies contrasted with the radical push of the dispossessed. Both promoted national independence, but with different social aims (Claudín, 1970: Chapter 4).

The opposing directions of the 'revolutions from above and from below' confirmed this distinction. In the first decades of the 20th century, Turkey was the main setting for the first direction, through reformist military coups and modernizing initiatives of the elites. The second direction prevailed in Mexico, with great protagonism on the part of the peasantry. The bourgeois-democratic movements wanted to reorder capitalism, increasing the influence of the local dominant classes in alliance with foreign capital. The revolutionary nationalists, in contrast, proposed anti-imperialist projects in conflict with this reorganization. The Third International favored support for these struggles in order to further the socialist aim.

5   Uneven Development

Lenin attributed the widening of the gap between advanced and backward economies to uneven development. He developed this concept in opposition to the evolutionist methodology of Bernstein and Kautsky, who imagined a repetition in the periphery of the path taken by the central countries. The Bolshevik leader thought that this linear path had been buried by the turbulence of the imperial age. He felt that the rivalry between powers destabilized accumulation, exacerbated the contradictions of capitalism, and undermined the harmonious image conceived by reformism (Davidson, 2010).

Lenin explained the misfortunes of the periphery by the historical asymmetries of uneven development. He illustrated how this process determined the theft of financial resources and the absorption of the profits of the colonies. He described multiple mechanisms of plunder suffered by the providers of raw materials, and asserted that they were harshly affected by any market volatility (Lenin, 2006). This theory of the weak link provided arguments for exogenous interpretations of worldwide polarization. It showed how the blockage of development suffered by the backward countries was a direct consequence of colonial partition.

Lenin transformed the hypothesis of obstruction to industrialization in the periphery suggested by the second Marx into a theory of complete suffocation. His characterization was in tune with the warlike panorama of the early 20th century, dominated by powers that destroyed territories to guarantee their control over markets. But in his studies of Russian agriculture, the Soviet leader also evaluated the endogenous dimension of backwardness. He analyzed how the rent appropriated by the nobility held back production and impoverished the peasants. He argued over two remedies for that suffocation before the Bolshevik revolution: the Prussian model of investment controlled by the landowners, or the American path of land distribution, elimination of absolute rent, and development with farmers (Lenin, 1973: 20–99).

In the first stage of revolutionary Russia (1890–1914), explanations for backwardness were focused on national and agrarian processes, while in the second period (1914–1922), characterizations of decapitalization of the periphery predominated. In one context Lenin attached primacy to endogenous causes of underdevelopment, and in the other he put more weight on exogenous determinants. However, he always prioritized the political dimension of the problems being debated. The diagnostics centered on agrarian backwardness provided foundations for the democratic revolution against Czarism, while the studies of colonial confiscation pointed toward anti-imperialist initiatives.

Lenin evaluated different levels of political dependency to demonstrate their impact in the backwardness borne by each country. He distinguished three varieties: administrative subjection, economic subjugation, and subordination of the local dominant classes. With these parameters, he differentiated the colonial character of Africa, the semi-colonial character of China, and the dependent capitalist character of Argentina. The leader of the soviets pointed to the roles of the agents, compradors, or junior partners of imperial domination to explain different levels of local political autonomy from the foreign oppressor. He also analyzed the situations of intermediate powers (Russia, Turkey, Italy) who did not fit into the simple division between empires and colonies.

All the analytical precisions of the Bolshevik leader were directed at establishing revolutionary strategies. He exhibited extraordinary political flexibility in the use of that instrument. In 1917, he transformed his strategy of democratic revolution into socialist revolution, and in the 1920s he promoted a shift in communist priorities from Europe to the East. He also revised his criticisms of the populist theories of the unviability of Russian capitalism. Lenin demonstrated a great capacity for framing social theories and economic processes in political strategies, considering various revolutionary alternatives and choosing the most adequate for each conjuncture.

6   Stages and Imperialism

The communist leader inscribed the center-periphery relation into his theory of imperialism as a new stage of capitalism. He introduced a periodization, complementing the distinction studied by Marx between the origin and the formation of capitalism. The debate over the existence of historical stages began during the recovery from the depression of 1873–1896. In opposition to Bernstein, who postulated the gradual disappearance of the crisis, and Kautsky, who emphasized its continuity, Lenin argued for the arrival of a new period. This concept was widely developed in later Marxist thought (Katz, 2009: 129).

The Bolshevik leader underlined several features of the imperialist stage: the predominance of protectionism, financial hegemony, the importance of monopolies, and the increasing weight of foreign investment. He drew on the importance placed by Hilferding on the intertwining of industrialists and bankers with the state bureaucracy, and on the supremacy placed by Hobson on high finance (Lenin, 2006).

The Russian revolutionary derived his approach from theories of crisis based on disproportionalities and overproduction by Hilferding and Kautsky. Later he favored Bukharin's theory of financial parasitism and national competition with strong state intervention. But the center of his attention about imperialism was not focused on economic characterizations, but on diagnosing the imminent military confrontation; the omnipresent context of war shaped his conception. The impact of his ideas is explained by that political choice. He presented not only denouncements, but also a devastating critique of the pacifist hope of avoiding war by means of ingenuous calls to disarm. In this challenge, Lenin joined with Luxemburg and clashed with Kautsky and Hilferding. Theoretical differences with regard to underconsumption (in the first case) and affinities around the dynamics of the crisis (in the second) were minor problems compared to the dilemma of the war.

Many later readings ignored the political primacy of the text and overemphasized the economic characterizations. In addition, they projected to the entire 20th century an assessment that was limited to the inter-war period. This extrapolation led to decades of dogmatism and repetitive Marxism. It became habitual to postulate the invariable validity of whatever Lenin said, and to update his affirmations with data on protectionism, financial primacy, or military confrontation. That reiteration left out the fact that the two central features of that theory – stagnation and inter-imperial war – did not represent permanent features of capitalism. In our book on the topic, we review those debates (Katz, 2011: Chapter 1).

Our assessment has been disputed for its "definitive break with the Leninist view." This objection reiterates the assumption of the immutable validity of assertions made in 1916 for the entire century that followed (Duarte, 2013). To demonstrate that freezing of capitalism, our critics highlight the continuing preeminence of the banks, as if such a prolonged interval of multiple industrial processes had not altered that supremacy. They assign the same weight to protectionism, ignoring the intensity of trade liberalization and the international intermixing of capitalists. They also stress the centrality of war, forgetting that the confrontations between the major powers were replaced by imperial aggressions of hegemonic or global reach. With the same criterion of blind fidelity to the original text, they highlight the shift from competition to monopolies, ignoring the complementary character of the two forms and the relevance of competition under current capitalism. They forget that the behavior of prices is not subject to simple agreements, but to an objective adjustment process guided by the law of value. In addition, they emphasize the continuing primacy of rentism, not mentioning that the key imbalances of the system are generated in the productive area. These tensions do not arise from parasitism, but from the uncontrolled dynamism of capital.

The formal loyalty to Lenin generally demands a ritual reminder of imperialism "as the highest stage of capitalism," forgetting that this evaluation was made on the eve of the Russian Revolution, counting on more victories in the rest of the world. Lenin never thought of that title as a refrain valid for any time and place. The theory of systemic decadence put forth by the Bolshevik leader was partly inspired by the expectation of soon-to-come triumphs of socialism. He did not formulate predictions of collapse divorced from the class struggle. In light of later developments, it is clear that the stage seen as the final moment of imperial development merely represented an intermediate period. Capitalism will not dissolve from a terminal collapse. Lenin rightly emphasized that its eradication depends on the political construction of a socialist alternative.

7   The Function of the Periphery

Luxemburg also analyzed the colonial world through a theory of imperialism, but she reasoned about it in a different way. She attempted a direct deduction from Marx's texts. She placed the topic within the expanded reproduction schemes of Volume II of *Capital* and assessed the obstacles capitalism confronted on an international scale. The socialist leader understood that the key imbalance was located in the realization of surplus value that the central economies were not able to complete because of the tightness of their markets. She argued that the only outlet for unclogging that accumulation was in sending the surplus products to the colonies. She recalled that Great Britain expanded by selling fabrics abroad, and based on this precedent defined imperialism as a system of external mobilization of inactive capital.

Luxemburg observed that Marx had omitted those imbalances and proposed a correction of that error, incorporating the absorption of the surplus into the reproduction schemes. She criticized the theorists (Eckstein, Hilferding, Bauer) who ignored this contradiction of capitalism (Luxemburg, 1968: 158–190). This approach led her to various evaluations of the schemes of Volume II that frequently overlooked the purpose of those diagrams. Marx introduced them to demonstrate how the system could function in spite of the huge obstacles that affect its operations. The author of *Capital* conceived of an ideal situation without imbalances, in order to show how the entire circuit of production and circulation would operate. Luxemburg and her critics ignored this function, and they embarked on inappropriate corrections of those schemes.

The revolutionary of Polish origin committed another error by looking on the outside for the limits that capitalism faced in its internal dynamics. Thus, she assumed that the exhaustion of the colonial markets would determine an absolute saturation of accumulation. She forgot that here too the system creates mechanisms to recreate its continuity through the devaluation (or destruction) of surplus capitals.

But none of those mistakes overshadow Luxemburg's significant contributions. Like Lenin, she grasped how the contradictions of capitalism take more extreme forms at the margins of the system. Luxemburg contributed the first analysis of the way in which the periphery is integrated into the center as a necessity of global capitalism, highlighting how this segment is indispensable for the reproduction of the whole system. She did not reason by assumptions of full-world capitalism, nor did she see the underdeveloped economies as simple complements to the advanced countries; she studied both sectors as parts of a single totality (Cordova, 1974: 19–44).

Luxemburg perceived that the center needs the benefits taken from the periphery to continue operating. She showed the connection of the West to Africa, Asia, and Latin America. She deepened this characterization with her studies of Poland, in which she inquired into how a peripheral zone ends up assimilated into the surrounding markets. In this way, she uncovered the unequal relations that connect dominant and subordinate economies (Krätke, 2007a: 1–19).

Luxemburg saw how the underdeveloped world endured a permanent primitive accumulation at the service of the central economies. She observed that this process did not correspond only to the genesis of capitalism, but also to its continuity. She highlighted the way in which metropolitan capital obstructs the growth of the periphery and illustrated how it keeps those regions from repeating the development of Western Europe, the United States, or Japan. This characterization constitutes a predecessor to theories of "the development of underdevelopment." It provided foundations for the theories that connect the backwardness of the periphery with the development of the center. It highlighted two sides of the same process of world capitalism that was not limited to the conjuncture of her times.

Luxemburg showed how capitalism destroys the peasant economies of the periphery without facilitating its industrialization. She described that process by examining the English conquest of India, the French occupation of Algeria, and the violent settlement of the Boers in South Africa. She saw how the disintegration of the pre-capitalist areas fostered poverty, impeding the expansion of demand and consequently of self-sustaining accumulation. Her analysis was well received by scholars of the period, but some claimed that capitalism integrates those regions without destroying them. It imposes relations of subordination on the preceding forms, following the model of incorporation of slavery to nascent capitalism or the path of assimilation of oligarchies to capitalized agrarian production (Howard and King, 1989: 106–123).

Luxemburg reasoned with underconsumptionist criteria. She argued that restrictions on demand induced the center to seek external markets, which do not prosper because of obstructions to purchasing power imposed on the periphery. This view was similar to Hobson's characterization, and kept a certain distance from the Lenin–Hilferding view (overproduction/disproportionality). While the Bolshevik leader shaped his theory in polemics with the under-consumptionism of the Russian populists, the revolutionary in Germany sharpened her theory questioning the harmonious view of social democracy.

Many authors objected to Luxemburg's under-consumptionism, claiming the primacy of imbalances on the level of profits, around which capitalism revolves. But these critics did not see the compatibility of the two approaches and their integration into the multicausal logics of crisis. They did not see how Luxemburg anticipated key differences between the center and the periphery in terms of the solvency of demand.

Luxemburg largely agreed with the Leninist analysis of imperialism, but did not ascribe the same relevance to protectionism, financial supremacy, or monopoly, nor did she associate this period with the export of capital, but rather stressed the preeminence of surplus commodities. However, Luxemburg did coincide with Lenin in asserting that the periphery was doubly exploited, by economic suction and colonial pillage. In the warlike context of the early 20th century, both processes fostered global polarization.

8 Accumulation by Dispossession

The identification of primitive accumulation with the depredation described by Luxemburg has been taken up recently by David Harvey in his analysis of the predatory effects of capitalism. He uses the term dispossession to indicate the contemporary character of this process. Harvey asserts that primitive accumulation includes processes preceding and concurrent with capitalist development. Like Luxemburg, he maintains that the metropolitan economies impose a pernicious exchange on the underdeveloped regions. But the English scholar attaches an additional dimension to the term dispossession, as a mechanism of expropriation in the advanced economies by means of financial speculation, fraud, patents, and privatization (Harvey, 2003: Chapter 4).

Serfati offers a similar characterization. He emphasizes that the depredation suffered by the periphery, especially through taxes to pay the public debt, coexists with the general confiscations of the system. He asserts that developed capitalism reproduces itself by overexploiting an "exterior" sphere that is not only geographic, but also social. This appropriation includes all available fields for accumulation (Serfati, 2005).

Some Marxists object to these views. They question the emphasis on extra-economic theft rather than the logic of capital, and warn against portraying the system as a simple regime of political domination. They remind us that Marx did not study primitive accumulation as theft to enrich the bourgeoisie. Rather, he sought to illustrate the process of creating a proletariat through social expropriation (Meiksins Wood, 2007; Brenner, 2006). The critics affirm that capitalism should not be analyzed with criteria of plunder. Unlike tributary or slave regimes, it is regulated by objective laws of competition, profit, and exploitation (Ashman and Callinicos, 2006).

Harvey asserts that these views underestimate the component of depredation in contemporary capitalism, and reaffirms his conceptualization of accumulation as a process combining economic and extra-economic confiscation. However, he does not clarify when and how each of these dimensions operate (Harvey, 2006). Extraction of surplus value and expropriation through plunder were considered in a different way in the early 20th century. Hilferding proposed a historical chronology of those processes. He considered plunder to be characteristic of traditional colonialism and the hegemony of commercial capital. He affirmed that this modality declined with metropolitan industrialization and had little relevance in the subsequent period of protectionism and export of capital (Hilferding, 2011).

Lenin and Luxemburg, however, argued that depredation had reappeared in the new imperialist stage. They held that the wars for colonial booty recreated the old scenarios of pillage. Many post-Leninist and post-Luxemburgist theories maintained this view, without taking into account that it was formulated in period of war.

A reconsideration of the problem should highlight the secondary function of plunder in the phases of ordinary accumulation, and its central weight in times of war. The same distinction could be extended to the regions of the periphery dominated by contexts of war (the Middle East) or of habitual exploitation (Latin America). It is true that primitive accumulation and capital accumulation are concurrent processes, not mere stages of historical development, but the relation between the two processes changes considerably in each period and region.

9   Uneven and Combined Development

Trotsky agreed with Lenin's and Luxemburg's characterizations about war, the imperialist period, and world polarization, but he introduced a concept that allowed him to overcome the simplified contrast of the periphery with the center. His concept of uneven and combined development placed the backwardness of the underdeveloped regions in the context of internationalized capitalism. He noted not only the asymmetries, but also the mixtures of advanced and backward forms in the formations that were incorporated into the world market.

The Russian revolutionary initially used a concept presented by several authors (Herzen, Chernychevsky) to illustrate the mixture of modernity and underdevelopment present in Russia. He then combined that application with other theories (Parvus) that depicted the world economy as a heterogeneous and interconnected totality. With this view, he illustrated the new configuration of underdevelopment – the periphery no longer reproduced the expansive European model, but neither did it maintain the old feudal, servile, or peasant modes.

Trotsky added a principle of combined paths to Lenin's uneven development. He illustrated how the diverse rhythms of development are complemented by a mixture of the archaic with the modern. He described this novel articulation in his assessment of the first Russian revolution, and completed the theory in his history of the Bolshevik victory (Trotsky, 1975; 1972: 21–34).

Uneven and combined development is able to overcome the diffusionist and stagnationist interpretations of the center-periphery relation. It refutes the myths of gradual expansion of the Western model, as well as the opposite impression of unchanging pre-capitalist forms. It highlights the predominance of mixtures inside of an imperial hierarchy (Barker, 2006). This amalgam was later denominated "structural heterogeneity," and was widely applied in the study of the Latin American economies that combined dependent industrialization with unproductive *latifundios*.

Trotsky provided the most complete explanation of the views of the second Marx on India. The English railroads did not transfer to the Asian subcontinent the development predicted in the *Manifesto*, but rather combined growth with subordinate insertion in the world economy. Endogenist Marxism utilized combined and uneven development to describe how distinct modes of production (slavery, feudalism, and capitalism) are articulated in unique economic-social formations. Exogenist Marxist theorists turn to the same concept to study how international patterns of dependency shape the semi-industrialized economies.

Trotsky further developed his concept in the political struggle against official communist theories of revolution by stages. He questioned the resurgence of the Menshevik idea of bourgeois development prior to any socialist transformation, emphasizing the unviability of that strategy in an interconnected capitalist world. Uneven and combined development constituted the main pillar of his strategy of permanent revolution. He supported this theory by contrasting the success of Bolshevism with the failure of the Chinese revolution (1925–27) (Trotsky, 2000; Demier, 2013).

Trotsky conceived this approach for understanding intermediate economies, old powers, or countries of high geopolitical importance. He proposed applying it in Russia or Turkey, and was cautious about its extension elsewhere. He did not include colonial regions or those of extreme underdevelopment. What was valid for China or India was not applicable to equatorial Africa or Afghanistan (Davidson, 2010). From this same perspective, he anticipated the peculiarities of the semi-peripheral formations, which at that time were undergoing substantial mutations. Together with the old powers (France, England) challenged by new central countries (United States, Japan, Germany), another segment remained in an indefinite position (Russia, Italy) or deepened its regression (Turkey, Spain). These second-rank powers were subsequently studied with the perspective of subimperialism. Uneven and combined development provided the foundations for this inquiry.

10   Challenges and Extensions

Since its formulation, uneven and combined development has given rise to numerous debates. It was widely recognized that it clarified the evolution of the economies subjected to a mixture of modernization and backwardness, and it raised reconsiderations of views on these articulations (Vitale, 2000). However, other applications highlighted its similarity to heterodox catch-up theories. These theories assert the advantages of the late-arriving country for assimilating available technologies. They associated that "privilege of back-wardness" with Trotsky's ideas. But the revolutionary leader conceptualized the fragmentary industrialization of late capitalisms, pointing to advantages and disadvantages. He noted the contradictions entailed in "arriving late," reminding us that Russia industrialized with tight markets, foreign debt, and disastrous military commitments.

The German case provided another example. Pressured by Anglo-French competition, German capitalism developed without a triumphant bourgeois revolution, under the boot of a militarized state. That Prussianism led to cata-strophic military pressures. Trotsky did not conceive of uneven and combined development as a category of sociology or heterodox economics. He sought to demonstrate the possibilities of proletarian protagonism in immature cap-italisms. Thus, he asserted that Russia had produced a working class prepared to carry out the Bolshevik revolution, which was the main corollary to his theory. Rather than pointing to a more vigorous bourgeois industrialization, the Russian amalgam allowed for the realization of an early experiment with socialism (Bianchi, 2013).

Trotsky integrated economics, politics, and class struggle in an anti-capital-ist logic. He built his approach in opposition to social-democratic positivism and the strategy of revolution by stages. He challenged proposals for imitation of central capitalism and the politics of construction of socialism in one coun-try. His ideas were completely contrary to "catch-up."

In other debates, it has been pointed out that uneven and combined devel-opment is a mechanism or a tendency without the status of a law – it lacks predictive logic and strict results derived from active forces. The methodolog-ical status of the concept is an open topic, but it is worth remembering that it was never conceived for the world of the social sciences. It pertains to social phenomena, political confrontations, and historical outcomes that depend on human action. It clarifies contradictions subject to the unforeseeable course of the class struggle.

Another debate involves the historical scope of the principle. Some authors assert that it goes beyond the capitalist framework and makes it possible to understand pre-capitalist processes. They use it to show how colonization combined mercantile processes with slave labor and exploitation of the indigenous peoples (Novack, 1974). Another backward extension uses it to depict the territorial expansion of the nobility in feudal societies (Rosenberg, 2009).

But this extension ignores that it is only under capitalism that economic actors get wrapped up in the interdependent web required for bringing about combined development. Earlier systems may have shared many features, but not the mixtures of industrial development described by Trotsky. Only capitalism introduces the global dimension required to break the isolation of preceding societies (Callinicos, 2009).

11   Enduring Concepts

Lenin, Luxemburg, and Trotsky attributed world polarization to the new imperialist stage. They portrayed that gap as an effect of the disputes between powers over colonial booty. They analyzed the confiscation of the periphery in the context of the commercial rivalries that led to the First World War. All three authors introduced ideas of great relevance for the study of the center-periphery relation. Lenin clarified uneven economic development and the political subordination borne by the backward countries. Luxemburg portrayed the structural economic obstructions these nations face and anticipated tendencies of accumulation by dispossession. Trotsky highlighted the peculiar contradictions of the intermediate countries affected by combined development. These theories were put forth in close connection to socialist strategies.

The ideas of the three revolutionaries had a great impact in the second half of the 20th century, but the modifications undergone by capitalism in this period also modified Marxist thought.

CHAPTER 3

Center and Periphery in Postwar Marxism

Four Marxist economists developed important analyses of the center-periphery relation in the postwar era. While Paul Baran and Paul Sweezy were precursors to that approach, Samir Amin and Ernest Mandel developed more elaborated work on the same topic. They all conducted their research in a period of postwar reconstruction and capitalist expansion, which widened the gap between advanced and backward economies. What was their view of this asymmetry?

1   Deindustrialization and Surplus

In the 1950s, the most widespread Marxist interpretation highlighted the barriers to industrialization of the periphery on the part of the center. It stressed that the purpose of this blockage was to impede the rise of competitors, in order to ensure the primacy of foreign companies. This approach held that the developed countries appropriated the raw materials of the periphery and perpetuated captive markets for their manufactured exports, impeding the transformation of decolonization into processes of development (Dobb, 1969: 83; 95–97). Baran reformulated this view. He attributed the low rate of growth of the backward countries to external suffocation, but also drew attention to the existence of certain processes of industrial expansion in the periphery. In this way, his view highlighted the insufficient character of the old dichotomy between industrialized and agro-mining countries (Baran, 1959: 33–34).

The Russian-American theorist located the main difference between the center and the periphery in the handling of the surplus. He introduced that concept to describe the utilization of the additional product generated in each cycle of accumulation. He considered that this excess was absorbed internally in the advanced economies by its military activity, luxury consumption, and unproductive spending. In contrast, in the periphery it was transferred abroad to facilitate the expansion of the metropolitan economies. He also asserted that in the underdeveloped economies, the gap between what could be invested (potential surplus) and what was actually allocated to productive activity (effective surplus) was huge, with most of the excess captured by the landowning aristocracy or sent out of the country by affiliates of the foreign companies (Baran, 1959: 223–259; Sweezy and Baran, 1974: 47–143).

Baran attached greater relevance to exogenous (transfers abroad) than to endogenous (landlord predominance) causes of the recreation of underdevelopment. He noted the structural character of the expatriation of funds from the periphery, and emphasized that the gap between advanced and backward economies went beyond wartime conjunctures or contexts of competition between empires (Howard and King, 1989: 167–168).

With these ideas, he illustrated how the developed economies need to absorb outside funds to guarantee their reproduction. The *Monthly Review* school led by Sweezy maintained this approach and fostered numerous studies of the great drainage of funds that decapitalized the periphery. The investigations by Magdoff also demonstrated how U.S. capitalism was nourished by that plundering of the backward economies (Magdoff, 1972).

2   Stagnation and Domination

The interpretations of the global gap proposed by the *Monthly Review* school were based on two characterizations: the stagnation of capitalism and imperial domination. The first concept was developed by Sweezy based on an underconsumptionist foundation. He argued that the tightness of demand created an unsellable surplus that pushed the system to regression. Later, he attributed the same effect to the expansion of monopolies. He held that corporate gigantism led to pricing agreements that discouraged new initiatives and led to recessive cycles. Sweezy stressed the blockage of innovation as an additional consequence of this process. He argued that technological change tended to decline with the weakening of the industrial revolutions that drove accumulation. In his later work, he located the main cause of stagnation in financial parasitism. He argued that capitalism had transformed itself into a rentier system controlled by bankers who stifled investment. This view was influenced by the pessimistic perspectives of several Keynesian authors of the period (Sweezy, 1973a: 33–35; Sweezy, 1973b: Chapters 11–13).

Sweezy conceived of world polarization as a compensatory process for the losses faced by metropolitan capitalism. He held that the large corporations compensated for their setbacks with bigger extractions from the periphery (Albo, 2004). However, amidst the economic boom of 1950–1970, these ideas confronted numerous problems. They assumed contractions of demand just when mass consumption was growing, and they stressed the stifling effects of monopolies in a context of creation of new companies. In addition, they emphasized technological regression at a time of increasing productivity; financial domination was postulated in the middle of that industrial boom.

The arguments put forth by the *Monthly Review* theorists provoked intense debates among Marxist economists. The underconsumptionist foundation was challenged with explanations for crises based on the declining rate of profit. Technological exhaustion was objected to by pointing to indications of a new technological revolution (automation, plastics, nuclear energy). The preeminence of monopoly was also criticized, for omitting the continuity of competition in a system ruled by the law of value. In turn, financial protagonism was challenged because of the primacy of the productive sector in the extraction of surplus value (Katz, 2001: 13–41).

However, none of these challenges affected the correct observation of a new gap between center and periphery. Baran, Sweezy, and Magdoff provided conclusive evidence of this cleavage. The critics pointed to problems in the theoretical foundations of their approach, but they did not object to their conclusive evidence of this polarization. The *Monthly Review* authors also provided geopolitical characterizations of the role of imperialism in the consolidation of global asymmetry. They explained how the great powers needed to control the supply of raw materials in order to continue their accumulation, and how the cheapening of those inputs counteracts the decline of profit.

Sweezy and Magdoff did not only describe the hegemonic weight of the United States; they analyzed the new role of the Pentagon as a guardian of capitalism on a world scale (Sweezy and Magdoff, 1981: 81–106). This theory anticipated several features of contemporary imperialism. What appeared to be a 'super-imperialist' exaggeration of the conjuncture illustrated an important long-term geopolitical tendency (Katz, 2011: 39).

3   Polemics with Liberalism

Baran, Sweezy, and Magdoff refuted liberal conceptions that attributed underdevelopment to the climatic adversities of certain regions. Those views naturalized the advantages of temperate areas, ignoring the variability of a condition that lost importance relative to economic and social processes (Szentes, 1984: 24–47). The liberals also attributed underdevelopment to the absence of entrepreneurial capitalists, without explaining the cause of this absence. They simply called for reinforcing individualism to encourage the rise of an entrepreneurial elite, identifying modernization with imitation of the West and trumpeting the desirability of this path. But the repetition they idealized never happened. Capitalist development was always marked by accelerations and superimpositions far from the chronology of takeoff, maturation, and growth proclaimed by the liberals.

The Marxists at *Monthly Review* refuted that neoclassical view, disarming the myths of comparative advantage. They countered those fantasies with strong evidence of imperial oppression, transfers of income, and appropriations of raw materials (Sweezy, 1973a: 25–33). In addition, they showed that backwardness was not explained by 'lack of capital', but by the unproductive use of existing resources. With this argument, they challenged the exaggerated benefits attributed to foreign financing. The members of *Monthly Review* operated in a climate of state persecution under McCarthyism, and at the height of the Cold War confronted the apologetics for the U.S. model propagated by anticommunist authors like Rostow (Katz, 2015: 93–94).

Baran also stressed the importance of political autonomy in the periphery to constrain the exactions of the center. He contrasted the experiences of India and Japan in the 19th century, recalling how nascent industry was devastated by English colonialism in the first case, and was able to emerge in the latter because of its political independence. To drive home this point, Baran updated the Leninist classification of the peripheral world. He distinguished colonial territories (Asia, Africa) and administrations with coveted resources (oil from the Middle East) from the countries that had won a sovereign status (Egypt) (Baran, 1959: 192–221, 263–287).

Baran argued that this autonomy would allow them to counteract underdevelopment if they initiated an anti-capitalist process. He was sympathetic to the planning model of the Soviet Union and proposed generalizing it to ensure high rates of growth. In this, he coincided with Dobb, and he encouraged international associations with the socialist bloc to implement the Soviet model of industrialization with high rates of investment (Dobb, 1969: 103, 114, 119).

These proposals coexisted with rejection of the policy of revolution in stages promoted by the Communist Parties. They rejected the call for joining with the bourgeoisie in projects for building national capitalism. The editors of *Monthly Review* sympathized with the Third World movements fighting for radical anti-colonial processes. This political position oriented all the economic research of Baran and Sweezy. When the totality of their work is assessed, their contribution to understanding the center-periphery relation is undeniable. In contrast to the orthodox myths of social welfare and the heterodox hopes of repeating the evolution of the United States or Europe, they showed how the draining of surplus obstructs development and reinforces imperial domination.

4   Amin's Five Theses

Samir Amin made similar assumptions to Sweezy-Baran but developed a more ambitious Marxist conception of the center-periphery relation. His approach can be synthesized in five characterizations. In the first place, he highlighted the intrinsic nature of world polarization under capitalism. He held that income inequality between advanced and backward countries was underestimated by socialist theorists who focused exclusively on the question of capital and labor (Amin, 2003: Chapter 4). The Egyptian theorist returned to Lenin's perspective of differentiated international forms of exploitation and to Bauer's interpretation of the profits obtained in the periphery as a compensatory mechanism for improvements conceded to workers in the center (Amin, 1976: 128–133).

Amin argued that in pre-capitalist systems, international leveling processes were still feasible in the different regions. He recalled, for example, how Western Europe surmounted, in record time, its historical lag with respect to previous regions of higher development. But he affirmed that the possibility for such evening out later vanished with the consolidation of capitalism, becoming impossible in the current age (Amin, 2006: 5–22). He illustrated this asymmetry pointing to the contemporary inequalities between regions. He stressed that imperialism is not a fixed state, but a mechanism for consolidation of these differences (Amin, 2001a: 15–30).

In the second place, and based on that observation of the gaps between regions, Amin attributed the widening of the global cleavage to the internationalization of a system that universalizes the mobility of capital and commodities, but not of labor. He showed how trade and investment expand to the entire planet while restricting wage-workers to relatively fixed locations. He explained the comparative immobility of labor by the historical-national structure of labor markets. In his approach, migration flows are nowhere near the high rates of movement that characterize money or goods (Amin, 1973: 67–68).

This is the basis for Amin's third thesis, which affirms the existence of higher rates of exploitation in the periphery. He argues that the immobility of labor consolidates great armies of the unemployed in these regions, cheapening wages. Moreover, in the industrial activities installed in the backward economies wage differentials that are larger than the productivity gap produce capitalists' profit. The Marxist theorist made numerous comparisons between the same industrial sectors in the advanced and underdeveloped economies to illustrate how the wage difference between home offices and affiliates determines the main source of profits of multinational corporations (Amin, 1973: 9, 14, 20, 56). He finished this analysis with a depiction of the mechanisms of value transfer utilized by metropolitan capitalists to appropriate the surplus value created in the periphery, presenting several estimations of the monumental amounts of these transfers (Amin, 2008: 237–238). The Egyptian theorist asserted in his fourth principle that this expropriation is possible because of the convergence of different economic-social formations around the same world market. He argued that within that sphere, dominant and subordinate structures operate to reproduce global inequality (Amin, 2005).

Finally, Amin contrasted the self-centered models of the advanced countries with the disarticulated economic processes predominant in the periphery, highlighting the durability of those differences and challenging the liberal expectation of leveling. He also challenged the developmentalist hypothesis of the periphery reaching the prevailing levels of welfare of the center by means of simple reproduction of the evolution followed by the more prosperous regions (Amin, 2008: 240–242).

In his five theses, Amin reaffirmed the durability of the structural gap between advanced and backward economies under contemporary capitalism. He did not limit himself to exposing the commercial or financial mechanisms of surplus value transfers that perpetuate these gaps, but also introduced a novel explanation centered on the peculiarity of the labor force in the underdeveloped countries. He emphasized that the abundance of that labor, and its relative immobility compared to the vertiginous movement of capital and commodities, generated extraordinary profits from the exploitation of labor, recreating the center-periphery polarity and clarifying aspects missing in previous analyses.

5   World Value and Polarization

Amin based his view on a theory of value on a world scale, extending the application of this Marxist principle to the global level. He returned to the rule that explains the prices of commodities by the socially necessary labor time for their production. This criterion attributes price changes to modifications in productivity or in demand, which in turn are regulated by levels of exploitation and profit rates. The primacy of the law of value distinguishes capitalism from previous regimes and determines the centrality taken by the maximization of profit in the general functioning of society (Amin, 2006: 5–22; Katz, 2009: 31–60).

But the novelty introduced by Amin is the applicability of this law on a world scale. He affirmed the preeminence of that dimension as the international fluidity of commodities and capital are consolidated, together with the immobility of the labor force (Amin, 1973: 14, 21–25). With this approach, Amin conceptualized the internationalization of production attained through the expansion of multinational corporations. By connecting processes of world production, these firms determine reference prices of all the activities under their control. The Egyptian economist challenged the theories that restricted the validity of the law of value to the national level, arguing that that initial scope has been overtaken by the global dimension characteristic of contemporary capitalism (Amin, 2001b: Chapter 5).

This view of price formation under the command of multinational corporations was later corroborated by many studies of the globalized management of firms. These companies operate with higher profit rates than those that prevail in each national territory. The law of value on an international scale explains the way in which a significant portion of contemporary production unfolds in the inner space of multinational corporations (Carchedi, 1991: Chapters 6–7).

Amin highlighted not only the increasing reach of globalization, but also its polarizing dynamic, which he held is intrinsic to a system that expands globally while maintaining national structures for labor markets. With this approach, Amin anticipated in the 1960s and 1970s many features of the coming globalization of production, seeing in the multinationals of that time various tendencies of the transnationalization to come. But he also approached the problem by assessing the qualitative change introduced by the working of the law of value on a world scale. By situating his analysis of the center-periphery relation on this terrain, he focused it on the industrial world of home offices and their affiliates. This approach emphasizes, much more than any previous study, the productive dimension of the global gap. While Baran showed that the center-periphery relation went beyond the old connection between manufacturing and primary economies, Amin explained how the global cleavage is reproduced within globalized industrial structures.

However, his approach was not without its problems. By postulating that polarization is an economic tendency intrinsic to capitalism in all its stages, Amin left several questions open about the reasons for the periodic halt of this process. He did not clarify the causes of the bifurcations that are frequently found in the periphery. The Egyptian economist also attributed the widening of contemporary polarization to the impact of monopolies. He described five contemporary types of monopolization that ensure metropolitan control over technology, financial flows, natural resources, mass media, and weapons of mass destruction. He demonstrated how that dominance reinforces the devaluation of labor in the periphery (Amin, 2001a: 15–30).

This theory has similarities to Sweezy's approach, but is based on a very different theory of value, which emphasizes the continuity of competition. In practice, Amin uses the term monopoly in the sense of competition among large groups, not as stable oligopoly as Sweezy uses it. With this approach, he analyzes super-profits derived from the segmentation that exists between the economies of the center and the periphery. His kinship with *Monthly Review* is closer in his analysis of polarization as a result of the senility of capitalism. Amin affirmed this historical decline with arguments that coincided with Sweezy, but without reference to stagnation. His concept of senility highlighted the explosive contradictions of the system, but did not postulate the existence of paralysis of the productive forces.

6   Unequal Exchange

Amin considered unequal exchange to be the main mechanism for value transfers. He argued that this flow increases with the generalization of foreign investment, which reinforces the global gap (Amin, 1973: 80–87). The Marxist theorist developed this characterization in a period of internationalization of trade and increasing dissemination of Prebisch's critique of the deterioration of the terms of trade. Both processes aroused great interest in the question of unequal exchange as a central cause of underdevelopment.

Amin coincided with the authors who emphasized the productive determinants of that process. He went back to Marx's observations about the higher international remuneration of labor involved in activities of higher productivity. He also reviewed the studies of Otto Bauer on the existence of transfers of surplus value between developed (Germany) and farther behind (Czech-Bohemian) economies. But the Egyptian theorist specifically analyzed the connections between unequal exchange and the globalized functioning of the law of value. He argued that the advanced economies absorb surplus value from the backward ones as a consequence of their greater development (higher organic composition of capital).

With this perspective, another difference between Amin and Sweezy was confirmed. The problem of unequal exchange assumes the current reality of competition and the centrality of productive dynamics, both of which are in conflict with the pure preeminence of monopoly and the supremacy of finance in the work of the U.S. economist (Howard and King, 1989: 188–189).

Amin also agreed with the importance attached by Emmanuel to unequal exchange, but he disagreed with explanations focused exclusively on differences in wages between the advanced and backward economies (Emmanuel, 1971: 5–37). He objected to that causality, rejecting the depiction of the wage as an 'independent variable' in the process of accumulation. He also argued that the wage was not determined by demographic trends. He affirmed that the wage remunerates the value of labor power according to objective parameters of productivity and subjective dynamics resulting from class struggle (Amin, 1973: 43–44, 16–17, 26–30).

Neither did Amin share Emmanuel's hopes for resolving global asymmetrics through wage increases in the periphery, and he rejected the depiction of the workers in the center as responsible for the exploitation of the Third World. He focused his interpretation of unequal exchange on the global cleavage created by the mobility of capital and commodities, combined with the immobility of labor (Amin, 1973: 34–56).

Another influential Marxist theorist – Bettelheim – challenged the errors of Emmanuel more categorically. He asserted that international differences in wages were due to gaps in the development of the productive forces, arguing that higher remunerations express the higher productivities in the central economies and the predominance of more complex and skilled labors (Bettelheim, 1972a: 38–66). Bettelheim located the origin of unequal exchange in the sphere of production, not of wages. In addition, he relativized the weight of that mechanism, asserting its variable importance at each stage of capitalism.

Amin partially took up these observations to improve his model of world value, and introduced the term 'unequal conditions of exploitation' to join the two logics (Amin, 1976: 159–161). What, then, has been Amin's contribution in this area? His approach contributed to distinguishing unequal exchange from the classical debates on the deterioration of the terms of trade in exchanges between raw materials and manufactured products. By analyzing transfers derived from differences between industries located in the center and the periphery, the Egyptian economist made a distinction between two different subjects that have traditionally been confused. Transfers of value from the periphery to the center – generated by wage differences that are bigger than the productivity gaps – can be applied to the *maquilas* installed in the Third World by large industrial corporations to increase their appropriation of surplus value.

This dynamic of unequal exchange differs completely from the relation between manufacturing and agro-mining prices, which suggests another dimension to the connections between advanced and underdeveloped economies, and involves other tendencies.

7   Dependency and Socialism

Amin posited that the center-periphery gap is a dominant economic tendency of capitalism, but distinguished that polarization principle from political situations of dependency. He considered the two processes to be related, but not identical or symmetrically operating, arguing that polarization marked the trajectory of capitalism since its birth, but that national situations of dependency were determined by the empire's capacity for domination in each case (Amin, 2006: 5–22).

Amin understood that resistance to this oppression introduces the only factor of significant counterweight to the center-periphery gap. He stressed the impact of this action as a restraint to underdevelopment and as a driver of the advances made by the industrialized peripheral economies. He thought that these developments were possible in the postwar era because of the presence of socialist blocs, anti-imperialist movements, and Keynesian compromises (Amin, 2001a: 15–30). The prolific economist believed that this confluence made it possible to counteract polarization through the local control of accumulation that several peripheral states had introduced. He argued that this mechanism, identified with delinking from the world market, allowed experiments with the self-centered models that facilitated the expansion of the advanced economies.

However, unlike the Keynesian heterodoxy, Amin did not have confidence in the potential of those autonomous development processes under capitalism, and he did not advocate trying to overcome underdevelopment by this route. For the Marxist analyst, local control over accumulation should introduce a sequence of delinkings favorable to socialist transformation. He argued that confrontation with the corporations of the center is the starting point of that long post-capitalist transition (Amin, 1988: 83–158).

Amin developed this theory in contention with conceptions that ignore the center-periphery gap or that see this cleavage in exclusively economic terms. He distinguished polarization from dependency to highlight the political primacy of the struggle to eradicate underdevelopment (Amin, 2003: Chapter 5). The difference he established between the two concepts constitutes a key contribution for overcoming simplified views of the center-periphery relation. It points to the existence of economic and political dimensions that do not follow identical paths. While polarization affects all underdeveloped countries in the same way, dependency varies according to the level of anti-imperialist mobilization prevalent in each case.

The differing situations of subjection, autonomy, or confrontation with imperialism found in countries that are equally subordinate to the international division of labor corroborates this distinction. Amin's theory also helps us understand why delinkings that do not deepen tend to recreate the center-periphery gap. But this novel approach opens up another question: how to explain the industrialization or continued growth of backward economies that did not carry out anti-imperialist processes?

The theory of delinking was conceived by Amin to support socialist strategies in the revolutionary processes of the periphery. This approach accepted alliances made with national bourgeoisies, and was inspired by Maoist views from the 1970s. It stressed the protagonism of different types of popular forces, and approved of the model of collectivist communes introduced in China during the Cultural Revolution (Amin, 1973: 9, 13; Amin, 1976: 112, 124, 184–186; Foster, 2011).

8   Collective Imperialism

Amin related center-periphery polarization to the existence of a new mechanism of collective imperialism led by the United States. He used this term to explain how global geopolitical domination operates in a framework of internationalization of capital and continued importance of the nation-state form. The Egyptian economist specified that the preeminence of the law of value on a world scale did not imply the formation of a global ruling class or state, but made it necessary to create structures to govern planetary companies and markets. He emphasized this economic determinant in the configuration of an imperial partnership around the Triad (United States, Europe, and Japan) (Amin, 2013a).

Amin also asserted that the new system adapted economic rivalries to a political-military strategy shared by the great powers. He stressed the generalized acceptance of the military patronage exercised by the United States in the context created by the Cold War. However, he attributed the appearance of collective imperialism not so much to the existence of the USSR as to the need to administer a capitalist economy that was globalized and threatened by large imbalances and popular challenges (Amin, 2003: Chapter 6). With this approach, he rejected the theory of hegemonic succession that postulated the necessary replacement of U.S. supremacy by another dominant power. He argued that the new context favored the articulation of imperial powers more than the resumption of fights for hegemony (Amin, 2004).

Amin emphasized that the predominance of collective imperialism reinforced world polarization in more insurmountable hierarchies. He thought that the barriers to the development of the periphery traditionally imposed by Europe were maintained by the Triad since the second half of the 20th century. Nevertheless, the Marxist theorist added nuance to the bipolar cleavage, affirming the existence of semi-peripheries between the two extremes. He pointed out that those intermediate formations were historically a standard feature, but that under contemporary capitalism these forms cannot catch up to the center. He argued, for example, that Brazil cannot catch up to the United States by following the path that in the past allowed Germany to catch up to England (2008: 221–222).

Amin thought that the stable hierarchy of collective imperialism leads to the integration of the intermediate variants in the dominant structures and to neo-imperial regionalization. He argued that these poles associated with the Triad (Turkey, Israel, South Africa) fulfill the function of maintaining the discipline that the center demands (Amin, 2003: Chapter 6). The collective imperialism posited by Amin contributed original and fruitful ideas for understanding current capitalism. On the one hand, he highlighted the qualitative changes generated by the international association among companies of different national origins. On the other, he illustrated the geopolitical correlate of this new power of multinational firms.

Our research on contemporary imperialism draws on those contributions of the Egyptian scholar. We show how the collective action exercised by the great powers unfolds under U.S. leadership. This joint management guided by the Pentagon has been verified in all the military conflicts after the Second World War. Collective imperialism does not imply an equitable management of the world order, but it does imply associations that radically modify the old logic of inter-imperial wars. The specific actions of each power (hegemonic wars) are carried out within a framework of joint imperial aggressions (global wars). For that reason, the pretext of collective security has replaced that of national defense as the guiding principle for armed intervention. This military solidarity in the geopolitical action of the powers is in tune with the intertwining of capitals and the enormous size of markets required to maintain and expand profitable activities. It expresses the level of centralization that capital has reached in the financial, productive, and commercial spheres.

Collective imperialism is the answer to the advance of economic globalization without an equivalent correspondence on the state level. Since national states persist without being replaced by any global organizations, the reproduction of capital is ensured by a more coordinated mode of imperial actions (Katz, 2011: 65–80).

9   Mandel's Perspective

Mandel developed his theory in the same period as Baran–Sweezy and Amin, being familiar with their work and sharing their general view of the center-periphery relation. He studied the same problem by means of three central ideas. First, he asserted that the cause of the gap was the conflict between primitive accumulation processes in the periphery and metropolitan capital's need for expansion. He understood this tension as leading to different levels of subordination of the underdeveloped economies. The Belgian economist affirmed that central capitalism always seeks to incorporate new regions to its control, while the development of the market undermines pre-capitalist formations. He stressed that both movements create tensions between foreign and local capitalists around the priorities for accumulation.

Mandel pointed out that the results of those conflicts vary in each stage, depending on the changing capacity of the central economies to dominate the underdeveloped countries. He held that metropolitan capital is only able to achieve this subordination when it has sufficient resources, and also noted that in periods of less expansive capacity, greater rivalries, or crisis, control over the periphery is attenuated (Mandel, 1978: Chapter 2).

Second, Mandel indicated that as capitalism expands, it profits from inequalities between regions, countries, and sectors, taking advantage of cost differences to accumulate extraordinary profits. This type of surplus profit is captured by capitalists who invest in the most profitable sectors or regions, profiting from the cheapness of inputs or labor. In those circumstances, the center-periphery gap is accentuated (Mandel, 1978: Chapter 2).

Third, Mandel proposed an outline of several historical periods in the relation between the two poles of the world economy. He maintained that in the formation of capitalism (through the late 19th century), the advanced economies had not reached the level of power required to subordinate the rest of the planet. In that stage of free trade, the major powers did not have the surplus capital or the means of communication necessary to exercise that supremacy. For this reason, there was a wide margin for the development of intermediate economies (Russia, Italy, Japan). In the following stage of classical imperialism (late 19th to early 20th century), the center had enough surplus capital, cheaper transportation, and foreign investment to dominate the periphery.

Finally, the postwar period was one of more contradictory obstructions for the underdeveloped regions. The reconstruction of the advanced economies concentrated investment in the center and gave rise to segmentation. One sector of the peripheral countries continued its agro-mining primarization to satisfy the new demand for inputs, while another group of nations achieved some level of industrial development with the import-substitution process, which went along with the priorities of the center in its own postwar reconstitution.

With this approach, Mandel offered an innovative interpretation of the center-periphery relation. He asserted that the foundation of the gap is the changing appearance of surplus profits in different areas, which establish durable cleavages between advanced and backward economies. This approach stresses the modification of situations in each stage of capitalism and the consequent remodeling of polarization. Mandel affirmed that those changes alter the segmentation of winners and losers, creating significant variations within the fractured historical structure of world capitalism.

With this perspective, Mandel observed that the periphery has confronted situations of more breathing room (free trade), suffocation (classical imperialism), and segmentation (late capitalism). In each of those contexts specific super-profits predominated, resulting from the prevailing differences between regions, nations, or branches of industry. The theoretical foundation for this theory is unequal and combined development, which Mandel took from Trotsky. He used this principle to describe the heterogeneous dynamic of accumulation, which increases the disparity between the components of a single world market as it expands (Mandel, 1983: 7–39). The Belgian theorist described how the countries that are most connected by commercial and financial transactions remain more distant on the level of technology and productivity as a consequence of that process of unification without homogenization that characterizes contemporary capitalism (Mandel, 1969b: 125–149).

Mandel avoided abstract reflections about unequal and combined development, challenging banal interpretations of that rule as a simple confirmation of asymmetries in international relations. He employed the concept in a useful form, to capture the peculiarities of capitalism in its different stages (Kratke, 2007; Stutje, 2007; Ven der linden, 2007). The Marxist theorist saw postwar center-periphery relations as a juxtaposition between different economic-social formations that operate in the same world market. In line with Amin, but based on a different foundation, he attributed the gap between development and underdevelopment to that lack of homogenization.

10   Bifurcations and Neutralizations

Mandel distinguished between two existing types of underdeveloped economies: a majority group of agro-mining countries, and a select segment of semi-industrializing countries. He asserted that this bifurcation emerged with the crisis of the 1930s and was reinforced during the expansion of the 1950s–1960s with the economic reconstruction of the Triad. On the one hand, the industrialization of many raw materials accentuated the subordinate specialization of the lesser periphery; on the other, import substitution shored up the industrial development of the better-off peripheries.

Mandel conceptualized this bifurcation by means of a reclassification of Leninist categories. He argued that the old ordering of the underdeveloped world in colonies, semi-colonies, and dependent nations should be replaced by a distinction between peripheries and semi-industrialized dependents (Mandel, 1986). He located Brazil, Mexico, Argentina, South Korea, Taiwan, South Africa, India, Egypt, and Algeria in the second group. Other theorists developed a similar characterization utilizing the notion of semi-periphery.

The Belgian economist argued that capitalist development widens the heterogeneity of the backward countries. The general underdevelopment of the entire conglomeration persists, but with forms that are differentiated with the expansion of manufacturing in the higher segment (Mandel, 1971b: 153–171). With this perspective, he highlighted the varied situations more than the polarizations of the peripheral world. Mandel emphasized the amalgam of productive forms and the development of some economies at the expense of others. He did not propose a model of simple distancing between the center and the periphery (Sutcliffe, 2008).

His reasoning separated him from the Marxists who stressed the metropolitan aim of impeding any type of competitive foreign industrialization. He argued that the problem of the intermediate economies was the partial and insufficient character of its industrial development, not the complete absence of that expansion. Mandel pointed to the changing nature of global polarization in the history of capitalism. He suggested that the crises inherent to the system cause periods of neutralization or bifurcation of the cleavage, and he presented three causes of counterweights to polarization: the scarcity of surplus capitals in the mid-19th century, the depression of the 1930s, and the metropolitan concentration of investment in the postwar era.

The influence of this approach can be found in the perspective of Harvey on capitalist development as a world process subject to periodic crises that cause changes in the location of investment (Harvey, 1982). Arrighi also stressed the turbulent course of capital and the existence of moments of greater suffocation or of more breathing room for the underdeveloped economies; within the stable architecture of global capitalism, there operates a changing geography of bifurcations in the periphery (Arrighi, 2005).

The importance of Mandel's theory lies in his demonstration of those objective processes, opening spaces for the expansion of some economies of the higher periphery. Those spaces emerge from the crises inherent to central capitalism or from the new forms of internationalized expansion of the system.

11   Imbalances and Fluctuations

Mandel combined external and internal determinants in his interpretation of underdevelopment. On the one hand, he argued that the insertion of the periphery as provider of raw materials perpetuated the transfers of surplus value to the advanced economies. On the other, he showed the limitations of industrial development caused by the rentier inclination of the dominant classes (Mandel, 1971b: 153–171).

However, the Belgian economist attributed these contradictions to the unbalanced dynamics of accumulation and not to stagnation. He at first used the term 'neo-capitalism' to describe the postwar stage, and later switched to the concept of 'late capitalism', and he went from an idea of 'second youth' to another of 'senility', but always emphasizing the maturity of the system rather than its final stage. Mandel challenged the social-democratic (and later regulationist) theory of organized capitalism and its image of unlimited prosperity. But he also objected to the catastrophist view of continual paralysis of the productive forces put forth by orthodox Trotskyism (Katz, 2008: 17–31).

The Marxist theorist emphasized the cumulative imbalances of capitalism, not the disappearance of competition because of the dominance of monopolies or because of financial waste. On this basis, he developed a different perspective from Baran and Sweezy, and only partially coincided with Amin. He noted the enduring cleavage between the center and the periphery, but mentioned some neutralizing tendencies to polarization. With this approach, he attained a more complete account of the global dynamics of capitalism.

With this perspective, he accepted the continued validity of unequal exchange while relativizing its reach. He noted the preeminence of cyclical movements in the prices of raw materials rather than continual processes of depreciation. He probably took from Grossman his attention to the lesser flexibility of basic inputs relative to technological innovation (Grossman, 1979: Chapter 3). The Belgian theorist asserted that this rigidity causes capitalists to counteract rising costs of production through the periodic industrialization of raw materials. He gave different examples of product substitution (natural to manufactured rubber, wood to plastic, cotton to synthetics). From this combination of tendencies, he deduced the existence of a fluctuating dynamic between the prices of primary and secondary products.

Mandel also suggested, as had Bettelheim, a limited current importance for unequal exchange. He observed that the profits of metropolitan capital came from different sources in each stage (commerce, finance, production). He argued that the profits generated by differences between productivities and wages were not only found in different countries, but also within each nation. He illustrated how this cleavage operated in some 'internal colonies' (the south of Italy or of the United States) and not only in the outer periphery.

Mandel's caution about simplified accounts of the center-periphery gap can be seen in his view of OPEC. He thought that the ruling classes of the oil-exporting countries captured a significant portion of the rent from crude oil, internationalizing the circulation of those funds as autonomous financial capital (Mande and Jaber, 1978). This was a key assertion, as it indicated the existence of situations of relative strengthening of some exporting bourgeoisies in the periphery. Here he also distanced himself from the simplified view of increasing and invariable global gaps. In addition, he opened an avenue for research into the evolution of rents in underdeveloped economies, exploring a dimension to which theorists of his time paid little attention. Mandel emphasized that local handling of rent did not modify the dependent character of those countries, nor did it reverse their enduring underdevelopment. He attributed this lag to the limited profits made during the stages of higher prices for raw materials and the acute losses suffered in periods of cheapening (Guillén Romo, 1978). This view completed his analysis of the causes of the backwardness of the periphery.

12   Socialist Convergences

As with Baran–Sweezy and Amin, Mandel analyzed the center-periphery relation as a contradiction of capitalism that would accelerate the transition to socialism. He noted the protagonism of certain underdeveloped countries in that transformation. The victories in Yugoslavia, China, Cuba, and Vietnam confirmed that expectation, and led the Belgian theorist to explore with greater precision the relation between anti-imperialist resistance, industrialization projects, and models for creating socialism (Mandel, 1980: 13–26).

Mandel stressed the close connection between these three processes. He proposed resistance to plunder by foreign capital and conquering greater state control over accumulation in order to introduce forms of planning the economy. This perspective was consistent with Sweezy–Baran and Amin, but it was inspired by Trotsky's theory of permanent revolution. He pointed not only to the incapacity of the national bourgeoisie to eradicate underdevelopment in the periphery, but also to the necessity of an anti-bureaucratic revolution in the socialist countries (Mandel, 1995: 57–88, 129–146).

With this approach, he stressed the potential convergence of the popular uprisings in Latin America, Africa, and Asia with rebellious processes in the West and in the socialist bloc. He especially emphasized the intersection of Third Word uprisings with the French May and the Prague Spring of 1968. Mandel launched a frontal critique of the strategy of revolution by stages. He rejected postponing revolutionary processes, and objected to the strategy of coexistence with imperialism propounded by the leaders of the Soviet Union.

All his life, he advocated convergent revolutionary action of the metropolitan proletariat with diverse popular subjects of the periphery. He imagined a close association between anti-capitalism and anti-imperialism.

His economic model challenged the coercive planning of the Soviet Union and promoted its replacement by democratic mechanisms. He argued for combining market and plan during the socialist transition. Mandel sympathized with the forces of the radical left and showed great political flexibility when seeking convergences with like-minded thinkers. Like Baran, Sweezy, and Amin, Mandel had a great influence over postwar Marxists and over the Latin American authors who, in the 1960s, began to develop dependency theory.

PART 2

Development

∴

The Rise of Dependency Theories

Dependency theories were developed in the 1960s and 1970s around three tendencies. Ruy Mauro Marini, Theotônio Dos Santos, and Vania Bambirra put forth a Marxist conception that was complemented by the metropolis-satellite perspective of Andreè Gunder Frank. Both perspectives came up against Fernando Henrique Cardoso's theory of associated dependent development. What were their disagreements?

1 Socialism and Liberalism

The Marxist Theory of Dependency was a direct product of the Cuban revolution. Before 1960, no one imagined an anti-capitalist process beginning 90 miles from Miami. It was thought that those transformations would be a consequence of prior changes in the centers of world power. The success of Cuba disrupted this scenario and created a great expectation of forthcoming socialist horizons for Latin America. Marini, Dos Santos, and Bambirra posited concepts in keeping with that expectation. They participated in organizations that were struggling against military dictatorships, and encouraged leftist projects in the turbulent period between the rise of the Popular Unity government in Chile (1970) and the fall of *Sandinismo* in Nicaragua (1990).

The three authors confronted U.S. imperialism and conceived proposals for Latin American integration and international association with the so-called socialist bloc. They favored a drastic rupture with the political strategies of the Communist Parties, which proposed forging alliances with the bourgeoisie to develop models of national capitalism. The Brazilian theorists sought convergences with radical nationalist tendencies, while keeping a distance from the conservative varieties. Their conceptualizations of underdevelopment unfolded in close connection with all the leftist debates of the era (attitude toward the Soviet Union, positions on reformist governments, opportunity for armed struggle) (Bambirra, 1986: 113–115, 78–82).

The dependency theorists criticized liberal interpretations that attributed regional backwardness to insufficient absorption of Western civilization, or to the indigenous, mestizo, or Spanish-Portuguese cultural heritage. Marini showed the inconsistency of that conception, pointing to the colonial exaction suffered by Latin America and the later dominance of wasteful oligarchies (Marini, 2007b: 125–247).

Dos Santos also challenged the liberal idea of repeating the U.S. model through the adoption of modernizing behaviors. He argued that the international insertion of the region as an exporter of agro-mining products obstructed its development, and he refuted the fallacy of a gradual convergence with the advanced economies (Dos Santos, 2003). In addition, he showed the inconsistency of all the indicators used by neoclassical economists to evaluate the passage from a traditional society to an industrial one (Sotelo Valencia, 2005). Dos Santos rejected the liberal dualist interpretation of underdevelopment as a conflict between modern and backward sectors of the economy, highlighting the artificial character of that separation and the close integration between the two sectors (Dos Santos, 1978: 198–283).

Frank also took part in that critique, stressing that the backward sector was not a hindrance to the prevailing model but the main factor in its recreation. He asserted that Latin American underdevelopment was not caused by the absence of capitalism, but by the burden of a dependent mode of that system. This idea of Frank not only confronted the liberal mythology that counterposed regional backwardness with Western modernization. By defining underdevelopment as an intrinsic feature of dependent capitalism, he replaced perspectives centered on ideal typologies with historical characterizations of social regimes (Laclau, 1973; Wolf, 1993: 38).

2   Developmentalism and Marxism

Marxist dependency theorists were influenced by the ideas of the U.N. Economic Commission for Latin America and the Caribbean (ECLAC), which attributed backwardness to the deterioration of the terms of trade and to the structural heterogeneity of economies with high unemployment, elite consumerism, and agricultural stagnation. Developmentalists promoted import-substitution industrialization and greater public-sector investment, challenged the attachment to an agro-export model, and encouraged economic policies favorable to the national bourgeoisie.

Marini agreed with several of Raúl Prebisch's diagnoses on the origin of underdevelopment, and with some of Celso Furtado's theories on the adverse impact of the labor supply on wages. However, he never shared their hope of resolving those imbalances with bourgeois modernization policies. He spoke highly of ECLAC's theoretical findings while questioning their expectations of autonomous capitalist development in Latin America (Marini, 1991: 18–19). In addition, he criticized them for ignoring the function served by the region in the accumulation strategies of the central economies. Marini explained the center-periphery gap by the dynamics of capitalism, and emphasized the inexistence of another variety of that system for the Third World. He asserted that underdevelopment could not be eradicated with simple corrective policies or with higher doses of investment (Marini, 1993).

Dos Santos formulated a similar critique. He stressed that Latin American backwardness is not caused by a lack of capital, but by the place occupied by the region in the international division of labor (Dos Santos, 1978: 26–27). Dependency theorists also objected to the depiction of the state as a driver of growth, free from the limitations of the dominant classes. They therefore did not believe in the space suggested by ECLAC for achieving Latin American development. With this perspective, they displayed an affinity with the Marxist economists from other regions who updated the characterization of postwar capitalism, avoiding the depiction of this stage as a simple continuation of the earlier Leninist scheme (Katz, 2016).

Dos Santos emphasized the new weight of multinational enterprises and the growing global integration of capital. He concurred with Amin's interpretation of the law of value operating on a world scale, and agreed with Sweezy's assessment of U.S. protagonism. Bambirra also stressed U.S. predominance in the new circuit of global accumulation.

These views connected the mutations of capitalism with analysis of the crisis of that system. Marini assessed the dynamics of the falling rate of profit tendency in the periphery, pointing out that the percentage decline of profitability comes from the reduction of new living labor incorporated in commodities relative to the dead labor already objectivized in raw materials and machinery. He noted that this modification reduces the profit rate in proportion to the total capital advanced. Marini also asserted that the affluence of capital to the periphery moderated that decline in the central economies through increases in the exploitation of workers in the periphery and cheapening of the provision of food and inputs for metropolitan industry. However, he emphasized that this compensation accentuated the suffocation of the capacity for consumption in the lower-wage countries (Marini, 2005). Dos Santos shared this combined reasoning of the crisis due to valorization imbalances (tendency of the rate of profit to fall) and tensions in the realization of value (insufficient purchasing power) (Dos Santos, 1978: 154–155). Both authors adopted a multicausal perspective – similar to Mandel's approach – which clarified various features of crises in the periphery (Katz, 2009: 117–119).

The dependency theorists also coincided with Mandel and Amin in recording the new bifurcations present in the underdeveloped countries. Thus,

Marini analyzed the industrial imbalances of intermediate economies affected by higher costs, technological disadvantages, and chronic trade balance deficits. His conclusions on Brazil (or Argentina and Mexico) were consistent with those of analysts of industry in equivalent countries of Asia and Africa. Marini analyzed the intermediate economies of Latin America in order to get past treatments of the periphery as an indistinct universe. He corrected old Marxist traditions that likened Latin America to regions of Asia or Africa. The same purpose motivated Dos Santos to investigate the specificities of Latin American industries, subject to externally-generated import price increases and internal hindrances due to the tightness of the domestic market.

Bambirra conceptualized the same problem, introducing distinctions between the Latin American economies. He contrasted the countries with early industrialization (Argentina, Mexico, Brazil), late industrialization (Peru, Venezuela), and agro-export structures without industry (Paraguay, Haiti) (Bambirra, 1986: 57–69). This attention to the unequal underdevelopment of the region was an analytical pillar of dependency theories.

3   The New Categories

Marini interpreted the deterioration of the terms of trade as an expression of unequal exchange. He claimed that transfers of value to the center were not due to the inferiority of primary production, but to the objective dynamics of accumulation on a world scale (Marini, 1973). In this way, he highlighted the generic weight of the law of value in that process.

However, the Brazilian theorist did not deepen that analysis, and sidestepped the differentiated study of those phenomena within and outside of industry that was started by the unequal exchange theorists (Emmanuel, Amin, Bettelheim). Nor did he explore the dynamics of oil rents recycled in financial circuits, as analyzed by Mandel. Dos Santos adopted the same perspective. He situated unequal exchange only in the realm of the struggles over international trade that habitually affect the periphery (Dos Santos, 1978: 322–323, 367).

The Latin American authors concentrated their attention on the imbalances of dependent reproduction. Dos Santos studied how trade imbalances combine with imbalances due to debt and inflation in the industrialized countries of the periphery. Marini conceptualized the cycle of financing, production, and commercialization in those economies in contrast to the central countries. He noted that private investment is less than in the metropolises, and that foreign capital drains funds through royalties, profits, or sales of machinery. He described how companies obtain extraordinary profits by taking advantage of the cheapness of wages, and illustrated the way in which low purchasing power holds back the internal market (Marini, 2012). In this way, he theorized ECLAC's structural heterogeneity in Marxist terms, as a dependent cycle. He took up Prebisch's diagnosis of strong limits to accumulation as a consequence of sectoral disproportions and restricted consumption, and affirmed that this *capitalist* adversity impeded development.

However, he saw these imbalances as contradictions that are specific to dependent capitalism, and investigated their dynamics using a model taken from Volume II of *Capital*. With that logic, he avoided abstract assumptions of equilibrium and detected the same tensions in industrial accumulation that were found by Amin and Mandel.

Marini noted the tightness of purchasing power, going back to Luxemburg's underconsumption hypothesis. However, he located the problem in the realities of the periphery. Instead of analyzing how the obstruction of internal demand pushes metropolitan capital outward, he studied the imbalances that process creates in the underdeveloped economies. He already understood the dynamics of mass consumption in the central countries; he therefore expounded a theory of obstructed Fordism in the intermediate economies of the periphery. He stressed the existence of a great stratification of consumption between low and middle-to-high segments, and highlighted the absence of a mass of middle-class acquirers comparable to the developed economies.

However, Marini situated the main peculiarity of the industrialized peripheral economies in the super-exploitation of labor, using this term to describe the condition of the workers subjected to being paid less than the value of their labor power. He asserted that this anomaly was the backdrop to the dependent situation and to the behavior of the dominant classes, who profited with higher rates of surplus value than the center. He held that the peripheral bourgeoisie compensated in this way for losses stemming from their subordinate place in the world market. arguing that Latin American capitalists used the consumption fund of the workers as a source of capital accumulation. He clarified that super-exploitation was only viable in regions with large labor surpluses, stemming from a large indigenous population (Mexico), rural exodus (Brazil), or immigration flows.

The Brazilian theorist located the main peculiarity of the intermediate Latin American economies in the form in which surplus value is generated. Like Amin, he highlighted the continued relevance of higher levels of exploitation. But instead of explaining this fact by wage differences bigger than productivity differences, he attributed the phenomenon to a qualitatively inferior remuneration of labor power. This assessment was formulated with his attention focused on the industrialization process in a country with enormous income inequalities (Brazil).

4   Subimperialism and the National Bourgeoisie

Marini did not limit himself to repeating old complaints about the oppressive role of the United States. He introduced the controversial concept of subimperialism to depict the new strategy of the Brazilian ruling class. He described the expansive tendencies of large companies affected by the tightness of the internal market, and noted their promotion of aggressive state policies to allow incursions into the neighboring economies.

This interpretation was based on a similar logic to that of Luxemburg when she characterized the imperial tendencies of Germany, France, or England. That perspective emphasized that those strategies were implemented to counteract reduced local purchasing power (Marini, 2005). However, the Latin American Marxist gave the concept a very different geopolitical dimension from the classical account. He did not claim that Brazil would be incorporated into the club of powers that dispute world domination. Rather, he stressed the subordination of that country to the U.S. strategy. Thus, Matini spoke of subimperialism and the role of regional anti-communist gendarme played by the Brazilian dictatorship during the cold war against the Soviet Union.

The dependency theorist further developed the meaning of subimperialism introducing other concepts like 'state of counterinsurgency'. He used that concept to describe the role of repressive tutelage exercised by the military in the transition to constitutional regimes (Martins, 2011a; Mendonça, 2011). Marini spoke of subimperialism to emphasize that the major South American bourgeoisie was a partner, not a puppet, of Washington. He especially stressed the autonomous geopolitical role of a ruling class that sought to project itself as an economic and political power on a regional scale (Marini, 1985). With this perspective, he returned to the perceptions of the classical Marxists on the role of the lesser imperialisms, and incorporated new analyses on the role of the United States in the postwar era. His theory was in tune with Amin's idea of collective imperialism on three levels: the increasing global association of capitals, the capitalist protector function exercised by the Pentagon, and the new role of regional custodians associated with Washington.

While subimperialism was a theme taken up specifically by Marini, the new direction taken by the national bourgeoisie was addressed by all three dependency theorists. They demonstrated the passage from an industrialist class with independent development projects to a sector associated with foreign companies, pointing to the bourgeoisie's support for the coup of 1964 as a convincing sign of their giving up on processes of autonomous accumulation (Chilcote, 1983).

The dependency theorists noted connections with foreign capital rather than simple subordination. They emphasized the new profile of more internationalized industrial bourgeoisies, specifying differences from the old landowning oligarchy and from the previous national capitalism. Dos Santos indicated that this turn created a conflict with sectors of the bureaucracy tied to classical developmentalism (Dos Santos, 1978: 34; López Segrera, 2009).

The Brazilian theorist also went into greater depth on the political dimension of that process by defining the status of a subordinate situation. He felt that dependency is verified when one group of countries conditions the development of others (Dos Santos, 1978: 305). He portrayed this situation for the Latin American case through an analysis similar to that proposed by Amin. In both cases, the political dimension of dependency was differentiated from economic polarization, clarifying the connections between processes that do not (necessarily) develop simultaneously. Both theorists explored the specificity of political subordination to imperial power, which earlier had been likened to economic subjection. But in a context of the absorbing primacy of socialist strategies, those characterizations were only sketched.

5   Theories and Particularities

Marini, Bambirra, and Dos Santos tried to mold Marxism to the study of the new postwar Latin American reality. Thus, they embarked on the same search for specific ideas as Baran–Sweezy with surplus, Amin with world value, and Mandel with long waves. This inquiry followed, as well, the path begun by Lenin on unequal development, by Luxemburg with her revision of primitive accumulation, and by Trotsky with unequal and combined development. However, the status of dependency as a theory provoked heated debates over whether it constituted a conception, a paradigm, or an approach, according to the different interpretations in fashion about social laws.

Dos Santos maintained that dependency theory had already reached a scientific level by defining the laws that govern the development of the peripheral countries. He affirmed that those principles clarified the evolution of dependent capitalism, with similar reasoning to that used by Lenin to explain imperialism. He held that the rules of dependency clarified the form in which commercial, financial, or technological-industrial subjection created blockages to accumulation in Latin America (Dos Santos, 1978: 300, 360–366). Marini worked in the same direction, attributing scientific legality to the mechanisms generating surplus value in the dependent regions.

Both theorists studied the peculiarity of Latin America relative to other dependent societies, and indicated that their investigations were different from those that predominated in Asia or Africa. In the major countries of those continents, the main questions had to do with the historical reasons that allowed Europe to dominate old civilizations and submit them to colonial (India) or semi-colonial (Egypt, China) degradation (Amin, 2005). In Latin America, the enigmas of dependency arose from the renovation of a subordinate status after a century and a half of political independence without comparison in other parts of the Third World. This view motivated research into the peculiarities of the Caribbean, Central America, Brazil, the Andean region, and the Southern Cone (Dos Santos, 1998).

Those studies were undertaken with a view 'from the periphery', which Marini adopted in opposition to the elitist paternalism of Latin American studies from the United States, England, or France. He proposed reverting this anomaly, generating knowledges from within the region (Marini, 1991: 9–10, 42). With the same approach, Dos Santos tried to correct the classical authors of imperialism, who in his judgment did not address that question from the point of view of the actual peripheral countries (Dos Santos, 1978: 301–303, 340–345).

With these characterizations of the status of dependency theory, the three Brazilian Marxists completed the presentation of an approach that shook the agenda of Latin American social sciences. The concepts introduced by Marini, the political characterizations of Dos Santos, and the perspectives of Bambirra on unequal underdevelopment created durable analytical points of reference for the theorists of this period.

6   The Metropolis-Satellite Perspective

André Gunder Frank actively participated in the rise of Marxist dependency theory, and his theory had a stronger immediate impact than the other authors. However, his perspective was different, and his metropolis-satellite approach represented only the first of three conceptions that he held during his life. The initial period was, curiously, both the shortest and the most famous of that trajectory. He began his work under the strong impact of the Cuban revolution, adopting the left critiques of the communist strategy of stages and questioning the policy of supporting the national bourgeoisie. He highlighted the inexistence of spaces for repeating the classical development of capitalism, noting the unviability of developmentalism and postulating the need for socialism (Frank, 1970: 211–213). In taking this attitude, Frank radicalized liberal political ideas and abandoned an evolutionary scheme that identified overcoming underdevelopment with the eradication of pre-capitalist institutions. He did not, however, mature his perspective by assimilating the Marxist theoretical debates that were incorporated by other dependency authors.

His affinity with this approach was acknowledged by Marini, who highlighted the accuracy of the formula used by Frank to depict Latin America's backwardness. He recognized that the 'development of underdevelopment' illustrated how the consolidation of the advanced economies was realized at the expense of those that were left behind (Marini, 1993). The German-American theorist put forth that corollary without identifying the mechanisms of dependent reproduction. Neither did he frame his characterization in the global functioning of capitalism, or connect his theory with some analysis of value, underconsumption, or the falling rate of profit tendency. Frank simply posited that capitalism creates underdevelopment in the periphery of the world system. He asserted that this subordinate insertion determined the appropriation by the advanced economies of the surplus of the backward ones.

Frank depicted the metropolis-satellite polarization as two faces of same world trajectory. He stressed the complementarity of those processes, and noted the exceptional character of interruptions of that cleavage. He pointed out that no subjugated economy had reached the status of central power in the contemporary era, and thought that the weakening of the metropolis did not change the durable status of dependency (Frank, 1970: 8–24).

The German theorist applied this logic to Latin American history. He situated the origin of the center-periphery relation in the subordinate integration of the region to world capitalism in the 16th century. He argued that in this chain of global accumulation, a metropolitan center (Europe) subjects the peripheral satellites (Latin America) through the mediation of certain countries (Spain, Portugal) that in turn become satellites of the dominant power (Great Britain). Within Latin America, this same circuit connects the peripheral satellite (Chile) with the major colonial satellite (Peru), which in turn is controlled by the extra-regional metropolis (Spain or England). This chain of subjugations is recreated together with the hierarchical confiscation of surpluses (Frank, 1970: 1–7).

Frank presented two examples of this connection. He illustrated how Chile remained subjugated to that subordination since the colonial era by means of a local ruling class tied to the demands of a handful of foreign companies. In the case of Brazil, he noted its dependent insertion through major satellites (Sao Paulo) that ensured the subordination of the secondary satellites (Recife) to the metropolis (first Portugal, then the United States). He did not find significant differences between the two countries (Frank, 1970: 119–123, 149–154).

7   Two Different Approaches

Frank prioritized analysis of the drainages suffered by the periphery, in keeping with approaches of absolute polarization between the center and the periphery. In contrast, Marini, Dos Santos, and Bambirra incorporated the existing bifurcations between agro-export (Chile) and partially industrialized (Brazil) economies. This difference led to distinct approaches. While Frank saw the Latin American economy as a uniform totality, his Brazilian colleagues studied specific national contradictions. They established distinctions where Frank saw equivalent subordinations. Moreover, the Brazilian theorists started from general characterizations of postwar capitalism that Frank did not take into account. His approach did not incorporate the considerations of multinational corporations, technological transformations, or changes in investment that Dos Santos highlighted.

Because of this omission, Frank only saw that at moments of crisis in the center, the spaces for development of the periphery widen. But with this insight he explained only the origin of Latin American industrialization, without clarifying what happened later. He skipped over all the writings on the center-periphery cleavage developed by Marxist economists and assimilated by the Brazilian authors. Thus, he only studied the dynamics of exaction, while Marini captured articulations with advanced capitalism and Dos Santos perceived the effects of globalization. That exploration allowed them to avoid simplifications and recognize new forms of dependency.

Dos Santos early on questioned Frank's omission of internal transformations in the underdeveloped countries. He objected to Frank's static view and the consequent suggestion of the immutability of Latin American society, attributing that unilaterality to his adherence to a structural-functionalist methodology (Dos Santos, 1978: 304–305, 350–352, 346). This mistake was demonstrated in his presentation of the links from the center to its satellites, as if they were simple pieces on a board moved by the great powers. In this view, social subjects either are absent or fulfill a mechanical role given by the place they occupy in the global mechanism. Antagonisms between social classes, conflicts between capitalist sectors, and state mediations do not fit into that scheme. In contrast, in Marini's logic the preeminence of dependent cycles, forms of super-exploitation, or transfers of value do not negate the central importance of oppressors and oppressed in the dynamics of dependency.

The economic mechanisms that recreate the center-periphery polarity in Frank represent only the point of departure for Marini, Bambirra, or Dos Santos. That is why the Brazilian theorists did not use the term satellite to describe the dependent economies. That metaphor alludes to a body that revolves in an invariable way around a certain center, without any autonomy or internal development.

Certainly, Frank contributed several worthy intuitions, but the development of these perceptions was hampered by his omission of social subjects. His account of tripolar relations is an example of observations that are accurate, but lack support in adequate conceptualizations. Frank recognized that the global hierarchy goes beyond the center-periphery duality, but at the same time he ignored the specificity of intermediate formations. Thus, he used the same reasoning to analyze the evolution of Chile as for Brazil.

This reductionism was even greater in his view of the national bourgeoisies. In contrast to Marini and Dos Santos, he limited himself to establishing the defection of that sector, without analyzing the contradictions that brought that change on. In addition, he identified association with foreign companies with a degradation of the local ruling classes to the condition of 'lumpen-bourgeoisie' (Frank, 1979). That idea implies a decomposition of the ruling groups that would make their running of the state impossible. Marini and Dos Santos never lost sight of the fact that the Latin American bourgeoisies combined agro-mining rents with the extraction of surplus value from the workers. They are ruling groups, not simple tributary layers of foreign capital.

The region's dominators are subject to the patterns of competition, investment, and exploitation inherent to capitalism. These principles differ from pure pillage implemented by a 'lumpen-bourgeoisie'. That name can be applied, for example, to the drug mafias that launder their fortunes in financial or productive activities; they are capitalists who are marginalized from the stable club of the dominators (Katz, 2015: 41–42).

Frank also failed to incorporate the Brazilian theorists' conception of the distinctions between economic polarization and political dependency. This omission was not unrelated to his limited political participation in the processes that marked the trajectory of Marini, Dos Santos, and Bambirra. These three authors were directly involved in the debates in Cuba, Chile, or the guerrilla movements. In contrast, while Frank gave his enthusiastic support to the Cuban revolution, he did not contribute significant reflections about the political dilemmas of the left. He was not part of the activist world that defined the work of the Marxist dependency theorists. This distance played a role in the change of direction in his later writings.

8   Development and Dependency

Fernando Henrique Cardoso developed an opposite approach to Frank, Marini, Dos Santos, and Bambirra, but was initially placed in the same category of dependency theorists. His text with Faletto challenged the traditional representation of regional backwardness as an effect of the cleavages between traditional and modern societies. He also objected to the Prebisch-Furtado explanations based on the deterioration of the terms of trade and structural heterogeneity.

Cardoso depicted the mechanisms of economic subjection that accentuated the subordinate integration of Latin America in the world market, describing two variants of this situation. In the national control models (Brazil, Argentina) elites, bureaucracies, or oligarchs manage the major exported resource, while in the enclave economies (the small nations of Central America and the Caribbean) that administration is in the hands of foreign companies. Based on this scheme, Cardoso described the diversity of social orders that in each country resulted in stagnation or growth.

More than a diagnosis of underdevelopment, the Brazilian theorist sketched a picture of multiple paths, highlighting the importance of the relations established between local ruling groups and the central powers. He identified those connections with different situations of dependency in the association between dominant national and foreign groups (Cardoso and Faletto, 1969: 6–19, 20–34, 40–53). Cardoso did not counterpose dependency with development. He only asserted that the two paths create differentiated models, which allow or frustrate long-term development. He noted that those paths are determined by the group leading the state, social cohesion, and the formation of legitimate orders of consent and obedience.

In his perspective, ruling groups define political models, which in turn determine advantageous or adverse economic directions for each country. Since this action demands autonomy, Cardoso concentrated his analyses on the intermediate countries with control over their own productive resources. He maintained that in the enclave economies, exclusionary political regimes prevailed, with little space for pursuing development (Cardoso and Faletto, 1969: 39, 83–101). Cardoso felt that Argentina had advanced significantly in the 1900–1930 period by incorporating the middle classes into a dynamic project of the exporting bourgeoisie. He considered Brazil to have maintained a confederation of oligarchies without hegemonies and without incorporating the middle sectors, and therefore its economy fell behind. Political action from the state determined both results.

Cardoso held that in the next period (1940–1960) distributionism affected the expansion of Argentina, while Brazil achieved greater industrial development by means of state aid and less popular pressure. The articulations brought about by Peronism in Argentina and Varguism in Brazil defined this outcome. Cardoso concluded his study by affirming the generalized tendency to overcome the limits to development through more foreign investment and associations between national capitalist groups (Kubistechek, Frondizi) and their foreign counterparts (Cardoso and Faletto, 1969: 54–77, 111–129, 130–135).

9   Theoretical Confusion

Cardoso's theses did not confront liberalism, did not share ECLAC's critical spirit, and were outside the Marxist tradition. They only showed affinity with conventional sociology, with the functionalist method, and with undefined viewpoints on the relation between the political dimension and the economic structure, which some analysts associate with Weber (Martins, 2011b: 229–233).

Cardoso formally ascribed analytical primacy to economic determination (national control versus enclave), but in practical applications he attributed to political actors (classes, bureaucracies, elites) the ability to create positive (development) or negative (underdevelopment) models. In all cases, he failed to recognize the limits that capitalism imposed on the possibilities under consideration. He conceived of that system as a conflictive regime, but superior to any alternative. In contrast to Frank, Dos Santos, Bambirra, or Marini, he did not take an anti-capitalist perspective or offer socialist proposals. He simply compared strategies of greater or lesser effectiveness, through typologies constructed around ideal models. He ascribed complete primacy to the political determinants of that counterpoint. He maintained that in the framework of certain structural possibilities, the trajectories of each country are defined by the type of political alliances that predominate. He believed that worker pressure favors accumulation at certain times, and at other stages obstructs it. He thought the same thing for agreements between the industrial bourgeoisie and the exporting oligarchies, or for the inflows and outflows of capital (Cardoso and Faletto, 1969: 136–143).

With this perspective, he assessed the compatibility of each process with development, following a functionalist model of adjustment or maladjustment to the requirements of capitalism. He took this social regime as an invariable fact, omitting any reflection on the exploitation of workers. Cardoso evaded sharp opinions. He adopted the attitude of a distant investigator who dissects his object of study, observing how the different capitalist subjects forge alliances that take advantage of the passive accompaniment of the people.

The most curious thing about this approach was its presentation as a dependency theory. In Cardoso's approach, that term represents one more ingredient for functionalist deduction. Some situations of dependency are dysfunctional for, and others compatible with, development. This view of dependency does not necessarily assume adversity. Thus, it is only acknowledged, without denouncing its effects. Cardoso did not consider any of the mechanisms of dependent reproduction that Marini, Dos Santos, or Bambirra pointed to as causes of underdevelopment.

Cardoso only observed significant adversities in the enclaves. In the countries with national control over the exported resource, he maintained that situations of dependency could be softened with adequate management. The complete distance of this approach from a theory of dependency was initially obscured by its ambiguities and by the recognition that surrounded the author.

10   An Illuminating Debate

Cardoso's perspective was clarified in the polemic he entered into with Marini. In an article coauthored with Serra, he accused the Marxist theorist of stagnationism. He questioned the consistency of super-exploitation, objected to the deterioration of the terms of trade, rejected the existence of a falling rate of profit, and highlighted the booming consumption of the middle classes (Cardoso and Serra, 1978). He complemented this critique in other articles, claiming that situations of dependency do not obstruct the dynamism of the industrialized economies of the periphery (Cardoso, 1980; Cardoso,1978; Cardoso, 1977b; Cardoso, 1972). He argued that foreign investment incentivized a bourgeois revolution, internationalized markets, and offset the tightness of local consumption (Cardoso, 1973; Cardoso, 1977b; Cardoso, 1972).

Marini responded by illustrating the level of exploitation of the wage-workers. He presented indicators of the prolongation and intensification of labor, and clarified that his concept of super-exploitation referred to those forms. He also affirmed that his model did not imply the predominance of absolute surplus value or the absence of increases in productivity. He also pointed to the severity of the realization crisis, observing that in a framework of high unemployment and deterioration of wages, the rise of middle classes does not compensate for the general weakness of purchasing power (Marini, 1978). He recalled that stagnationism was a defect of Furtado's developmentalist pessimism and of his thesis of Brazilian 'pasturization' or regression to agricultural stages, which was disproved by the new period of industrialization (Marini, 1991: 34).

Marini was never a stagnationist. He wrote *Dialectic of Dependency* to uncover contradictions of capitalism, not its final stages (Osorio, 2013b). In his assessment of the expansive dynamic of that system, he was closer to Mandel than to Sweezy. Marini's response clarified that his differences with Cardoso didn't revolve around the existence of a new local bourgeoisie closely associated to foreign capital. Both authors highlighted this novelty. The point of discord was the consistency and reach of the industrialization in process. For Marini, that process did not correct the old limitations of the Brazilian economy, nor would it bring Brazil to comparable levels of development with the central countries. On the contrary, Cardoso thought that those restrictions had been left behind, and that the South American country would enter into the virtuous cycle of development.

In the course of the debate, Marini modified his initial view of his adversary, arguing that Cardoso had broken with his past to embark on a "grotesque apologetic for the capitalism currently in effect in Brazil." That fascination impeded him from seeing the basic facts of a country with higher inequalities than the world average, as well as more segmented internal markets and more significant imbalances of industrialization. Cardoso ignored these problems and failed to recognize the impossibility of Brazil reaching the historical performance of the United States, France, or Japan (Marini, 2005).

Dos Santos propounded the same criticisms. He expressed his agreement with Cardoso on the existence of a turn toward more associations with multinational capital on the part of the Brazilian bourgeoisie, but he stressed his complete disagreement with the representation of this turn as a road to development. He specified that the model adopted by the ruling class increased their investments, but without repeating the self-sustaining development of the advanced economies (Dos Santos, 2003).

The entire debate confirmed that Cardoso's fascination with foreign capital had already taken root in his classic book with Faletto. The title of that book – *Dependency and Development* – was expressed even then in implicit opposition to Frank's *Development of Underdevelopment*. There he had depicted situations of dependency that were very far from the structural dynamics of subjection that Marini, Dos Santos, and Bambirra had portrayed. It was assumed that development would materialize with correct economic policies, and that capitalism would not obstruct the eradication of underdevelopment.

11   Socio-liberal Regression

The dissolution of the meaning of dependency was accentuated by Cardoso in the revision of his book. There he used the formula 'associated dependent development' to characterize the joint management of multinational corporations with local bureaucracies and bourgeoisies (Cardoso and Faletto, 1977). Cardoso argued that under that management, foreign investment would facilitate an intense economic expansion without generating the obstacles asserted by the Marxist theorists. He rejected the approach of the authors who illustrated how growth driven by foreign capital creates greater imbalances than those suffered by the central countries. This qualitative difference was forgotten by Cardoso, who transformed dependency into a concept opposed to that envisioned by the creators of that idea. The only real limit to development that Cardoso saw in the intermediate countries was the existence of exclusionary political regimes that obstructed the markets from including the entire population. He thought that the removal of this political barrier would also eradicate the main cause of underdevelopment.

In that period, Cardoso still considered several paths to the achievement of that democratization. However, a short time later he thought that only transitions negotiated with the dictatorships could pave that path. Thus, he actively participated in the development of supervised democracies, which in the 1980s ensured the continuity of the neoliberal economic model inaugurated by those tyrannies. Based on this approach, Cardoso promoted post-dictatorial transitions as the ideal political framework for attracting foreign capital. He initiated a fervent vindication of neoliberalism, and his differences with the left were concentrated on this apologia. The debates about their divergent assessments of dependency were relegated to the past.

Cardoso also distanced himself more from ECLAC and abandoned any representation of the state as a driving force for industrialization (López Hernández, 2005). It is true that, in contrast to the developmentalists, he grasped the conversion of the old national bourgeoisies into associates, but he never lamented or challenged this conversion. On the contrary, he defended it as a correct path toward Latin American prosperity.

His critique of Marini coincided with his acceptance of more conservative positions. He challenged all the concepts of his adversary that clashed with his enthusiasm for the market and multinational corporations. In this period, Cardoso brought the Ford Foundation into Brazilian academia and created incentives for private financing of the social sciences. He stopped making any reference to the problems discussed by Marini, and avoided debates related to his own past (Correa Prado, 2013).

Later, as president of Brazil, Cardoso became the chief architect of adjustments, privatizations, trade openings, and labor flexibilizations. In the last decade, he went even further until becoming, together with Mario Vargas Llosa, the main champion of reactionary causes. Currently, he is a spokesman for imperialist intervention in Venezuela and for all the abuses of the Pentagon. Thus, it is no surprise that he actively participated in the recent judicial and media coup that removed Dilma Rousseff from the presidency. Cardoso had a major role in that outrage, presenting himself as a noble statesman who extolled the values of the republic in demanding the destitution of an elected president. He wrote 22 articles with that hypocritical message in the major newspaper of those behind the coup (O Globo), and mounted this campaign as a personal revenge against his rival Lula (Anderson, 2016; Feres Júnior, 2016). This attitude has generated overwhelming repudiations from progressive intellectuals (CLACSO, 2016).

José Serra, Cardoso's partner in his critique of Marini, was also an active coup-plotter, rewarded with the post of Foreign Minister. From that position, he promoted the biggest pro-U.S. turn in the recent history of Brazil (Nepomuceno, 2016). Cardoso's neoliberal regression was anticipated by Marini's critique. The polemic between the two was not a conjunctural episode of the 1970s, nor can it be reduced to errors on both sides. Cardoso denied the persistent reality of backwardness and Marini explained its continuity. That difference puts them in opposite poles.

In recent years, there has been a renewed appreciation for Marini's work (Murua, 2013: 1–3; Traspadini, 2013: 10–12). His writings have been disseminated and his work has been taken up again to update his conception. Some researchers claim that he built a 'political economy of dependency' and provided the foundations for understanding underdevelopment. This characterization raises several questions: Are the pillars provided by Marini sufficient? Does the value of his approach refer to his era, or does it project to the present? How should the challenges he received from within Marxist circles be evaluated?

CHAPTER 5

Critiques and Convergences

In the 1970s, Agustín Cueva was the most important Marxist critic of dependency theories. He objected to the thesis of associated development, challenged the metropolis-satellite view, and engaged in intense polemics with Bambirra, Dos Santos, and Marini. Nevertheless, in the following decade, based on political convergences, he participated with them in a theoretical encounter that modified the approach to underdevelopment.

1 Functionalism without Subjects

Cueva stood out as a very creative intellectual. His early formation was in the limited environment of Ecuador; later he absorbed structuralist conceptions in France, and matured his novel historiographic perspective in Mexico. He shared some political strategies with the communist parties, but questioned the dogmatism prevailing in the Soviet Union (Prado, 1992). His debates with dependency theory began with three objections to the Cardoso-Faletto approach. In the first place, he criticized the use of functionalist criteria to explain the history of Latin America, arguing that 'inward development' or 'colonies of exploitation' lacked explanatory consistency. They portrayed peculiarities of certain areas or singularities of the exported products, but they did not provide criteria for the interpretation of underdevelopment. Cueva pointed out that the advantages or disadvantages generated by the resources of each region did not clarify capitalist logic, nor did it clarify the differential capacities for accumulation. He argued that only the Marxist concepts of forces of production, relations of production, and class struggle allowed that analysis (Cueva, 1976).

The Ecuadorian theorist maintained that Cardoso sidestepped social-historical processes in all his characterizations. He asserted that Cardoso offered a description of the advantages of national control over resources (Mexico) rather than foreign control (small Central American countries), and that he also demonstrated the advantage of certain political alliances for incentivizing industrialization (Brazil in the 1960s) or obstructing it (Argentina in the same period) (Cueva, 1973: 102), but that this snapshot omitted the imbalances of capitalist accumulation, as well as the conflicts between dominant groups.

In the second place, Cueva objected to Cardoso's 'externalist' logic. He stressed that instead of an analysis of each Latin American economy, Cardoso's approach gave a simple verification of insertions in the world market. He argued that the comparison between situations of enclaves and of national control over resources registered external connections without examining the endogenous dynamic of development in each country. He maintained that the omission of the agrarian dimension illustrated how Cardoso ignored internal processes, emphasizing especially the absence of references to the conflicts between peasants and large landowners, which determined the major progressive (Mexico) or regressive (Peru, Colombia) outcomes of regional history. He observed that in many circumstances those processes were more determinant of underdevelopment than external exactions.

In the third place, Cueva warned of the complete absence of popular subjects in Cardoso's depiction. He pointed out that Cardoso treated the masses as passively accompanying the alliances woven by bureaucracies with the dominant classes. He asserted that Cardoso only recognized some importance for the middle class, completely ignoring the workers, the peasants, or the dispossessed, and that this obstructed any analysis of what was occurring on a continent convulsed by popular rebellions and resistances (Cueva, 1976). With this early perception of functionalism, externalism, and the omission of class confrontations, Cueva highlighted defects in Cardoso's work, which the Marxist dependency theorists would take longer to do.

2   Mechanical Exogenism

Cueva also objected to the externalist perspective of the metropolis-satellite model and the interpretation of underdevelopment as an exclusive result of subordinate insertion in the world market (Cueva, 1979a: 7–11). He questioned Frank's unilateral emphasis on exogenous imbalances, arguing that Latin America was not dependent because of its integration into the world market, but because of internal obstruction to its development. He argued that the predominance of unproductive rents caused by the primacy of large landholdings blocked the accumulation of capital more than colonial or imperial extraction.

The Ecuadorian theorist attributed Frank's errors to his acritical assimilation of ECLAC's approaches, focused exclusively on the deterioration of the terms of trade. He asserted that this perspective lent itself to excessive generalizations and to assuming that all Latin American societies are cut from the same cloth; thus, the simplified model of satellites and metropolises leaves out the differences between economies as dissimilar as Chile and Brazil. He also questioned the exclusive attention to trade as the key determinant of underdevelopment, neglecting production (Cueva, 1986). Several authors of the period classified this defect with the term 'circulationism'.

The Andean critic also challenged the conclusions of his German colleague. He argued that the well-known formula for describing Latin American backwardness ('development of underdevelopment') suggested an erroneous picture of stagnation. He objected to the identification of a dependent situation with blockages of any expansion, and proposed analyzing Latin America as a weak link of the unequal development of capitalism. He emphasized that competition and investment are incompatible with stagnation in a system subject to spirals of contradictions (Cueva, 1977: 98–113, 437–442). Cueva also criticized the disregard for the antagonisms between oppressors and oppressed. He questioned the analytical replacement of struggles and revolts by mere classifications of satellites.

Frank did not respond. He merely took those points as an indicator of the impact generated by his own work. This attitude was consistent with his abandonment of dependency theory not long after having formulated it (Frank 1970: 305–327). Later, he would return to the topic, affirming that his approach never privileged trade or ignored the endogenous dimensions, but he did not provide arguments to justify that opinion (Frank, 2005a). Cueva's observations were in tune with the objections of other analysts, who stressed "unilateralities" of the metropolis-satellite approach (Vitale, 1981), its "exaggerated dependentism" (Martins, 2009), or its "apocalyptic pessimism" (Boron, 2008).

3   Problems of Pan-Capitalism

Cueva's critique extended to the analysis of commercial capitalism installed in Latin America since the 16th century. Frank had affirmed that a system of market-oriented production predominated in the region since that period. He propounded that thesis in contention with theories of a feudal past, arguing that a closed or merely rural economy had never prevailed (Frank, 1970: 31–39, 167–168). Cueva also traced the origin of underdevelopment to the colonial period, but he did not attribute that problem to trade. He recalled the devastation suffered during the 'primitive de-accumulation' imposed by the conquest, and argued that this depredation did not establish capitalist modalities (Cueva, 1973: 65–78).

The Andean theorist criticized the identification of capitalism with commercial exchange. He counterposed the association of that system with the monetary economy (Adam Smith) with capitalism as a mode of production based on the exploitation of wage-labor (Marx), emphasizing that capitalism presupposes industrial processes of surplus value extraction that were inexistent at that time, not only in Latin America but also in Europe. Cueva underlined the initial preeminence in Latin America of pre-capitalist regimes closely connected with the nascent world market. He objected to the simplified counterpoint between interpretations of feudal or capitalist colonization, stressing the impossibility of corroborating either characterization. He proposed incorporating the idea of economic-social formations to resolve that problem (Cueva, 1988), arguing that the articulations of varied modes of production reigned from the conquest until the 19th century (Cueva, 1979a: 60–68). He especially distinguished three modalities: servitude in the *hacienda*, slavery on the plantations, and wage-labor in the *latifundios*. He understood that such attention to the prevailing form of exploitation was more consistent with Marxism than the analytical hierarchy privileging foreign trade, and rejected Frank's pan-capitalism for reducing four centuries of history to the primacy of a contemporary mode of production (Cueva, 1978).

The Ecuadorian theorist also emphasized that the concept of economic-social formations was indispensable for understanding the unequal underdevelopment of Latin America. He maintained that what had occurred in each national process was explained by the dissolution of pre-capitalist foundations, which preceded the consolidation of the oligarchical models that have predominated since the 19th century (Cueva, 1982). He located the contemporary origin of underdevelopment in the consolidation of large rural property, and described how the balkanized republics impeded the rise of the farmers. He situated the central cause of Latin American backwardness in the lack (Ecuador, Brazil) or insufficiency (Mexico, Bolivia) of agrarian transformations.

The relevance he assigned to internal determinants of underdevelopment was in tune with other perspectives equally inspired by the Althusserian approach (Howard and King:1989: 205–215). They all rejected the traditional opposition between feudalism and capitalism, highlighting the predominance of mixtures conditioned by the unequal or insufficient penetration of capitalism. These views were similar to objections within Marxist dependency theory to the omission of internal structures, and to the critique of the false equivalence between colonial and contemporary situations (Dos Santos, 1978: 303–304, 336–337; Marini, 1973: 19). These challenges emphasized neglect of the roots of dependency in the productive sphere (Chilcote, 1983) and coincided with other critiques of the thesis of capitalism reigning in Latin America since 1492 (Salama, 1976: 13).

Cueva also objected to neglect of the protagonism of the popular classes in Latin American history. He asserted that Frank ignored their impact in the struggles for independence and in the agrarian, national, or anti-imperialist revolutions of the previous century (Cueva, 1979a: 69–93). The Ecuadorian theorist approached the study of the past from the point of view of the oppressed ('history from below') in order to underline how that legacy nourished the culture of the left. He put forth an approach that also drew on the work of Marxist theorists from other regions. English historians, for example, were exploring a new synthesis between the role of economic structures and the critical role of the social struggle in this period (Kaye, 1989).

4   Methodological Singularity?

Cueva also criticized the theoretical status of the concept of dependency. He objected to the formulation of specific laws of subordinate capitalism, arguing that those principles only correspond to the universality of modes of production, without alluding to the center or the periphery. He specified that specific social formations are not subject to any type of law (Cueva, 1976). He formulated these observations in generic terms, but he reproached the mistaken search for particular laws in "such a rigorous author" as Marini.

Cueva did not question the existence of dynamics specific to the Latin American economy. He objected to their presentation as laws, arguing that those rules explain the functioning of feudalism or capitalism, but do not extend to the particular parts of those systems (Cueva, 1979b). He did not further develop the epistemological consequences of this idea; he did not intend to initiate a philosophical controversy, but to contribute arguments to the debate with the theorists of regional particularism. Thus, he challenged Cardoso's search for Latin American originalities, and rejected the identity-based vehemence of many promoters of Latin American social sciences.

Cueva had opposite concerns to those of Marini. Rather than lamenting the absence of authors located in the region, he emphasized the excess of provincialism and the scant absorption of universalist ideas. He rejected the existence of "our categories" and confronted regionalist mythologies (Cueva, 1979a: 83–93). In this debate, Cueva continued the battle he had launched in Ecuador against the ideology of *mestizaje*. He criticized the imaginary portrait of a harmonious coexistence among peoples that was disseminated by the theorists of the dominant classes. He maintained that this idyllic universe concealed the oppression exercised by the moneyed elites, and questioned that nationalist demagogy from a socialist position (Tinajero, 2012: 9–35).

This opposition to populist nationalism explains Cueva's hostility to the pretension of elevating the conceptual status of dependency theory. He rejected

that aspiration, affirming that Latin America was ruled by the general principles of capitalism. For the Ecuadorian theorist, Latin American societies were
particular, but not original, and the investigation into its dynamics did not
imply discovering laws specific to the region. However, his criticisms were only
pertinent for the thinkers who resorted to spiritualist explanations of Latin
American identity, or for the builders of imagined national destinies. None of
those defects were found in the Marxist theories of dependency. Accusations
of nationalist nostalgia against several members of that school lacked justification. Not only did Dos Santos, Marini, and Bambirra posit socialist approaches
with universalist perspectives, but Cardoso had affinities with liberal cosmopolitanism, and Gunder Frank with libertarian variants of that same ideology.
Cueva's mistake was very much influenced by the tense political climate of
the 1970s.

5   Perspectives on 'Popular Unity' in Chile

All the participants in the dependency debate were personally involved in the
experience of the Popular Unity (UP or *Unidad Popular*) government in Chile.
Like his colleagues, Cueva had enormous expectations for a socialist outcome
from that process in a country with exceptional traditions of institutional continuity. He asserted that this legacy facilitated the electoral triumph of the left,
but was also used by Pinochetism to prepare for the coup. He thought that
the right demonstrated a will to power that was absent in the UP. That coali-
tion sought agreements with the opposition, and did not know how to utilize
popular support to break the mutiny. He described the arbitrator role taken by
Allende and the social-democratic confidence in legalism, but also criticized
the 'adventurous' behavior of the MIR (Revolutionary Left Movement) for its
encouragement of direct actions "used by the right" (Cueva, 1979a: 97–140).
      Marini reached a completely opposite conclusion. He identified the tri-
umph of the UP with the opening of a revolutionary process, and he blamed
the Communist Party for its failure. He especially criticized the hostility of that
organization toward going at all beyond the bourgeois political framework. The
Brazilian economist thought that Allende was trapped in a suicidal tolerance
for the coup. He argued that the MIR never carried out actions unfavorable
to the UP. On the contrary, they collaborated with its government, promoted
committees to support it, and encouraged the agrarian reform and continuity of production that was sabotaged by the capitalists (Marini, 1976a). At the
same time, he defended the validity of the attempt to create alternative forms
of power to hold back Pinochet (Marini, 1976b).

Dos Santos agreed with Marini. He was a member of the Socialist Party, and he proposed the unity of the entire left to radicalize the process opened by the government of Allende (Dos Santos, 2009a: 11–26). With a retrospective view, the balance of the debate leans in favor of Marini. The dependency theorist grasped the prevailing dilemma in 1970–1976 between the debut of socialism and the triumph of the reaction. Cueva eluded this dilemma with contradictory statements, objecting to both institutionalist myopia and direct action without clarifying which of the two problems was determinant in the tragic outcome.

While the left wing of the UP promoted popular power, the conservative sector of the front sought an alliance with the Christian Democrats to develop a stage of national capitalism. Cueva suggested a third option, without explaining how it could be implemented. He criticized both the suppression of intermediate stages and neglect of the correlation of forces (Cueva, 1979a: 7–11). But Marini took both problems into account in supporting initiatives from below in the industrial belts and the agrarian communes. Both Cueva and Marini promoted the conversion of electoral triumphs of the left into radical dynamics for the conquest of power, but they clashed harshly on the definition of strategies for reaching this objective. This divergence was projected into other areas and provoked drastic critiques (Cueva, 1988) and virulent defenses (Marini, 1993; Dos Santos, 1978: 351, 359, 361); Bambirra, 1978: 40–73).[1]

6   Endogenism: Traditional and Transformed

Although Cueva agreed with the strategy of many communist parties, he did not question dependency theory from this alignment, and his approach contrasted with the objections formulated from that current. The exponents of official communism criticized the rejections by Frank, Marini, and Dos Santos of the policy of alliances with the national bourgeoisie. They argued that this opposition denied the primacy of the anti-imperialist struggle, ignored the necessity of multi-class fronts, undervalued the peasantry, and omitted the centrality of the democratic struggle (Fernández and Ocampo, 1974). In practice, however, alliances with the 'progressive bourgeoisie' led to those mistakes. Those dominant groups adopted regressive positions involving abuse of workers and support for repression. Communist officialdom also

---

1 Our general assessment of the Popular Unity can be found in Katz (2015: 256–259).

failed to register the socialist potentialities opened by the Cuban revolution, which two of the dependency theorists explored in depth (Dos Santos and Bambirra, 1980).

Cueva did not participate in those debates, nor did he repeat the accusations launched against dependentism for its kinship with 'bourgeois ideology'. That challenge highlighted the 'idealist' philosophical content of the conception, underlining its inattention to the materialist problems of the capital-labor relation (Angotti, 1981). It also warned of the existence of a confusing variety of concepts of dependency, which were taken advantage of by pro-imperialist authors.

The inconsistency of these observations seems obvious in any contemporary reading, but empty verbal disputes were very common at a time of orchestrated reasoning around loyalties or heresies toward the party. Cueva operated in a political context close to communism, but without sharing these codes. He never sacrificed reflection in order to demolish dissidents. Nor did Cueva crucify the dependency theorists for their resistance to deifying the Soviet Union, or accuse them of 'playing into the hands of the imperialists' for avoiding eulogies for the 'socialist camp'. Rather, he developed the endogenist arguments suggested by various communist critics of dependency theory. He turned vague observations into solid ideas, objecting especially to the unilateral attention paid to processes of commercial circulation in lieu of the productive dynamic of capitalism.

Cueva also stressed the importance of prioritizing agrarian backwardness as an explanation for underdevelopment, underlining the weight of the *latifiundio*, the significance of rent, and the importance of the peasantry. He posited that the endogenous suffocation caused by agrarian stagnation carried more weight than exogenous-imperial exaction. But in contrast to traditional endogenism, Cueva never attributed the backwardness of the region to the persistence of feudal traditions; neither did he suggest a need for an alliance with the bourgeoisie to overcome this hindrance.

The Andean theoretician developed his critique of Frank's exogenism without sharing the precepts of traditional endogenism. He rejected the mechanical scheme of successive historical stages, and reasoned using criteria of unequal and combined development. In his more mature phase, Cueva spoke highly of dependency theory's attention to the international role of Latin America, but he continued to insist on the lack of clear analytical connections with local parameters. He emphasized the national genesis of capitalism and underlined the internal determinants of accumulation. In this way, he sought to contribute endogenous foundations to dependentism.

7   Agreement against Post-Marxism

With the consolidation of the dictatorships, dependency theory lost its influence. In the 1980s, some authors pronounced the dissolution of that school
of thought, together with the decline of emancipation projects (Blomstrom
and Hettne, 1990: 105, 250–253). That retreat was not due to mistaken views
on Latin American reality, but to the defeats suffered by the revolutionary
movements. The concepts of dependency did not vanish, but were silenced
by the neoliberal counter-reform (López-Hernández, 2005). The theory that
dominated the previous period was relegated for political motives, and lost the
interest of new generations that were distanced from anti-capitalist radicality.

The electoral defeat of *Sandinismo* in Nicaragua in 1989 began a retreat
of socialist processes, which was deepened with the implosion of the Soviet
Union. Dependency theory declined as a consequence of that retreat. Cueva
and Marini immediately felt the blow and began a process of drawing closer
to each other, although they disagreed on their characterizations of the
dictatorships.

The Ecuadorian thinker defined those tyrannies as fascist regimes, comparable to the inter-war barbarity (Cueva, 1979a: 7–11). The Brazilian theorist,
in contrast, highlighted the differences from what had occurred on the Old
Continent. He stressed the weakness of the Latin American bourgeoisies, who
accepted the substitute role of the military forces without forging their own
bases of political support (Marini, 1976b). Beyond those nuances, both theorists immediately agreed on the priority of democratic resistance. When the
tyrannies ended, they denounced the pacts agreed to by the traditional parties with the militaries to perpetuate neoliberal surgery. Cueva launched an
intense polemic with the authors who justified those negotiations. He argued
that those agreements helped the gendarmes, established their impunity,
and guaranteed regressive neoliberal transformations (Cueva, 2012). Marini
expressed the same denunciation through categorical rejections of military
supervision in post-dictatorship transitions.

But the main battle in which Cueva and Marini came together was the
critique of the post-Marxist intellectuals (Laclau). These authors abandoned
class analysis and the centrality of imperial oppression, and considered action
by the left to be obsolete. They also rediscovered social democracy and found
their way back to the old ruling parties (Chilcote, 1990). In this context, Cueva
and Marini concentrated all of their efforts on the defense of anti-imperialism
and socialism, and argued against the mystified presentation of capitalism as
an unchangeable regime.

The Ecuadorian writer also modified his assessment of populism in this period. Rather than emphasizing its functionality for bourgeois ideology, he stressed the stimulus it had provided to Jacobin conceptions, which in Latin America had connected radical nationalism to socialism (Cueva, 2012: 183–192). In the same period, Marini returned to Brazil after 20 years in exile and confronted the hostility of the ex-dependentistas settled comfortably into the academic world. He denounced that adaptation and again took up his debates with Cardoso (Marini, 1991). His confluence with Cueva was a natural outcome of that battle against common adversaries.

8   Return to Dependency

Cueva and Marini also jointly participated in a debate with neo-Gramscian theorists (Aricó, Portantiero) who reformulated the thought of the Italian communist to derive a laudatory view of democracy from his approach. They ignored the distinctive contours of that political system in diverse social regimes, and considered anti-imperialism and dependency to be obsolete concepts. Cueva rejected that view, presenting new data on the economic subordination and political subjugation of Latin America. He illustrated how dependency had accentuated with the growth of foreign debt (Cueva, 1986) and argued that underdevelopment persisted together with modernization processes. He highlighted the combination of poverty and opulence current in Brazil and demonstrated the inexistence of any approximation of the Latin American economy to the central countries (Cueva, 1979a: 7–11).

With this affirmation, Cueva clarified his earlier characterizations. He asserted that in the 1970s he had criticized dependency theory from positions on the left that were antagonistic to the right-wing challenges he observed 20 years later. He declared his total opposition to those viewpoints and praised the accuracies of the conception he had challenged, ratifying his closeness to dependency theory and clarifying that he had never denied Latin American submission to the imperial order. He confirmed his belonging to the same anti-imperialist realm as the authors he had criticized in the past, and indicated that he only wished to complete the dependency approach in order to overcome its lack of consideration for the internal determinants of underdevelopment (Cueva, 1988).

The Ecuadorian theorist presented this reconsideration with praise for the work of Marini (Cueva, 2007: 139–158) and for the positions taken by Dos Santos upon his return to Brazil (Cueva, 1986). In turn, Marini upheld the validity of

Cueva's critiques of the post-Marxist intellectuals and took his side in his differences with other endogenist authors (Marini, 1993).

9   The Opposite Path

Cueva was the last exponent of Marxist endogenism and the precursor of a synthesis with dependency theory, seeking solutions in Latin American Marxism to the challenges that confronted that approach. He followed an opposite path to other thinkers in his tradition, who opted for rejection of the center-periphery model and adopted a comparative theory of national capitalisms. In this direction went, for example, Alain Lipietz, who had inspired French Regulation Theory. This theorist did not work specifically on the question of Latin America, but he assimilated in his early work the same Althusserian Marxism as Cueva. With that conceptual foundation, he studied the dynamics of articulated modes of production, seeking to understand the singularity of national models. From that perspective, he also expressed strong objections to dependency theory for its lack of consideration for internal conditions (Lipietz, 1992: 20, 34–39, 62).

However, in the mid-1980s Lipietz declared his 'tiredness' with anti-imperialism and with Marxist interpretations of underdevelopment. He objected to the principle of world polarization, claiming that there is not a predetermined place for each economy in the international division of labor. He underlined the existence of many available spaces for situations of dependency or autonomy (Lipietz, 1992: 12–14, 25–30, 38–41). The French theorist continued this reasoning pointing to the existence of a wide variety of national capitalisms, whose path is defined by the governing elites based on changing social and institutional circumstances. This thesis nourished Regulation Theory – which mixed Marxism with Keynesian heterodoxy – and later led to social-developmentalist conceptions that promoted models of redistributive capitalism.

This approach contained two problems that Cueva had managed to avoid. On the one hand, abandoning the socialist horizon led Lipietz to conceive of unlimited room for capitalism to deal with its own imbalances. That view assumed that the market can be improved by perfecting institutions, that profitability can be delimited by state regulations, that exploitation can be neutralized, and that crises are manageable with macroeconomic mechanisms. With these assumptions of self-correcting capitalism, a more convenient regime of accumulation is promoted for a system that would always find solutions for its contradictions. The initial description of varied forms of capitalism passes to a diagnostic of self-improvement of the system through movements from one regime of accumulation to another (Husson, 2001: 171–182).

The second problem of this bourgeois endogenist approach is its omission of the objective conditionality imposed by globalization. It assumes that the capitalism in place in each country represents a sovereign decision of its citizens. By highlighting the purely internal determination of the path prevailing in each nation, it ignores how globalized capitalism shapes those national dynamics. Hostility to dependency theory ends up resurrecting beliefs in free choice and imaginaries of elective capitalism. Cueva avoided those mistakes by sensing the new forms of underdevelopment generated by globalization.

10   Theoretical Synthesis

Cueva's road to convergence with Marini opened the path for a theoretical synthesis. Their coming together arose from Cueva's alignment with the dependency camp, not only as a reaction to criticisms from the right. The Andean writer recognized the general validity of the Marxist version of that conception, and distinguished that approach from Frank's simplifications and Cardoso's inconsistencies. This reconsideration made it possible to understand that the endogenist interpretation was not incompatible with the dependentist characterization of Latin American underdevelopment. They came together in the same way that postwar Marxists had come together in assessing the center-periphery relation. The same affinities that connected Sweezy-Baran, Amin, and Mandel united the South American theorists.

The meeting of Cueva with Marini allowed dependency theory to move forward, refining its concepts and incorporating contributions from other theorists. That synthesis was a process of simultaneous maturing. At the same time that Cueva was revaluing the work of his old adversaries, Marini, Dos Santos, and Bambirra reinforced their distancing from Frank and Cardoso. The coming together of the endogenists and exogenists did not imply unanimity or full agreement. Cueva reaffirmed his disagreement with several of Marini's concepts. He highlighted his interest in analyses of the dependent productive cycle, but also stressed the supremacy of the financial dimension; nor did he consider satisfactory the concept of super-exploitation, which he still saw as a variant of absolute pauperization. But he emphatically defended Marini from accusations of 'stagnationism', recalling that this defect marked the work of Furtado (Cueva, 2012: 199–200).

In the synthesis of Marini with Cueva can be found the pillars of a comprehensive characterization of the status of Latin America. Starting from the subordinate and backward condition of the region, that perspective made it possible to distinguish three levels of analysis. On the economic dimension, the region is underdeveloped in comparison to the advanced countries. In the international division of labor, Latin America occupies a peripheral place, counterposed to the privileged insertion held by the central powers. On the political level it suffers from dependency, that is, narrow spaces of autonomy as opposed to the dominant role exercised by the empires. Underdevelopment, periphery, and dependency thus constitute three concepts connected to the same condition. These three ideas are not clearly differentiated by Cueva or by Marini, but this has been done more carefully by later authors (Domingues, 2012).

The Ecuadorian Marxist and his Brazilian colleagues suggested a close interrelation between the three concepts. They argued that peripheral subordination to the world market defines distinct levels of underdevelopment that are accentuated by political dependency. Cueva and Marini highlighted the reduced spaces that Latin America has – under capitalism – to change its status. This viewpoint differs from the open road to development that Cardoso imagined since the 1980s. It also differs from the completely closed path to any alteration that Frank assumed in the 1970s.

Moreover, the Marxist theorists carried out very original explorations of the differences that exist within the region. Cueva presented a model of unequal development determined by the level of capitalist penetration present in each country, Bambirra provided a detailed classification of those varieties, and Marini investigated the peculiarities of the most industrialized economy of the region.

In this effort, each author prioritized distinct locations. Cueva focused his attention on the countries with pre-capitalist remnants, while Marini focused on the structures of greatest industrial development. For that reason, Cueva utilized endogenous criteria suitable for the study of agrarian underdevelopment. Marini, on the other hand, privileged parameters of connection with the world market, which are more useful for understanding the imbalances of the semi-industrialized economies.

11   Methodological Convergence

A synthesis of Cueva and Marini makes it possible to overcome the contradiction between the primacy of the internal or external focus in interpreting underdevelopment. Cueva criticized simplified externalism as he inquired into how a variable articulation of modes of production prevailed in Latin America as a consequence of insufficient capitalist development. He analyzed the chain of reciprocal determinations that were established between backward internal elements and advanced external components. On his part, Marini investigated the way in which international capitalism conditions all the internal relations of the region.

The maturing of both perspectives contributed to leaving behind equally reductionist binary positions. Emphasis on external subordination or on lack of internal development as a cause of backwardness should be modified according to the historical stage analyzed or the geographical area specifically under study. It is clear that external devastation was the central factor in the first decades of the conquest of America, while internal regression prevailed during the later phase of consolidation of the *latifundio*. In turn, the external-colonial depredation inflicted on the mining enclaves differed from the endogenous-agrarian stagnation generated by the consolidation of the *haciendas*.

Dependency theory provides an accurate form of explanation for the subordination suffered by Latin America, but it needs the analytical complement of endogenism to analyze the internal blockage generated by the prolonged preeminence of pre-capitalist forms. Osorio points out how that integration combines a totalizing treatment of dependent capitalism with an analysis specific to the historical formations of the region, stressing that these formations can only be understood by assessing their insertion in the world market. Marxist dependency theory defines an analytical framework enriched by endogenism (Osorio, 2009b: 94–98).

The advance of that synthesis requires leaving behind three errors. In the first place, the perspective without historicity of the metropolis-satellite model, which confuses the colonial situation with the later dependency, assuming that a single contradiction repeats itself over time in invariable structures (Osorio, 2009b: 86–89). In the second place, the 'dialogue of the deaf' that has taken place between the theories of feudal and capitalist colonization, ignoring how Latin America's insertion in the world market required it to turn to pre-capitalist forms of production (Osorio, 2009b: 44–47). In the third place, the false dilemma between pure exogenists, who ignore how dependent capitalism internalizes external conditionalities, and pure endogenists, who ignore the way in which Latin America has been inscribed into the international market, must be overcome (Osorio, 2009b: 82–85).

The convergence of Cueva with Marini, Dos Santos, and Bambirra resolves these pitfalls through an integrated approach that ascribes great significance to the class struggle in the course of history. In these three authors, 'internal' and 'external' do not refer exclusively to economic developments, military conquests, or political hegemonies. They refer to the impacts and outcomes of class confrontation. These approaches are far from Cardoso's functionalism or Frank's distancing from political action. They reason within a tradition of simultaneous attention to the development of the productive forces and to the results of the social battle.

The convergence of endogenists and exogenists also contributes to clarifying the controversial methodological status of Marxist dependency theory. At first, Cueva claimed the inexistence of laws of dependent capitalism, maintaining that those rules only hold for modes of production (capitalism) and not for specific modalities of those systems (dependency). Marini and Dos Santos, on the other hand, specified laws of functioning particular to the underdeveloped regions.

By demanding such a restrictive categorization of the object of study, the initial view of Cueva shut off the possibility of analyzing the specific functioning of the periphery. Several authors proposed escaping this trap by freeing the conception from the stringent demands of a theory. They suggested studying dependency as a paradigm, that is, as a model accepted by the community of the social sciences, through radical innovations in the prevailing perspectives (Blomstrom and Hettne, 1990). Along the same lines, other authors proposed characterizing dependency as a perspective, an approach, or a point of view (Johnson, 1981).

In all these perspectives, dependency is seen as a program of positive research. Its studies can clarify center-periphery relations, whatever the epistemological status of that inquiry (Henfrey, 1981). Thus, the paradigm of dependency and underdevelopment analyzes the dynamics of accumulation that distinguish the periphery and the modes of functioning specific to dependent capitalism. This approach has room for the different historical varieties of modes of production and economic-social formations that have prevailed in Latin America. In addition, it incorporates new concepts, such as pattern of reproduction, to analyze the models peculiar to dependent capitalism in contemporary periods (Osorio, 2012: 37–86). The investigations initiated by Marini and Cueva inspired this fruitful recent development.

12   Assessments and Declines

The importance of the convergence of Cueva with Marini was perceived by various analysts, who noted how the differences between the two authors shrank in line with their political agreements. That connection clarified prior misunderstandings and allowed them to overcome them by the late 1980s. The

two theorists came together again in the neoliberal period, developing a common battle in defense of socialism (Gandásegui, 2009). In this convergence,
they defined a similar approach to characterize the logic of underdevelopment
and to unravel the causes of the gaps that separate the advanced and backward
economies (Chilcote, 1981). In the new political framework, they modified old
positions (Moreano, 2007) and it became clear that they expressed variations
of the same conceptual matrix (Bugarelli, 2011).

   Their convergence can be seen as another example of the more general revision of interpretations that counterpose 'productivist' and 'circulationist' readings of Marx (Munck, 1981). Their synthesis illustrated the maturity of Latin
American social thought, which shares anti-imperialist viewpoints for the
analysis of the region. The conflict between dependentism and endogenism
lost meaning by the end of the 20th century, but the maturity of Cueva also
expressed the decline of an approach affected by the definitive extinction of
the pre-capitalist states. Endogenism illustrated the Latin American dynamics
of the colonial era and clarified the weight of agrarian backwardness in the
era of classical imperialism. However, it had little ability to uncover what had
occurred in the postwar period, and is not relevant for understanding the current period of full capitalist rule. In this stage, the relics of modes of production articulated in differentiated economic formations have disappeared. In
the 21st century, only models, varieties, or patterns of accumulation of existing
capitalism in each country can be distinguished. None of those retain pre-capitalist relics.

   Endogenism was weakened with the extinction of those hindrances in the
agrarian sector. The Mexican case – so closely followed by that approach – illustrates the radical reorganization of rural life under the reign of agri-business,
the end of self-sufficiency, the replacement of old forms of feeding the country by imports, and specialization in new profitable products. The same can
be verified in all the Andean economies. The types of conflicts that generate
this transformation – inequality, rural exodus, dispossession, pauperization,
narco-trafficking, labor informality – are typical of contemporary capitalism.
Exogenism's own definition of growth as expansion of capitalism explains its
loss of meaning. The consolidation of that system eliminates the usefulness of
all preceding observations about the insufficient development of this mode of
production.

   The decline of endogenism also owes to the loss of centrality of national
economies as a consequence of globalization. That expansion drastically
reduces the power of any national-level explanations of underdevelopment
(Chinchilla and Dietz, 1981). The endogenist approach was fundamental in
explaining how various modes of production were articulated in certain

regional spaces under the watch of the state. However, the growing weight of the global economy first reduced, then annulled, the autonomy of those processes (Barkin, 1981). The advance of internationalization drastically increases the primacy of exogenous factors, and explains the loss of interest in endogenism. Nevertheless, that decline put all the questions onto the opposite side. What happened with the approaches that emphasized external conditionality as the cause of Latin American backwardness? How did the World System school relate to dependency theory?

CHAPTER 6

Dependency and World-System Theory

World-system theory has influenced many areas of contemporary social sciences. It was elaborated by Immanuel Wallerstein, based on a large study of contemporary history and a detailed critique of global capitalism. His approach has much in common with Marxist dependency theory. He took some ideas from that conception, and in turn influenced the dependency debates. Several authors have explored the relations between the two perspectives. In what areas do they converge, diverge, or complement each other?

1 Cycles and Hegemonies

Wallerstein maintains that capitalism arose in Europe 500 years ago with a direct character as a world-system. It emerged from the exhaustion of a prior world-empire regime that had appeared after subsistence mini-systems. The scholar from the United States holds that the most primitive formations have functioned around an extensive division of labor, in very diverse cultural frameworks. He argues that the later model developed in extensive geographies with centralized political regimes, and that the third model is in force through the present. Globalized capitalism rests on multiple political structures, a geographical division of labor, and a great variety of national states (Wallerstein, 1979: 489–492).

This system appeared with the crisis of feudalism (1300–1450) and expanded to a world scale. It quickly distanced itself from other regions like China, which had reached very similar levels of population, area, and technology. The motor of that drive was the economic-military rivalry prevailing in the absolute monarchies. The clash between those states motivated the association of the new bourgeoisies with the old aristocracies, incentivized accumulation, and paved the way for the appearance of global commerce (Wallerstein, 1979: 182–230, 426–502).

Since that time, the world-system has ruled the planet through four secular cycles inherent to capitalism. The initial phase of great expansion (1450–1620/40) was followed by a long crisis (1600–1730/50), which led into a stage of exceptional development (1730–1850). The fourth period persists up to the present, and would be the last one of this modern world (Wallerstein, 2005: Chapter 2). The systemic thinker argues that expansionary and

contractionary cycles of 50–60 years have regulated those stages. These fluctuations are labeled Kondratieff cycles, and operate as foreseeable sequences
within processes of longer duration that determine the course of the world
system (Wallerstein, 1984: 5).

Wallerstein argues that an interstate structure has functioned on an international scale with changing hegemonies, each arising as a result of bloody wars
that consolidate the predominance of the winning power. After some time,
the economic superiority of the winner is undermined by their rivals, who
copy innovations while avoiding the military costs borne by the dominator.
This same sequence is repeated with the winner of the next stage (Wallerstein,
1999a: 279).

Following an Iberian period, the Netherlands commanded the first significant leadership position, using its advantages in trade, intensive agriculture,
and textile manufacturing. That primacy was challenged by England and
France, which had reached some level of parity of development. Overseas control was the key to British success; it allowed it to establish colonies that compensated for its inferiority in population and domestic resources. The colonies
facilitated the accumulation of money and the handling of a large foreign market (Wallerstein, 1984: 50–98, 102–174; 1999a: 83–89).

The hegemony of the United States in the 20th century also depended on
victories at the international level. For Wallerstein, the helm of the world-
system is always on that exterior plane. It is there that U.S. superiority over
its competitors (Germany and Japan) and subordinates (England and France)
was established. This succession of hegemonies is explained by the competitive nature of the system, which impedes the consolidation of completely
dominant imperial centers. For that reason, the three attempts to gain absolute control (Charles v, Napoleon, and Hitler) failed. The world-economy
renews itself through the self-destruction generated by the very exercise of
hegemony.

2   Orders and Hierarchies

Wallerstein detailed several principles of the functioning of the world system.
He stressed the permanent expansion of that circuit through the incorporation of outside areas into a structure segmented between central countries and
providers of raw materials. As the world-economy expands, all the regions of
the planet end up incorporated into that mechanism (Wallerstein, 1979: 426–
502). The Americas were absorbed during the Spanish conquest, and Eastern
Europe when it consolidated its export of food products. India, the Ottoman

Empire, Russia, and Western Africa entered when they were subjected to the demands of the international division of labor.

That subordination reinforced the labor and productive specializations of each area. The early industrialization of England, France, and the Netherlands determined the primacy of free labor. In the United States, slavery predominated in order to ensure the provision of inputs to the Old Continent. In Eastern Europe, servitude was imposed to guarantee the supply of grains, and in intermediate zones, such as Italy, combinations of waged and forced labor predominated (Wallerstein, 1979: 93–177). In this approach, capitalism is considered to have originated as a world system, which was consolidated with the inclusion of countries at the top, middle, and lower levels of its structure. The central, peripheral, or semi-peripheral location of each country determines the prevalent type of labor exploitation.

The product each country exported was also definitive. Those with a subordinate insertion provided the goods required for the manufacture of more elaborate commodities. When this integration was settled, their old role as sellers of secondary (or luxury) goods was replaced by a new role as providers of specific inputs (Wallerstein, 1999a: 183–207). That mutation determined the specialization of the Indian subcontinent in the production of indigo, silk, opium, or cotton, and the transformation of the Ottoman Empire into an exporter of cereals. Western Africa established its production of palm oil and peanuts, and Russia consolidated its sales of hemp. flax, and wheat.

These incorporations into the world-system caused, in turn, the destruction of the old local manufactures. Textile production was destroyed in India, while in the Ottoman Empire the productive centers of Anatolia, Syria, and Egypt collapsed. In Africa, embryonic industrial forms were pulverized. Only Russia was able to withstand the onslaught, due to the relative strength of its army (Wallerstein, 1999a: 207–212). The systems theorist understood that the placements and hierarchies of each region are reproduced through a chain of products that connects all its participants into a single global circuit. Through unequal exchange and the polarized flow of commerce, that connection reinforces the predominance of certain central areas. The system therefore includes a constant recreation of underdevelopment.

The same global hierarchy is also reproduced with industrial transformations that modify the locations of the different branches. In the 16th century, the presence of a textile industry indicated a central economy. But that same activity in the 19th century was representative of a semi-peripheral country, and became characteristic of a periphery in the late 20th century. The product chain adjusts to the periodic reorganization of the stable hierarchy of world capitalism (Wallerstein, 1986).

This analysis also maintains that the world system functions through a political structure that reaffirms the central, peripheral, or semi-peripheral location of each country in the global hierarchy. That arrangement adapts to the preeminence of strong, weak, and intermediate states. The different state formations coexist through mutual recognition that ensures the international legitimacy of each country (Wallerstein, 2004: Chapters 18–19). Those states are essential for commodifying labor power, ensuring tax collection, guaranteeing profits, and socializing risk. Capitalism needs territorial jurisdictions and defined borders in order to externalize the costs of large investments and sustain policies of trade protection or liberalization (Wallerstein, 1988: 36–48).

The decisive weight the U.S. theorist ascribes to the state contrasts with the secondary role he attributes to the nation. He maintains that these entities were formed as simple derivations of the states, and have served to cohere individuals around patriotism, school systems, and military service (Wallerstein, 2005: Chapter 3). With a similar logic, he suggests that race arose as an identity adapted to the place occupied by each human grouping in the international division of labor. Free white workers, black slaves, and mestizo serfs were separated by the mode of exploitation prevalent in each segment. Ethnicity was in turn used to assign specific labors to the different communities of each country. Thus, the genetic idea of race, the socio-political concept of nation, and the cultural category of ethnicity were defined by their roles in the world-economy (Wallerstein, 2004: Chapter 1).

3   Relationship to Dependency Theory

Wallerstein worked out his conception adopting several postulates of dependency theory. He shared its critique of liberal theories of development and of positivist conceptions of modernization. He challenged the presentation of the West as a model to imitate, and argued against the myth of achieving welfare through the simple expansion of capitalism. However, he objected to those conceptions without accepting the developmentalist alternative, and he especially rejected the nation-state perspective. He emphasized the advisability of taking the world economy as the starting point for all investigations. With this perspective, he was situated on the opposite pole from institutionalism. He debated with Weberian approaches that explain development by comparing different routes to national development. He developed this approach with the same vehemence displayed by the postwar Marxists in their controversies with the Keynesians.

In highlighting the impact of unequal exchange and describing transfers of income to the metropolis, this view of capitalism coincided with dependency theory. Wallerstein characterizes the capitalist system as a regime of exploitation subject to growing imbalances and insurmountable contradictions. He stresses the polarizing dynamics of a structure that reinforces the separation between advanced and backward economies. His affinity with dependentism is also confirmed by his assessment of the fate of the underdeveloped countries that provide inputs to metropolitan industry. That specialization obstructs the internal development of the periphery.

Wallerstein was also in tune with the Latin American Marxist theorists in his interpretation of world accumulation as a process that compensates for declines in profits with the cheapening of wage costs. Thus, he studied the way in which the exploitation of workers in the periphery counteracts the reduction of profit in the center (Wallerstein, 1988: 24–30). His concurrence with dependency is also verified by his critique of evolutionary political strategies and projects of national capitalism in the underdeveloped countries. Wallerstein used this foundation to reject the rigid historical scheme of successive modes of production, and to postulate the international character of the passage from one system to another.

4   Convergences and Separations

The positive reception of world-systems theory among the dependency theorists included certain differentiations. Dos Santos distinguished between three areas of similar treatments of the center-periphery relation. In the first place, he held that Wallerstein placed the topic within a conceptualization of historical capitalism, as a structure that expands in conflict with other systems. Second, he maintained that Amin had studied the same problem from the Asian-African contexts, putting greater emphasis on the evolution of the Third World. Finally, he indicated that his perspective (together with Marini and Bambirra) treated the topic from the Latin American situation, distinguishing between central capitalism, the dependent countries, and socialism (Dos Santos, 1998).

These general agreements were ratified by Amin, who stressed that they were predominantly complementary formulations of the same problem. The Egyptian economist highlighted convergences in the characterization of the origin and the polarized functioning of capitalism (Amin, 2005). He also affirmed the utility of Wallerstein's idea for tracking the international dynamics of the law of value and the importance of transfers of surplus value. He maintained that the world-system view makes it possible to see the unity of those phenomena, overcoming the conceptualization of the world market as a mixture of juxtaposed components (Amin, 2008: 234–236).

Other researchers underlined the affinities between these three perspectives (Martins, 2011a: 265–266), highlighted the enrichment that resulted from their encounter (Herrera, 2001: 201–220), and presented the systemic view as a continuation of dependentism (Blomstrom and Hettne, 1990: 243–244, 247–248). Some observers spoke highly of Wallerstein's influence on Dos Santos, arguing that he contributed to overcoming the identity-based aspects of the old dependentism. With the comprehensive perspective of the world system, the unilateral treatment of underdevelopment as a 'Latin American thought' was dissolved, and the dependency concept was revised as a mutable relation within a world-economy (Niemeyer, 2005).

These interpretations of confluence have coexisted with characterizations that underline their differences. They emphasize that the systemic treatment privileges global logics, as opposed to the dependency view that stresses the dialectical interaction between center and periphery (Sotelo Valencia, 2005). They also maintain that Wallerstein was not able to perceive the specific significance of Latin American dependent capitalism (Osorio, 2009b: 41–44). These problems can be clarified by specifying the ideas that unite and that separate the two theories.

5   Convergent Concepts

Wallerstein introduced several ideas that broadened a shared view of contemporary capitalism. He demonstrated how the industrialization of the intermediate economies studied by Marini is intertwined with integrated processes of global production, situating the dynamics of dependent reproduction in the tendencies of world accumulation. He explained the way in which the underdeveloped economies participate in international product chains, and why only certain countries of the periphery develop a manufacturing profile.

Wallerstein stressed that capitalism re-creates a stable global stratification. He demonstrated the preeminence of a hierarchy that reproduces unchosen situations of dependency and perpetuates the center-periphery polarization (Schwartzman, 2006). This perspective reinforces all the postulates of dependentism, which highlight the strict limits that capitalism imposes on any change in the international status of countries. Like the Latin American Marxists, Wallerstein deduced that stability from the rigidity of the international division of labor. He stressed the existence of a stable architecture in changing geographical contexts. He noted that alterations in the center-periphery pyramid unfold mainly on the inside of each segment. Only in a few historical circumstances have some central economies been demoted to the peripheral level, and the same exceptionality rules in the opposite direction (Agurre Rojas, 2007).

Wallerstein posits a zero-sum principle in the internal mobility of each part of the world system. He maintains that the rise of one component tends to be compensated by the fall of an equivalent portion. The dependency theorists reasoned about underdevelopment in these same terms. World-system theory provided new arguments to support shared theories of the structural re-creation of global inequality. However, the U.S. author also introduced a concept of semi-periphery to illustrate the existence of intermediate situations, which historically operated as links of ascent or descent in the world system. He indicated that, together with the hegemonic powers, there always existed intermediate formations that cushioned global inequality. The semi-peripheral situation expressed the decline of old powers to intermediate situations (Spain) or the transition to positions of world domination (United States, Germany) (Wallerstein, 1984: 248–267, 313–329).

This logic of tri-modal development was used to overcome the simplifications of the dual model bequeathed by Prebisch (center-periphery) and re-created by the most rudimentary anti-imperialist approaches (empire-colony). This new model not only clarified how income transfers function on an international scale. It also renovated studies of the alliances that the hegemonic centers enter into with their subaltern partners to guarantee the stability of capitalism and incorporate new areas into the world-system (Chase Dunn, 2012).

The same model was suggested, but not made explicit, by the dependency theorists. Marini investigated the peculiarities of the industrialized Latin American economies and distinguished them from the countries that purely exported raw materials. Bambirra presented a differentiation between models with distinct levels of underdevelopment. The idea of semi-periphery is present in these treatments, and that similarity was recognized by the dependency theorists (Dos Santos, 2009b).

Wallerstein also utilized an approach very similar to the dependent cycle theorized by Marini to underline the place occupied by each economy in the global productive circuit. This perspective moved away from Prebisch's early model, which only studied the insertion of the periphery in exchange networks. Thus, there are many thematic convergences between world-system and dependency theories. What are the areas of divergence?

6   Systems or Modes of Production?

The dependency theorists indicated that Marxism has been one way they are different from the world-system approach. Wallerstein only accepted the classification as Marxist when that name implied a generic identification with radical thoughts or attitudes, but he does not share the habitual application of that theory (Wallerstein, 2013: 202–210).

Some interpreters of his approach emphasize his compatibility with Marxism (Penston and Busekese, 2010). Others even feel that he reformulated Trotsky's representation of the world economy as a totality structured around the division of labor (Doronenko, 2005). What is debated, however, is not so much the classification of the author as the meaning of his concept of *system*. That concept articulates his entire perspective. Wallerstein recalls that he began by studying social conflicts, and then investigated how the consensus of values operates in African reality and European history. From this research, he deduced the need to prioritize the world context, understood as a system (Wallerstein, 1979: 7–18). He has developed this last category as a perspective of analysis or paradigm, and leaves open a later deepening of the concept as a more complete theory (Wallerstein, 2011).

'The system' is close in many ways to the Marxist idea of mode of production used by Latin American dependency theorists. However, the ideas presuppose different logics about the development of society. Wallerstein indicates a difference in the importance ascribed to the exploitation of labor as a pillar of distinct social regimes. Mini-systems, world-empire, and world-economy are not conceived around this foundation. Thus, he counterposes his models to the old scheme he attributed to Marxism of a succession of modes of production (primitive collectivism, slavery, feudalism, capitalism). The divergence is not in the existence of a successive order, since the systemic thesis also contains steps. Neither is the inexorable passage from one mode to another central, since that simplification was only characteristic of the most dogmatic varieties of Marxism.

Not even Wallerstein's method is the motive for the controversy. He adopted an idea of system with a multi-disciplinary approach that breaks with the tradition of studies fragmented into separate subjects. He rejects the division between economics, political science, or sociology, and builds his concepts calling for the reunification of the social sciences (Wallerstein, 2005: Chapter 1). This attitude is very similar to Marxism. With this focus, he vindicates Marx, historical materialism, and the primacy of the economic in the study of capitalism. He approves of the holistic perspective of that tradition and its interest in grasping the contradictions that stifle processes of accumulation.

However, Wallerstein is further away from that matrix when he defends his idea of system with three other theoretical foundations. From Braudel he takes the location of those structures in long temporalities and extended spatialities. From Polanyi he takes the classification of specific forms of social organization around principles of reciprocity, redistribution, and commercial exchange. Finally, he absorbs from Prigogine the characterization of systems as organisms with delimited lives and existences marked by periods of equilibrium and chaos. At certain stages those structures survive by assimilating disturbances, and at other times they are affected by chaotic whirlwinds. These systems are studied with the same outlook astronomers use to investigate the universe (Wallerstein, 1979: 7–18; 2002: 69–80).

This transfer of criteria from the natural sciences to social thought sets him apart from the Marxist view of modes of production. The contradiction between development of the productive forces and social relations of property posited by that approach assumes other patterns of transformation and privileges the combination of productive variables and class confrontations. That difference in approach is greater with the historicist variant of Marxism, which emphasizes the role of subjects in the passage from one system to another and rejects in the most categorical fashion analogies with the natural sciences. The world-system approach does not utilize class logics, which with differing levels of centrality inspire all variants of Marxism. The primacy ascribed to social struggle by this conception contrasts with the structuralist viewpoint of the systemic perspective. Wallerstein assesses each event as a functional requirement of the course of history (Robinson, 2011).

Some critics claim that by presenting successive systems as the only drivers of social evolution, this approach imposes a harmful 'tyranny of the totality'. They argue that Wallerstein builds forced worlds, assuming that the whole is always more important than the parts. This viewpoint ignores the autonomy of the components, which are seen as simple transmitters of a dynamic that is already pre-assumed by the world system (Smith, 1979). Other analysts maintain that this view dilutes particularities and loses sight of processes that operate in short time frames (Osorio, 2009b: 48–50).

Wallerstein synthesizes his differences with the Marxist view by counterposing his concept of totality with that of Perry Anderson. He uses the idea to conceive of mutations in closed systems, with the beginning and end predefined and with rigorous internal mechanisms of change. The opposite approach works with open paths, uncertain outcomes, and a great variety of transformation mechanisms (Wallerstein, 2013: 202–210). Wallerstein's totality and Anderson's totalization illustrate the discrepancies between two ways of reasoning that inspire distinct perspectives on the current course of capitalism.

7   Terminal Crises and Social Subjects

Wallerstein believes that the starting and concluding dates of the world system are predictable. He deduces a rigorous chronology of the self-destructive
behavior of that structure. He argues that the exhaustion of the current cycle
will imply the end of the world-economy. It will not be one secular movement followed by another, but the last fluctuation of the system. In a very
chaotic scenario, this closure will conclude a period of 500 years (Wallerstein,
2005: Chapter 5).

Wallerstein indicates three determinant causes of this outcome. First, that
the greater power of unionized workers has caused a strong reduction of profits. Capitalists have tried to counteract that pressure by displacing production
to regions with cheap labor power, but they are not able to offset the sustained
process of urbanization that increases the cost of labor. Second, he highlights
the generalized rise in costs of production as a consequence of the ecological
crisis, the depletion of raw materials, and the accumulation of waste products.
Finally, he affirms that the tax system cannot afford the political democratization that workers have imposed (Wallerstein, 2002). These three processes
hasten the terminal crisis of the world-system. It is no longer possible to regen-
erate a world-empire, nor to recreate another hegemonic succession.

With this analysis, Wallerstein describes several contradictions that Marxists
present as historical limits to capitalism. However, his perspective incorporates precise dates for a terminal outcome. He affirms that the decline began
in the years 1960–70, and will culminate in 2030–2050. At that time, a great
disturbance will put an end to five centuries of modernity, and a more egalitarian form of social organization will arise (Wallerstein, 2011; 2005: Chapter 2).

This characterization has points of contact with the theories of collapse
that Marxists debated in 1920–40 to elucidate what the determinant factor
would be in the explosion of capitalism (decrease in consumption, falling
profit rate, financial breakdown). The later maturation of that debate made it
possible to understand that a final crisis is unforeseeable, and should not be
conceived with the automaticity of purely economic mechanisms. Only the
popular majorities, acting in the political sphere, can put an end to capitalism
and replace it with a more progressive social regime.

In any case, what is most important is not the magnitude of crises, but
popular perception of the anti-capitalist potentials of those upheavals – and
that level of consciousness is much less now than it was in the 1970s or 1930s
(Therborn, 2000: 266–284). This last problem requires more attention than
all the speculations about the date of the final collapse. The consistency of
that prognosis is as doubtful as the different reflections about the moment the

system will end, which is conditioned by political-social actions that are completely unforeseeable. Certainly, the current regime confronts historical limits, but that frontier does not presuppose the temporality foretold by Wallerstein.

8   Two Views on Long Cycles

The systemic theorist conceives of a process of decadence similar to that of Europe during the passage from feudalism to capitalism (Wallerstein, 1986). That analogy, as well as the parallels between the decline of the United States and that of the Roman Empire, has been debated. In these cases, there is a tendency to compare social regimes with very different functioning, economic mechanisms, and types of crises. The extension of those comparisons to state structures or types of political-popular intervention is even more controversial.

In practice, those analogies only suggest long transitions, which in turn contradict the prediction of a pre-defined moment of collapse. The descriptions Wallerstein presents of the current chaos illustrate reorganizations of capitalism, changes in power relations, or alterations in hegemonic leadership (Wallerstein, 2012a). These processes include very turbulent situations, but do not imply an end that can be anticipated. This type of closure is a necessary ingredient of the systemic viewpoint, but does not constitute a corollary of the Marxist view held by the Latin American dependency theorists.

Dos Santos, Marini, and Bambirra always conceived of the future of capitalism in close relation to the progress of a socialist alternative. The periods of time they imagined for that change were associated with the course of that battle. They never assumed collapses that were intrinsic or self-inflicted by capitalism itself. This difference in approach is also verified in the two treatments of Kondratieff cycles. Wallerstein incorporates them in the tradition of Schumpeter, as mechanisms with fixed time-frames that renovate technology and broaden markets. Thus, he assumes their predictability and cyclical reappearance every five or six decades. He posits the validity of those movements throughout 500 years, and predicts that the current stage of stagnation will end with the collapse of the world system. A descending Kondratieff will coincide with the exhaustion of the last secular cycle (Wallerstein, 2016; 2012c; 2011: Chapter 1).

The application that Dos Santos made of those cycles is located in another tradition, closer to the Marxist theories of long waves developed by authors like Mandel. It records prolonged economic movements only since the 19th century, and sees its development in close relation to the dynamics of the class struggle. Dos Santos sought to unravel how a Kondratieff period operates in the contemporary reality of technological-productive reorganization of capitalism. He did not situate those cycles in secular time-frames or in sequences of collapses in the world-system (Dos Santos, 1983).

The differences between Wallerstein and the Latin American dependency theorists also includes conflicting views on stagnation and absolute pauperization. For Wallerstein, these two features indicate the presence of a terminal crisis of modernity. He believes that the majority of workers confront greater adversities than 500 years ago in terms of food, work conditions, and life expectancy (after the first year of life). He attributes that regression to the elimination of community structures, and maintains that the improvement in consumption has solely benefited the 10–15 percent of the world population that has achieved the status of middle class (Wallerstein, 1988: 92–96).

The many arguments developed by Marini to demonstrate that this theory did not involve stagnationism or increasing misery illustrate his disagreement with Wallerstein's view. The theory of super-exploitation, in which his major challenges are concentrated, was formulated in contrast to the theories of generalized pauperization in any stage of capitalism. Marini theorized the existence of higher rates of exploitation in the periphery than in the center; with this comparison of the situations of the workers in the advanced and backward economies, he recognized a more significant improvement in the developed countries. He also distanced himself from the theory of more generalized deterioration posited by the world-system theorist.

9   Discrepancies on Socialism

In the period in which he formed his conception, Wallerstein included the ex-Soviet Union, China, and the so-called socialist bloc within the world system. He understood that these regions were integrated into that circuit and confronted the same decline. He considered the world-economy to be a dominant totality on the planet. He also felt that the socialist project had an initial revolutionary impulse that was later diluted in the networks of world capitalism. It could not escape the dynamics and the destiny of that regime.

Thus, Wallerstein did not ascribe importance to the implosion of the Soviet Union, and he analyzed that collapse as part of the general crisis of the current era. He countered Hobsbawm's definition of the 'short 20th century', framed by the rise and fall of the Soviet Union, with a 'long 20th century' determined by other circumstances like the rise and decadence of the United States (Wallerstein, 1992). However, by including the ex-Soviet bloc within the world system, he also had to assume that this segment functioned with the same principles of profitability, competition, and property as the capitalist economies.

This characterization left out the internal analysis of those countries. He deduced their similarity with the rest of the world from a simple external connection with the Western powers. He applied the same logic that he used to inscribe within the world-system all the regions that were absorbed by that circuit over 500 years. However, he never explained that analogy between the ex-Soviet Union, China, and Eastern Europe and all that had happened several centuries earlier with India or the Ottoman Empire (Chen, 2010). He did not show how, when, and in what way an invariable permanence, or an exit and immediate reintroduction of those countries to capitalism, was produced. That re-entry could only be clearly demonstrated after the collapse of the socialist bloc.

The consequences of overstating totalities at the expense of the specific dynamics of each component of the world system can be verified on these grounds. Wallerstein forced the classification of the Soviet Union and China within the same bloc that the United States hegemonized since the postwar. This assimilation was another area of disagreement with dependentism, as the Latin American Marxists did not treat the Soviet Union as a sub-system of capitalism and were attentive to its role in the battle against imperialism. Dos Santos, Marini, and Bambirra dissented from the laudatory view of the socialist bloc propagated by the communist parties, but emphasized the conflict of that sector with the Western powers. They hoped for socialist renovation in those countries in the heat of that dispute.

All of the logic of the dependency theorists was guided by their hopes for the socialist project. Wallerstein only conceived of that course as an immediately global leap by highlighting the existence of a single worldwide totality. The Latin American group did not assume victorious results, but positioned themselves on a field of battle for socialism. The systemic theory disregarded that perspective in its belief that capitalism would collapse by itself at a predictable time.

10   Anti-imperialism and National Traditions

Marxist dependency theory imagined anti-capitalist triumphs as a result of popular insurgencies in the periphery that would be projected onto the center. That hope was framed by the Cuban revolution, which did not occupy any significant spaces in Wallerstein's conceptualization. His approach was informed by other political experiences, based on his formation on the U.S. left together with radical, libertarian, and anti-Stalinist movements. Later he worked in Africa, in contact with the leading currents in the anti-colonial struggle, and was very influenced by Fanon's ideas (Wallerstein, 2012b).

Through this experience, he processed the critique of the evolutionary perspective of the communist parties in a different way. In particular, he assimilated the historiographic consequences of that challenge, and drew conclusions to elaborate his model of systemic mutations. In contrast, dependentism concentrated its attacks in the political sphere, and objected to the proposals for national capitalism supported by the communist parties (Chilcote, 2009). The dependency critique had an immediate aim that was not present in Wallerstein's perspective.

This differentiated viewpoint extended to the meaning of the national struggle in the periphery. The systemic view rejected that type of action, and instead of anti-imperialist strategies it promoted policies critical of oppression, with cosmopolitan biases, and identified any validation of the national dimension with the developmentalist project. In addition, Wallerstein's approach does not share the mediation between anti-imperialist action in the periphery and anti-capitalist dynamics on a global scale proposed by Amin in his delinking model (Goldfrank, 2000). He assumes that the collapse of the world-system will light the way to a global post-capitalist outcome, with no need for those links.

Thus, Wallerstein supports direct social transformations on a global level thorough anti-systemic action. This does not include the convergence of socialism with revolutionary nationalism as proposed by dependentism. That rejection is inspired by his characterization of the nation as an entity derived from the form in which each state was inserted into the international division of labor. However, it omits the fact that state formation was a very convulsive process, which included progressive and democratic projects conditioned by popular revolts. Dependency theory drew precisely on this national legacy and attempted to combine it with the socialist perspective.

This difference between the two perspectives can be seen in their assessment of the wars that led to independence in Latin America. Wallerstein did not ascribe revolutionary relevance to that rupture, and highlighted the dominant group's fear of the slaves and the Indians. He saw what happened in this period as an example of passive and subordinate adaptation of a region to the world-system (Wallerstein, 1999a: 352, 306–317). On the contrary, dependency theory was always willing to accept this event as a precedent to contemporary anti-imperialism. With this view, it encouraged thinking about socialism from the viewpoint of Latin American traditions. These disagreements about the past are reflected in their strategies for future emancipation.

11   Only Now Is It Possible?

In the process of objective collapse of the world-system, Wallerstein ascribes a leading role to the anti-systemic movements forged during the decolonization and rebellions of 1968. He argues that those uprisings marked the beginning of revolutionary rejection of U.S. hegemony and the cultures of oppression. He also thinks that those uprisings initiated the replacement of the old left by new social movements that broaden democratization, challenge Eurocentrism, and introduce multiculturalism.

Wallerstein maintains that for the first time in history, an age of real emancipation is emerging. He maintains that in the last five centuries the system could not be modified and the revolutionaries ended up adapting to the world order. They confronted unresolvable dilemmas when they tried to modify structures that could not be overturned (Wallerstein, 1999b: 127–176). With this assumption, he held that a great nightmare affected socialist experiences, social democracy, and nationalist movements, which fought fruitlessly between 1870 and 1968 for another course of social evolution (Wallerstein, 1989).

This same thesis of the unviability of transformations in the past and their feasibility in the present has been very common among other historians. Many have argued that the impotence suffered by insurgent slaves in antiquity, by rebel peasants in the Middle Ages, or by the defeated workers of the Paris Commune obeyed the rigid conditions of those eras, as the immaturity of the productive forces made it impossible, in all cases, to realize other alternatives.

However, this perspective assumes that only in the stage that one happens to live in are real transformations possible. Wallerstein presents this idea with two considerations: on the one hand, he is critical of the adaptation of all rebel movements of the past to the status quo; on the other, he declares that another evolution is feasible since 1968, given the appearance of a new subjectivity with no precedents (Wallerstein, 2004: Chapter 23). This logic of dead-end situations in the past introduces a tragic element in historical analysis. It assumes that in past times revolutionaries were condemned to failure, self-sacrifice, or capitulation, and that only now are winning choices open to them.

This approach explains Wallerstein's attitude toward the Latin American wars of independence. He claims that this confrontation led to the formation of oppressor states subjected to British oversight as a consequence of the place the region had to occupy in the world system (Wallerstein, 1999a: 356–357). But he also took this final result as an unchangeable outcome, ignoring the potentialities of a revolutionary confrontation. In addition, he does not mention the legacy of experiences and traditions left by that struggle for the oppressed classes. It is very arbitrary to assume that history confers the keys to the future only to the living subjects of a certain conjuncture, assuming they have the doubtful privilege of acting in a terminal stage of capitalism.

Historicist Marxism thinks through the problem on other terms. It emphasizes the role of popular subjects, indicating that progressive projects have been feasible at all times. Thus, it does not classify contemporary projects above its precursors, knowing that such an ordering could be disproven in the future, or used to dismiss the importance of what is currently happening. In Wallerstein, the role of subjects is an enigma. He assumes that popular actions were irrelevant until now because of their inability to twist the dynamic of the world system. Yet he attributes to them a central function in the construction of the society that will emerge in the mid-21st century. Some analysts attribute these oscillations to an extreme determinism in his conceptualization of world systems, arguing that this perspective keeps him from noticing the multiplicity of paths taken in the establishment of modernity. This outcome was a result of diverse rebellions that followed the French Revolution, not simply a corollary of the world-system (Therborn, 2000: 284–266).

12   Political Strategies

Wallerstein attributes the popular failures of the past to the preeminence of political projects tied to the seizing of power. He believes that this policy allowed the achievement of some reforms in the 20th century, but did not serve to modify the status quo. He argues that it would have been difficult to have obtained more than they did, and notes the negative consequences of many experiences, which led to generalized disappointment among the popular sectors (Wallerstein, 1989; 1992).

Based on that characterization, he claims that liberation will now be feasible, under the impulse of anti-systemic movements that do not seek to take power. He celebrates the abandonment of that objective, arguing that to govern within a world-system is equivalent to renouncing the goals of justice and equality. He highlights the existence of new political paths that introduce non-hierarchical forms of action, with greater horizontality and decentralization (Wallerstein, 2002: 41–48).

This theory is very compatible with the autonomist strategy of sidestepping the administration of the state in order to prepare for emancipation in all the pores of society. It is in tune with the theory of 'changing the world without taking power', which over the last decade was intensely debated in Latin America. What has happened in this period shows that this approach does not offer viable alternatives for building popular power. Wallerstein proposes a strategy in three stages. He holds that in the long run, a utopia of a democratic and egalitarian world should be sought, without setting out predefined institutional forms for that future. In the medium term, he proposes working for libertarian alternatives that sidestep the administration of the state, and in the short term he favors opting for the 'lesser evil', in both elections and in direct action (Wallerstein, 2008).

His first objective has similarities with the communist ideal, but leaves out the need for socialist transitions that make it possible to build that future by means of a state controlled by the popular majorities. Wallerstein dismisses that instrument, and does not offer suggestions about the way to achieve his proposals in the medium term. Given the absence of an alternative state project, his short-term view is even more problematic. It leaves the doors open for going down all types of paths.

On that terrain, his differences with the dependency tradition are more significant. That approach always prioritizes the socialist goal and encourages different paths to accede to the government, administer the state, and transform society. The world-system perspective shares many characterizations of the center-periphery relation with Marxist dependency theory. It also contributes fruitful ideas for adapting dependency theory to the transformations undergone under current capitalism. But the two approaches are farther apart on other key areas of economics, politics, and historiography.

CHAPTER 7

Three Stages of the Metropolis-Satellite Perspective

André Gunder Frank was a well-known intellectual who, in the 1960s, participated in the creation of Marxist dependency theory. He sought to elucidate the peculiarities of the center-periphery relation by analyzing the origins and characteristics of capitalism. Frank adopted successive views centered on Latin American underdevelopment, the dynamics of the world system, and the international protagonism of Asia. In each treatment, he provoked intense debates because of his tendency to radicalize the discussion while contradicting his previous ideas. His evolution was very illustrative of the different contours taken by the debate on underdevelopment.

1   Variety of Approaches

The first Frank, in the 1960s, asserted that Latin America suffered from a burdensome appropriation of surpluses because of its subordinate insertion in the world market, indicating that those confiscations perpetuated the stagnation of the region. He traced the origin of that subjection back to the colonial era, and noted that Ibero-America was integrated into global capitalism in a dependent form. Thus, it was linked to a circuit that favored first the metropolitan centers (Spain, Portugal) and then the dominant power (Great Britain). With this long-term view of capitalism, Frank postulated that underdevelopment was inherent to a system that had operated in a polarized form since its birth, and underlined that capitalism was synonymous with backwardness for the past, present, and future of Latin America (Frank, 1970: 8–24).

In the early 1970s, Frank reformulated his conception in harmony with world-system theory, which was just emerging as an influential conception in the social sciences. He asserted that Wallerstein's perspective prioritized the global question and surpassed the limitations of partialized studies of underdevelopment. With this new approach, he argued that by itself dependency theory did not provide feasible alternatives. He underlined the omnipresence of the global economy, and stressed the obsolescence of autonomous national development (Frank, 1970: 305–327; 1991: 10–62).

In this second period, the German theorist reaffirmed the preeminence of capitalism in the Americas since colonization, but from a world-system perspective, framing his research on the metropolis-satellite relation in the more general context of the secular cycles of capitalism. This turn led him to reconsider all the connections between the subjection of the periphery and the functioning of the system (Frank, 1979: 54–142).

In the early 1990s, the German writer expressed a new dissatisfaction with his theory and proposed a third conception, based on the importance of the Asian continent. He questioned the scarce relevance ascribed to that region, and looked back to the ancient global supremacy of the East (Frank, 2009: 115–130). With this new viewpoint, he challenged the conceptions that underlined European centrality in the formation of capitalism. He argued that the West only temporarily usurped the primacy of China, which was again emerging at the end of the 20th century. From this characterization, he also deduced the existence of a millennial temporality of capitalism. He reinterpreted this system as a regime with mercantile foundations, cyclical continuities, Asian pillars, and immemorial origins (Frank, 2009: 110–115). In this last model, he introduced changes in the protagonists of the metropolis-satellite approach. China was now located at the summit, with India in an intermediate position and Europe in a subordinate role. In the three stages of his evolution, Frank maintained similar concerns, but his changing definitions generated strong challenges.

2   Controversies over Colonization

Frank based his initial theory of underdevelopment on the capitalist character of Latin America since colonization. He argued that a conquest led by the commercial sector of the Iberian Peninsula created, since the 17th century, production regulated by the market and oriented toward export (Frank, 1970: 31–39, 167–168). He took up the viewpoint of the historians (Bagu, 1977: 62–64, 75–86) that highlighted early accumulation in an open economy. He also argued against the theorists of feudal colonization, and supported the views of authors who pointed to lack of rural self-sufficiency, primacy of urban development, and priority of export in the use of forced labor (Peña, 2012: 69–70). Thus, he accepted descriptions of the *encomendero*, the *latifundista*, and the plantation owner as instruments of commercial capitalism.

Frank questioned the portrayal of the colonial system as a subsistence economy. He rejected the thesis of the theorists who contrasted the English introduction of the seeds of capitalism with the Spanish transmission of medieval forms (Mariátegui, 1984: 13–16, 50–64). Moreover, he disagreed with the historians who interpreted the preeminence of servitude or slave forms of exploitation as evidence of feudalism (Puiggrós, 1965). He directly confronted the studies that saw indications of that system in the weight of the *latifundio* or in the importance of rent (Fernández and Ocampo, 1974). His perspective underlined categorically the supremacy of the market and investment since the arrival of Christopher Columbus (Frank, 1965).

This approach is in tune with Sweezy's view in an analogous controversy over the passage from feudalism to capitalism in Europe. In that case, what was debated was the driving forces of the new system, not the protagonists of overseas colonization, but the content of the debate was similar. Sweezy argued that long-distance trade and the urban boom determined the decline of feudalism on the Old Continent, as it forced the nobility to compensate for their losses with greater exploitation of the peasants (Sweezy, 1974: 15–34, 114–120). That pressure caused a scarcity of rural labor power, accentuated the flight of the serfs to the cities, and transformed rent from products into money. The same markets that weakened the nobility according to Sweezy were, for Frank, determinants of the initial configuration of Latin America.

That characterization was rejected by Dobb, who attributed the transition to capitalism in Europe to the erosion of the agrarian structures challenged by peasant rebellions. He argued that feudalism was internally corroded by that conflict (Dobb, 1974: 12, 52–55). Other authors challenged the presentation of that system as a stable mode of production, divorced from urban life. They underlined the incidence of endogenous crises that forced increased tributes and accentuated competition among the nobility, and demonstrated how that process gave birth to a sector of rich peasants, who employed wage-labor and inaugurated capitalist agriculture (Hilton, 1974: 123–135). The European and Latin American debates explored two poles of the same process that generated development in one region and backwardness in the other. Those debates sought to clarify why capitalism took off in England and led to dependent stagnation in Latin America.

3   More Elaborate Answers

The development of historiographic analysis modified the terms of the debate in the late 1970s. Several scholars incorporated the concept of socio-economic formation to explore amalgamations of modes of production, with differing levels of preeminence of one system over another (Anderson, 1985: 74–76). This idea replaced purely economic interpretations with more comprehensive assessments of social processes (Aricó, 2012: 134–179). The specific form taken by feudalism and capitalism in each period and region was clarified, noting the mixed forms of dominant and secondary systems.

This approach prioritized the abrupt change introduced by colonization in the pre-Columbian regimes (Cardoso, 1973). The destruction of those civilizations led to a colonial system based on servile labor, which the surviving structures of the indigenous world supplied. The most developed communities were subjected to that form of labor, while the least developed were exterminated (Vitale, 1984). The crown, the church, and the conquistadors connected the indigenous aristocracy to the collection of tributes, revolving administration of labor, and massive relocation of the population. This symbiosis was as foreign to Spanish feudalism as it was to commercial capitalism. It did not create the homogeneous situation imagined by analysts of both versions of colonization. Forced labor in the *haciendas* was very different from feudal servitude, and impeded the formation of small-scale capitalist agrarian property.

The same particularities prevailed in other economic models of the colonial era (Cardoso and Pérez Brignoli, 1979: T I, 177–178, 186–192, 212–222). In the plantation areas, slavery was generalized for the growing of sugar, cacao, or cotton. This combination of coercive labor forms to satisfy European commercial demand was another peculiarity of the hemisphere. In the third model of frontier economy, the usufruct of cattle rents predominated. This variant, too, did not fit into the crude classification of feudalism versus capitalism.

This analysis of these *haciendas*, plantations, and *latifundios* took Frank's world market hierarchy into account, but with another logic. Rather than pure external exactions, it favored exploring property relations and forms of labor exploitation (Cardoso and Pérez Brignoli, 1979: T II, 9–14). This perspective showed how Latin America was integrated into international trade with a wide variety of pre-capitalist relations. The standard form of slavery (with distribution of lands to guarantee self-provision of food) did not prevail; nor did feudal serfdom (because of the persistence of indigenous communities), and even less the minority or exceptional use of waged labor.

Frank's 'pan-capitalist' perspective overlooked these combinations. He correctly argued that Latin America was linked to nascent capitalism, but he did not recognize that this connection was made through slave, servile, and oligarchical structures. These formations were, in turn, articulated with secondary types of production (peasant or patriarchal) in pre-monetary realms and precapitalist agricultures. Out of this variety, the unequal underdevelopment that characterized dependent capitalism in the 19th century arose (Cueva, 1982).

4   Commercial Capitalism

In this first period of his intellectual evolution, Frank did not offer satisfactory responses to the criticisms raised in response to his theory of commercial capitalism. He assumed that an economic system that had recently taken off in Europe already operated in Latin America. He defined the mode of production by the scope of exchange, forgetting the centrality of labor, which in Latin America involved distinct coercive labor forms.

The theorists of feudal colonization pointed to those problems, but assumed a simple transfer of European productive systems to Latin America. They did not recognize that those formations were not simply exportable. Their establishment depended on local conditions very different from those that were predominant in the Old World. In the Americas, viceroyalty was prevalent, not the fragmented sovereignties of feudalism. Lordship, loyalty in exchange for protection, territorial reconfiguration based on family alliances, or the typical conflicts between nobles and serfs were not found. Frank's errors were not corrected, forcing a presentation of the conquest as a feudal venture.

The authors who studied socio-economic formations avoided those mistakes. They explored the origin of capitalism and colonization in the productive sphere, highlighted the internal contradictions of the modes of production, and ascribed a definitive weight to the class struggle. This perspective confirmed that the presence of commercial capital was compatible with various social systems and was not unique to capitalism (Laclau, 1973).

Frank sidestepped these problems and privileged the sphere of circulation over that of production. Thus, his model only found expropriations of surpluses by means of commercial circuits and monetary movements. The metropolis-satellite model also conceived a mechanical relation of Latin American evolution to external processes. It paid little attention to what occurred in the internal structures and local exchanges of the colonial economy (Assadourian, 1973). That agrarian world had a strong impact in a region with abundant land and scarce productive improvements. Rural transformations, which in Europe anticipated the rise of capitalism, were not found in any part of Ibero-America.

With his perspective of pure capitalist continuities, Frank did not perceive that contrast. Neither did he grasp the impact of the great political changes brought on by the Wars of Independence. His approach tended to emphasize sequences of a single underdevelopment, without taking into account the difference that separates the formation and the maturation of capitalism. While the debate over colonization corresponded to the first period, contemporary forms of dependence should be conceptualized starting from the 19th century.

Frank noted that the conquest of the Americas was a key moment in the constitution of the world market, but he identified that event with the full presence of capitalism. He left out the long process of transition that tied the original de-accumulation of the Americas to capital accumulation led by Europe (Vitale, 1992: Chapters 4, 6). In his metropolis-satellite model, that diversity of stages got dissolved into indistinct totalities. This treatment was a

consequence of the primacy ascribed to the exogenous-commercial components relative to the endogenous-agrarian elements. Frank formulated all his
explanations of underdevelopment in terms of colonial exaction. He emphasized the great impact of pillage, which certainly devastated the New World to
feed the reserves of European accumulation. However, by seeing only this side,
he overlooked the fact that the divergent paths of the two regions were defined
by more structural processes of agricultural prosperity and stagnation. That
long-term effect had an enormous impact on the consolidation of pre-capitalist rural structures (Cardoso and Pérez Brignoli, 1979: T i, 100–102).

The lack of farmers or tenants was determinant in Latin American underdevelopment. That adversity was re-created in the 19th century with the dissolution of the slave plantations, which was followed by *latifundios* surrounded
by peasant economies with low productivity. The same process is found in the
concentration of properties and the destruction of communities that went
along with the remodeling of the haciendas. In the frontier zones, the hoarding
of territories by parasitical oligarchies was more accelerated. The five-century
commercial capitalism model is unable to see how that agrarian backwardness
affected the later rise of industrialization.

5   Political Simplifications

Frank underlined the capitalist nature of Latin American evolution in order
to demonstrate the exhaustion of a system with five centuries of history. He
emphasized that long timespan for the purpose of stressing the immediate need
for socialism. Thus, he rejected the thesis of feudal colonization and objected
to delays in revolutionary action, which were justified by the persistence of
pre-capitalist features. The theory of capitalist colonization was presented as a
critique of the strategy of socialism by stages. That motivation led it to demonstrate the early capitalist roots of dependent underdevelopment. In addition,
this analysis posited the inappropriateness of alliances with the national bourgeoisie. Those propositions pointed their critiques at the strategy of passing
through a prolonged bourgeois-democratic stage, as proposed by the communist parties. That same goal was supported by many studies of the plantations,
haciendas, and *latifundios* that flourished in that era.

The first Frank was positioned in the space of the revolutionary left.
However, that positioning did not require arguments going back to the colonial era. The timing of a contemporary socialist transition did not depend on
the character taken by colonization. That path would be the same whether it
had feudal or capitalist roots in the Spanish-Portuguese conquest. The German

theorist looked for answers to the problems of the 20th century in events of four centuries back, overlooking the qualitative difference between political and historiographic questions. The debate on the socialist possibilities opened up by the Cuban revolution was different from the controversy over what had happened with the arrival of Columbus. Nor did understanding the conservative behavior of the national bourgeoisies require an assessment of what went on in the 16th century.

Frank overstated the controversy, establishing a direct relationship between historical 'feudalists' and political 'stageists'. He did not remark on the fact that several communist theorists (such as the Chilean Teitelbaum or the Brazilian Caio Prado) defended the thesis of capitalist colonization while supporting the political strategies of their organizations.

That schematism was not shared by the Marxist dependency theorists, who rejected equating the colonial situation with the later context (Marini, 1973: 19–20). They challenged the exaggeration of the role of trade and the representation of a capitalist economy since Latin America's infancy (Dos Santos, 1978: 303–304, 336–337). At the height of these controversies, Frank declared that he was abandoning the historiographic debate as well as dependency theory. With that declaration, the first stage of his thought came to a close.

6   The Turn toward World-System Theory

The German theorist began his new period arguing that dependentism was weak because of its lack of global horizons. He proclaimed the demise of that conception, and therefore the need to surpass it with a more comprehensive perspective of the global framework. He found that viewpoint in world-system theory, which to some extent extended and radicalized his earlier approach. There are several areas of affinity between Wallerstein and Frank. The world-system view offers a characterization of historical capitalism very similar to commercial capitalism. It considers that system to have been forged by commercializing productive activity with global mechanisms of competition, expansion of markets, and displacement of inefficient firms.

Wallerstein explicitly agrees with Frank's analysis of capitalist colonization (Wallerstein, 1984: 204–216). He postulates that after emerging in Europe, that regime already operated on a global scale when Columbus arrived in the New World. The incorporation of that hemisphere consolidated the world system and anticipated its absorption of other parts of the planet (Wallerstein, 1988: 1–8).

The two theorists also coincided in considering that the trajectory followed by the peripheries was always determined by the world market. They described historical developments centered on the impact of global forces, arguing that at each stage of the system, those external tendencies defined the status of the victorious powers and the underdeveloped economies (Katz, 2016). Their kinship extended to other areas, but the historiographic agreement was key for the convergence of the metropolis-satellite model with the world-system approach. Wallerstein contributed new arguments to the theory of commercial capitalism and situated the debate over colonization on a more conceptual plane.

This approach gave rise to new controversies about the origin of capitalism in three areas that had been little explored in the earlier controversy: the significance of wage-labor, the duration of the transitions, and the role of subjects. On these questions, Wallerstein followed the same analytical directions suggested by Frank.

7   Debates over the Proletariat

Like Frank, Wallerstein took Sweezy's side against Dobb in prioritizing trade over agriculture as the main driving force of capitalism. Unlike Sweezy, however, he questioned the relevance of wage-labor in that process. He rejected the dominance of that labor form, arguing that this feature was not determinant of a world system assembled in a commercial form and ruled by profit maximization (Wallerstein, 1984: 180–201; 2005: Chapter 1). In representing capitalism as a regime of market coordination, Wallerstein understood that the slave plantations and servitude-based *haciendas* did not disprove the presence of that system.

Brenner objected to this characterization, pointing out that capitalism arose from an original accumulation that gave birth to an exploiting class established through the extraction of surplus value. He went back to Dobb's arguments, arguing that trade contributed to dissolving the old social relations only under certain conditions and in certain countries. When the power of the nobility was consolidated (Eastern Europe), pre-capitalist structures were strengthened and generated a second feudal servitude (Brenner, 1977; 1988: 39–44, 381–386).

In contrast to Sweezy, who saw trade as the originating force of a capitalist regime based on the extraction of surplus value, Wallerstein denied the relevance of the proletariat as a constituting fact of that system. He asserted that the 'orthodox Marxists' overestimated that factor by making the industrial structure the only determinant of capitalist take-off. He attributed this position to logics that were bound to the national framework, and argued that capitalism extracts surplus value from a wide variety of exploited workers, without discriminating their status as wage-laborers, serfs, or slaves. He stressed that the world-system functions by means of the control exercised by capitalists in that subjection (Wallerstein, 2005: Chapter 11; 2011).

However, this approach did not clarify the differences that separate capitalism from the preceding modes of production. This distinction arises from the existence of a surplus value generated specifically by wage-laborers. Only the reinvestment of that surplus appropriated by the bourgeoisie fuels accumulation. The importance of wage-labor lies in the fact that only capitalism introduces a form of economic coercion that is not based on explicit force. The free labor of wage-workers is what typifies contemporary subjugation to the tyranny of the market. This peculiarity is highlighted even by authors who agree with Wallerstein on the advisability of extending the characterization of capitalism beyond the status of the exploited and the form taken by surplus-labor (Amin, 2008: 198–200).

8   Long Transitions

Frank argued that the capitalism of the 16th century defined the type of colonization predominant in Latin America. Wallerstein broadened this view, arguing that this system should be conceived as a global totality from the start and that there are no reasons to assume that it came about in long periods of maturation (Wallerstein, 1984: 8–10, 43). However, he did not provide justifications for that postulate of abrupt leaps from one regime to another.

His critics observed that he, like Frank, confused the origin of capitalism with its development. He placed two different stages in the same package by failing to differentiate its birth in agriculture from the development of industry. Meiksins Wood argues that in the first stage (16th–17th centuries) primary activity was predominant, while industrial processes were predominant in the second stage (since the 18th century). This distinction highlights, in addition, that the initial phase did not involve the generalization of wage-labor, but only the preeminence of new rules of commercial coercion. Those rules implied competitive pressure, maximization of profit, and compulsion to reinvest surpluses to improve productivity. Thus, conditions for the establishment of capitalism were generated that did not entail the full utilization of wage-earning workers. The massification of that labor form was a result, not a forerunner, of capitalism (Meiksins Wood, 2002: 36–37).

This approach contributed to getting beyond discussions about the colonization of the Americas that were based only on resolving the primacy of wage-labor or feudal labor. What was determinant in the gestation of capitalism in agriculture was the generalization of rules of competition and profits, not the massification of labor exploitation. The distinction between the emergence and the consolidation of the system makes it possible to trace the long process of transition left out of the Frank–Wallerstein approach. As Mandel pointed out, in Europe that passage included phases of primitive and ordinary accumulation, with differentiated significance for peasant expropriation and colonial pillage (Mandel, 1969a: 71–74; 1971: 153–171).

That prolonged transition implied the articulation of the world market around diverse national projects, which combined capitalist, semi-capitalist, and pre-capitalist forms. Global exchange aligned that variety of hybrid relations. It is true that the international dimension of capitalism was prominent, but only as a referent for distinct national processes of accumulation (Mandel, 1977; 1978: Chapter 2). It did not replace that protagonism or eliminate the presence of socio-economic formations with pre-capitalist components.

This viewpoint allows another perspective on the center-periphery relation. It begins with the world economy, but without forcing the existence of a global system since the 16th century. It defines stages, in contrast to the pure continuity of Wallerstein, and highlights differences between the peripheries as opposed to Frank's invariant metropolis-satellite model. Rather than a simple primacy of capitalism in the generation of underdevelopment, it describes the amalgamations of backward and advanced forms, applying a logic of unequal and combined development (Wolf, 1993: 38; Trimberger, 1979). Mandel recognized the significance of colonization, without assigning it an absolute determination in the rise of capitalism. He emphasized that capitalism had a national origin conditioned by the dictates of the world market, but only reached a complete international configuration in the contemporary era.

9   The Missing Subject

Frank never explained the absence of social subjects in his representation of Latin American history. Wallerstein partially introduced those actors, but maintained that in the past, the popular sectors could not bend the course of the world-economy. With different foundations, both approaches disregarded the class struggle. In contrast, other historians sought to conceptualize the impact of those social confrontations on the rise of capitalism. Brenner, in particular, described how conflicts between peasants and aristocrats influenced that rise. He did not paint a linear process of greater dissolution of feudalism in the face of more intense (or victorious) social battles of the oppressed, but rather a path full of unexpected (or undesired) corollaries.

This approach held that capitalism took off in England because of its peculiar combination of the collapse of serfdom, consolidation of large-scale property, and extension of leasing. This mixture generated a structure of nobles, bourgeoise contractors, and wage-workers that drove agrarian productivity and the start of industrialization. A less solid state than in Spain or France, but more unified and with greater capacity to eliminate the sovereignties of the nobility, fostered a broad network of roads and markets. But it was peasant resistance that was determinant; those uprisings did not impede the entrenchment of large-scale property, but they forced the lords to turn to leasing and the collection of monetary rents. Both processes facilitated the appearance of a prosperous rural capitalism (Meiksins Wood, 2002: 50–55).

Brenner contrasted this agrarian model with France, where peasant resistance compelled a great division of property. That fragmentation consolidated a model of subsistence and low productivity. The alliance of the absolutist state with the farmers to limit the power of the aristocrats also reinforced the delay of capitalism and planted the seeds for the greatest revolution of the era. The class struggle in France obstructed the process of accumulation that it incentivized in England (Brenner, 1988: 62–81). These conflicts also determined the de-capitalization of Eastern Europe, with the resurgence of serfdom to export food to the West. The nobility reinforced the collection of rents from the peasants, who did not have the legacy of triumphs obtained by their peers in Western Prussia during the great wars of the 15th–16th centuries.

The same importance of the social struggle is found in the New World. The settlers' resistance to any type of extra-economic coercion initially favored the introduction of production outside the rules of the market in the 13 colonies of the United States. The settlers took advantage of the ease of obtaining land that they expropriated from the indigenous tribes. When trading companies, banks, and elites forced the purchase of land and debt on growers, a transition to capitalist agriculture was established (Post, 2011: 67–84, 98–103). Here too, the outcome of the social struggle defined the form of development of capitalism. In all cases, that struggle determined differential capacities of the aristocracy to adapt to the new era. There was not automatic acceleration of capitalism in function of the strength or passivity of the oppressed, but rather a wide variety of situations with contingent outcomes.

The complex effects of social confrontation on the intensity of accumulation, which Brenner analyzed for the origin of capitalism, were also considered by Mandel in his theory of long waves. He related different paths of prosperity and stagnation to the outcome of the class struggle. Some connections of the same type can even be found in Cueva, in his explanation of the specificities of Latin American capitalism in the 19th century. In these three cases, the introduction of subjects into history is not aimed solely at clarifying the singularities of capitalist development; it also seeks to assess the impact of their actions on the traditions of popular liberation. The Wallerstein–Frank approach offers little room for this question.

10   Debates over the East

In the 1990s, a new occurrence had a big impact on Frank: the growth of Southeast Asia and the rapid expansion of China. In studying this take-off, he found historical causes that clashed with the primacy ascribed to Europe by world-system theory. He argued that this centrality had always corresponded to the East, and that the leadership of the Old Continent only appeared in the 19th century, during a temporary stagnation of China.

Frank asserted that in prior centuries, the famous spices reflected the higher productivity of Asia. He maintained that Europe could only take the lead by mediating with gold and silver obtained in the Americas, but was not able to reverse the subordinate character of its accumulation process. He argued that the small countries of the West (Portugal, Holland, England) were never able to exercise world domination. He questioned the myths of European exceptionalism, highlighting the fictitious character of its pillars in the Renaissance and the Greek tradition. He also maintained that these fallacies tended to diminish in the late 20th century with the resurgence of Asia and the exhaustion of Western domination (Frank, 2009: 114–120).

This intellectual turnaround displeased his colleagues, who expressed various objections to the primacy of the East in the emergence of the world-system. Wallerstein underlined the incongruence of postulating a structural superiority of Asia over long and imprecise periods, at the same time accepting the success of Europe over its rival in the 19th century. He asserted that all of Frank's reasoning fell apart when it came to explaining how the Old Continent could achieve this sudden advantage (Wallerstein, 2006–7: 1–14).

Arrighi launched a similar refutation. He argued that Frank did not clarify in what way a relegated European continent could, in 1800, displace China from the leadership of the world economy (Arrighi, 2006: 1–18). Amin was more categorical. He challenged the revision of history proposed by Frank, under-lining the total absence of indications of Chinese hegemony. He argued that a millennial pre-capitalist period of central and peripheral tributary societ-ies was followed, during the rise of capitalism, by a relative parity between Europe and China that was finally settled in favor of the former. That advan-tage was due to the unique existence of a feudal system run by the nobility that directly extracted its rents from the peasants, in contrast to the model of large state bureaucracies predominant in the East. The flexibility of a privat-ized aristocratic regime facilitated an original accumulation, which remained blocked in Asia. China fell into a long-lasting lag behind Europe, and only its prior development allowed it to escape colonial status, which affected the rest of the periphery during the zenith of Western expansion (Amin, 2006: 5–22).

In contrast to the substantial dominance of China imagined by Frank, Amin postulated the premature birth of capitalism in Europe. He argued that this emergence was a consequence of the peripheral fragility of that region with regard to the more advanced societies of India, China, or the Ottoman Empire. The political prerogatives of the nobility and the decentralization caused by the primitivism of that formation accelerated the processes of accumulation on the Old Continent (Amin, 2008: 198–213).

11   Problems with 'Asia-Centrism'

Frank defended his thesis of Eastern primacy, arguing that China maintained a trade balance surplus and a positive flow of money over most of its history. He pointed to the conversion of the country into the final destination of the silver circulating in other economies, and presented this acquisition of metal-lic money as indisputable proof of Eastern supremacy (Frank, 2009: 108–111).

Wallerstein objected empirically to this argument, arguing that the per cap-ita amount of silver was always higher in Europe and questioning the use of this indicator as a parameter of economic superiority. He pointed out that the dependency theorists had always stressed that England's trade deficit with the rest of the world did not contradict its colonial primacy (Wallerstein, 2006–7). In addition, he argued that a hegemonic position is not confirmed only by commercial or financial indices. He especially emphasized that the old con-sensus on the dominant role of the West represented overwhelming evidence and not simple mystifications. However, he also pointed out that Frank did not provide any data on China's superiority in the area of industrial productivity. He only assessed the destination of the monetary resources circulating over long periods of history.

In this characterization of leadership based exclusively on the absorption of monetary or trade surpluses, there appears again the 'circulationist' defect that had been repeatedly stressed by the critics of the first and second Frank. The scarce relevance that the German theorist ascribed to the productive dimensions extends to an account of Chinese advantages based only on exchange flows and capital movements. Frank adopts a new 'Sino-centric' perspective, but continues to privilege the sphere of trade or finance in his assessments of world hegemonies.

The same continuity of problems is seen in the 'externalism' of a logic that privileges resource transfers while not considering endogenous processes. In his book *ReORIENT* there is a total omission of the geopolitical and military sphere. He does not analyze the competition which China confronted with the European powers on those grounds. The lack of subjects also indicates that the third Frank retained the structuralist determinism of his early work.

12   Misunderstanding Capitalism

Frank responded harshly to the criticisms from his colleagues. He claimed that they did not see the historical primacy of China because of their attachment to old notions of capitalism. He held that the search for singularities of that system was an obsession inherited from Marx and proposed a revision of that legacy, stressing that capitalism always existed intermixed with other productive forms (Frank, 2005b). However, he did not provide clues to clarify how the reformulation of capitalism should be addressed beyond that generality. He only alluded to its presence since distant times and to its identification with the market.

Wallerstein saw a return to the old ingenuousness of liberal economists in this reconsideration. Amin interpreted the turnaround as a relapse into neo-classical vulgarities of capitalist eternity. Certainly, Frank lost his way in seeking a perpetual centrality of China in the world system. He forgot the basic principles of the characterization of capitalism. Here too, he retained his previous rejection of defining that mode of production in terms of the exploitation of wage-labor. He never accepted that capitalism is a regime of competition for profits arising from the extraction of surplus value. His earlier erroneous definitions focused on trade turned into a denial of the historical transience of that system.

This mistake was carried further by extending the spatiality of capitalism. The third Frank no longer conceived of a world-system led by Europe that followed and deposed the world-empires of other regions. He postulated the millennial presence of a single global structure headed by China. Since it proved difficult to substantiate that leadership, the German theorist dissolved the very existence of capitalism, presenting that system as a simple, enduring, and underlying fact. The erroneous planetary dimension that Frank ascribed to capitalism since an undecipherable origin also spotlighted the drawbacks of analyzing that origin in global terms.

Arrighi invoked an ironic qualifier ('globo-logic') to object to the exaggerated use of international criteria. However, this brings up a problem that runs all the way to world-system theory. In Frank's super-holism, many difficulties appear from the 'tyranny of the totality' that reigns in that approach. The dissolution of capitalism that appeared in the last Frank complements the supra-temporal primacy of China. But by placing the birth of that system back in some indefinite time, its singularities are diluted. In that millennial picture of capitalism, the mechanisms of the development of wage-labor are lost. The problems with a world system that arose in 1500 in northern Europe (Wallerstein) or in 1200 in Italian cities (Arrighi) become, with Chinese primacy, a dilemma with no solution. This shortcoming is another consequence of analyzing national processes of accumulation in commercial and global terms.

Frank projects all the contemporary features of capitalism backward in time. Thus, he reverts to assumptions of an eternal system. He assumes that at the start of the last millennium its current characteristics were already present. With this approach, there is no way to understand the specificities and mutations of capitalism.

13   Contemporary Influences

The third Frank retained the polemical vehemence of his earlier work. He rejected the world-system theory he had adopted against dependentism, challenging the 'Eurocentric vanity' of that perspective and its insistence on postulating the primacy of the Old Continent since 1500 (Frank, 2009: 130–136). His critics mocked his use of that epithet, considering that Frank himself attributed to Europe an inexplicable power to suddenly dominate China in the 19th century. In fact, it made little sense to accuse Wallerstein of Euro-centrism, as he has been a staunch objector to the liberal identification of the Old Continent with progress or civilization (Wallerstein, 2004: Chapter 23).

Putting Amin in that category was even more confused. The Egyptian economist had repeatedly argued against all beliefs in Western supremacy. He showed how they were inspired by false assumptions of millennial advantages of Europe that ignore how capitalism arose from a tributary formation in that

THREE STAGES OF THE METROPOLIS-SATELLITE PERSPECTIVE 125

region because of its backwardness, not its enlightenment, (Amin, 2008: 198–213). At most, it can be said that Eurocentric preaching appears in the revival of the Smithian commercial model, which attributes exceptional abilities for exchange, and the consequent emergence of capitalism, to the Old Continent (Meiksins Wood, 2002: 21–33). But a challenge of this sort would affect Frank himself, as he always privileged the sphere of circulation. In fact, Eurocentrism is an ingredient of liberal thought that is as far from Marxism as it is to the systemic perspective.

Frank fired criticisms at Eurocentrism to underscore Asian protagonism, without noticing his symmetrical slippage into the glorification of the Eastern world. Even so, his interpretation of the millennial weight of China had a notable influence. In particular, Arrighi reformulated that thesis as a counterpoint to paths of development. He contrasted the defensive economic model of the East with the expansive imperial strategy of the West and took up Frank's ideas to explain the advantages of the Chinese commercial-cooperative model (Arrighi, 2007: Chapters 3, 8, 11). The German scholar opened up a sequence of views on the left favorable to the path followed by the Asian giant. But this approach had to also accept the assumptions of the eternal or cyclical continuity of capitalism that were adopted by the third Frank.

14   No Response to Dependency

Frank interpreted the economic rise of the East as a development of great importance. That conclusion was the crowning point of his revision of the question of underdevelopment that began with his reappraisal of the expansion of Southeast Asia. He first argued that this growth seriously affected dependency theory, and later he corroborated that impression with his characterizations of China.

In this conceptual exploration, Frank did not succeed in finding a satisfactory reformulation of center-periphery dynamics. He traversed winding paths of hesitations and questions without answers. His initial misstep in that journey was his distancing from dependentism, questioning the attachment of that conception to reasoning in national terms. By objecting to the 'chimera' of autonomous growth within the capitalist world system, the German theorist got tangled up in inconsistent objections (Frank, 1973; 1991: 61). He forgot that Marxist dependency theory never conceived of or proposed capitalist development in the periphery, nor did it identify so-called 'delinking' with that project. That strategy was the objective of other currents like ECLAC or the Communist Parties.

The first Frank's metropolis-satellite model contained several unilateralities, but defined relations of dependence; the second Frank dissolved those connections in an extreme globalism, while the third Frank diluted that framework with its 'Asia-centrism'. This pathway was accompanied by his successive characterizations of capitalism in commercial, global, and secular terms. Changing views of the center-periphery relation emerged from these approaches. Frank reaffirmed the persistence of dependency in light of the degradation suffered by the Latin American economy in the 1980s and 1990s, but he also emphasized the absence of proposals for resolving the problem. With some bitterness, he merely indicated that "we were unable to put an end to dependency" (Frank, 2005a). Frank's writings attracted many readers captivated by their irreverent tone (Ouriques, 2005) and the changing directions of his trajectory (Marins, 2009). Despite all his many contradictions, Frank contributed significant ideas to the debates on underdevelopment.

CHAPTER 8

Anti-dependency Arguments

Dependency theories faced numerous criticisms from Marxist theorists claiming that it is contrary to socialist thought. The English author who initiated these objections in the 1970s claimed that capitalism tends to eliminate underdevelopment through the industrialization of the periphery, and that dependency theory failed to recognize that process, which is driven by foreign capital (Warren, 1980: 111–116, 139–143, 247–249). In the 1980s, another British theorist maintained that the take-off of Southeast Asia disproved the main characterization of dependency theory (Harris, 1987: 31–69).

Later, several Latin American intellectuals expressed similar ideas. Some of them revised their earlier writings to highlight the expansion of the periphery under the helm of the transnational corporations (Cardoso, 2012: 31). Others replaced old challenges about dependency theory being insufficiently Marxist with new criticisms of its blindness to the impetus of capitalism (Castañeda and Morales, 2010: 33; Sebreli, 1992: 320–321). All of these critics have moved toward neoliberalism and distanced themselves from the left, but their ideas influenced the new anti-dependency generation.

1 Reformulating the Same Approach

Some more recent critics claim that dependency is an appropriate term to designate situations of technological, commercial, or financial dominance by the most developed countries. However, they believe that the conception left out the contradictory character of accumulation, overlooked the partial industrialization of the Third World, and propounded erroneous stagnationist characterizations (Astarita, 2010a: 37–41, 65–93). From these objections, they deduce the inappropriateness of investigating the laws of dependency with assumptions of a capitalist system differentiated by center and periphery. They consider it more appropriate to deepen the study of the law of value than to build a theory specifically of the backward economies (Astarita, 2010a: 11, 74–75; 2010b).

Other authors object to Marini's abandonment of Marx. They believe he attributed to monopoly capital an arbitrary ability to manage economic variables and obstruct Latin American development (Kornbilhtt, 2012). Some also believe that dependency theory failed to recognize the primacy of global capitalism over national processes (Iñigo Carrera, 2008: 1–4).

These challenges have appeared in a political framework very different from that which prevailed in the 1970s and 1980s. The attacks are no longer directed at defenders of the Cuban revolution, but at supporters of the radical path led by *Chavismo*. In this context, the debate over the international status of the Latin American countries reappears. Argentina, especially, is seen by several anti-dependentists as a developed economy.

The critics also return to old rejections of the replacement of class antagonisms by accounts of exploitation among countries. They accuse dependency theory of promoting benign modes of capitalism for the periphery (Dore and Weeks, 1979), encouraging local accumulation processes (Harman, 2003), and favoring alliances with the national bourgeoisie (Iñigo Carrera, 2008: 34–36). Some of them claim that this orientation leads to a radicalized nationalism that recreates false expectations of national liberation. They propose adopting internationalist proposals focused on the contradiction between capital and labor (Astarita, 2010a: 99–100).

These views maintain that dependency theory abandoned the prominent role of the proletariat in favor of other popular agents (Harris, 1987: 183–184, 200–202). They object to the negation of, or lack of consideration to, the historical function of the working class (Iñigo Carrera, 2009: 19–20). They believe that the international character of the anti-capitalist project gets diluted, leading back to autarchic proposals for building socialism in one country (Astarita, 2010b). These negative assessments of dependency theory contrast with the convergent views expressed by several endogenist and systemic authors. The anti-dependency arguments are forceful, but are they consistent, valid, and coherent?

2   Interdependence?

The first critics aimed at minimizing the effects of underdevelopment denounced by the dependency theorists. They argued that foreign capital remitted profits after generating a great expansion, and held that the drainage of resources suffered by the periphery was not so severe (Warren, 1980: 111–116, 3–143). However, they avoided looking into the reason why that profit was considerably higher than that of the central economies. Dependency theory never denied the existence of accumulation processes. It only highlighted the obstructions to integrated processes of industrialization introduced by foreign investment.

The objectors argued that social inequalities were the cost required to mobilize entrepreneurial initiative in the debut of development. For them, that inequality tended to correct itself with the expansion of the middle classes

(Warren, 1980: 199, 211). But that portrayal of capitals disembarking in the periphery to the benefit of the entire population contrasted with the facts. The trickle-down they expected never went beyond the collective imagination of the neoclassical manuals. Warren also highlighted the incentive provided by social differentiation for the take-off of the primary sector, leaving out the dramatic plundering of the peasantry imposed by agri-business. He even justified labor informality, repeating absurd accolades to the 'entrepreneurial potentialities' of the marginalized (Warren, 1980: 236–238, 211–224).

These affirmations are in tune with liberal theories that extol a future of well-being as a result of the convergence between the backward and advanced economies. With this idealization of capitalism, they echoed all the mainstream arguments against dependency theory. Warren especially stressed that the dependency approach failed to recognize the mutual influence generated by the new relations of interdependence between the center and the periphery (Warren, 1980: 156–170), but he did not provide any evidence of greater equity in those connections. It was evident that the influence of the United States over Haiti did not have any equivalent in the opposite direction.

A recent presentation of the same argument claims that dependency theory only registers the subordinate status of basic input exporters, without considering the symmetrical bonds suffered by producers of manufactured commodities (Iñigo Carrera, 2008: 29). But do banana exporters play in the same league as their counterparts who specialize in computers? The obsession to highlight only the inequalities that prevail between capital and labor leads to imagining that relations of reciprocity reign in all other areas.

3   Simplified Comparisons

The critics of dependency theory claimed that the strong expansion of the underdeveloped economies of Southeast Asia disproved the pillars of that conception, but Marini, Dos Santos, or Bambirra never claimed that accelerated growth of some backward countries was impossible. They only claimed that this process introduced greater imbalances than those confronted by the advanced economies. With this approach, they analyzed the manufacturing debut of Argentina, the succeeding take-off of Brazil, and the later establishment of *maquilas* in Mexico. In those three cases, they stressed the contradictions of industrial development in the periphery. Far from ruling out any expansion, they investigated the Latin American precursors of what would later occur in the East. Asian development did not disprove the diagnoses of dependency theory.

In more detailed treatments, the critics claimed that South Korea, Taiwan, and Singapore showed the unviability of protectionist models that generate waste and high costs (Harris, 1987: 28, 190–192), but this last outcome also did not disprove Marxist dependency theory. On the contrary, it confirmed its objections to the developmentalism of the postwar era and to the ECLAC model, which were made in underlining major challenges to liberalism, which some anti-dependentists omit. They praise the waves of liberalization and its impact on Asia, and criticize the more closed economies for not following it (Harris, 1987: 192–194). They forget that the possibilities for greater industrialization were never open to all countries, and did not follow patterns of commercial opening. Dependency theory intuited this situation, observing how globalization harmed the peripheral nations with internal markets of some magnitude (Latin America) while shoring up areas with greater abundance and cheapness of labor power (Asia). While this dependency perspective explained changes in the flows of investment through the objective logic of accumulation, the critics highlighted the trade opening, with messages very close to those of neoliberalism.

The same logic was used to extol the prosperity of certain economies traditionally based on agro-mining. They claimed that Australia and Canada demonstrated how primary product exporters could locate themselves in spaces closer to the center than to the periphery (Warren, 1980: 143–152). However, they never clarified whether those countries represented the rule or the exception of the economies specialized in basic inputs. Marxist dependency theory did not try to fit the great variety of international situations into a simplified center-periphery package. It offered a model to explain the durability of underdevelopment on the bulk of the world's surface, as opposed to post-liberal approaches that denied that cleavage. If that gap is recognized, it becomes possible to put forward a more specific analysis of semi-peripheral structures and subimperial political processes that explain the place of Canada or Australia in the world order.

An updated dependency perspective would allow clarification of those positions, specifying the different levels of analysis of global capitalism. This system includes economic unevenness (development-underdevelopment), global hierarchies (center-periphery), and political polarities (domination-dependence). With this perspective, the place occupied by countries located in positions complementary to the center can be understood.

In contrast to critics with a close relation to neoclassical thought, the Marxist dependency theorists underlined how global capitalism recreates inequalities. They did not characterize these asymmetries as invariable, nor did they conceive a model of pure polar actors, but instead suggested the existence of a complex spectrum of intermediate situations. With that perspective, they avoided representing any example of development as an imitable path with free-market recipes.

4   Stagnationism?

Some more recent critics agree with their predecessors in the belief that the expansion of Southeast Asia delivered a severe blow to dependency theory (Astarita, 2010a: 93–98). However, they ignore that this development did not affect this approach more than any other of the era. The growth of South Korea and Taiwan generated the same surprise as the later implosion of the Soviet Union or the recent irruption of China. Neither did the objectors assess whether the industrialization of the Eastern economies inaugurated a process that the rest of the periphery could copy. They only reaffirmed that the Eastern take-off showed the non-fulfillment of dependency theory predictions of stagnation (Astarita, 2010b). They went back to an argument that has frequently been expressed as an explanation for the decline of that approach (Blomstrom and Hettne, 1990: 204–205).

But the failure of a particular forecast does not disqualify a form of reasoning. At most, it indicates insufficiencies in the assessment of a context. Marx, Engels, Lenin, Trotsky, or Luxemburg formulated many failed prognoses. Marxism offers methods of analysis, not recipes for foretelling the future. It allows more consistent diagnoses of situations than other conceptions, but it does not reveal the events of the future. Predictions make it possible to correct observations in light of what has occurred, and must be judged in function of the general consistency of an approach. They represent only one element for evaluating a given theory.

The stagnationism attributed to dependency theory is a different type of defect, one that implies characterizations that ignore the competitive dynamic of a system governed by cycles of expansion and contraction. A structural freezing of the productive forces is incompatible with the rules of capitalism. That logic was ignored by several theorists of the heterodoxy (Furtado) and by some thinkers influenced by the monopoly capital thesis (the first Gunder Frank), both of which upheld the existence of a permanent blockage of growth. In contrast, dependentist Marxism studied the limits and the contradictions of the periphery in comparison to the center, without identifying underdevelopment with the paralysis of the economy. It underscored that Brazil or Argentina suffered from different and higher imbalances than those present in France or the United States.

The false accusation against Marini of stagnationism was first spread by Cardoso. He stressed his rival's similarity to the economists Lenin had criticized for denying the possibility of capitalist development in Russia (Narodniks). However, the actual object of Marini's analysis disproved that accusation, given that he investigated imbalances generated by the industrialization of Brazil. He did not describe permanent recessions, but rather tensions derived from a significant process of growth.

The mistaken criticism of stagnationism is at times toned down with objections to the omission of the contradictory character of accumulation. In this case, ignorance of widening markets or rising productivities is claimed (Astarita, 2010a: 296). But if Marini had ignored those dynamics, he would not have been able to analyze the particular imbalances of the underdeveloped economies. His contribution lay precisely in replacing generic assessments of capitalism with specific investigations of the imbalances of those regions. He analyzed in detail the realms that his critics excluded.

5   Monopolies and the Law of Value

The characterization of monopolies is seen by the critics as a mistake of dependency theory. They argue that it exaggerates the ability of large companies to harm the peripheral economies by manipulating price formation (Kornblihtt, 2012). However, Marini kept a long distance from the influential theories of monopoly capital of the 1960s and 1970s. Like Dos Santos, he paid more attention to imbalances in the productive sphere than in the financial sphere. His investigations were more focused on the contradictions of accumulation than on price management on the part of the large corporations. Certainly, he took into account how those firms cornered super-profits on a global scale. But he took an approach closer to the Marxist authors who were further away from the monopoly thesis, such as Mandel. In contrast to many Keynesians of his era, he did not attribute to the large corporations the discretional power to fix prices.

Marini kept a great distance from rudimentary perspectives of monopoly, and also rejected the opposite mystification of competition. That fascination is clearly seen in Warren and Harris, who extolled the merits of competition with characterizations that were very close to the neoclassical treatment. Because of that idealization of competitive capitalism, they failed to recognize the relevance of center-periphery stratification.

Other critics claim that Marini distanced himself from Marx by losing sight of the centrality of the law of value. They propose a return to that concept in order to clarify relations of dependency (Astarita, 2010b). But the question of underdevelopment is not solved with this type of investigation. Several authors have emphasized that studies at that level of abstraction do not facilitate an understanding of the global cleavage (Johnson, 1981). Additional mediations are needed to those used in *Capital*. In that text, the exploitation (Volume 1), reproduction (Volume 2) or crisis (Volume 3) of the system is analyzed. Marx hoped to treat the international structure (and probably the development gaps) in a volume he never got to. Surely, that investigation would have broadened knowledge of global imbalances in the period of the formation of capitalism. However, it is equally worth remembering that the center-periphery dynamic in the 19th century presented very different characteristics from those that prevailed in the late 20th century. More than the "return to Marx" posited by some analysts (Radice, 2009), clarification of that question requires looking back on the reflections of the Marxist theorists of the last century (see chapters 2 and 3 of this book).

The law of value provides a general principle for explaining prices and a generic theory of capitalist functioning and crisis. None of those dimensions goes far enough to clarify the dynamics of underdevelopment, which requires reasoning at more concrete (and at the same time consistent) levels than those used to capture the logic of value.

6   Underdevelopment as a Simple Fact

Some authors question explanations of underdevelopment centered on the subordination of the periphery. They claim an inverse causality, of dependency situations derived from the underdevelopment of those economies. This interpretation bears a resemblance to the endogenist logic, which attributes international inequalities to the internal contradictions of each country. That approach objected to the primacy of external causes in explaining economic backwardness, highlighting the greater impact of the continuation of oligarchic or semi-feudal forms. In this view, the exactions generated by imperial domination were less determinant than the persistence of pre-capitalist impediments.

The anti-dependency idea, however, is different. It rejects the survival of those features and underlines the presence of totally capitalist realities. Thus, it objects to both the dependency theorists and traditional endogenism. From this perspective, the exponents of these critiques stress the internal capitalist determinants of the profile presented by each country. They also claim that the international insertion of any nation is a result of the way in which it entered the world market (Astarita, 2010a: 296). But, how does that approach explain the cleavage between advanced and backward economies? Why has that gap persisted over the last two centuries?

One answer points to the international division of labor, in which the more productive forms are concentrated in the central economies and the most rudimentary forms in the periphery (Figueroa, 1986: 11–19, 55–56, 61). Another way of expressing the same interpretation is the well-known description of differentiated specializations in the provision of foods or manufactures by the two types of countries (Iñigo Carrera, 2008: 1–2, 6–9).

However, the verification of that difference does not clarify the issue. While the dependency interpretation attributed underdevelopment to resource transfers, and endogenism to the persistence of pre-capitalist structures, these critics' interpretation is conspicuous by its absence. That perspective seems to accept that the initial cleavage was caused by diverse historical particularities (European feudalism, singularities of English agriculture, European manufacturing transformations, features of the absolutist state, early onset of certain bourgeois revolutions), but it does not explain the contemporary persistence of the lag. What occurred in the 16th–19th centuries is not enough to explain the current reality.

Anti-dependentism even lacks the basic answers proposed by neoclassical (obstruction of entrepreneurs) or heterodox (lack of state skills) approaches. It is limited to stating that the advanced and relegated economies differ by their level of underdevelopment. That obvious fact does not explain the qualitative gaps that govern the world order. The contrast between the United States and Japan is not comparable to the abyss that separates both countries from Honduras. Underdevelopment distinguishes the two situations.

The critics reject the role played by drainage of value from the periphery to the center in the reproduction of that lag. But without recognizing the varied forms and intensities of those transfers, there is no way to explain the stability of global polarizations, bifurcations, and hierarchies. Denial of those flows makes any interpretation impossible.

7   Classifications and Examples

Most of the critics treat dependentism as an indistinct block, ignoring the huge differences that separate the Marxist and conventional variants of that approach. While Cardoso sees underdevelopment as an anomaly of capitalism, Marini, Dos Santos, and Bambirra characterize the same feature as a characteristic of that system. Some objectors recognize those disagreements and note the inexistence of a common school of thought; yet, after acknowledging these differences, they unify the authors they had distinguished, as if they formed a more or less radical group of exponents of the same thesis (Astarita, 2010a: 37–41, 17–63).

The greatest confusion appears in the assessment of Cardoso and Marini. The ex-president is presented as a more open theorist than the author of *The Dialectic of Dependence*. His methodology is examined, challenging the Weberian pillars of that approach or the ordering of political relations, rather than his economic analysis (Astarita, 2010a: 65–82). But this does not clarify Cardoso's contribution before his neoliberal turn; nor does it recognize Marini's contribution to understanding the center-periphery relation. It especially forgets that the hostility or affinity of the two thinkers toward revolutionary socialism was not unrelated to these contrasting conclusions. The critics' disregard for that contrast hampers their assessments of both theorists.

Marini contributed concepts (such as the dependent cycle) to understand the continued reproduction of the global gaps. This achievement was correctly perceived in the 1980s by an important analyst (Edelstein, 1981), who stressed the merit of grasping the reasons that impede Latin America from repeating the development of Europe or the United States. He also emphasized that the logic of dependency offers a coherent answer to that limitation.

Moreover, this approach provides great support to numerous national and regional studies of underdevelopment. The devaluing of that contribution leads to many false characterizations by the critics. For example, in analyzing the recurrent failure of attempts at industrialization by the oil economies (Saudi Arabia, Iran, Algeria, Venezuela), one anti-dependency author emphasizes the harmful weight of rentism. He also points to the entrenchment of bureaucracies, inability to use hard currency productively, and a historical pattern of waste (Astarita, 2013c: 1–11).

But none of these endogenous explanations is sufficient to understand the continuity of underdevelopment. The dependency thesis highlights another key aspect: the international division of labor. That subjection generates outflows of capital that are higher than the incomes obtained by oil exports. The oil economies have endured trade deficits, financial decapitalizations, and transfers of funds through profit repatriation or payments for patents, while capital flight and indebtedness exacerbate those imbalances characteristic of dependency. That which is in plain view in any study of those countries is not mentioned by Marini's objectors.

8   Argentina as a Developed Country?

An important corollary of anti-dependentism is the portrayal of several Latin American countries as developed nations. That interpretation is especially applied to the case of Argentina. An exponent of that view harshly questions those who "dogmatically cling to the ideology of a backward country" for not recognizing that Argentina has reached the level of accumulation required by world capitalism (Iñigo Carrera, 2008: 32). But the problem to be solved is the meaning of that expansion and of that international location. It is obvious that Argentina is a big exporter of food products. What needs to be clarified are the implications of that role.

The critics claim that the high magnitude of cattle, cereal, or soy rent determined the incorporation of the country in global capitalism with the status of an advanced economy. But the magnitude of rent is not synonymous with development. It could indicate opposite situations of obstruction to sustained growth. Development is not measured by the amount of export surplus, but by the level of industrialization or the parameters of human development. None of these figures puts Argentina at the top level of the global hierarchy. Rent does not define that classification. While it is a key economic ingredient of Canada, Argentina, and Bolivia, the first of these is recognized as developed, the second as intermediate, and the third as backward.

Throughout all of Argentina's history, there have been intense struggles over the distribution of rents between its agro-mining recipients and its industrial captors. Those rents operated as an indirect support for industrial activities, which never reached levels of international competitiveness or self-sustaining productivity. That outcome illustrates the functioning of an economy that is backward, dependent, and affected by periodic and far-reaching crises. Thus, capitalists avoid investment, protect their funds outside the country, and facilitate the financial appropriation of rent, in detriment to its being channeled to productive use. That mechanism demonstrates the underdeveloped character of Argentina.

The critics see this problem in an inverted form. They prioritize analysis of the most profitable sector, and find the competitiveness of agriculture to be comparable to the prevailing average in Europe or the United States. With this assessment, they conclude by situating Argentina in the league of the developed economies. However, the level of development of a country is not defined by its most profitable branch. Using this criterion, Saudi Arabia and Chile would be placed at the top of the global ranking because of their oil and copper wealth. The high profits of a primary sector are generally an indicator of productive backwardness.

The relegated status of Argentina can be seen right in the agricultural sector. Beyond the controversy over the continuity or reversion of extensive models with limited utilization of capital per hectare, the complete dependence of that model on imported inputs is evident. Those components are supplied by foreign companies, which reinforce the predominance of crops powered by direct, transgenic, and agro-toxic cultivation. That bond is a clear indicator of underdevelopment (Anino and Mercatante: 2010: 1–7).

Some authors argue that the Argentine economy absorbs the bulk of its rents and generates inflows of funds from the center to the periphery, thereby disproving dependency theory (Kornblihtt, 2012). This characterization recreates the views that appeared in the 1970s with the irruption of OPEC. The capture of oil rent by the economies that generate that surplus led to a diagnosis of extinction of the old subordination of primary exporters to the center. But experience showed the temporary character of that conjuncture; by means of financial payments and trade surpluses, the advanced economies recovered those incomes.

Argentina also went through temporary periods of great absorption of its agro-livestock rent, but its dependent political status accentuated the dissipation of that capture. A country with longer periods of subjection than of autonomy in its international operations has little ability to manage its surpluses. Argentina is far from the anti-dependency portrayal. It is not a developed economy, it does not occupy a central place in the division of labor, and it does not display the strategies of a dominant power.

9   Political Challenges

The critics question the anti-imperialist alignment of the dependency theorists, identifying that view with the abandonment of anti-capitalist positions (Kornblihtt, 2012). However, they do not indicate when and how that desertion came about. No Marxist exponent of that tradition separated resistance to imperial subjugation from its capitalist foundations. They always joined together both of those pillars.

Dependency theory is accused of replacing class analysis with nation-based approaches (Dore and Weeks, 1979). This attitude is associated with erroneous postulates of exploitation between countries (Iñigo Carrera, 2009: 27). But no debate can develop in those terms. Exploitation is exercised by the dominant classes over the wage-workers of any nation. That relation does not extend to the profits obtained by one country at the cost of another in the world market. Since the Marxist dependency theorists never confused these two dimensions, the objection lacks sense.

It is true that in anti-imperialist political propaganda, adherents sometimes use confused terms to denounce the plunder of natural resources or financial drainage. In those cases, they use incorrect names in formulating relevant denunciations. But anti-dependentism suffers from a bigger drawback. Its errors are on the level of concepts, not of terminology.

Marini, Dos Santos, and Bambirra always pointed to capitalists as those responsible for all forms of domination. They never contended that the oppressed classes of the periphery were exploited by their peers in the center. This characterization was only suggested by authors close to Third-Worldism (such as Emmanuel), who picked up on old interpretations about the complacent behavior of the labor aristocracy with regard to imperial actions. The critics also argue that dependency theory promoted national capitalism in the periphery in order to bolster private national capital against foreign companies (Harris, 1987: 170–182). They maintain that it saw the national bourgeoisie as a natural ally in the battle for development (Iñigo Carrera, 2008: 34–36). But these goals were promoted by conservative nationalism or the supporters of developmentalism, not by dependentism. Under the impact of the Cuban revolution, that approach adopted a clear attitude of commitment to the socialist project.

The truth is that the Marxist dependency theorists recognized the difference between the ruling classes of the periphery and their counterparts in the center. They rejected the common identity of the two as postulated by a critic of dependency (Figueroa, 1986: 80, 91, 203). Marini, Dos Santos, and Bambirra remembered the subordinate place occupied by the local bourgeoisie in the international division of labor, indicating the consequent existence of more accentuated contradictions and imbalances. From that characterization, they deduced the existence of unresolved national problems in Latin America, and consequently the presence of significant conflicts with imperialism. Dependency theory formulated critiques of the national bourgeoisie from leftist positions opposed to the ideas of Cardoso or Warren. For the liberal exponents of anti-dependentism, the verbiage against national capitalism always had a reactionary connotation.

The critics rant against any demand for national liberation, ignoring what has occurred over the last 100 years. All the socialist revolutions in the periphery were connected with demands for sovereignty, from which a dialectic of radicalization developed that culminated in the anti-capitalist roads taken by the revolutions in Yugoslavia, China, and Vietnam. The socialist victory in Cuba also arose from resistance to a puppet dictator of the United States. The objectors forget that those experiences followed a very different route from those foreseen by classical Marxism. Instead of assimilating the lessons of that mutation, they proclaim their anger with what has occurred and erase those sagas from their diagnoses of the world.

It might be thought that the restoration of capitalism in the Soviet Union (or the greater internationalization of the economy) has altered the close

connection between national and social struggle that predominated in the
20th century. The anti-dependentists do not clarify that potential basis for
their opinions. But even in that case, it would be evident that the Pentagon
and NATO persist as custodians of the oppressive world order. It is enough to
observe the destruction of several Middle Eastern states or the disintegration
of Africa to note the centrality of imperial action. No socialist process can be
conceived if it ignores the priority of that enemy.

Rather than recognizing that threat, the critics accuse dependentism of
replacing materialist economic analysis with superficial logics inspired by
imperial concepts of domination (Iñigo Carrera, 2008: 29). They undervalue
observation of reality in order to extol abstract reflection, forgetting that the
reproduction of capitalism is sustained by the use of force. The simple accumulation of capital is not enough to ensure the continual recreation of the
system. It needs the additional support of an imperial structure.

The rejection of recognizing the national dimension of the struggle for
socialist transformations in the periphery leads to disregard for popular
demands. The most recent example of that blindness is the objection to the
mobilizations against the foreign debt. One objector to dependentism rejects
that cause, denouncing the participation of the local dominant classes in the
creation of that debt, and arguing that campaigns against the debt dilute the
centrality of the antagonism between capital and labor (Astarita, 2010a:110–111).

However, they do not explain the difference between these two planes.
Payment of the debt affects workers, who suffer wage cuts to settle those
liabilities. As demonstrated in Argentina, Venezuela, Bolivia, and Ecuador
between 2000 and 2005, resistance to that outrage challenges the very capitalist system. It is true that the local bourgeoisies have been accomplices in
creating that indebtedness, but the crises unleashed by that financial burden
corrode the functioning of the state and stifle its exercise of domination. In
that context, the debt emerges as an axis of anti-imperialist resistance. The
events in Greece in 2015 exemplify that conflict. The creditors forced brutal
sacrifices to allow payment of a liability, illustrating the relations of dependence within the European Union. The critics ignore the explosive effects of
that subordination.

10   Marx, Lenin, Luxemburg

For the liberal variants of anti-dependentism, the return to Marx presupposes
reclaiming a devotee of individualism and the forced dissolution of non-
Western societies. The author of *Capital* is presented as a defender of empire

who extolled the English contribution to overcoming the backwardness of Africa and India (Warren, 1980: 39–44, 27–30).

But Marx was always in the opposite camp that denounced colonial plunder. He intuited the huge contrast between what was taken from and what was provided to the occupants of the underdeveloped countries. The bloodshed generated by slavery in Africa, or the demographic massacre suffered by the original peoples of the Americas, provided compelling proof of that assessment. In his analysis of Ireland in his mature phase, the German theorist portrayed Britain's obstruction to the industrialization of the periphery and defended popular resistance to the crown (see chapter 1 of this book). This position is unknown to those who claim that Marx praised the development introduced by English railroads in India (Astarita, 2010a: 83–90). They forget that those investments reinforced the subordination of the country as a primary-good producer, and gave rise to an anti-colonial movement that was supported by the German revolutionary.

The anti-dependency criticism of any kind of struggle against that oppression includes severe challenges to connecting the national and social struggles, as espoused by Lenin (Warren, 1980: 83–84, 98–109). The Bolshevik leader promoted that connection in his polemic with Luxemburg, who rejected any form of national separatism, arguing that it harmed proletarian internationalism and the primacy of class demands (Luxemburg, 1977: 27–187). Lenin responded by illustrating how the right to self-determination decreased tensions between the oppressed groups of different nationalities. He pointed to the fraternity achieved between the workers of Sweden and Norway after the peaceful separation of the latter. Lenin defended that right without necessarily approving of the secession of the different countries. His endorsement of each proposal depended on the genuine, majority, or progressive character of that demand (Lenin, 1974b: 26–90).

This is the same distinction that can be established today between fictitious claims (the "Kelpers" of the Falkland/Malvinas Islands), pro-imperial balkanizations (ex-Yugoslavia), or elitist territorial separatisms (northern Italy, Flanders) and legitimate national demands (Kurds, Palestinians, Basques). Anti-dependentism repeats the errors of Luxemburg by counterposing national and social demands as if they were antagonistic desires. It recognizes only the centrality of exploitation of wage-workers, without noting the existence of innumerable forms of racial, religious, sexual, or ethnic oppression. All of these lead to the types of resistance that Lenin sought to connect with the proletarian struggle.

Some authors claim that the Russian leader only promoted self-determination on the political level, not extending it to the economic sphere. They accept only that limited application of the concept, and reject any kinship with the battle for the second independence of Latin America. They believe that proposal contains inappropriate and nationalist economic demands (Astarita, 2010a: 118, 293–296).

But Lenin never accepted those types of abstract distinctions. Thus, he objected to any logic of self-determination based on its economic viability. Instead of speculating on that level of feasibility, he called for assessing by whom, and how, the demand for sovereignty was being propelled, in order to distinguish valid demands from pro-imperial uses of national sentiments (Lenin, 1974a: 99–120, 1974b: 15–25). The battle for the second independence fits with that position of the Bolshevik leader. It takes up the regional objective of full emancipation that was frustrated in the 19th century with the balkanization of Latin America.

By only acknowledging the antagonism between capital and labor, anti-dependentism sails on an ocean of abstract internationalism. Thus, it does not perceive the basic differences that oppose progressive and regressive nationalism. That which, in the past, distinguished Mussolini or Theodore Roosevelt from Sandino or Lumumba, today separates the Western right (Trump, Le Pen, Farage) from Latin American anti-imperialism (Chávez-Maduro, Evo Morales). Lenin underlined this distinction in order to delineate political strategies that are not recognized by the critics of dependency theory.

11   Mythical Proletariat

The main political accusation of anti-dependentism against its adversaries was that it failed to recognize the leading role of the working class. This omission was attributed to the influence of Third-Worldism or the lumpen-proletariat (Sender, 1980). But those characterizations were not aimed at specifying the leading subjects of a revolutionary process, but at defining paths to capitalist modernization. They looked at the possibility of socialism in strict relation to the growing weight of the working class under the current system, and therefore highlighted the preeminence of the proletariat over other popular actors (Harris, 1987: 183–184, 200–202). With this logic, it assumed that the liberation of the workers would emerge from an opposite process of consolidation of bourgeois oppression. How the exploited could be liberated from a system that consolidated its subjection was an unresolved mystery.

This thesis also emphasized the protagonism of the developed economies, with larger contingents of wage-workers, in the gestation of socialism. In this way, they ignored the fact that in the 20th century revolutions occurred in the regions encumbered by the most acute capitalist imbalances. In that anti-dependency approach, proletarian leadership did not imply promoting radical changes; on the contrary, it embraced a model of humanitarian socialism configured by means of parliamentary action. It believed that in this way, the West would once again show the rest of the world the path to civilization (Warren, 1980: 7, 24–27).

That perspective repeated the Eurocentric mythology forged by German social democracy and the English Fabians, ignoring the point to which that utopia was disproved by the fierce wars and depressions of the 20th century. With allusions to the rule of the proletariat, they anticipated the socio-liberal libretto of Felipe González and Tony Blair.

The preeminence of the working class was especially extolled as an antidote to the contamination of anti-imperialism. With that anti-nationalist fanaticism, Warren was opposed to the struggle of the Northern Irish (Catholics) against English occupation. He rejected the national unification of the island and approved of the position of the Protestant currents loyal to the British monarchy (Proyect, 2008; Ferguson, 1999; Munck, 1981). That pro-imperialist attitude crowned an imagery of proletarian purity, ascribing to the workers located in the major centers of the West a function of guiding international socialism.

The theories of invariable worker protagonism looked different in Latin America in the 1970s. They were promoted by thinkers identified in militant circles as pure socialists, who opposed any strategy that included anti-imperialist programs or organizations, and promoted revolutionary processes with exclusively socialist dynamics. That approach worked toward the exact recreation of Bolshevism, as against both the stages strategy of official Communism and the extension of the Cuban model favored by dependentist Marxism.

Pure socialism defended a model of worker soviets against the "deformations" introduced by the revolutions of peasant (China, Vietnam) or radicalized middle class (Cuba) preeminence. It held that the replacement of proletarian leadership generated the major contemporary errors of the socialist project. That approach combined dogmatism, political myopia, and great irritation with the course of history. Instead of acknowledging the revolutionary role played by a wide variety of oppressed subjects, it discredited the great anti-capitalist transformations for their deviation from a presupposed sociological-classist path. It assumed that a revolution lacked socialist attributes if the place of the proletariat was occupied by another popular sector. Proponents of this perspective argued with the defenders of the Cuban revolution about the tactics and strategies that should be followed by different countries.

These characterizations of the Latin American proletariat, conceived to advance the paths to gaining power, have disappeared from the current debate.

Criticisms of theories that reduce the role of the proletariat persist (Iñigo Carrera, 2009: 19–20), but are expressed in abstract terms unrelated to real experiences. They no longer refer to forthcoming political events., but navigate in phantasmagoric worlds that are not anchored in worker actions. They expound ideas connected more to philosophical deduction than to political reasoning.

The present-day critics are not tied to the foundations posited by pure socialism. They do not aim to demonstrate the superiority of the proletariat with respect to other oppressed sectors. By breaking away from that pillar, their challenges lack relevance for any battle for socialism. That loss of direction empties their arguments from its old pretension of shoring up the revolutionary tendencies in their dispute with reformism.

An analogous process of evaporation of the critical sense is found in the Marxist economic debates between analysts of the falling rate of profit tendency and underconsumption theorists. In the 1970s, that controversy aroused passions among those who saw the debate as an expression of the battle between revolutionaries and reformists. The first thesis presumably conceptualized the inability of capitalism to achieve improvements, while the latter provided foundations for that possibility. In the present, both theses provide elements for understanding crisis, but they no longer express the political contrasts of the past. Any review of that debate must be situated in the new context. The same thing happens with criticisms of the class omissions of Marxist dependency theory. Those objections are no longer formulated in accordance with the old debates on the leading role of the proletariat in the socialist revolution. Thus, many controversies flutter in a vacuum, with no direction.

12   Globalist Socialism

Another ground on which Marxist dependency theory has been challenged is in the assessment of 20th century attempts at socialism. Some think that this project was doomed to failure from its birth. They do not situate the failure in the bureaucratic totalitarianism of the Soviet Union, but in the mere existence of a model that attempts to skip stages of capitalist maturation (Warren, 1980: 116–117).

Other thinkers attribute the same outcome to the preeminence of national liberation objectives in detriment to socialist goals, arguing that those deficiencies will be overcome in a socialist future preceded by the global expansion of capitalism. They see neoliberal globalization as a promissory foretaste of that future, and extol the international interlinking of the dominant classes (Harris,

1987: 185–200). That perspective identifies the current trend with increasingly homogeneous processes. It assumes that global hierarchies will dissolve, facilitating the direct international introduction of socialism. This diagnosis explains its hostility toward Marxist dependency theory, which underlines the preeminence of opposite tendencies toward global polarization of capitalism.

The portrayal of globalization as a prologue to universal socialism is astonishing for its level of fantasy. It is evident that neoliberal globalization is the most reactionary attempt of the last decades for the preservation of capitalism, and it is ridiculous to assume that inequities will tend to disappear under a model that generates monumental social cleavages on a world scale.

Warren and Harris inverted the basic meaning of Marxism. They transformed a critical conception of capitalism into its opposite. They called for restraint in condemnations of capitalism, forgetting that this challenge is the basic foundation of any socialist project. Their strange model of globalist socialism has disappeared from the political map, but the principles of their approach survive in present-day anti-dependentism. By ruling out the national component of the struggle in the periphery, ignoring the progressivism of sovereign victories, and failing to recognize anti-imperialist mediations, that current assumes equivalent anti-capitalist paths in all countries.

While dependentist Marxism conceives of distinct intermediate links for socialist strategy, its critics only offer hopes for the sudden irruption of socialism on a world scale. That assumption of magical simultaneity is implicit in the absence of specific programs for a transition to socialism in Latin America. They reject those paths, arguing that delinking from the world market will re-create illusory variants of socialism in one country (Astarita, 2010b). They do not realize that this strategy was formulated to promote a combined sequence of overcoming underdevelopment and advancing toward social equality. That aspiration was supported by real experiences over several decades. It did not fantasize about magical outbreaks of socialism in all countries through immediate contagion or simultaneous appearance, nor did it expect Western patronage or planetary solutions to be settled in a single round.

It is true that socialism cannot be built in a single country, but that limitation does not imply renouncing the start of that process in the framework prevailing in each circumstance. If the national foundation is ignored and socialism is conceived of as an ultimatum (everywhere at once or nothing), there is no room for developing feasible political strategies. The exotic models of global socialism were also inspired by objectivist variants of Marxism. They reasoned in positivist terms, idolatrizing a pattern of evolution identified with the progress of the productive forces. That criterion led the early critics of dependentism to support the expansion of capitalism and to object to any brakes on that surge. They imagined a growing process of maturation under the leadership of the civilized sectors of the working class. With this logic, they updated the gradualist positivism of Kautsky–Plekhanov into a novel variation of global Menshevism.

The pure socialists also conceived a model of progressive movements in accordance with the impact of each process on the development of the productive forces. They approved of whatever bolstered this development and criticized whatever obstructed it, prioritizing the abstract sphere of economics over the popular struggle.

The followers of that perspective are not able to formulate constructive reflections on the socialist project. They limit themselves to expressing criticisms without proposing positive solutions to the problems under discussion, dodging any suggestion of alternatives to the theories that they criticize. With that ongoing series of rejections, they obstruct the continuity of the fruitful paths opened by dependentism in the 1970s.

PART 3

Concepts

••

CHAPTER 9

Subimperialism I

Review of a Concept

The characteristics of subimperialism were studied by Marini in his exposition of dependency theory. That concept raised controversies in the 1970s and has been reconsidered in recent years. How relevant and how useful is it?

1   Foundations and Objections

Marini ascribed two dimensions, one economic and the other geopolitical-military, to subimperialism, and he applied both meanings to the Brazilian case. In the economic sphere, he saw that foreign investment had increased productive capacity, generating surpluses that could not be sold in domestic markets. He underlined how multinational corporations promoted the placement of those surpluses in the neighboring countries, and used the new term to describe that compensatory action (Marini, 2005: 151–164). Subimperialism described the conversion of a dependent Latin American economy into an exporter of goods and capital, as companies counteracted the tightness of the local market with sales in the surrounding radius. This outward incursion went beyond the industrial sphere and included finance (Marini, 2007a: 54–73).

Marini reformulated a thesis presented by Luxemburg in the early 20th century that illustrated how the major European economies dealt with the problem of their tight internal markets. She argued that they counteracted that limitation with imperialist policies of expansion to the colonies (Luxemburg, 1968: 158–190). The dependency theorist took up this idea of an external outlet for the imbalances of underconsumption, but he located the phenomenon in lesser economies and on a more limited scale (Marini, 1973: 99–100).

Marini connected the second sense of subimperialism to the geopolitical protagonism of Brazil. He argued that the major country of South America acted outside its borders with Prussian methods in order to fulfill the double role of anti-communist gendarme and autonomous regional power, presenting this role as a feature that was complementary and functional to economic expansion. He highlighted that Brazilian governments acted in concert with the Pentagon, following the rules of the Cold War. Subimperialism implied being repressive, but not merely subordinate to the dictates of the North. The ruling classes sought their own dominance, in order to guarantee the interests of the corporations in the country (Marini, 2007a: 54–73).

Marini emphasized this combination of dependency, coordination, and autonomy in Brazil in the period of open turmoil because of the Cuban revolution. He portrayed subimperialism as an instrument of the oppressors to stifle the revolutionary threat, arguing that it operated in a period marked by choices between two antagonistic models: socialism and fascism. Another exponent of the same theory agreed with this characterization, arguing that the main purpose of subimperial action was to impede the gestation of a postcapitalist scenario on a regional scale (Bambirra, 1986: 177–179).

However, there were objections to the concept from within Marxism. Those who were close to orthodox Marxism questioned its revision of Leninist theses and its ignorance of the dominant role of finance. They rejected the existence of a subimperial power in Brazil, emphasizing its incompatibility with the country's subjugation to the First World powers (Fernández and Ocampo, 1974). The critics perceived that Marini distanced himself from the old analyses of imperialism, and they dismissed that reconsideration without assessing its foundations. Cardoso also contested that new concept. He questioned the consistency of subimperialism, and argued that Marini overestimated crises of realization (Martins, 2011a: 233–236).

Another type of observation was put forth by an important Marxist theorist who converged with dependentism. Cueva did not challenge the validity of subimperialism, but its application to Brazil. He argued that because of its high level of subordination to the United States, the South American country did not reach this status (Cueva, 2012: 200). Marini's closest colleague also had reservations about the new category. Dos Santos argued that it suggested a possibility of development, but he doubted its materialization. He observed that a subimperial status created undesired conflicts between the ruling classes and U.S. power (Dos Santos, 1978: 446–447).

2   Evaluation of a Concept

Marini reformulated the classical theory of imperialism while assimilating several updates. One reevaluation underscored the new military hegemony of the United States (Sweezy–Magdoff), and another highlighted the attenuation of military confrontations together with the deepening of economic disputes (Mandel). The Brazilian theorist absorbed those ideas, together with the characterization of collective imperialism led by the Pentagon to manage the growing international interlinking of capital (Amin) (Katz, 2011: 33–49). He not only combined various elements of these perspectives (Munck, 1981); he also took up the thesis of another thinker who underlined the new joint action of the powers, in contrast to the old inter-imperialist contradictions (Thalheimer, 1946). With these influences, Marini spoke of a novel 'hegemonic cooperation' between the centers.

To this model, he added the role of the intermediate countries, describing the connection of the subimperial powers to the dominators of the planet. His approach highlighted the role of the new intermediate centers of accumulation in the imperial pyramid of the postwar; analysis of those countries was his main object of study. He called the semi-peripheries studied by World System Theory subimperialism (Dos Santos, 2009b) and inquired into the specific laws of those formations in global dynamics (Marini, 2013: 24–26).

The Brazilian theorist chose the term subimperialism in contention with another denomination (privileged satellite) that overestimated the geopolitical importance of the phenomenon while underestimating its economic impact. He formulated the same objection against another concept (intermediate power) that omitted the role of the multinational corporations (Marini, 1991: 31–32). With even greater emphasis, he rejected the portrayal of Brazil as an imperialist power. Moreover, he rejected the classification of the country in the category of the lesser postwar imperialisms (Switzerland, Belgium, or Holland).

Marini located subimperial status in the intermediate dependent economies, which maintained unique relations with central imperialism. In response to the erroneous identification of the prefix 'sub' with subordination to outside will, he clarified that that connection implied a combination of subjection with association and autonomy. He argued that subimperialism involved economies in the process of industrialization, subject to the turbulent effects of the dependent cycle. This model was later theorized as a pattern of reproduction of certain underdeveloped economies (Osorio, 2012). On the geopolitical level, he argued that subimperial action implied expansionist paths, adapted to the global hegemony of the United States. He underlined the role of regional leaderships associated with the supremacy of U.S. imperialism.

Marini also related the presence of subimperialism to the type of dominance prevalent at the top of the ruling classes. He emphasized the dominance the industrial companies and their financial partners had reached in Brazil. He stressed that this sector headed the expansion to the outer vicinity (Bueno, 2010). With this observation, he suggested wide margins of variability of subimperialism, according to the dominant capitalist sector. He argued that there were changing phases of that status, and suggested that it lacked the stability that prevailed in the imperial powers.

Marini also pointed to the selective access available to the subimperial condition. He argued that only some intermediate economies meet the requirements needed to reach that status. He placed Brazil, but not Argentina, in that position. For the dependency theorist, a subimperial position assumes great political cohesion of the bourgeoisie around its state. He understood that the absence of that homogeneity impeded both Argentina and Mexico from emulating the place achieved by Brazil. In the former case, he attributed that limitation to the prolonged crisis of the political system, and in the latter to the high level of dependency to the United States (Luce, 2015: 31, 32, 37).

Marini clarified that in similar economic contexts, the type of state was determinant of subimperial action. With this logic, he reduced the number of countries with those aptitudes to only a few cases. He situated Brazil, Israel, Iran, and South Africa in this camp (Luce, 2011). Marini's theory had some precedents in characterizations of subsidiary (Spain) or relegated (Russia) empires, but it was conceived as a feature exclusively of postwar capitalism. It did not project Brazilian subimperialism back to the 19th century. His concept contributed to overcoming anachronisms, and motivated a fruitful research program.

3   Another Context

A present-day analysis of subimperialism should take note of the radical difference that separates 21st century capitalism from that of Marini's era. Since the 1980s, the postwar Keynesian model has been replaced by a neoliberal model of permanent aggression against workers. Precarization deteriorates the wage, and the displacement of industry to the East cheapens labor power. Unemployment intensifies urban marginality, and capitalists use informatization to increase profitability, destroying jobs and boosting inequalities.

This context differs from that which was studied by Marini. The intermediate economies on which he focused his attention still play a key role, but operate in a new framework of transnational corporations, free-trade agreements, and globalized finance. Compared to the 1970s, the internal markets of the intermediate countries have lost relevance in the face of growing export activity. In addition, the global chain of production increases the varieties of those formations (Domingues, 2012: 47–55).

Three modalities of economies equivalent to those analyzed by Marini can currently be found. Some semi-peripheries with greater prior development maintain their old specialization in basic exports with a reduced global impact (Argentina). Others integrated into global manufacturing processes without expanding their regional influence (South Korea). A third type exhibits enormous weight in its surrounding area with a low percentage of per capita GDP (India).

These economies are still far from the clearly peripheral countries (Mozambique, Angola, Bolivia) and from the central powers (United States, Germany, Japan). They are located in the space that Marini analyzed. However, unlike the preceding stage, a sharp differentiation has arisen within this segment, in accordance with the connection each country has established with neoliberal globalization.

In addition, the gap between semi-peripheral economic structures and subimperial roles has deepened. What determines the passage from the former to the latter status is not the weight of the country in the value chain. Countries that are more connected to productive internationalization (Korea) or little integrated in that network (Argentina) have not changed their subimperial shortcomings. The potential divorce between the two situations that Marini suggested has taken new forms.

4   Economic Interpretations

The distinction between intermediate economies and subimperial powers is a key feature of the current context. This difference was omitted from the characterizations that extended to Mexico or Argentina the role that Marini ascribed to Brazil. It was assumed that subimperial performance corresponded to Latin American nations with some degree of industrial development and, therefore, some distance from the purely agro-mining countries (Bambirra, 1986: 177–179).

One great scholar of dependency theory maintains this criterion, highlighting the scale obtained by the 'multilatina' companies (Techint, Slim, Cemex) (Osorio, 2009b: 219–221). He argues that regional blocs and customs unions have driven the subimperial calling of all the states that house that type of company (Osorio, 2007). However, the weight of those firms does not necessarily place them in the same subimperial category as countries with very different geopolitical, military, and state profiles.

In recent years, this question has gone beyond the Latin American orbit. The appearance of the bloc composed of the BRICS opened a debate on the validity of the subimperial category for that group. Authors who value Marini's approach retain his objections to the simple characterization of the members of this group as intermediate powers. They recall the insufficiencies of a label used by conventional political science (Bond, 2015: 243–247). But the classification of the BRICS in the subimperial world would ignore the heterogeneity of this bloc. One of the participants in this partnership (China) has already passed intermediate status and has entered the nucleus of central economies. This fact does not allow us to place the entire alignment in the category analyzed by Marini.

That application also faces another problem: the BRICS have established an economic alliance without a clear geopolitical program. Its members maintain very different relations with the central powers. It is enough to compare India's bond with the United States to China and Russia's relation with that country to notice that chasm. Each component of the conglomerate acts according to its regional priorities, and the quest for that dominance leaves open potential conflicts between China, India, and Russia.

In contrast to the collective imperialism of the triad, the BRICS did not emerge in postwar contexts to guarantee common strategic objectives. That group arose in order to form a space for negotiation within neoliberal globalization. It is an alliance on the inside of that structure. Thus, all the summit meetings of the BRICS have revolved around economic initiatives (banks, investment, currency use), and recreate corporate debates close to those of the World Economic Forum (García, 2015: 243–247). This has again shown that the concept of subimperialism does not extend to a bloc; it is only valid for regional powers that dispute regional influence.

5   Reformulation of a Status

Subimperial forms have changed in a geopolitical context marked by the end of the Cold War. The fundamental anti-communist motivation that shaped all relations with the United States and its partners has disappeared. Conflicts among the ruling classes are now processed in a framework of globalized business and redesigned borders, in contrast to the frozen map of the postwar. The old context of bipolarity, still present at the origin of neoliberalism (1985–89), was followed by a phase of unipolar supremacy (1989–2008), and another of multipolarity (2008–2017).

But in such rapidly changing periods, one central fact of Marini's analysis has remained: the military preponderance of the United States. The most powerful nation maintains its leadership of concerted imperial action, which in the mid-20th century replaced the old inter-imperialist confrontation. That predominance persisted, together with the loss of U.S. economic primacy. The guarantor of the capitalist order retains its function as protector of the ruling classes of the planet. It no longer has the capacity for unilateral action, but it retains a great power of intervention. For example, the United States sets the rules for the nuclear club, which penalizes those who attempt to accede in an autonomous way to those resources. It also directs the Western coalitions that perpetrate occupation or remove disobedient governments. The aggressions that Bush committed under banal pretexts were continued, with covert methods, by Obama.

The logic of subimperialism adapts to that patronage by the Pentagon, but adopts a content shaped by growing conflicts for regional primacy within neoliberal globalization. Those tensions do not have the global reach that characterized the first half of the 20th century (Panitch, 2015: 62). They appear on a limited scale that does not repeat what occurred in the past; nor does it prepare the third world war that some authors erroneously anticipate (Sousa, 2014). The subempires act to reinforce their primacy without involving the great powers in general conflagrations.

Another feature of the period is the absence of proportionality between economic supremacy and politico-military hegemony. Japan and Germany have established themselves as dominant on the former level and orphans on the latter, while the inverse is true for France and England. As in Marini's era, the current subempires are regional powers on the economic as well as the politico-military and state levels. They must combine these two conditions rather than just one of them. The presence of transnational corporations (South Korea, Mexico, Chile), systematic actions of war (Colombia), or sporadic military incursions (Argentina during the Falkland/Malvinas War) are not enough. Only those that concentrate all the components of the subimperial profile assume that role. As Marini argued, the name commonly used for those countries – intermediate powers – is insufficient to characterize them; yet, they are nations located in that stratum. None is a typical Third World country.

At present, the geopolitical-military aspect is determinant of subimperial status. That condition requires a sufficient level of autonomy to act in favor of the major dominant classes of each area. However, the subimperial condition also requires acting in harmony with the first power. These two features underlined by Marini (association with the United States and power of its own) have persisted.

The very term 'subempire' indicates the importance of military action. Powerful economies with small armies are excluded from this group. The subempires therefore correspond, in general, to countries that in the past already developed a significant military role beyond its borders. The effective exercise of that power is uncertain due to the vulnerable place of those countries in the global hierarchy. The regional gendarmes are corroded by sharp imbalances, which contrast with the stability achieved by the central empires. That fragility determines the temporary nature of the subempires. Few candidates on the possible spectrum are able to effectively embody that condition (Moyo, 2015: 189–192).

6   Controversial Extensions

In our reformulation, only a few countries – such as Turkey or India – presently meet the requirements of a subempire. They are semi-peripheral economies with high levels of intermediate development that maintain a close relationship with the United States and seek to increase their regional dominance. The geopolitical-military component defines a status that fits with several formulations of Marxist dependency theory.

Another interpretation suggests a broader view of subimperialism as a new determinant of major conflicts. This approach rejects the meaning Marini ascribed to the concept. It holds that postwar growth reduced the center-periphery gap and facilitated a great deal of development of native capitalisms. It argues that this expansion generates subimperial confrontations that recreate the classical inter-imperialist clashes of the past (Callinicos, 2001).

With this approach, an extended list of subempires was posited in the last decade. In the Middle East, Iraq, Egypt, and Syria were added to Turkey and Iran. In Asia, India was joined by Pakistan and Vietnam; and in Africa Nigeria was added to South Africa. In Latin America, Brazil was complemented by Argentina. In this interpretation, every country with a regional projection and significant accumulation processes participates in the subimperial category. This broadening of the concept considers the local impact of the phenomenon. It highlights its regional importance and plays down its connections with the global structure of imperialism.

Marini proposed a lower number of subempires because of the double role he ascribed to the phenomenon. He defined that condition by relations of association and autonomy with the central powers and by regional policing actions. Thus, his list excluded Iraq, Syria, Vietnam, Nigeria, or Argentina. His approach did not magnify the presence of subempires, and avoided separating them from the world order. There was an implicit distinction between potential and effective subempires: Pakistan and Argentina could claim pretensions to that status, but they were not able to achieve it. Under dictatorial governments, both countries maintained their close subordination to the Pentagon without developing autonomous strategies.

Marini also avoided confusing subimperial aspirations with anti-imperialist actions. Although Vietnam faced serious conflicts with its neighbors, it was involved in the major war on the Asian continent against the United States. For their part, Egypt and Syria primarily confronted Israel, which was the principal representative of U.S. interests in the Middle East. The extended view of sub-imperialism omits these characterizations, which are indispensable for adequately applying the category in each circumstance. In addition, it conceives of wars between these formations as a feature of subimperialism in the present period, using the concept to explain the armed conflicts that pit Greece against Turkey, India against Pakistan, and Iraq against Iran. It assumes that those bloody conflicts replace the conflagrations between central countries in the age of classical imperialism.

But that comparison is inadequate, and not only for the different magnitude of the conflicts. It leaves out the relation those regional clashes represent with the leading role of Washington. Although Iraq started the war against Iran with its own objectives, that adventure was promoted by the United States in order to crush the regime of the Ayatollahs.

The subempires do not replicate the old inter-imperialist rivalries. They unfold in a period of extinction of those conflagrations. The United States no longer fights with Japan for control over the Pacific, nor with Germany for supremacy in Europe. It coordinates joint imperial action that is sometimes intertwined with the actions of regional subempires. The extended thesis exaggerates the power of intermediate conflagrations. It neglects the fact that those countries act in reference to a collective imperialism led by the United States. It does not take into account that military conflicts between subempires tend to remain limited within the thresholds set by the global powers.

An oversized characterization of subempires leads, as well, to erroneous political assessments. By assigning a subimperial status to Argentina, the Falklands/Malvinas war was interpreted as an inter-imperial conflict between powers of different weights. This perspective ignores the fact that the basis of this conflict was a colonial usurpation of a portion of Argentine territory. What happened in the Falklands/Malvinas war was not the collision of a mature empire with another in gestation, but that British colonialism reaffirmed its violation of the sovereignty of the South American country. The legitimacy of an Argentine national demand is weakened with the subimperial characterization of that country.

7   Misunderstanding a Category

An author critical of subimperialism objects to the replacement of class analysis of exploitation by interpretations based on the subjection of countries. He especially challenges the existence of a tripartite rule of national oppression, considering it wrong to imagine a chain of exploitation of Bolivia by Brazil, and of Brazil by the United States. He asserts that to analyze the tension between bourgeoisies over the distribution of surplus value, there is no need to resort to the categories of imperialism (Astarita, 2010a: 62–64).

But that view attributes to Marini a thesis that he never postulated. He never claimed that subimperialism implied mechanisms of exploitation between countries. He always specified that multinational corporations profited from the extraction of surplus value from the workers of the nations neighboring Brazil, explaining the way in which that process responded to the contradictions of capitalism and arguing that the course of accumulation confronted limits to the realization of value, leading capitalists to compensate for imbalances by pushing beyond borders. Neither did Marini reformulate the tripartite metropolis-satellite model posited by Gunder Frank. He developed a unique Marxist thesis, which has been misinterpreted by the anti-dependentist readings (Katz, 2017).

But the main problem of that critique of subimperialism is its failure to recognize the geopolitical-military sense of the concept. It does not grasp its important role in the prevailing global hierarchy under contemporary capitalism. The objector assumes that to understand the functioning of this system it is enough to indicate the aggressive-competitive dynamics. However, he overlooks the fact that this characterization is only the starting point of the problem. Capitalism operates on a world scale and depends on a coercive order that requires imperial mechanisms. By omitting this fact, he ignores how the analysis of subimperialism contributes to clarification of the multiple present-day forms of global oppression. These mechanisms are indispensable for the reproduction of capitalism.

Subimperialism is a category of the capitalist world order, and its validity stems from the existence of regional wars and conflicts. By neglecting this structure (or assuming that it is not the economist's job to address that topic), the critic impoverishes the analysis begun by Marini. More than analyzing chains of surplus extraction among large, medium, and small economies, subimperialism refers to the geopolitical role of the regional powers. It is an explanatory concept for the pyramidal structure of dominators, partners, and subordinates that sustains capitalism.

8   Comparison with Semi-Colony

Some authors believe that subimperialism contradicts the traditional contrast between center and periphery. They especially highlight Brazil's backwardness, and point to its distance from the central countries. They argue that the country is still subjected to a semi-colonial position shared with Argentina and Mexico (Matos, 2009). In fact, this viewpoint underlines the persistence of a situation described by the classical Marxists in the early 20th century.

But this treatment ignores the obsolescence of the old portrayal of a handful of powers stifling indistinct peripheries. That type of imperial domination was long ago replaced by other subjections. The three typical forms of subordination in the last century (colonies, semi-colonies, and dependent capitalisms) gave way to more complex varieties of stratification that were analyzed by a Marxist theorist in the 1970s (Mandel, 1986),

Productive lag, agrarian rentism, or tight markets do not currently define the semi-colonial status of a country; they merely indicate development gaps or modes of international insertion. That category does not distinguish between an agro-mining or an intermediate-industrial country; nor does it clarify whether a country has reached a certain level of development of the internal market or depends on exports. The semi-colonial idea describes a political status – it illustrates the level of autonomy from the major powers. In colonies, the authorities are appointed by the metropolis, while in the semi-colonies they are selected in a hidden manner by the centers.

Colonies are now marginal, and semi-colonies persist only in those countries under total subordination to the State Department. Honduras is an example of that type; the same occurs in Haiti. But that status does not apply to Brazil, which is one of the occupiers of Haiti. It is not logical to place them on the same level, forgetting that the largest South American country is a member of the G20. Because of the margin of autonomy of their states, Brazil, Mexico, and Argentina are located outside the semi-colonial group. That condition died out in the last century, and did not reappear with the predominance of governments allied to Washington. The state is managed by local ruling classes and not by emissaries of the U.S. embassy.

It is true that the Brazilian economy depends on natural resources and suffers from a high level of external appropriation. But those features do not in themselves define its position in the global order. There are imperialist powers with large natural reserves (United States), and others with a significant foreign presence in their economy (Holland). Nor do recurrent crises determine the international position of each country. Many nations of the lower periphery languish without major periodic turbulences, while others of the center face a high level of economic instability.

Those who situate Brazil in the semi-colonial world stress the productivity or per capita GDP gap, which separates it from the advanced economies, but a similar gap is found with the impoverished nations of the lower periphery.

Brazil's distance from Nicaragua or Mozambique is as substantial as its distance from France or Japan. Marini analyzed the world of subimperialism precisely to overcome the simplified location of Brazil in the periphery of the planet. In an updated conceptualization of distinct geopolitical locations, the dominant powers must be distinguished from the countries that have very different levels of dependence. The subordination of Honduras contrasts with the autonomy of Brazil.

9   Dogmatic Inconsistencies

Insistence on the concept of semi-colony, in opposition to the idea of sub-imperialism, assumes the complete present-day validity of the assessment of imperialism espoused by Lenin. A similar view was adopted by the communist orthodoxy against Marini in the 1970s. Both of them underestimate the changes undergone in imperial dynamics since the mid-20th century.

In our book on imperialism (Katz, 2011), we presented an update with treatments close to those of Marini. We noted the same postwar changes that the Brazilian scholar intuited, on three levels: the existence of greater global integration of capitals, the absence of inter-imperialist wars, and the dominant role of the United States. We highlighted the importance of the same process of 'hegemonic cooperation' among the imperial powers. Our use of subimperialism rests on this coinciding view.

Some critics object to our approach with the same arguments that question the subimperial thesis. They accept the validity of strong tendencies toward convergence between capitals of different national origins, but they stress the contradictory dynamics of that process. They emphasize that transnational ruling classes disconnected from the old states have not been created, and believe that this framework generates explosive tendencies that we have ignored. They do not, however, clarify what our omission has been (Cri and Marcos, 2014).

From the time the bourgeoisie did not build globalized classes and states, those imbalances have been apparent. The objections are limited to exposing the same tensions we have noted and that we, in turn, have taken from other authors. But this portrayal is telling. On the one hand, they accept the dominance of multinational corporations; on the other, they posit their irrelevance. They highlight the international association of capitals, while at the same time underlining the continuity of rivalry. With this duality, they do not specify which is the dominant tendency.

The objectors understand that both processes coexist with the same force as in the past. But in that case, continuation of the Leninist scenario would prevail, even though it has been altered by greater integration of capitals. They exemplify the persistence of the old rivalries in the disputes that currently pit Germany against the United States over the management of monetary crises, and they assert that we omit those contradictions. But our approach does not ignore those clashes; it simply contextualizes them in a context of absence of wars between powers. We postulate that the conflagrations that inspired Lenin's thesis are not found at the present time. Thus, no one foresees a repetition of armed conflicts between the United States, France, Germany, Japan, or England.

It is not clear whether the critics believe the contrary and expect the reappearance of confrontations between the armies that make up NATO. Rather than specifying this prediction, they describe the divergences that have arisen around the values of the Euro and the dollar. But it is obvious that those financial discrepancies are not comparable to the clashes that led to the First or Second World War.

It is not enough to expound generalities about inter-imperial tensions. Their scope and potential outcome must be assessed. Thus, we argue that hypotheses of repetition of events from the early 20th century lack corroboration. The triad currently exercises nuclear blackmail against third parties that does not extend to its members. Economic conflicts within that alliance do not project to the military sphere. No one wants to disarm the system of capitalist protection controlled by the Pentagon, and an eventual confrontation with Russia or China would not repeat the inter-imperial conflicts of the past either.

Rather than confronting these problems, the objectors limit themselves to confirming the existence of opposing tendencies. They find greater global integration of capital, and at the same time they dispute the dissipation of inter-imperialist wars. But with that presentation of diverse tendencies, they do not assess the consequences of their own formulations. If there is greater global bourgeois integration and at the same time identical possibilities for wars, the logic of their analysis is not clear. That inconsistency derives from assuming that contemporary capitalism is a carbon copy of the capitalism of the last century. To preserve their loyalty to the classical theory of imperialism, but with facts that modify that context, they create a cloud of ambiguities.

That eclecticism extends to the assessment of the role of the United States. The critics recognize the abyss that separates the military forces of the leading power from those of any other – but they do not deduce any corollary of that unique situation. They highlight the exhaustion of U.S. leadership without presenting any prognosis for the replacement of that supremacy. They settle for ambiguity. They reject theories of the decline of U.S. primacy, and also theories of its continuity. With that position, they repeat the obvious (the United States no longer has its postwar strength) without explaining why the dollar endures as a refuge from crises, U.S. companies lead in the development of information technology, and the Pentagon persists as the pillar of NATO.

In order to underscore analogies with the Leninist scenario, the critics find "Kautskian traces" in our approach, claiming it has affinities with the "ultra-imperialist" model. They argue that this view means imagining an "unchal-lenged empire" managing a "stable and strong capitalism" (Chingo, 2012). Our text provides abundant data and assessments of the imbalances generated by present-day capitalism. A simple reading of those characterizations disproves any impression of the system's stability. But we place those contradictions in the logic of an economic system that is more internationalized and managed collectively under U.S. command.

In contrast to dogmatic approaches, Lenin located each problem in the specificity of its time. Thus, he highlighted the military particularity of con-flicts in the face of Kautsky's pacifist expectations. This could be updated by comparing anti-imperialist views with the social-democratic illusions of 'humanitarian' imperial interventionism. Rather than attempting that applica-tion, the critics draw a dividing line between crisis interpretations (them) and stability theories (us). This classification makes no sense.

To understand present-day imperialism, one must take analytical risks, rec-ognize new discoveries, and abandon archaic theses. Our objectors sidestep these commitments and commit the evil they attribute to us: navigating in ambiguity. By recognizing one thing and also the contrary, they do not contrib-ute ideas about the current dynamics of imperial oppression and its subim-perial complements. Marini delineated various ideas for understanding those processes. But, how do they operate in the present?

Subimperialism II

Current Application

Theoretical debates on subimperialism are interesting, but the concept is only relevant if it sheds light on contemporary reality. How would it be applied in the current context? The category has validity particularly for a region with a prolonged presence of war like the Arab world. Those conflicts involve central powers (United States, France, England) and one in recomposition (Russia), together with various local actors (Turkey, Saudi Arabia, Israel, Iran). That group of countries has intervened in confrontations that have caused endless tragedy. The responsibility of the United States stands out – it craves the appropriation of oil and control over strategic areas of international trade, and its presidents directed the destruction of Afghanistan (Reagan-Carter), Iraq (Bush), Libya and Syria (Obama). That devastation included terrifying massacres that meant 220,000 deaths in the first of these countries, 650,000 in the second, and 250,000 in the fourth.

In the last six years, the main political objective of that bloodbath has been to crush the Arab Spring. The uprisings were stifled by means of dictatorships (Egypt, Syria), return to the old regime (Tunisia), invasions (Libya), and jihadi massacres (Syria). Imperial protagonism in this destruction is evident, but the United States does not act alone. It maintains a close connection with three regional powers (Turkey, Saudi Arabia, and Israel) and oscillates between threats and negotiations with another decisive contender (Iran). Do those countries operate as subimperial powers?

1   The Main Prototype

Turkey, which intervened in the recent war in Syria following all the rules of subimperialism, fits into the concept perfectly. The Erdogan government sought to topple its old rival Assad in order to build its regional leadership, in alliance with the Muslim Brotherhood. With the fall of its partner in Egypt and the danger of formation of a Kurdish state, the Turkish president undertook a spectacular turnaround. He joined the Russian and Iranian bloc that sustains the Syrian regime. Since he did not achieve primacy by the removal of his enemy, he chose to support it. This turnaround illustrates how Turkey unfolds its strategy for regional hegemony. Its rulers have amassed great experience in that type of maneuvering that combines association with, and distancing from, the United States.

Turkey is a member of NATO and maintains a well-oiled connection with the Pentagon. It houses a military base with nuclear warheads pointed at Russia, and has sent troops to operations in Afghanistan, Iraq, and Somalia. However, the country's rulers have never acted as a simple regional police force; they harbor long-standing expansive appetites. That is why they invaded and occupied Cyprus. The strategy of neo-Ottoman resurgence is not a nostalgic fable. It inspires a project of regional hegemony.

That pretension is based in despotic-statist traditions recreated under military tutelage. In contrast to Latin America or southern Europe, the end of the dictatorship in Turkey did not diminish the dominant weight of the army in its political structure. That influence is a decisive component of its subimperial strength. With this aggressiveness, it seeks to maintain the growth rate that secured the country's intermediate economic status. Corporations of Turkish origin have operated in various countries since the 1980s by way of free-trade agreements.

These characteristics make the term subimperial, as used by one author (Çağh, 2009) to portray the country's profile, appropriate. Its expansionist policy seems to fit more with the Islamic political faction of the bourgeoisie (Rabiismo) than with the old Atlanticist segment (Kemalism). The first group does not forgive the second for having accepted subjection to the West, in detriment to Sunni identity, and now tries to lead a project of regional Islamization (Savran, 2016).

The subimperial profile of Turkey includes the historical oppression of several national minorities. The Kurds, in particular, are victims of an authoritarian order that demands the total supremacy of a single race and language. The same thing happened with the Armenian genocide, perpetrated at the end of the First World War in order to build a homogeneous state. The denial of that massacre forms part of the imagined nationality in the creation of Turkey. It is a bedrock of the neo-Ottoman restoration project (Batou, 2015). The subimperial character of Turkey is also verified by its persistent dispute with Iran, which recreates old rivalries with the Persian empire. That competition guides the country's foreign policy, and has been decisive in its intervention in Syria. But another unexpected contender with hegemonic aspirations has been added to that traditional rivalry.

2   An Adventurous Experiment

The subimperial pretensions of Saudi Arabia have been very visible in the Syrian war. The monarchy headed the support for the jihadists in their effort to topple Assad, and its criminal regime is the principal referent of the fundamentalists. The kingdom disputes hegemony with Iran, invoking a long-standing clash between Sunnis and Shias that cost a million deaths in the Iraq-Iran war. It does not tolerate the preeminence achieved by its adversaries in the governments that succeeded Saddam Hussein. It also demands the subjection of all the Shiite inhabitants of the Arabian Peninsula who led the Arab Spring protests (Jahanpour, 2014).

To establish itself as a subimperial power, the Saudis have acted with great military autonomy, first in Bahrein and then in Yemen. They have led an atrocious escalation of massacres in that strategic enclave. They take advantage of the important collaboration of England and France, but they have developed the bulk of their military operations on their own.

Following a basic principle for a subempire, Saudi Arabia maintains a close association with the Pentagon. It is an important customer for arms, and its financial power helps bolster the dollar as world currency. However, after many years of managing colossal rents, the monarchs have built their own power, generating multiple conflicts with Washington. Oil is one area of controversy – the United States increased its internal supply, reduced its dependence on outside providers, and uses the low price of oil as an instrument to pressure Russia and Iran, all of which affects the Saudis' business. The monarchs have responded with some ambivalence. On the one hand, they sought the fall in the price of oil in order to obstruct the vulnerable profitability of U.S. production (shale extraction). But they also prioritized convergence with the United States to discipline OPEC and weaken Teheran. Their new subimperial ambitions are fed by this management of oil resources.

The key milestone in the Saudis' consolidation of its own force has been its patronage of the jihadis. The monarchs protect and finance a variety of terrorist groups that destabilize the West. Those organizations perfect Taliban terrorism, which the United States fomented several decades ago to expel the Soviet Union from Afghanistan. They form networks that the Western powers use to destroy adversarial regimes in the Arab world and have served to bury the vestiges of secularism and cultural modernization that were sprouting in those societies.

However, the fundamentalists ended up forging a cross-border force that feeds into the hatred caused by imperialist destruction. They promise social regeneration founded on strict rules of religious authenticity. Those principles include getting to paradise through suicidal immolation. Following the example of Bin Laden, distinct groups tend to develop autonomous actions that escape the control of their creators.

Saudi Arabia protects those organizations to underpin its hegemonic goals. But the future of the kingdom is very uncertain. Some State Department strategists are considering the usefulness of ending fundamentalism by neutralizing the Saudi monarchy. They even promote the balkanization of Saudi Arabia, in order to turn that country into a collection of powerless mini-states (Katz, 2017). The sheiks guarantee the crushing of the secular adversaries of the West, but their retrograde regime damages alliances with liberal-conservative variants that are more subordinate to the United States. This conflict shows the potential tension caused by the subimperial evolution of the Saudis (Petras, 2014).

3   An Uncertain Reconstitution

Iran demonstrates the changing status of subimperialism. Marini included that country in his classification when Shah Palevi acted as a regional power against the Soviet Union, in partnership with the Pentagon. The theocratic regime that replaced the monarchy not only stopped exercising those functions; it clashed sharply with the United States. Its recent intervention in Syria reaffirms that confrontation, and also illustrates how the Ayatollahs shore up the Assad regime to reinforce their dominance in Iraq and counteract Saudi aggression in Yemen. They take part in these conflicts with arms, advisors, and some deployment of regular forces. Their regional ambition can be seen in their recruitment of Shiites to dispute leadership with their Sunni adversaries throughout the Arab world (Behrouz, 2017).

Iran negotiates directly with the great powers. It has allowed Russia to use its territory for raids against the jihadis, but keeps open the nuclear negotiations initiated by Obama. After several decades of economic isolation, the regime accepts partial disarmament in exchange for Western investment. It plays a leading role in the gas pipelines designed by oil companies (Armanian, 2016). The privileged partners of Iranian capitalism will be determined in the intense internal battle between the pro-Western wing (Rohani) and the traditionalists (Khomeini). They all seek to defuse reformist discontent, which threatens the supremacy of the theologians and the military in the administration of the government.

The United States tried to destroy Iran by war, sabotage, and embargos. Obama tried a turn to negotiation, but the course of those negotiations is uncertain. Everyone is aware of Iran's potential ability to reconstitute its influence as a great subimperial player. The rivalry maintained in those terms by Turkey, Saudi Arabia, and Iran does not extend to other countries like Egypt, whose ambitions were watered down by a series of defeats by Israel. Those frustrations led to a total subjection to the State Department.

The Middle East is an area of subimperial tensions because of the continued predominance of unstable societies. All the countries shoulder the frustrations generated by the failure of secular modernization. Autocratic military powers associated with the business world persist, using religion to legitimate their domination (Amin, 2011b: 201–216). In this context, the traditional subempires (Turkey), the new ones (Saudis), and those in recomposition (Iran) dispute supremacy. The United States makes use of those conflicts, periodically backing one sub-power against another. It seeks to wear down all of them in order to maintain a balance of power. In this Machiavellian action, central imperialism remodels its own control over allies and rivals.

4   Co imperial Appendages

Among the partners of the United States that develop their own interests, Israel was classified by Marini as a subempire. Although it certainly exhibits many features of that type, it has more similarities with the countries organically integrated into collective imperialism. This last group operates as a direct prolongation of the centers, and should be assigned another designation. More than partners, they are appendages of that structure.

The mutual understanding of those countries with their big brothers has led to identifying them as "external provinces" of the United States (Amin, 2013b), "secondary imperialisms" (Bond, 2015: 15–16), or "mini-empires" (Petras, 2014). This role likens Israel to Canada and Australia. In all three cases, a contemporary adaptation of imperial behavior prevails. They are not old powers subordinated to the leader in a silent (England) or conflictive (France) way; nor have they gone through previous experiences of global ambition (Germany, Japan) or colonialist preeminence (Spain, Portugal, Holland).

Israel, Canada, and Australia occupy a key place in the maintenance of the global order. Because of their complete integration with the Pentagon and NATO, they are not part of the subimperial conglomeration. In terms of economic coordination as well as political action and military coercion, the three countries act more as extensions than as associates of the United States. They represent states that never displayed great autonomy and were never involved in the conflicts that characterize subempires. They design their actions in agreement with their leader and guarantee, on a regional scale, the same interests the United States ensures on a global scale.

Their articulation with U.S. power has a historical foundation in the shared legacy of societies created by white-skinned colonizers. They share the same inheritance of racism, extermination of original peoples, land occupation, and Eurocentric ideological prejudices. That affinity of Israel, Canada, and Australia facilitates a predominance of explicitly pro-Western policies, which is not found in Turkey, Saudi Arabia, or Iran.

For these reasons, Israel does not fulfill equivalent functions in the Middle East as its competitors. It acts as an exponent of the Zionist lobby, directly connected to the U.S. state apparatus. This qualitative difference separates it from other U.S. partners in the region. While Turkey has NATO bases, Egypt is a major recipient of U.S. arms, and Saudi Arabia provides key financial support for the U.S. dollar, Israel has privileges that the top power does not extend to any other ally.

The origin of that preferential treatment is the alignment of the United States with Israel's late colonialism, which recreates all the mechanisms of Western oppression. It practices territorial annexation, exclusionary democracy, expulsion of the indigenous population, and the creation of a mass of refugees. In the name of historical reparation for the Holocaust, it exercises state terrorism in the occupied territories (Katz, 2007).

Israeli integration with U.S. power was established after several wars with its Arab neighbors. Israel also has recurrent conflicts with the State Department. Zionist warmongering ensures imperial control in the region, but gets in the way of flexibility for U.S. foreign policy. It destroys potential markets and alliances, compels additional wars, and creates problems in the handling of oil policy. These tensions reached a critical point toward the end of the Obama administration when, in alliance with the Republicans, Netanyahu challenged the Iran agreement in unprecedented terms. Israel now attempts the complete capture of the West Bank to eliminate the farce of the two-state solution, and with this objective it encouraged the destruction of a Syrian adversary that harbored the Palestinians. The Israeli government will not accept losing its regional atomic monopoly in the face of the installations built by the Ayatollahs, and it boycotts the agreement signed to dismantle those structures.

Will those tensions modify the status of Israel? Will its role as a U.S. appendage be replaced by one more similar to the subempires? This is a possibility that derives from the changing character of those configurations. Iran is an example of those mutations. However, the trajectory of Israel would seem to lead the country to permanence in its condition of imperial extension.

5   Contrasting Situations

Australia is another case of total integration with the central powers. Some studies use the term "co-imperialist" to define this position (Democratic, 2001).

It has developed this function since it lent its services to Great Britain to block the entrance of rivals (Germany and Japan, France) to a remote area of the Pacific. Later, Australia recreated all the forms of traditional imperialism. It established the primacy of military action, chauvinism, and racist ideology. That oppressive heritage allowed it to join with U.S. military policy and play a counterrevolutionary role in Korea, China, Vietnam, and Indonesia. In recent years, it has taken on a policing role in Timor and facilitated the initiatives taken there by the United States in detriment to Portugal.

In that role of imperial guardian, Australia also strengthened the presence of its own companies. It exported capital and became a great architect of capitalism in the Pacific. In the last decade, it underwent another transition and resumed its specialization in the export of the minerals required for Asian industrialization. This succession of changes was carried out while remodeling its co-imperial status. Canada is a similar case of a high level of participation in foreign military incursions, and its companies have also established a strong integration with those of the United States. The corollary of those business relations has been greater adherence to the dictates of the Pentagon. Israel, Australia, and Canada do not, therefore, conform to the meaning Marini ascribed to subimperialism. The application of that concept could, though, be extended to India, which plays a similar role to Turkey in its sphere of influence and maintains an analogous relation of association, autonomy, and dependence with the United States.

India's placement in the subimperial category is consistent with the regional omnipresence of its army. It actively intervenes in the turmoil in Sri Lanka, in the tensions in Bangladesh, and in conflicts with Nepal, and its armed forces continue to act in Kashmir after four wars with Pakistan. That same presence is found in its border disputes with China; after the military clash of 1962, the future of Tibet remains indeterminate. The army also plays a central role against the Taliban's wave of terror in a context of great oppression against the Muslim minorities. The subimperial profile of India can be seen in the changing views of its ruling classes. They adopted the neoliberal creed after the collapse of the Soviet Union, and took advantage of the complicity of the Pakistani army with the Taliban to shore up their alignment with the United States.

India's huge geopolitical protagonism differentiates it from other semiperipheral economies. Its expansive regional pretensions are corroborated on the level of ideology and religion (Morales, 2013). India and Turkey illustrate models of subimperialism that are not applicable to Israel, Canada, or Australia.

6   Peculiarities of Another Power

It is intuitively evident that Russia differs from the subempires – it is not placed in that category even by those who emphasize that feature of the BRICS. Everyone perceives that it is a configuration of another sort. Russia does not play the role of complementary gendarme that characterizes subempires. It is a military power in continual conflict with the United States. In addition, over the greater part of the 20th century it was at the center of a non-capitalist system that was conflictive with any mode of contemporary imperialism.

Russia's international economic insertion is vulnerable (Dzarazov, 2015). Its economy is based on extractivism and extensive exploitation of natural resources, and it has not overcome the demographic crisis and industrial stagnation that followed the collapse of the Soviet Union. It exports raw materials and maintains an industrial base that is not very competitive. The oligarchs who have taken over state properties invest little, speculate in financial markets, and protect a large portion of their fortunes outside the country.

After the devastating experience of extreme neoliberalism led by Yeltsin, capitalist restoration was remodeled under authoritarian leadership. Putin reintroduced state control, limited the plunder, and recovered the country's military capacity. That recovery included the revival of Russian patriotism and a return to patronage over the border zones (Presumey, 2014). The collapse of the Soviet Union precipitated the separation of the 14 non-Russian republics and the resurgence of conflicts with another 21 nations, which occupy 30 percent of the territory. The permanence of that region under the aegis of Moscow is the geopolitical priority of the Kremlin. That control was rekindled while facing the harsh pressure of the West. With the second Chechnya war (2000), the military response in Georgia (2008), and the reintegration of Crimea (2014), Putin curbed the U.S. pretension to converting Russia into a vassal state.

This defensive attitude toward imperialism, together with an aggressive behavior toward its neighbors, explains the peculiar foreign positioning of Russia. It resembles the subempires in its search for regional supremacy, but the harassment it faces from the United States separates it from that condition. Russia combines the protection of its borders with an ambition to forge its own structure of domination. That contradiction differs from the dilemmas faced by Turkey, Saudi Arabia, or India. Russia does not maintain a relation of association and autonomy with the United States, but rather a far-reaching structural tension. Thus, it does not fit the subimperial category. The ruling classes aspire to a more significant status, in spite of the embryonic character of that desire.

7   Empire in Formation

The formula that best fits the current profile of Russia is empire in formation. This implies the preeminence of a very incomplete and provisional process. Other designations could be used, such as semi-empire, pre-empire, or proto-empire. The latter concept alludes to a formation that is already contained within the current structure; it is similar to proto-industrialization (rural hand-icraft), which precedes manufacture in the debut of capitalism.

Some analysts argue that Russia is already an empire that behaves as a great power in its conflicts with its rivals (Pozo-Martin, 2015: 207–219). But they fail to recognize that it is not a confrontation between equals. There is a huge difference of power between Russia and its Western rivals. The description of the country as an established empire highlights a history of internal colonization, in both the feudal and Soviet eras as well as in the current period (Kowalewki, 2014). However, it is problematic to assert that Russia is an empire because it has been so previously. This ignores the enormous mutations that have occurred over so many centuries. It is especially problematic to assume that this pattern of imperialist continuity endured over 70 years of a non-capitalist regime. With this criterion, the definition of that status in relation to the social regimes present at each moment is diluted. It is not clear what interpretation of imperialism can draw an equivalency between the czarist, Soviet, and contemporary empires.

On the opposite side, there are characterizations that consider Russia to be a beacon of contemporary anti-imperialism (Escobar, 2014). This approach tends to include praise for Putin as the clear leader of resistance to the United States. It repeats the logic of the old communist orthodoxy, forgetting that the Soviet Union disappeared. Russia is now governed by capitalists who prioritize their own welfare. It faces tensions with the United States from the perspective of a fledgling oppressive power.

Being an enemy of the United States does not make the Russian government a defender of the dispossessed. It is completely valid to focus resistance on the main enemy, but it is ingenuous to glorify a nascent empire. To compare Russia to the United States is as mistaken as it is to contrast them by imagining definitive antagonisms between capitalist formations. One empire in formation and another that is dominant are not equals, but neither are they located on opposite poles.

The status of Russia is made clearer by analyzing its relation with the central powers and its region. Lenin's criteria from the early 20th century do not resolve that problem, and its schematic application leads to abstract reasoning. Some authors assert, for example, that Russia is not imperialist because of the reduced role of its international banks and capital exports (Annis, 2014). Others claim that it is imperialist due to the influence of its monopolies and foreign investments (Slee, 2014). But the Bolshevik leader used these types of parameters to define the peculiarities of a stage of capitalism. His intention was not to classify countries. With classifications so attached to these characteristics, a power from the last century as battle-hardened as Japan would be excluded from the imperial club.

Russia acts as an empire in formation. Its behavior in the recent conflict in Ukraine confirms this profile. The United States took advantage of the wave of protests against the autocratic government of that country to promote the right-wing takeover of the revolt and incite a coup. It intended to turn Ukraine into a satellite of NATO in order to fortify the circle of missiles it had established in Poland, Estonia, Latvia, and Lithuania (Rozhin, 2015). Putin responded with the assimilation of Crimea, and supported the resistance in Eastern Ukraine (Donetsk) against the reactionary government in Kiev. However, he blocked the autonomous and radical actions of those rebels (Kagarlitsky, 2015).

What happened there illustrated how Obama tried to debilitate Russia in order to break any autonomous alliance with Europe. It also showed how Putin resisted that encroachment to reconstruct the country's regional hegemony. The State Department made use of its agents in Kiev, and the Kremlin responded with shows of force in Crimea and Syria. Both central imperialism and its rival in formation confirmed their nature in those battles.

8   Another Variant in Formation

China could also be characterized as an empire in formation. That status can be corroborated by observing how its passage from a bureaucratic to a capitalist regime has modified its foreign policy. It is now a power embarked on projects of global reach (Rousset, 2014). Because of this global (not merely regional) character of the Asian giant's strategy, it is accurate to reject its classification within the subimperial conglomeration (Luce, 2015: 38–39). Application of that concept is inadequate in this case because of the structural tension it maintains with the United States. In that sense, it is similar to Russia and different from Turkey or India. The Eastern power is not a member of NATO, but rather is subjected to the Pentagon's hostility. It is not a part of the current imperial order, but a rival of that structure. Thus, its profile is that of an empire in formation rather than another link in the subimperial circuit.

In spite of its dazzling economic presence, the weight of its exports, and the magnitude of its foreign investment, China is not yet an imperial power.

In some regions, like Africa, it appropriates natural resources and indebts the insolvent economies, but it does not act as an empire. Some analysts argue that it will repeat the trajectory of Japan and Germany, which in the past sought external solutions to its difficulties with internal growth (Dockés, 2013: 131–152). However, this view does not take into account the inverse path that China has followed. It deepened its global expansion by means of prior integration into globalization. This model was not in force in the early 20th century. Japan and Germany competed with the United States and England without sharing economic associations with their rivals.

China is a player in globalization, but the geopolitical-military element of imperialism found in the case of Russia is little developed. It has the second highest GDP on the planet, is first in the manufacture of industrial products, and receives the largest volume of funds in the world. But this economic weight does not have a military correlate.

The Eastern giant has shortcomings in the modernization of its armed forces, and does not participate in military alliances or have bases in other countries. Its colonial past is still felt in the separation of Taiwan and the partial reintegration of Hong Kong (Loong Yu, 2015). Until now, the emerging Asian power has employed defensive strategies, especially in its principal supply route (the China Sea). Unlike Russia, it does not practice military responses (like those in Georgia or Syria) in the face of U.S. aggression. It keeps a low profile and avoids confrontations. That self-restraint coincides with the cultural profile of a giant who arrived late to the world market; with a language of purely internal use, it is limited to copying transnational corporate management.

However, its foreign policy bears no relation to the angelical image of a power devoted to forging equitable international relations (Escobar, 2015). This view omits the fact that the country acts with capitalist parameters that exclude equity and cooperation. China did not invent a benevolent capitalism, nor does it intend to recuperate its past primacy of the first millennium. It is expanding under the rules of capitalist oppression, which did not exist in that long-ago era.

The combination of economic preeminence and geopolitical limitations faced by China gives rise to different prognoses. Some think that it will continue its rise, strengthening its alliance with Russia to take advantage of Western decline (Zibechi, 2014). Others argue that China is already very integrated into the global economy and will continue to accumulate dollars or Treasury Bonds to support its export model (Hung, 2015: 196–201). But as a power that cannot replace the United States, it must deal with the tensions of an economic integration undercut by political rivalries. The vacillations of the U.S. establishment with respect to China illustrate the confusion caused by this indetermination of China's way forward. The imperial status of the country is an unknown of the same type.

9   Is Brazil Subimperial Today?

Brazil was Marini's main model for characterizing subempires. Does this concept fit its present reality? There is no doubt that the country maintains its condition of intermediate economy, in light of the size and importance of its markets. In 2005 it replaced Mexico as the largest economy of the region, and in absolute terms its GDP is the sixth largest in the world. Its impact can also be seen in the role of its multinationals. There are 11 Brazilian companies among the 100 largest on a world scale, and their foreign investments passed from 1.1 percent of the global total in 1970 to 2.3 percent in 2006. The large companies have specialized in natural resources (Gerdau, Vale, Petrobras, Votorantim), construction (Odebrecht, Andrade Gutiérrez), and engineering (Marcopolo, Sabó, Embraer, WEG, Tigre). They have been supported by a big state bank (BNDES) and have had a better performance than their counterparts in Argentina or Mexico (Bueno and Seabra, 2010).

However, the current Brazilian economy differs from the profile it had in the 1960s and 1970s. In recent decades, specialization in basic exports has reappeared, together with a significant decline of industry. That regression coexists with the growing indebtedness of the state. Banks and agribusiness have recovered primacy from the industrialists in the ruling class bloc. Brazil has lost the aura of a rising industrial economy. Asian countries, transformed into the world's workshops, have taken over that image. Brazil's industrial decline is very relevant for the subimperial diagnosis in Marini's terms. The Marxist dependency theorist ascribed that condition to external meddling derived from the rise of industry. If that sector declines, in his view, the status of the country must be reevaluated.

In our updating, the economic dimension is not as relevant as the geopolitical role in characterizing a subempire. Brazil has established its international relevance on that level: it is part of the BRICS, it operates as the main intermediary in any regional crisis, it is the prioritized interlocutor of the State Department, and it aspires to a seat on the United Nations Security Council. However, it has also demonstrated the ambivalence of its governments about leading processes of economic integration and the formation of regional blocs. In recent decades, all of its presidents have vacillated between two strategies, without clearly establishing either one – they have not progressed in either their own multilateral insertion or in leading an autonomous South American presence. Doubts about the former strategy led them to put the brakes on the promotion of a common currency in the region, block the implementation of the *Banco del Sur* (Bank of the South), and thwart the coordinated management of the region's accumulated reserves. MERCOSUR was formally promoted without any practical accompaniment. Proclamations were abundant, but effective initiatives were not.

As Brazil's agro-export expansion was sold largely outside the region, interest in the rest of the world, rather than in South America, prevailed. More attention was paid to the BRICS Bank than to the *Banco del Sur*, and participation in the portfolio of the International Monetary Fund increased at the cost of Latin American financial articulation. This divorce between global and regional interests diminished the country's geopolitical profile.

Compared to Marini's era, Brazil has strengthened its autonomy from the United States. It participates in organizations, such as UNASUR and CELAC, that are far from the traditional subjection of the Organization of American States (OAS). But this broadening of autonomous action does not translate into subimperial actions. Brazil's ambiguity can be seen in the military sphere. Its governments have chosen to rearm in order to protect natural resources; they have modernized ships, airplanes, and detection systems to guard the borders and protect the Amazon. But they have entered into only one foreign incursion, with the occupation of Haiti, which they coordinated with the United States to fulfill the same policing functions earlier exercised by the Marines. Far from providing humanitarian aid, they contained uprisings and ensured the semi-colonial order.

The reactionary character of that invasion is clear, but its subimperial nature is not. Brazil led a Latin American squad composed of countries like Uruguay, which no one places in that category. Subimperialism is not defined by simple participation in international operations to protect the capitalist order. Certainly, Brazil heads the legion that intervenes in Haiti, but Marini did not characterize subimperialism by military presence in actions originating in the Pentagon, which is why he did not apply the term to the Brazilian intervention in World War II. His thesis aimed at highlighting specific actions of the ruling class to reinforce the profits of the multinationals. This characterization applies only very partially to the case of Haiti.

Brazil's space for implementing subimperial policies in the present conjuncture is narrow. The removal of Dilma Rousseff was carried out by a triad of corrupt parliamentarians, judges, and media, taking the place of the military in the orchestration of reactionary revolts. They brought to Brazil the new type of "soft coup" that the establishment had previously carried out in Honduras and Paraguay. These para-institutional actions undermine the stability required to implement subimperial strategies. The conservative restoration, marked by total alignment with the State Department, only presages a prolonged period of crisis.

10   Comparisons with Other Cases

If Turkey's level of foreign military intervention is compared to that of Brazil, a huge difference is found between the two countries in terms of interference. Since Turkey offers a model of present-day subimperial intervention, extending this characterization to the South American nation would be forced. The same contrast can be drawn with India. It is worth remembering that Brazil does not have centuries-old traditions of oppression, nor has it undertaken systematic military actions outside its borders. It has maintained a conservative subordination to the world powers without entering into, for example, the sort of adventures that the Argentine military carried out in the Falkland/Malvinas Islands.

In recent decades, the most active gendarme of South America has been Colombia. Under the pretext of combatting drug traffic, the Pentagon installed six bases and trained an armed force that shelters paramilitaries, threatens Venezuela, and spies on all its neighbors. That army, guided by the U.S. Marines and incorporated into NATO, is the principal repressor of the region, but does not represent a subimperial force. It lacks the autonomy needed to act on that level, and it answers to a ruling class with no projects for regional supremacy. Colombia is much farther than Brazil in any classification of subempires.

Brazil's recent evolution has some similarities with that of South Africa. The major economy of Africa developed an active intervention in its neighboring zones over most of the 20th century, to expand the business of companies located in Johannesburg and thwart anti-colonial rebellions. The term subimperialism was used appropriately to describe that strategy of the Apartheid regime. The racist system of internal oppression clearly operated as an external counterrevolutionary force, and exhibited much similarity with military Prussianism as described by Marini (Bond, 2005).

As in Brazil, however, the problem appears when updating that characterization. The subimperial thesis could be maintained if the expansion of South African companies under post-Apartheid neoliberalism is prioritized. The governments of the new period have the blessing of the IMF. They coopted the new Black elites in order to implement regressive policies that magnify social inequality, indebtedness, and the sacking of natural resources from South Africa's neighbors. Financial domination and the predominance of mining companies from Johannesburg are very visible in Congo and Angola (Bond, 2016). Here the analogy with Brazilian transnationals can be seen.

However, the extinction of Apartheid has ended the explicit foreign military intervention of troops from that regime, and lateral incursions like those the Pentagon implements have not persisted. The blatant intervention of French imperialism in its old colonies has no correlate in southern Africa. The legacy of the racist regime impedes South African governments from using explicit military force outside its borders. That curtailment in the margin of foreign military action makes the term "subimperial" little applicable to the major economy of Africa. Like Brazil, South Africa remains only a potential subempire. It does not fulfill that role at the present, confirming the variable character of that category.

11   Controversies over Application

A current subimperial characterization of Brazil stresses the continuing influence of multinational corporations that operate out of São Paulo (Luce, 2015: 29–31). This view notes that during the Workers' Party administration, the large corporations again looked outside the country to compensate for the limitations of local purchasing power. The increase in domestic consumption did not lessen that necessity for foreign markets. The multinationals ventured into profitable businesses in South America, created conflicts in Paraguay and Ecuador, and bought assets in Argentina. Lula and Dilma acted as lobbyists for those companies, perfecting the diplomatic mediation of Itamaraty.

But that expansionism does not signify a subimperial profile. No government of the new century has resorted to military supremacy or explicit geopolitical pressure to support those companies. They appealed to mediation in the conflicts those companies had with the radical governments of Bolivia and Venezuela, an attitude that contrasts with the that of the military governments of Marini's era (Martins, 2011b). The solvency of those companies points to another contrast between the two periods. The expansion of the past has been followed by the deterioration that arose with the Odebrecht crisis. Lula acted as a lawyer for that company in its foreign troubles, and Temer confronts a corruption mega-scandal. Odebrecht used a collapsed system of international bribes to win bids for contracts. Several foreign competitors now want to take over the businesses of Brazil's flagship company. The limitations to sustaining the geopolitical flank of subimperialism start to spread to the economic sphere.

Some authors argue that the structural gap between the two spheres applies historically to Brazil. They assert that Brazil always maintained a presence in the world market that was stronger than its geopolitical weight. They consider this imbalance to have established a hybrid formation that combines features of a privileged semi-colony with characteristics of a dependent semi-metropolis (Arcary, 2016). This characterization is a variant of the intermediate status highlighted by numerous researchers. However, that definition should also consider the new cleavages between the economic sphere and the political-military realm. There has been a strengthening of some countries with strong attributes in the former but not the latter (South Korea), as well as others with exactly the inverse situation (Russia).

It is not easy to pin down the intermediate particularity of Brazil that Marini explored, but that status is very far from the rise of the country to the rank of "new global power" that occupies the vacuum left by U.S. decline (Zibechi, 2015). There is no sector of the Brazilian economy comparable to its counterparts in the United States, Europe, or Japan. Nor is Brazil comparable to any of the empires in formation on the geopolitical or military levels. They do not carry out foreign actions analogous to the military display of Russia in Georgia or Syria, and there is not the slightest sign of comparability with the presence of China in Africa or southern Asia (Sotelo Valencia, 2015b: 70–86). Moreover, putting Brazil in the category of a central power does not fit with any theory of imperialism. The only conceptual foundation would be the post-developmentalist perspective, which associates the rise of new powers with the predatory dynamics of extractivist capitalism. But in that case, the conceptualization of empire again takes on vague connotations disconnected from the logic of accumulation.

12   Reconsideration and Usefulness

What is the usefulness of the concept of subimperialism today? Above all, it helps to understand the hierarchical structure of contemporary capitalism. It shows that at the apex of the system there are central powers, which have acted under the command of the United States, and that at the base there is a great conglomeration of dominated countries. In between the two poles there are distinct formations that operate as appendages, rivals, or autonomous associates of the dominant powers. All these sub-powers seek to establish, from different positions, their regional hegemony.

The appendages to imperialism expand that power in total harmony with Washington's strategies; the empires in formation clash with that center;

and the subempires pursue autonomous actions in coordination or conflict with the metropolises. The subimperial category is particularly appropriate for understanding the state of permanent war that prevails in certain areas to establish regional supremacy. The sub-powers resort to military action to assert their dominance. The Middle East is the main example of these situations; rivalries between Turkey, Saudi Arabia, and Iran can be analyzed in those terms. That competition destabilizes the world order, as shown by the havoc created by the jihadi forces. They generate turmoil that projects back inside the United States and Europe. Terrorism has spread as a consequence of the autonomous action of the subempires.

This chaos is never found in the countries incorporated into the structure of the Pentagon or NATO. This is the case for Israel, Canada, or Australia, which act not as subempires but as extensions of imperialism. The category also does not apply to the major powers in structural conflict with the United States. Russia and China represent empires in formation that act on a global, not just regional, scale. They maintain ties of hostility, not association, with Washington. In these cases, the concept of subempire does not apply. Here, the category serves to illustrate, by contrast, the status of the main adversaries of Western imperialism.

Subempires undergo intense mutations due to their vulnerable insertion in the international division of labor and in the global geopolitical order. Those rises and falls modify their profile. While there are subempires in action (Turkey), recomposition (Iran), or emergence (Saudi Arabia), others do not presently exercise that role (South Africa and Brazil). The absence of large-scale military action beyond their borders determined that transition from effective to potential subempires. The end of Apartheid in the first case, and atomic disarmament in the second, were determinants of the passage from one position to the other.

Subempire offers a useful concept for understanding contemporary reality, but it requires a reinterpretation of the idea, somewhat distant from its original application. This reformulation puts more emphasis on the geopolitical meaning of the concept, in accordance with the major global changes of the last 40 years.

CHAPTER 11

Insights and Problems of the Super-exploitation Concept

Super-exploitation was a central thesis of the dependency theory posited by Marini. He held that the ruling classes of the periphery compensate for their subordinate place in the world market by remunerating labor power below its value. Through this additional suction of surplus value, capitalists sustain their profits and impose lower wages for longer and more intense workdays. Using these mechanisms, they counteract the deterioration of the terms of trade caused by the provision of raw materials and the acquisition of manufactured goods. Since the dominant groups prioritize export businesses, they disregard the low level of popular incomes and the consequent contraction of the domestic market.

Marini attributed the consolidation of this model to the historical overpopulation of Latin America, arguing that the large volume of indigenous labor, reinforced by immigration flows, provided the demographic surpluses needed to underpin super-exploitation (Marini, 1973: 38–49). He proposed this interpretation of underdevelopment in opposition to the liberals, who explained regional backwardness by the failure to exploit comparative advantages and to encourage foreign investment. He also contrasted his approach with that of the Keynesians, who highlighted the low level of state support for industrialization (Marini, 2005: 139–150). Thus, super-exploitation was conceived as a determinant feature of the socio-economic configuration of the region.

1   Logic and Interpretation

Marini's main adversaries at the time objected to this idea, arguing that it is an accidental feature that lacks theoretical significance. They claimed that it expressed primitive forms of absolute surplus value, which was contradicted by the decisive investments in Brazilian industrialization in the 1960s (Cardoso and Serra, 1978). The Marxist theorist responded by clarifying that super-exploitation included increases in productivity, and did not imply simply squeezing more out of the labor force (Marini, 1973: 91–101; 1978: 57–106). He maintained that it constituted a form of relative surplus value in the intermediate economies, and added that industrial modernization occurred in those regions with less cutting-edge investment and more physical impacts on the workers.

Marini highlighted the predominance of this amalgam during the import substitution industrialization period. He analyzed the specificities of wage-labor without projecting his novel concept back to the 19th century. Thus, the application of that idea to semi-capitalist structures like Apartheid, which violated the principles of free movement of workers, is debatable. The Brazilian thinker also emphasized that his theory did not imply stagnationism. Like Marx, he saw the impact of absolute pauperization as limited to specific sectors (Marini, 1973: 81–101). The author of *Capital* located this misfortune mostly among the unemployed during 19th century English industrialization, and Marini in the most vulnerable sectors of the contemporary periphery. Marini's most important interpreter of those years clarified that super-exploitation does not imply a general deterioration of the conditions of life of the workers; it only sought to explain the peculiarities of the work force in the industrialized periphery (Bambirra, 1978: 70–73).

Marini distinguished his thesis from other formulations of extreme oppression of labor. He did not characterize super-exploitation as an additional abuse. He shared their moral indignation against those abuses, but his aim was to explain a feature of dependent economies. For that reason, he did not associate his idea with the Taylorist degradation denounced by investigators of management control. That approach analyzed how management separates conception from realization of tasks to reduce the control of workers over their own activity. Marini pointed in another direction – he sought to explain the conditions of wage-workers in the periphery in close connection with the prevailing logic of underdevelopment in those regions.

2   Compatible Objections

Some theorists shared Marini's theory of dependency without accepting the concept of super-exploitation. They pointed to the incompatibility of capitalism with the generalized remuneration of the labor force below its value (Cueva, 2012: 200). They recalled that Marx had demonstrated how the objective logic of that system ensured the normal reproduction of wage-workers through remunerations set by the labor market. With those wages, the extraction of the surplus labor that creates surplus value is perpetuated.

Cueva stressed that capitalism does not need additional mechanisms to get by, and asserted that the underpayment of wage-workers violated the principles of accumulation. These norms entail the reproduction of the labor force through prices commensurate with the value of that commodity. The violation of those criteria would threaten the very survival of the workers. If they do not receive the goods needed to subsist, they would tend to suffer a deterioration that would undermine the necessary human element of the system. The Ecuadorian sociologist analyzed an antecedent of that type in his investigation of the demographic massacre suffered by Latin America during the primitive de-accumulation of the 19th century (Cueva, 1973: 65–78).

It might be argued that super-exploitation works by other means, through capitalist appropriation of the future years of the worker. That would work through the premature exhaustion of wage-workers' labor capacities (Bueno, 2016: 91–95). However, this type of pressure in fact coexists with an increase in the average lifespan of the workers. The system impedes a substantial reduction of the working day in accordance with increased productivity, but it does not obstruct the normal reproduction of the workers. Capitalism recreates itself in brutal ways, but does not destroy its principal foundation. It is true that a large reserve army provides new bodies to counteract the attrition of workers, but that substitution does not operate purely through replacements of labor contingents, as occurred with the *Mita* in Peru or with colonial-era slavery. Super-exploitation is also defined by deterioration of the socio-historical component of labor power, which does not necessarily affect the biological basis of that resource (Bueno, 2016: 102). But if the first element of socio-cultural improvements confronts permanent and systematic degradation, the workers could not act as the leading force of an emancipation process. They would form a defenseless multitude far removed from the transformative potentials of the oppressed that Marini envisioned.

Cueva criticized Marini's concept while sharing its diagnoses of the dramatic situation faced by Latin American wage-workers. He also indicated that some term referring to those nightmare situations should be used. He therefore asserted that the theoretical inaccuracies of super-exploitation did not invalidate the practical presence of something similar to that category (Cueva, 2012: 200). His disagreement with the concept while drawing closer to Marxist dependency theory opened the way to some important reflections.

3   Low Value of Labor Power

How could Marini's intuition be reformulated without the conceptual problems of super-exploitation? Is there some formulation compatible with both Cueva's objections and the characteristics of the labor force in the dependent economies? The simplest solution is to postulate that a low value of labor power predominates in those regions. This thesis is consistent with Marx's view of the wage as a payment commensurate with the cost of reproduction of the wage-earners. In addition, it recognizes the size of the reserve army and the existence of substantially lower wages in the industrialized periphery.

Several authors have noted that this divergence in remuneration has a historical foundation in productivity gaps (Figueroa, 1986: 113–122). The class struggle modifies average national wages within this differential condition, which structurally separates an underdeveloped region from an advanced one. The values of labor power (and the corresponding consumption baskets) are therefore substantially different. Those wage disparities become stabilized in accordance with two processes: the place occupied by each country in global stratification (center, semi-periphery, or periphery) and its internal level of development (advanced, intermediate, or backward economies). The two dimensions are closely related, but also have some autonomy from each other.

National wages do not constitute fixed and immutable magnitudes. They rise or fall together with the mutations occurring in the international division of labor. Low values of labor power in the periphery are reflected in the extent of poverty, which affects both the precarious and the formal sectors of wage-workers. In the developed economies, the high value of that resource restricts the drama of impoverishment to only the excluded (Portes, 2004: Chapters 1, 4). In both cases, the prices of the labor commodity are established by the capitalist rules of exploitation. In both cases, too, the movement of wages is determined in the long run by objective tendencies (productivities and demographic base), and on a conjunctural basis by the phase of the cycle (prosperity or recession). Workers' action (intensity of the class struggle) defines the final outcome. This pattern of changing and stratified values of labor power (high in the center, low in the periphery, medium in the semi-periphery) requires the use of classical Marxist concepts different from the principles of super-exploitation.

4   Statistical Irresolution

Conceptual controversies over the value of labor power are not resolved by calculations of different national magnitudes. The same is true for the theory of super-exploitation. It is not a fact that can be corroborated with examples of greater suffering on the part of wage-workers in the periphery. Some authors point to the shortening of the working life or the scale of the reserve army as indicators of payment below the value of labor power (Ruiz Acosta,

2013: 5–89). However, that same data could be used as evidence of a low value of labor power. Those parameters illustrate standards of living, not types of remuneration.

Marx never equated the wage with the maintenance of workers at a pure subsistence level. He differed substantially on this with the classical economists. He identified the magnitude of workers' incomes with the time socially necessary for their reproduction, which includes physiological and social components. The former could be measured by levels of food, clothing, and housing, but the latter encompasses rights that have been won by workers as well as the advance of productivity, whose quantification is more complex. There is no strict magnitude of wages that indicates what is required to cover both components – it all depends on the way in which the necessities that constitute the value of labor power are assessed. Which goods are included and which are disregarded? Do these necessities include a car, vacations, and health services?

Using a very demanding criterion that incorporates, for example, free education at all levels, it could be asserted that super-exploitation applies in the United States. The same could be said about Japan, if Western patterns of welfare are taken as the reference point. Using a looser criterion, on the other hand, it could be argued that the burden of super-exploitation does not apply to Bangladesh. In that country, there is an elemental reproduction of labor power through an ultra-basic consumption basket.

The great diversity of national parameters that currently exist for defining patterns of poverty illustrate this statistical complexity. Estimates in Argentina (33.2 percent of the population) put this percentage on the same level as Bolivia (32.7 percent), and above the Latin American average (28.2 percent). The inconsistency of these comparisons shows the extent to which simple measurement does not resolve the problem.

Another example of the same limitation can be found in the recent debate over the continuity, elimination, or worsening of super-exploitation under the government of Lula (Bueno, 2016: 133–136, 205–209). During this administration, unemployment and poverty decreased as the minimum wage rose, but the precariousness and the turnover rate of labor also increased. Opposite conclusions are reached depending on the weight assigned to each of these factors. Super-exploitation therefore lacks any directly mathematical expressions. Physiological and social needs are not defined with models or figures that can be taken as reference points. On the other hand, comparative parameters are useful for assessing high, low, or medium values of labor power. The contrast of national magnitudes indicates relative positions in a ranking of payments equivalent to that required for the reproduction of the workers.

5   The Centrality of Transfers

The classification of differing values of labor power is consistent with interpretations of underdevelopment centered on transfers of surplus value from the periphery to the center. That approach does not situate the cause of the social and economic backwardness of certain countries in super-exploitation. Dussel expressed this view in disagreement with Marini. He drew on the perspective of the Marxist economists (Bauer, Grossman, Rosdolsky, Mandel) who explained how the movement of surplus value from the backward to the advanced economies operates. That drainage is carried out through the prices prevailing in the world market. The concentration of activities that require complex labor, developed technologies, and significant investment in the advanced economies determines that the prices of their products are higher than their values. For example, they exchange one day's work for three from another country, while the inverse occurs with the underdeveloped economies.

These international transfers are qualitatively different from the appropriation of value within each nation. In the latter case, the more concentrated capitals increase their profits at the expense of the more rudimentary, under the rule of national standards of prices, currency, and exchange rates. On a world scale, in contrast, rules that stabilize relations of dependency prevail. Transfers of surplus value between distinct bourgeoisies do not imply any type of exploitation. They represent modes of domination regulated by the need to compete under conditions that are unfavorable for the periphery. The dynamics of the law of value on an international scale cause that redistribution of surplus value in favor of the more advanced economies. Capitalists from the major powers exchange their commodities for more labor than is incorporated in the products they sell.

Marini accepted the importance of that mechanism, but he did not analyze its functioning. In his classic text, he highlighted the centrality of unequal exchange as a determinant of super-exploitation. However, in developing his thesis he ended up attributing greater importance to the latter process than to the former condition (Marini, 1973: 24–37). Dussel questions this analytical shift that turns super-exploitation into the main cause of international imbalances. He asserts that working conditions in the periphery represent an effect, not a cause, of underdevelopment. In his view, Marini confused causes with consequences (Dussel, 1988: 355–357). This argument is compatible with Marxist dependency theory; as with Cueva previously, the correction of mistakes allows the theory to be improved.

By highlighting the role of transfers of surplus value, the logic of dependency is situated within the global dynamics of accumulation. Central and peripheral insertions and dissimilar levels of development are defined in this context. Differences in the value of labor power are consistent with the place occupied by each competitor on the global stage. Marini emphasized the weight of global stratification and deduced from that pyramid the behavior of the Latin American bourgeoisies, who compensated for unfavorable locations with super-exploitation. He did not perceive that this counterbalance would be at most a secondary effect, and not the epicenter of dependency. The correction introduced by Dussel allows us to overcome the over-emphasis on super-exploitation. It also contributes to replacing payment below the value of labor power with payment commensurate with the low value of that resource. With this reformulation, the updating of dependency theory can advance.

6   Dependency without Super-Exploitation

The advantage of formulating a dependency approach without recourse to the concept of super-exploitation is corroborated by Amin's perspective. That view highlights the intrinsic nature of global polarization and the mechanisms of surplus value appropriation used by metropolitan capitalists. He attributes this capture to the convergence of different economic-social formations in a single world market, emphasizing that the dominant and subordinate structures that reproduce global inequality operate at this level. That disparity reinforces the self-centered models of the advanced countries and the disarticulated processes that prevail in the periphery (Amin, 2008: 237–242; 2003: Chapter 4). This characterization underscores how relations of dependency are determined by the polarized structures of the world market, which reinforce the particularities of the labor force in the underdeveloped countries.

Amin explains the extraordinary profits generated by the exploitation of wage-workers in the periphery by the relative immobility of labor, in comparison with the dizzying movement of capital and commodities. Unlike Marini, the Egyptian economist analyzes those singularities of the labor force in the underdeveloped economies without using the concept of super-exploitation. With the exception of some passages referring to unequal exchange, he does not mention this term, nor does he refer to the remuneration of labor power below its value. He only assesses situations caused by wage differences that are higher than productivity gaps, as a result of the greater immobility of labor in the periphery. In his view, migratory flows are not comparable to the more intense movement of money and commodities (Amin, 1973: 67–68).

In explaining the extraordinary profits derived from the disproportion between wages and productivities, Amin establishes a comparative relation between the two poles of the global economy. He finds variable parameters of dependency that are not unique to Latin America or to any other region, and clarifies that status without considering payment of labor power below its value.

7 Variety of Uses

Theorists very close to Marini also developed detailed expositions of dependency theory without using the concept of super-exploitation. They only referred tangentially to that category, to illustrate how the local ruling classes divide the surplus with their foreign partners (Dos Santos, 1978: 320). The dispensable character of the category can also be corroborated by the existence of authors who question or accept the term from strongly anti-dependentist perspectives. In the first case, the idea is challenged on the grounds that it defines the value of labor power in an ahistorical manner, without considering the course of the class struggle (Castañeda and Hett, 1991: 51–66). This objection ignores the fact that Marini's entire career was marked by his commitment to the revolutionary struggle. It presupposes an unimaginable divorce between his theoretical reasoning and social battles, forgetting that Marini formulated his category in close contact with processes of worker resistance in his country. The theoretical problems of super-exploitation do not affect socialist strategy, which Marini promoted in explicit harmony with the Cuban revolution. Paradoxically, Castañeda – who questioned the omission of the class struggle – ended up in open opposition to that principle. As foreign minister of a right-wing government, the Mexican critic regressed from Marxist orthodoxy to a fanatical defense of neoliberalism.

But the reception of super-exploitation was, in fact, quite varied in theories contrary to dependentism. Some perspectives not only approved of the idea, but extended it. In an analysis of the Argentine case, for example, the concept is applied to explain how the accentuated expropriation of the workers exclusively benefits local capitalists. This analysis postulates that local capitalists absorb the bulk of the surplus by means of captures in the opposite direction from the outward flows described by Marini. Rather than drainages, there are inflows of surplus value from the center to the periphery (Iñigo Carrera, 2008: 20).

The disadvantages of this perspective were addressed by the Brazilian theorist in his research on the dependent cycle. What is here corroborated is how a version of super-exploitation can be incorporated into approaches located at the polar opposite of Marini's approach. That concept is not the master key of Marxist dependency theory.

8   Super-exploitation with and without Marx

In some interpretations, payment of labor power below its value is attributed to Marx himself. This application is highlighted in analyses of the exploitation suffered by coolies and slaves in the colonies (Higginbottom, 2012: 253–267). But these references refer to non-wage modes, which are therefore outside the principles of capitalism. Marx investigated the function of those variants in primitive accumulation and in the formation of the world market. However, he concentrated his studies on the English case, in order to reveal the logic of labor prevailing in the contemporary era. In this investigation, he left no doubt about the remuneration of labor power at its value. Rather than exploring the peculiarities of an additional surplus value, the German theorist sought to solve the mystery of a commodity that creates more value than that required for its reproduction.

It is a mistake to suppose that super-exploitation is present in Marx as an immanent law of capitalism (Nascimiento, 2013: 115–127). This reading not only dilutes the logic of surplus value; it also contradicts Marini's own approach, which saw remuneration below value as a specificity of the periphery. In the reinterpretation of the phenomenon, it is presented as an indistinct feature of capitalism. These views tend to identify super-exploitation with a waste of labor power and suggest that capitalism depletes the workers' capacity to labor to the point of exhaustion, neglecting the fact that the wage-worker is not a slave, separated from the market. In fact, these views return to the Proudhonian interpretation of exploitation as theft, disconnected to the objective logic of accumulation.

Other theses trace super-exploitation to Marx with more moderate interpretations. They only describe his treatment of it in his discussion of counteracting forces to the tendency to a falling rate of profit (Smith, 2010: 31–32). But in this case, it refers to a very specific problem that is not comparable to the general logic of surplus value. The authors who highlight the total absence of criteria of super-exploitation in *Capital* offer more accurate assessments (Carcanholo, 2013: 101–104). The reasons for this omission are apparent. Marx sought to clarify the nature of the contemporary economic system, contrasting the profits arising from surplus value with previous forms of enrichment. Those pre-capitalist profits were frequently derived from violation of the exchange of equivalents by means of commercial trickery. In the current system, those types of inequities are secondary.

Some theorists accept the primacy of this treatment in Marx. They emphasize that what is central is not what said or omitted by Marx in *Capital*, but the consistency of those modalities with the functioning of capitalism. However, they also recall that Marx suggested the existence of forms of 'redoubled exploitation' (Osorio, 2013a: 10–20). They recognize that super-exploitation violates the principles on which the system is founded (law of value), but they believe that this negation does not contradict the logic of capitalist development, arguing that the dialectic of development includes those types of transgressions. They also recall that the abstract logic of Volume I of *Capital* takes on other modalities in the concrete forms in Volume III. Payment of labor power at its value in the initial presentation would change to remuneration below that floor in the verifiable reality of wages in the periphery (Osorio, 2013a: 10–20).

But if this violation is taken as a rule, what sense does the theory of value have as the organizing principle of the logic of capitalism? A transgression should be seen at most as an exception. It does not make sense to assume that the theoretical edifice of *Capital* operates in reverse in practice. Dependency is not based on the violation of the law of value, but on its fulfillment. That criterion is decisive in the characterization of labor power, and also provides a guide for resolving old enigmas of Marxist theory, such as the transformation of values into prices.

9   Absence of Fordism

Super-exploitation is sometimes explained by the tightness of markets in the periphery. Its impact on the fragility of consumption as compared to the center is emphasized for two reasons: the workers count more as producers than as purchasers of products, and the bourgeoisies who export primary products realize their profits abroad. For that reason, they sidestep the formation of the massive circuit of consumption that some heterodox theorists call Fordism.

Some authors believe that the principal characteristic of super-exploitation is precisely the use of the consumption fund as a foundation of accumulation (Osorio, 2013a: 10–34). The insignificance of the wage in the realization of surplus value is reflected in the lack of relevant purchases. The workers buy televisions but spend less on health or food, and therefore increase their relative poverty. The insufficiency of the wage obstructs the normal reproduction of labor power (Osorio, 2017: 8–10; 2009: 107–115). This characterization is based on an accurate diagnosis of the severe limitation of purchasing power in the underdeveloped economies. A real chasm separates the United States from Brazil in the normal volume of purchases of the population. Marini noted this difference and described how capitalism incentivizes consumption without allowing its satisfaction. The system itself encourages broadening sales while obstructing its realization by reducing wage costs.

These tensions between production and consumption, which ultimately derive from the class stratification of society, lead to periodic crises. These upheavals, which impede the sale of commodities at prices compatible with expected profits, are more acute in the periphery because of the tightness of markets. The critics of dependency theory object to this view, arguing that low incomes in the popular sectors are not an obstacle to accumulation if capitalists continue to invest. In contrast to Marini, they assert that this expansion of business transforms luxury products into normal purchases and necessary goods for workers (Astarita, 2010a: 55–58). With other arguments, emphatically opposed to any underconsumptionist theory, it is argued that problems of realization are equivalent in the advanced and underdeveloped countries (Valenzuela Feijoo, 1997).

But in fact, Marini never identified the limitations of purchasing power with underconsumption or with economic stagnation. He postulated a multicausal approach to crisis, combining imbalances of realization with the falling rate of profit tendency. In our reading of that same thesis, we have highlighted how the former aspect operates with greater force in the underdeveloped economies, and the latter in the advanced economies (Katz, 2009: 117–119). Recognizing the obstacles to Fordism in the periphery is indispensable for explaining the greater intensity of crisis in the underdeveloped countries. In these regions, what anti-dependentism dismisses is precisely what happens: the tightness of the market leads capitalists to invest less in consumer goods.

Marini accurately noted this enduring contradiction of the peripheral economies. However, he stretched his analysis without noting that this imbalance is not based on super-exploitation. The retraction of consumption is explained by the simple reality of reduction of wages. It does not imply payments below the value of labor power. If remunerations were so insignificant, the fragile circuits of purchases could not even arise. What predominates in those regions is the perpetuation of low incomes that contract the market, periodically stifling self-sustaining development.

10   Where Is Exploitation Greater?

Super-exploitation has also provoked debates over the differentiated levels of subjection suffered by wage-workers in the center and the periphery. Some authors maintain that dependency theory ignores that labor is more productive in the former and loses relevance in the latter (Callinicos, 2001). Others have argued that this approach ignores the existence of higher rates of surplus value in the developed economies (Valenzuela Feijoo, 1997). On the same basis, they assert that growth in the United States, Japan, or Germany depends on the greater productivity of those economies, not on the appropriation of surplus value created in the backward countries (Astarita, 2010a: 109–110). However, Marini always recognized that the rate of surplus value is higher in the center. More significant investments are concentrated there, and there is a greater volume of surplus labor. This diagnosis is also accepted by contemporary proponents of the concept of super-exploitation (Osorio, 2009b: 167–186).

The problem is more complex for another reason. The higher rate of surplus value in the center does not also mean higher profit rates. On the contrary, in the industrialized periphery the profit rate is higher, since the organic composition of capital is lower (labor-intensive techniques) and the same investment yields more significant revenues. Amin highlights in addition the existence of wage differences that are larger than the productivity gaps. When it is asserted that the rate of exploitation is higher in the center, this concept is identified with the extraction of surplus value. But if the appropriation of surplus labor is associated with the level of effort demanded of the worker, that obligation is more onerous in the periphery.

Exploitation therefore presents two meanings that are used to validate one or the other characterization. If it is identified with the magnitude of appropriated labor, it is clearly higher in the more productive economies of the center. If, on the other hand, it is associated with the misery of the wage-workers, the scale of this burden is greater in the underdeveloped countries. The anti-dependentists use the first of these parameters, while some proponents of super-exploitation use the second. In the latter case, it is suggested that the bulk of the surplus value circulating on the planet is created in the periphery (Smith, 2010: 50). But already in the debates of the 1960s, the error of that thesis was demonstrated (Bettelheim, 1972b: 169–174). This same error is rightly questioned today (Mercatante, 2016). In reality, the two phenomena coexist. There is greater productivity in the metropolitan economies, and there are also higher profits in the periphery owing to the brutality of labor conditions. Both processes confirm the postulates of Marxist dependency theory.

11   Current Applications

Debates over super-exploitation are very useful for analyzing the wage gap in the current stage of neoliberal globalization. This analysis requires the introduction of the two corrections we have proposed: on the one hand, replacing the concept of payment of labor power below its value with low remuneration of this resource; on the other, prioritizing international transfers of surplus value in explaining dependency.

These two principles facilitate the interpretation of what has happened over the last three decades of capital's offensive against workers. The Keynesian postwar scenario that Marini analyzed has been totally modified by that international upsurge of labor precarization. The forms of employment have diversified, with more disparity in remunerations and elimination of defined rules for wages. The individualization of incomes has been established, with demands for permanent validation of qualifications and a premeditated disruption of worker solidarity. This aggression segments workers into formal and informal sectors; in the former, the levels of stability required for the continuity of accumulation are maintained, while in the latter, limitless precarization prevails.

Old characterizations based on the contrast between stable working worlds (of the center and the periphery) must be revised. The new framework is marked by the degradation and division of workers at both ends. What implications do these changes have for the value of labor power? This question cannot be settled by observing only what has happened to wage-labor. Another mutation of equal importance has taken place in the international division of labor. On this front, we observe the new weight of transnational corporations that act in the global value chain through the displacement of industry to the East. These changes have radically altered the process and location of production based on the cheapness of labor. To maximize this advantage, transnational corporations geographically divide manufacturing processes, as commodities produced in a given region are acquired on some other part of the planet. This process includes the outsourcing of labor processes to companies that assume part of the risk (and cost) of productive globalization.

The main effect of these transformations is an increase in global disparity. Inequality between nations has grown more rapidly than the gap within countries. The labor force of the underdeveloped economies has a growing importance as a reserve for exploitation. In this context, several of Marini's ideas to explain foreign investment in the periphery regain relevance. The utilization of cheap labor power awakens more hunger for profits than in the past. A plant in Bangladesh promises greater profits than its equivalent in Brazil did forty years ago.

The new international segmentation of production generates the same transfers of surplus value that were analyzed by the dependency theorists. Some researchers maintain that the magnitude of those transfers is not accounted for by current statistical systems based on criteria of aggregation at the national level (Smith, 2010: 34–40). The new global value chain also presents more complex stratifications. The center-periphery polarization is complemented by the introduction of new intermediate categories. How can this scenario be conceptualized in the tradition of Marxist dependency theory?

12   A Tentative Model

The distinction between countries with high (United States, Germany) and low (Philippines, Bangladesh) values of labor power is now mediated by intermediate economies (South Korea, Brazil). This differentiation, which was beginning in Marini's era, has become more visible. The simple contrast between economies using parameters of exploitation and super-exploitation does not capture this diversity; nor does it allow us to see the passage from one status to another.

Segmentation between the formal and informal sectors of wage-workers is a shared feature of all economies. A large income gap separates the two exploited sectors inside each country. These groups in turn maintain structural differences with their equivalents in other places. In the center, the semi-periphery, and the periphery, different modes of surplus value extraction prevail.

In all three types of countries, there is also a sector of impoverished or semi-unemployed workers. The concept of super-exploitation can be applied to this segment, considering that to a certain extent it is remunerated below its value. This situation is observed among the immigrants in the center, the newly-arrived migrants from the countryside in the semi-periphery, and the marginalized urban sectors in the periphery.

The high, medium, or low value of labor power is determined by the degree of internal development and the mode of insertion in the world market of the three types of countries. However, what tends to stabilize that location in the current stage of neoliberal globalization is the function of each economy in the global value chain. That role depends on the weight of transnational corporations and the impact of the new Asian industrialization.

Since transfers of surplus value are determined by the final place of each economy, a country that receives these flows will maintain or achieve a central position. If, on the contrary, it is an emitter of those resources, it will maintain or deepen a peripheral status. In between are economies with limited amounts of both emission and reception of those movements.

Those transfers consolidate or modify the predominance of high, low, or medium values of labor power, according to the magnitude and type of investment prevailing in each country. What defines one national situation with respect to another is the comparative relationship between wages and productivities.

The table 1 below presents different locations of that variation of status using imaginary figures. The value of labor power of the formal (E1), informal (E2), and super-exploited (S) workers of the representative countries of each group is ordered according to the place it occupies in the global value chain (GVC).

The advanced central economies (such as the United States, Germany, or Japan) maintain this position because of their primacy in productive internationalization. The most complex tasks of conception of different activities – for example, the large companies of the new information technology sectors that require highly skilled labor – are concentrated there. The values of labor power are higher in all three segments under consideration. New centers like China have risen to great power status because of their increasing protagonism in the global productive process. Although the value of their labor power is less than in countries that are lower on the global pyramid, the Asian giant has climbed to a higher level by absorbing more surplus value than it transfers outside its borders.

In the semi-peripheries, medium-level values of labor power predominate. However, rising economies of that type (like South Korea) have taken a leap from basic levels to more significant specializations. In the process, they raised the value of their labor power. In contrast, the declining semi-peripheries of the same level (such as Brazil) have undergone industrial regression and a return to an agro-export profile. Thus, they have descended in the ranking of productive globalization, and consequently in the comparative value of their labor power. This contrast between two semi-peripheries is in line with the change

TABLE 1   Value of labor power by type of worker

Place in GVC	Value of labor power		
	E1	E2	S
Advanced center	100	70	30
New center	40	20	10
Rising semi-periphery	60	40	20
Declining semi-periphery	50	30	15
Periphery	20	10	5

Note: GVC = Global Value Chain; E1 = Formal; E2 = Informal; S = Super-exploited.

from the import substitution model to export-oriented industrialization models. The former case favored, in the Keynesian era, the intermediate economies with domestic markets of certain weight (Brazil). The latter strengthened, in the period of neoliberal globalization, nations that had been further behind and that had more sizeable and disciplined labor reserves (Korea).

Finally, countries of the lower periphery (such as Bangladesh or Philippines) with very low values of labor power are incorporated into the lowest rung of the global value chain. That insertion has been possible because of a level of internationalization of transport, communications, and trade that was unimaginable in Marini's era. Unlike the model presented by the Brazilian theorist, this model conceives of super-exploitation as a very limited category, though present in all economies. International disparities persist and grow wider in all the segments. The chasm that separates the super-exploited in the United States from their counterparts in Bangladesh is as significant as the cleavage that distinguishes the exploited of the two countries. This same divergence can be observed in the other situations in the table.

13   Controversies over the Extension of Super-Exploitation

An interpretation that combines the different values of labor power with the dynamics of international transfers of surplus value provides insights into the current determinants of underdevelopment. It provides more elements for reflection than the various generic theses on globalization or neoliberalism. The most radical versions of the latter tend to correctly highlight the capitalist objectives of the current stage, underscoring the purposeful raising of the rate of exploitation through dualization of labor and massification of unemployment. However, these observations do not clarify the way in which the current model reconfigures relations of dependency and the gaps between the advanced and backward economies.

The concept of super-exploitation is used by other analysts to clarify this issue. But the principle of paying labor power below its value creates irresolvable problems. This treatment does not capture the existence of labor markets that are internally segmented, internationally differentiated, and equally marked by the presence of more disadvantaged workers. These difficulties can be seen in the debate over the world-wide extension of super-exploitation. This enlargement was suggested by Marini himself in his later writings. Several authors take up that proposition to underscore how super-exploitation has been generalized in the central countries since the 1990s. They argue that the development of global companies has created common spaces of accumulation that allow them to utilize that under-remuneration of wages as a new instrument of competition. The universalization of poverty, labor informality, and wage stagnation corroborates that change (Martins, 2011a: 293–294, 302–303; 2011b).

This view understands that super-exploitation has extended to the developed countries, as firms increase labor precarization through the diversification of their investments (Sader, 2009: 27–36; 2012). But if super-exploitation has expanded to a universal scale, it no longer represents a mechanism peculiar to dependent capitalism; it has lost the specificity ascribed to it by Marini. That contradiction becomes very visible when it is asserted that the same mechanisms used by the Latin American bourgeoisie to compensate for losses are now implemented by their counterparts in the center. The wages of workers at both poles are said to be equally squeezed to counteract technological lags or productivity problems (Bueno, 2016: 49–56, 66–68). In this version or in similar ones (Santana, 2012: 135–137), the divorce from Marini's thesis is greater. Dependency theory comes to resemble a conception about the new forms of exploitation in the 21st century.

Some followers of the Brazilian theorist perceive this problem, but still argue that super-exploitation has been extended after losing its exclusive location in the dependent economies (Sotelo Valencia, 2013: 78–81). They assert that this constitutive feature of Latin American societies has become an operative fact of the international economy (Sotelo Valencia, 2012: 161–167). They stress that this process is emerging only as a tendency, without noticing that the attenuation of this diagnosis does not reduce the contradiction with Marini's thesis.

To sustain this approach, it is also asserted that the extension of super-exploitation coexists with disparities in purchasing power between the center and the periphery (Sotelo Valencia, 2013: 92–93). But what is the basis of that disparity if wage-workers in both regions suffer the same underpayment of wages? The initial basis of that dissociation gets diluted when it is assumed that workers' incomes in both cases do not cover the normal reproduction of labor power.

The extension of super-exploitation has implications for all the dependentist criticisms of the transnationalist approach, which postulates the complete disappearance of the cleavages between center and periphery. This last viewpoint takes the thesis of the 'third-worldization' of the planet to an extreme. It equates a Mexican *maquila* with a precarious workshop in Los Angeles, overlooking the fact that wages in the two countries still revolve around different national baskets of goods. It does not recognize the persistence of the income gap between the United States and Mexico, which is reflected in the different scales of suffering between the pauperized of the two nations.

Critics of the extension of the concept of super-exploitation underline these contradictions. They recall that it is a category of the dependent economies, and assert that the expansion of its application undermines Marxist dependency theory (Carcanholo, 2013: 108–124). They argue that it compromises the pillars of that conception (Massa, 2013: 83–85). But is it enough to underscore that contradiction? Hasn't neoliberal globalization modified the international structure of the labor market? How should we interpret the growing precarization and segmentation of labor across the planet? These questions, which the extension thesis is unable to answer, are ignored by the opposite view, which emphasizes the inconsistency of its counterpart without offering alternatives. It assumes that Marini's initial thesis still fully applies, avoiding recognition of the extent to which it has been called into question by neoliberal globalization.

Marxist dependency theory provided the key analytical model for revealing the peculiarities of Latin American capitalism. However, it had certain conceptual inaccuracies that it tended to fix with the observations of thinkers who converged with this conception. Super-exploitation is one of the ideas that is corrected with this maturation of dependentism. Its modification replaces the idea of payment of labor power below its value with low remuneration of that resource. This revision not only allows us to resolve old questions about the Latin American case; it also introduces a criterion for interpreting the contemporary diversity of wages. That diversity depends on the place occupied by each economy in the global value chain in the new context of transnational corporations and Asian industrialization. This analysis offers answers to the enigmas of Korean and Chinese development. This revision of the super-exploitation concept is consistent with the primacy ascribed to international transfers of surplus value as the key determinant of underdevelopment.

Similarities and Differences with the Age of Marini

In the last writings of his intense career, the most important theorist of dependency explored the dynamics of globalization. He observed the beginning of a new period based on the internationalized functioning of capitalism (Marini, 1996: 231–252). Some interpreters argue that this research crowned his previous work and inaugurated the study of the political economy of globalization (Martins, 2013: 31–54). This analytical shift confirmed Marini's enormous ability to treat the most relevant process of each conjuncture. His findings anticipated several characteristics of the stage that followed his death. Assessing those observations in light of what has since occurred is a good way to begin to update his theory.

1   Productive Globalization

In the late 1980s, Marini observed that capital was internationalizing in order to increase the surplus value extracted from workers. With this foundation, he analyzed the cheapening of transportation, the growth of new technologies, and the concentration of businesses (Marini, 1993). In particular, he assessed the new manufacturing-export model in the periphery, led by multinational firms that secured common spaces between headquarters and branches to expand their manufacturing process, separated skilled activities from assembly-line work, and profited from national differences between productivities and wages. Marini understood that this mode of operating on a global scale was a structural rather than cyclical trend of accumulation.

That scope is clear today. Globalization introduces a qualitative change in the functioning of capitalism, fostering the liberalization of trade and the adaptation of finance to the instantaneity of information. The Brazilian theorist accurately located the epicenter of this shift in globalized manufacturing, seeing the close connection between internationalization and the pattern of flexible production that replaces Fordism.

Transnational corporations are visible protagonists of the current economic stage, fragmenting their production into a web of intermediate inputs and final goods for export. That strategy operates under principles of high competition, cost reduction, and cheap labor power. The consequent offshoring of production has turned several Asian economies into the new workshop of the planet. Transnational corporations complement their direct investments with subcontracting and outsourcing of labor. Responsibility for worker control and dealing with uncertain demand is unloaded onto their providers. In this way, they spread the risks and increase profits.

Marini only lived through the beginning of that process, and he highlighted its contradictions in very generic terms. He was therefore not able to observe the trade imbalances, financial bubbles, and surplus of commodities that exploded with the crisis of 2008. That shock destabilized the system without reversing productive globalization and temporarily called into question financial deregulation, which in any case was preserved without any relevant change. The recent challenges to trade liberalization (Trump, Brexit) illustrate the reaction of those powers that are losing ground. They try to recover spaces by restoring a certain degree of unilateralism, but they do not seek a return to the old protectionist blocs. The political economy of globalization, which Marini foresaw, persists as an accurate approach to contemporary capitalism.

2   Exploitation and Industrial Remodeling

The importance that the Brazilian theorist ascribed to the increase in the rate of surplus value has been corroborated in recent decades. The employers' offensive dispersed remunerations, eliminated wage regulations, and segmented labor. This reorganization maintains the stability required for the continuity of accumulation in the formal sector and generalizes precarization in the informal world.

The main foundation of globalization is the reduction of labor costs. That is why the incomes of the popular sectors stagnate in times of prosperity and decline in times of crisis. Transnational corporations enrich themselves through low wages in the periphery and the cheapening of the goods consumed by workers in the metropolises. They use offshoring to weaken unions and flatten wages in all regions. Firms especially profit from wage differences resulting from the structural unevenness of overpopulation. Those disparities are stabilized by the lack of international mobility of labor. While in the early period of globalization (1980–1998) foreign investment tripled, the total of migrants hardly varied (Smith, 2010: 88–89). The labor force is marginalized from all the whirlwind of movement that drives globalization.

Marini noted the first shift of industry to the East with the emergence of the so-called 'Asian tigers' (Taiwan, Hong Kong, South Korea, and Singapore), but he did not see the later mutation that completely changed the industrial map. China is currently the epicenter of a growing installation of subsidiaries in

Asia. The bulk of world production is generated there. Wages oscillate between 10 and 15 percent of those in the West for equivalent jobs.

The magnitude of the change can be seen in U.S. consumption of manufactured goods. One third of that total is currently produced outside the country, doubling the average from 1980 (Smith, 2010: 153–154, 222–227). It is clear that the foundation of neoliberal globalization is found in the exploitation of workers. Investments relocate to the countries that offer lower costs and greater discipline and productivity of the workforce.

Marini also perceived how the import substitution model (which inspired his dependency analysis) was being replaced by a new pattern of manufactured exports. But he was only able to see the generic features of a model that has been reconfigured by global value chains (GVCs). Through the modality of GVCs, the entire process of production is fragmented in accordance with the comparative profitability offered by each activity, including linkages directed by the manufacturer (aeronautical, automotive, and information technology firms) or commanded by the buyer (commercial emporiums like Nike, Reebok, or The Gap) (Gereffi, 2001). The companies that lead these structures not only control the most profitable resources (brands, designs, technologies); they also dominate 80 percent of world trade in these circuits.

This differs radically from the model prevailing in the 1960s and 1970s. Instead of integrated processes, the subdivision of parts predominates, and national manufacturing is replaced by the assembly of imported components. The proximity and size of markets loses relevance vis-à-vis the comparative advantages of the labor cost. A new global division of labor (GDL) replaces its international precursor (IDL) (Martínez Peinado, 2012: 1–26). In the activity of transnational corporations, the importance of intermediate goods is multiplied through linking and mechanisms of industrial vertical integration (Milberg, 2014: 151–155). These modalities introduce forms of export management that were unknown at the end of the last century.

3   The Crisis of Capitalism

Marini analyzed the economics of globalization believing that capitalism had entered into a long cycle of growth. It was in this context that he situated productive specializations and the emergence of the Asian newly industrializing countries (NICs). He believed that regional integration processes were on the rise in order to broaden the scale of markets (Marini, 1993). His dependentist colleague shared this logic, investigating the impact of new technologies on long waves (Dos Santos, 2011: 127–134).

The subsequent course of globalization neither confirmed nor denied the presence of that long-term upward cycle. Controversies among those who postulate the existence of those movements and those who deny them did not end in any clear conclusions. For that reason, we have emphasized the need to clarify the qualitative transformations of this stage, without forcing the conformity of that period to a long wave (Katz, 2016: 366–368).

Marini framed his assessment in Marxist characterizations that underscored the disruptive nature of accumulation. He emphasized the traumatic potential crises that globalization was incubating and highlighted the presence of simultaneous tensions in the spheres of demand (decreased consumption) and valorization (insufficient profitability). He emphasized both imbalances, with more observations on the former (demand) type of contradiction.

Those shocks have come to light in recent decades. The explosive setback of employment has also been verified, driven by the relative immobility of labor in the face of the vertiginous movement of commodities and capital. That contradiction distinguishes present-day globalization from the old European industrialization. Between 1850 and 1920, more than 70 million emigrants abandoned the Old Continent; that massive relocation drained the surplus population at one pole and generated new centers of accumulation in the regions that received the workers. An equivalent demographic movement today would imply the entry of 800 million immigrants in the central countries (Smith, 2010: 105–110). But today's unprotected workers are denied that movement – the developed economies build fortresses against the dispossessed of the periphery and only absorb irrelevant contingents of skilled labor. The escape valve that in the past drove the very process of accumulation has been vastly diminished. Countries that have concluded their primitive accumulation processes in an accelerated form cannot unload their surplus population on other localities.

That restriction fosters other tensions of capitalism, like the destruction of employment due to the expansion of the digital world. Parameters of profitability, which guide the introduction of new technologies, impose a dramatic elimination of jobs. Unemployment greatly increases with globalization. At this stage, there is less work for all than in the preceding phases. Available jobs shrink and their quality is going down in the underdeveloped regions, which is why the informal economy (lacking state regulations) accounts for 50 percent of labor activity in Latin America, 48 percent in the north of Africa, and 65 percent in Asia (Smith, 2010: 115–127). Accelerated automation and the expulsion of the agrarian population due to new technologies in the countryside drastically reduce employment opportunities. Capitalism based on exploitation, so well analyzed by Marini, cannot even apply this affliction to the entire oppressed population.

4   Imperial Reformulations

The Brazilian theorist emphasized the weight of imperialism and the inescapable function of that system of military domination for the preservation of capitalism. However, he wrote in a period that was very far from Lenin's era. He understood that the Cold War was qualitatively different from the old conflicts between powers, and pointed to the unprecedented military supremacy of the United States. He noted the ability of that empire to forge subaltern alliances, subordinating its rivals without destroying them.

Marini avoided drawing parallels with classical imperialism. He understood the novelty of a period marked by reduced protectionism, postwar recovery of industrial protagonism, and reorientation of foreign investment toward the developed economies. He synthesized those transformations with an idea (hegemonic cooperation) that he used to define the relations prevailing among the central powers (Marini, 1991: 31–32).

The current context presents several continuities with that characterization. The framework forged around the Triad (United States, Europe, and Japan) continues to ensure military stewardship of the neoliberal order. That military alliance has already caused the devastation of numerous regions of Africa and the Middle East. The primary role of the Pentagon in directing the major military actions also persists. However, U.S. hegemony has lost the forcefulness it exhibited in the 1980s and 1990s at the onset of globalization.

The United States played a key economic role in launching this process. It provided the state connection needed to propagate accumulation on a world scale. The Washington-based institutions internationalized financial instruments and fomented productive globalization. They continued these actions with greater intensity in the aftermath of the crises of the past decades. Banking regulation by the Federal Reserve, the dollar as world currency, reorganization of state budgets under the supervision of the IMF, and Wall Street's stock market rules all strengthened globalization. That influence was again conspicuous in the aftermath of the 2008 crisis.

However, the decline of U.S. supremacy is currently corroborated by that country's trade deficit and foreign debt. The United States retains the management of the major transnational banks and corporations and leads in the introduction of new digital technologies, but is has lost key positions in production and commerce. Its boosting of globalization ended up favoring China, which has become an unexpected global competitor. The arrival of Trump illustrates that retreat; the tycoon tries to recover U.S. positions by rearranging free trade agreements, but faces enormous difficulties in his effort to rebuild economic leadership.

On the military front, the United States still prevails, and replacements for stewardship of the capitalist order are lacking. Yet it fails in the operations undertaken to sustain its hegemony. That ineffectiveness is evident from the failures of all its recent wars (Afghanistan, Iraq, Syria). For these reasons, the relations of the primary power with its partners have changed. The total subordination that Marini witnessed has mutated toward more complex relationships. The European (Germany) and Asian (Japan) powers no longer accept orders from Washington with the same submissiveness; they develop their own strategies and openly express their conflicts with the North American giant (A. Smith, 2014).

No partner challenges the supremacy of the Pentagon or attempts to build a competing military power, but the vassalage of the second half of the 20th century has lessened. This trend is consistent with the inability of the United States to maintain the patronage it displayed over the other capitalist economies in the postwar period (Carroll, 2012). Whether, in the future, Yankee leadership disappears, revives, or gradually dissolves remains to be seen. This uncertainty is a factor that was absent when *Dialectic of Dependency* was published in 1973.

5   The Collapse of the USSR and the Rise of China

The implosion of the Soviet Union and the conversion of China into a central power distinguish the current period from Marini's era. With the collapse of the USSR, the neoliberal offensive was strengthened. The ruling classes regained confidence and, in the absence of international counterweights, resumed the typical outrages of unbridled capitalism. The Brazilian theorist was a Marxist who was critical of the Kremlin bureaucracy. He was committed to socialist renewal, not the fall of the Soviet Union. The regression of Russia to a capitalist regime, in a context of popular immobility, depoliticization, and apathy, transformed the scenario envisaged by the Latin American fighter.

The second turnaround has been equally striking. Marini could not even imagine that the takeoff of Taiwan and South Korea anticipated the transformation of China. The per capita GDP of that country grew 22 times larger from 1980 to 2011, and its trade volume doubles every four years. China not only maintained very high growth rates in conjunctures of international crisis; the help it provided to the dollar (and euro) prevented the recession of 2009 from turning into global depression. The scale of the historical change underway is comparable to the steam revolution in England, the industrialization of the United States, and the initial development of the Soviet Union. No other BRICS country has a level of prosperity comparable to the conversion of China into a central power. It is enough to observe its dominant role as investor, exporter, importer, or creditor of the major countries of Africa or Latin America to measure the enormous gap that separates the Asian giant from its former peers in the Third World.

The new power does not share simple relations of cooperation with its counterparts in the South; it exercises a clear supremacy that extends to its neighbors in the East. No other economy has transformed its position in the global order so radically. China acts as an empire in formation that faces the strategic hostility of the Pentagon. It is forging its own capitalist model through a novel relation to globalization. It does not pass through the old stages of initial takeoff based on the domestic market. It deploys a process of accumulation directly connected to globalization. To elucidate the specificity of its capitalism, we must resort to characterizations that were absent in Marini's time. The classical formulas of dependency theory do not resolve this question.

6　　Polarities and Neutralizations

The dependency theorist highlighted the preeminence of polarization on a world scale. He considered this polarization to be inherent to capitalism, in accordance with the international cleavages observed by the classical Marxists of the early 20th century (Luxemburg, 1968: 58–190). The world-system theorists also interpreted those disparities as intrinsic features of the existing social regime.

Numerous empirical studies have corroborated that divide in the rise of capitalism. The industrial revolution produced the greatest chasm in all of history between an ascending and a descending pole. That 'great divergence' accompanied the takeoff of the West. The developed countries converged in their average rates of expansion that were radically distant from the underdeveloped economies (Pritchett, 1997). The limited initial distance turned into a monumental gap: from 1750 to 1913, the leap in per capita GDP in England (from 10 to 115) and the United States (from 4 to 126) was as spectacular as the regression suffered by China (from 8 to 3) and India (from 7 to 2). The differences between nations expanded at a much higher pace than within nations (Rodrik, 2013).

Marini began with these sorts of evidence to theorize the distance between advanced and underdeveloped economies, with arguments inspired by unequal exchange. However, he also perceived the changes in that tendency introduced by postwar late capitalism. In that model, accumulation processes in the industrialized periphery counterbalanced previous polarizations (Marini, 1978: Chapter 2). The dependency scholar also noted how the presence of the so-called socialist bloc compensated for the spontaneous international inequalities of accumulation. The existence of the Soviet Union and its allies determined that neutralizing effect.

The result of these multiple tendencies was a certain degree of stabilization of inequality between countries. The purely ascending gap of the 19th century took a more variable course and tended toward equilibrium between 1950 and 1990 (Bourguignon and Morrisson, 2002). In that period, the polarities within countries declined due to improvements granted by the capitalist class in response to their generalized fear of socialist contagion. That panic explains the presence of Keynesian models, in a context of decolonization and the rise of anti-imperialism. Marini took note of the national and social disparities generated by capitalism as well as the forces that limit those polarities. This combination of processes was significantly altered in the last decades of the 20th century by the new dynamics of neoliberal globalization.

7   Diverse Inequalities

Numerous studies agree in highlighting the current widening of social cleavages in all parts of the planet. One well-known analysis of that polarization in 30 countries shows that the richest one percent controls 25–35 percent of total wealth in Europe and the United States (2010). In both regions, ten percent of inhabitants control 60–70 percent of the wealth. Similar levels of inequality are found in other central, emerging, or peripheral regions (Piketty, 2013).

But the path followed by inequality between countries is more controversial. That indicator is assessed by comparing the different population-weighted GDPs (Milanovic, 2014). In that way, the impact of growth rates on global inequality is measured, taking into account the populations involved. A substantial increase in GDP in India has very different effects from the same increase in New Zealand (Goda, 2013).

In recent decades, the growing social gap was accompanied by new polarities between countries. However, if the population factor is included, the final result varies. The growth of nations of great demographic weight narrowed the total national differences. The course of inequalities outside and inside of borders, usually synthesized with the Theil coefficient, has been reduced by 24 percent since 1990. The 14 percent increase in inequality within those nations was compensated by a 35 percent decrease in the gap between countries (Bourguignon and Châteauneuf-Malclés, 2016). Because of its large population, China altered the world indicator. While the global economy stagnated at around 2.7 percent annually (2000–2014), the Asian giant grew at a rate of 9.7 percent. Although this trajectory has similarities with earlier cases in Japan and South Korea, its effect on between-country polarities is very different.

Given the explosion of social inequalities, the continuity of that narrowing of the global cleavage is very doubtful. China rose at the expense of its Western rivals, and reconfigured the framework of the dominant powers. But the remaining spectrum of the global hierarchy is still segmented into the traditional compartments. There are few modifications of the global pyramid. A reversal of the 'great divergence' brought about in the 19th century would have to break that hierarchy. In studies prior to the recent rise of China, world-system theorists presented many examples of the enduring character of that structure. They illustrated the reduced international mobility of countries in the long term, exemplifying that permanence in 88 of the 93 cases they considered (Arrighi, 1990).

Anther assessment made at the beginning of globalization (1960–1998) observed the paradox of growing participation of the new economies in productive globalization with scarce effects on the relative level of their per capita GDPs. That work showed that manufacturing production in those countries (as a percentage of First World GDP) rose significantly (from 74.6 percent to 118 percent), as compared to a per capita GDP (as a percentage of its equivalent in the advanced economies) that remained almost unchanged (from 4.5 to 4.6 percent). Industrial convergence did not translate into equivalent improvements in the standard of living (Arrighi, Silver, and Brewer, 2003: 3–31). The later take-off of China has also been achieved while remaining far behind the per capita GDPs of its Western counterparts. The course of global inequality is a determinant of the center-periphery relations that Marini analyzed so carefully. But very different forces than those that prevailed in the glory years of dependency theory operate in the different trajectories that have opened up since then.

8   Internationalization without a Political Counterpart

The current widening of social inequalities beyond that of national inequalities unfolds in a very unique scenario: the internationalization of the economy does not have an equivalent correlate in the ruling classes and states. That contradiction was barely suggested in the 1960s. The coexistence of productive globalization and national-state structures is a 21st century conflict. The importance of global economic (International Monetary Fund, World Bank, World Trade Organization) and geopolitical (United Nations, G20) organizations has not reduced the disruptive scale of that separation. The configuration of states forged at the outset of capitalism still plays a central role. They ensure localized management of the labor force in a context of great global movement of products and capital.

This strengthening of labor regulation at the national level in turn has repercussions on the specific identities of the different ruling classes. Although they globalize their businesses, those groups maintain opposing political and cultural behaviors. Companies internationalize, but their management is not disconnected from their states of origin. For the same reasons, international competition to attract capital unfolds while consistently rewarding the nearest investors.

The neoliberal order expands a globalization administered by national structures. The same states that the classical and postwar Marxists analyzed now operate in a new framework of productive globalization. In that framework of global economic association, geopolitical confrontations develop that recreate relations of dependency. The major powers renew that subjection in their spheres of influence while they dispute supremacy in the most coveted areas of the planet. The United States tries to recapture its hegemony beginning with the regions that were traditionally under its control (Latin America). The existence of a common currency among countries with huge differences in productivity reinforces the supremacy of Germany in Europe. China widens the gaps with its Asian neighbors. The dependency that Marini analyzed adopts new forms and intensities.

9   Problems of Transnationalism

The current stage of productive globalization, without direct correspondence in the ruling classes and states, contradicts the thesis of full transnationalization. That view assumes that the major subjects and institutions of the system have been divorced from their national pillars (Robinson, 2014). It holds that the old anchoring of companies on the map of countries has been dissolved.

This approach turns the prolonged transitions of history into instantaneous transformations. It accurately observes that economic internationalization generates the same type of dynamics in other spheres, but it ignores the huge temporal gaps that separate the two processes. That a firm takes on a transnational profile does not imply an equivalent globalization of its owners; nor does it presuppose processes of that type in the social groups or states that harbor the company. Capitalism does not develop with automatic adjustments; it articulates the development of the productive forces with the actions of the ruling classes adjusted to different state contexts. The different spheres of that tripod maintain levels of connection that are as intense as they are autonomous.

Already in the Marini years, some Marxist theorists (such as Poulantzas) perceived that productive internationalization did not imply identical sequences in the state or class superstructure. This proposition inspired the later characterization of globalization as a process rooted in the most powerful state institutions on the planet (Panitch and Gindin, 2014). The transnationalist approach ignores that mediation by Washington in the evolution of the new stage. Thus, it also ignores the current role of Beijing. The association between the two powers coexists with an intense rivalry between very differentiated state structures. The links between Chinese and U.S. companies do not imply any type of transnational dissolution.

It is enough to recall the complex trajectory of early capitalism around pre-existing classes and states to see how varied the patterns of change of those entities have been. The transnationalist thesis is in tune with the historiographic currents that postulate the abrupt establishment of an integrated world capitalist system, neglecting the complex transition coming from multiple national trajectories (Wallerstein, 1984). In the same way that it conceives of that untimely appearance 500 years ago, it assumes that current globalization very rapidly gives birth to global classes and states.

The opposite tradition, which explores the differentiated paths followed by each national capitalism, instead looks at how local subjects and structures shape current globalization (Meiksins Wood, 2002). It questions the existence of a synchronized irruption of global capitalism, and demonstrates the preeminence of uncertain transitions guided by state intermediations. A generically common course of internationalization develops with a very high diversity of rhythms and conflicts.

Relations of dependency persist precisely because of the inexistence of a sudden process of complete globalization. The structures of center and periphery get remodeled without disappearing, in a context of globalized production and redistributions of value among competing classes and states. This diagnosis, consistent with Marini's tradition, contrasts with the transnationalist perspective.

10   Semi-peripheral Reordering

Marini studied international transfers of value in order to analyze the dependent reproduction of Latin America. He believed that the region recreated its subordinate status through the systematic draining of resources to the central countries. Trade disadvantages, profit repatriation, and interest payments on the debt perpetuated this submission. But the Brazilian theorist did not limit himself to portraying the bipolar cleavage (between center and periphery) generated by these outflows. He explored the new complexity introduced by the existence of intermediate formations. He investigated especially how industrialization placed certain countries in a semi-peripheral segment. He observed this transformation in Brazil, which remained distant from the imperial centers without sharing the extreme backwardness of the periphery (Marini 2013: 18).

This characterization was shared by his dependentist colleague, who differentiated the Latin American economies by their internal development and by the type of products they exported (Bambirra, 1986: 23–30). This was also addressed by the principal exponent of endogenist Marxism when he assessed how unequal underdevelopment separated the most backward agrarian countries from the economies embarked on some level of industrial development (Cueva, 2007).

These distinctions are very useful for analyzing the current context. The simple center-periphery polarity is more insufficient than in the past for understanding globalization. Value chains have increased the weight of the semi-peripheries. Multinational corporations no longer prioritize the occupation of national markets to take advantage of subsidies and customs barriers; another type of foreign investment is of greater importance to them. In certain cases, they ensure the capture of natural resources that depend on the geology and climate of each place. In other situations, they take advantage of the existence of large contingents of cheap and disciplined labor. These two variants – appropriation of natural resources and exploitation of wage-workers – define the strategies of transnational corporations and the location of each economy in the global order.

Both the peripheries and the semi-peripheries are still integrated into the conglomeration of dependent countries, and the subordinate role that Marini ascribed to those two categories has not changed. They are part of the value chain, but without participating in the most profitable areas of that network or exercising control over that structure. They act in globalized production under the control of the transnational corporations. This relegated position is corroborated even in those economies where their own multinational corporations were created (India, Brazil, South Korea); they entered a field that was monopolized by the center, without modifying their secondary status in globalized production (Milelli, 2013: 363–380). Another indicator of that relegated position is the reduced participation of those countries in the direction of globalized institutions, consistent with the scarce representation of those regions in the management of transnationalized firms (Carroll and Carson, 2003: 67–102).

But two significant changes can be seen in comparison with Marini's era. The role of each semi-periphery in the value chain introduces an important element that is quite definitive of its place in the global pyramid. Unlike in the past, it is not enough to record its per capita GDP level or the size of the domestic market. On the other hand, within the semi-peripheral segment the advance of the Asian economies (South Korea) and the regression of their Latin American counterparts (Argentina, Brazil) is very clear. Since the same reordering is observed in other regions, some authors suggest the introduction of new classifications to conceptualize the change (such as strong and weak, or high and low, semi-peripheries) (Morales Ruvalcaba, 2013: 147–181). Marini could not foresee these transformations.

11   Extent of Subimperialism

The Brazilian theorist analyzed the role of the intermediate economies in the same years that the world-system theorists explored the double role of the semi-peripheries. They argued that those countries ease global tensions and define the mutations of the global hierarchy. They highlighted how they moderate the cleavages between center and periphery, and the way in which they play the leading role in the upward and downward mobilities that reshape the international division of labor.

The world-system theorists attributed that role to the intermediate character of the semi-peripheral states, which neither have the power of the center nor suffer from the extreme weakness of the relegated states. They described cases of ascent (Sweden, Prussia, United States), stagnation (Italy, Flanders), and decline (Spain, Portugal) of that segment in the last five centuries. They postulated that their equidistant location allows them to lead great transformations while balancing the global pyramid (Wallerstein, 1984: 233–247; 1999: 239–264; 2004: Chapter 5).

Marini partially agreed with that thesis in his assessment of the intermediate countries. He used that lens to differentiate Brazil from France and Bolivia. However, he also introduced the new concept of subimperialism to characterize a group of regional powers with foreign policies that are associated with, but at the same time autonomous from, U.S. imperialism. With that idea, he emphasized the disruptive role of those actors. Rather than seeing them as buffers for global tensions, he analyzed their convulsive function. The high level of conflict in those regions has later been attributed to the explosive coexistence of welfare and abandonment of the 'Bel-India' type (Chase-Dunn, 1999).

Marini's approach was similar to that used by an exceptional 20th century Marxist to explain the vulnerability of intermediate countries with the logic of unequal and combined development (Trotsky, 1975). As those nations were greatly delayed in being incorporated into the accumulation race, they faced greater imbalances than the center, but which are not present in those that immediately follow them in the periphery. Thus, potential locations for a new emergence of socialism are concentrated there. Like other thinkers of his time, Marini saw the dynamics of those formations on a horizon of confrontation between capitalism and socialism (Worsley, 1980).

However, his notion of subimperialism requires a significant revision in the era of neoliberal globalization. The dependency theorist ascribed to this category an economic dimension of outward expansion and a geopolitical-military dimension of regional protagonism. That simultaneity is not found at present. Contemporary subimperialism does not demonstrate the economic connotation that Marini observed. It is typical of countries that fulfill a double role as associated and autonomous gendarmes of the United States. Turkey and India play that role in the Middle East and South Asia, but Brazil does not perform an equivalent role in Latin America, nor does South Africa fulfill that function on its continent (Katz, 2017b).

The geopolitical aspect of subimperialism and the economic nature of the semi-periphery are more visible today than in the past. The first aspect is determined by military actions to increase the influence of the regional powers; the second derives from the place occupied by each country in the value chain. Marini did not observe this difference.

12   Global South?

The new combination of increasing globalization of capital and continued nation-state configuration of classes and states makes it necessary to revise other aspects of traditional dependentism. Productive globalization is habitually researched by proponents of that tradition, but imperial geopolitical reconfiguration is often neglected. That omission can be seen in the widespread use of the term 'Global South', a concept that is posited to highlight the persistence of the classic disparities between developed countries ('North') and underdeveloped countries ('South'). The relocation of production to the East and the capture by the West of the new value created are presented as evidence of that undeniable polarity (Smith, 2010: 241).

These characterizations accurately challenge the happy future of convergences between advanced and backward economies announced by neoliberals (and often accepted by the heterodoxies). They also show that the foundations of the current model are exploitation and the transfer of surplus value to a handful of transnational corporations. They provide detailed explanations for the advantages that the most powerful countries maintain for capturing the lion's share of the profits.

But these valuable insights do not clarify the problems of the period. The simple diagnosis of a differentiation between South and North runs into a difficulty in classifying China: in which of the two camps is that nation located? That country is sometimes excluded from this divide, with the same argument used twenty years ago to underscore the uniqueness of South Korea or Taiwan. But what was plausible for two small countries cannot be extended to the second largest economy of the planet, one that is home to a fifth of the world population. It is impossible to characterize present-day capitalism if the transformation undergone by the Asian giant is ignored.

Excellent research analyses have in fact erroneously situated China in the bloc of underdeveloped countries. They argue that the surplus value extracted from its enormous proletariat is transferred to the West (Smith, 2010: 146–149). But it makes little sense to include in this category a power that comes to the aid of Western banks, sustains the dollar in a crisis, accumulates a huge trade surplus with the United States, and is in the lead in foreign investment in Africa and Latin America. Nor is it logical to infer that the bulk of the surplus value created in China is fully transferred to the West and appropriated by the parent companies of globalized firms. A drainage of that sort would have made the very high rates of accumulation that characterize the country impossible. It is evident that a large portion of the profits created in China is captured by the local capitalist-bureaucrats. That monumental profit is wrongly interpreted as a simple 'slice' of what is appropriated by the Western companies (Foster, 2015).

China is a challenger, not a puppet, of the United States. Its dominant groups are far from being a dependent bourgeoisie with small slices of the globalization pie. The new Asian ruling classes bear no relation to the old postwar national bourgeoisies. The emerging Eastern power has demonstrated its ability to limit the drain of surplus value while increasing its appropriation of the value created in the periphery. None of these actions is consistent with its classification in the 'Global South'.

13   Renewing Dependency Theory

In his analyses of the political economy of globalization, Marini laid the foundations for understanding the current period. He highlighted three focal points of study: exploitation of labor, transfers of value, and imperial restructuring. He left us important clues, but not answers. The updating of his theory requires more complex inquiries than the simple corroboration of concepts set forth half a century ago. The pillar of that reevaluation is the characterization of productive globalization in the new imperial geopolitics. This study requires that we take note of how the transfer of surplus value redesigns the map of drainage, retention, and capture of flows of value. It is also essential to analyze the new relations of subjugation, subordination, and autonomy that are emerging in the international mosaic. Marini has bequeathed us a monumental research project.

The Dependent Cycle Forty Years Later

In the 1980s, Marini studied the dependent cycle of the Latin American economies. He assessed the crisis of industrialization and the commercial, financial, and productive imbalances of the region (Marini, 2012: 21–23). Forty years later, the same contradictions reappear in a new context of industrial decline, regressive exploitation of natural resources, and financial fragility. In this context, comparisons with Southeast Asia replace the old comparisons with metropolitan capitalism. Studies of countries that depend on rent from primary exports are also relevant. The role of China draws more attention than U.S. domination, while Brazil's path no longer arouses as much interest. Moreover, developmentalist expectations have dissipated among the Latin American bourgeoisies, and new characterizations of public administration emerge. These changes significantly alter the traditional subject matter of Marxist dependency theory and provoke new debates over modifications or extensions of that conception.

1   Tensions and Crises

The Brazilian theorist associated the imbalances of Latin American industrialization with unequal exchange and specialization in the provision of raw materials. He argued that industrial development in Brazil, Mexico, and Argentina did not eradicate the drainage of resources; on the contrary, it reproduced that drainage within manufacturing activity (Marini, 1973: 16–66). From this perspective, he posited the existence of a dependent cycle that impeded repetition of the development carried out by the central economies. He described that obstruction in the different phases of accumulation, using a model inspired by Marx's schemes in *Capital* to illustrate the temporal sequence of accumulation (Marx, 1973: Vol. I, 27–47).

The dependency theorist portrayed how financial resources (money capital) were transformed into inputs for industry (commodity capital), which facilitated the super-exploitation of the workers (productive capital), and gave a detailed analysis of the tensions arising from that process (Marini, 2012: 23–35). He saw that the preeminence of foreign capital motivated the transfer of value abroad (royalties, patents, profits), limiting the extent of accumulation. He argued that multinational corporations complemented that absorption with the capture of enormous profits derived from subsidies, tax exemptions, and the provision of obsolete machinery, and that foreign acquisition of inputs and equipment increased the loss of hard currency.

But the main focus of his study was the productive phase. He analyzed how the large companies obtain extraordinary profits, paying the workers below the average paid in the central economies, and emphasized that this flattening of wages was fortified by the use of capital-intensive technologies that created little employment and perpetuated the reserve army of the unemployed. He added that local capitalists reinforced the extraction of surplus value to compensate for their weakness relative to their foreign competitors (Barreto, 2013).

From those peculiarities of the dependent cycle, Marini deduced the existence of two crises specific to the industrialized periphery. On the one hand, he stressed that the outflow of hard currency caused a breakdown of the balance between the components that sustain accumulation (disproportionalities), reformulating the heterodox reading of balance of payment imbalances in those Marxist terms (Marini, 1994). Since industry did not generate the dollars needed to import its inputs and equipment, the periodic strangulation of the external sector stifled the level of activity.

The dependency theorist located the second type of crisis in the sphere of consumption. He argued that low wages limited purchasing power, blocking the realization of the value of commodities. He understood that this impediment limited the formation of a mass consumption standard similar to those of the metropolises. He analyzed the segmentation of purchases between the elites and the popular sectors, underscoring the differences from the consumption basket in the advanced economies; he understood that a wage good in the center was equivalent to a luxury good in the periphery. His description of those combined crises of accumulation and purchasing power clarified many of the tensions of the Latin American economies (Marini, 2013). He believed that crises of valorization (falling rate of profit tendency) fully affected the metropolis, and that realization crises (gaps between production and consumption) hit the underdeveloped countries with greater severity. With these arguments, he synthesized his assessment of dependent capitalism.

2   Industrial Regression, Obstruction to Consumption

The Brazilian economist introduced the idea of 'pattern of reproduction', which was widely used later to characterize the retreat of regional industry (Marini, 1982). That regression is an enduring feature of recent decades and modifies some of the effects of his diagnoses. The weight of the industrial sector in Latin

American production fell from 12.7 percent (1970–74) to 6.4 percent (2002–6), while industrial density per inhabitant, which measures the value added by that activity in per capita GDP, declined in an equally significant manner (Salama, 2017a). Regional industry has been confined to the basic links of the global value chain; its participation in the production or design of new goods is insignificant and limited to reproducing already standardized commodities. In Brazil, the industrial structure has lost the dimension it had reached in the 1980s. Productivity stagnates, the external deficit expands, and costs increase with the deterioration of the energy and transportation infrastructure. Thus, the country faces a visible backslide in high and medium technology exports (Salama, 2017b).

Argentine industry has sustained an even greater decline. The recovery in the last decade did not revert the systematic fall since the 1980s. High concentration in a small number of sectors, foreign predominance, the wave of imports, and a low level of integration of local components all persist. In addition, the trade deficit increases to the rhythm of increasing foreign acquisitions of inputs and equipment (Katz, 2016: 159–170). Mexico might seem to have another status because of the sustained expansion of its *maquilas*, but those enterprises only assemble parts in accordance with the economic requirements of the United States. They perform basic activities with little multiplier effect on the rest of the economy, and that frailty explains the country's low GDP growth (Schorr, 2017: 9–16).

Whether in the Brazilian or Argentine variant of explicit decline or in the more misleading case of Mexico, Latin American industrial regression has provoked generalized diagnoses of 'deindustrialization'. That regression differs from the dislocation occurring in the advanced economies because of its premature character; it reflects the decline of a sector before having reached its maturity (Salama, 2017b). To the extent that the manufacturing sector does not disappear, 'deindustrialization' might be a controversial term, but it draws attention to the unquestionable shrinkage of that activity and its specialization in very basic processes. Whatever the denomination one uses, Latin American industry suffers from a more dramatic surgery than the tensions described by Marini.

The poverty that accompanies this industrial regression has, in addition, intensified the contraction of purchasing power, as the growth of services that multiply informality do not compensate for the loss of industrial jobs. The decline of industry dilutes the traditional improvements in consumption that were generated by increases in manufacturing productivity. The Fordist model of massification of consumption has passed, and the possibilities for its appearance in the current context of assistentialism, lack of protections, and precarization of employment are lost.

Already in the 1960s, the limited scale of the middle class limited the broadening of consumption. That sector consisted of more small merchants and self-employed than skilled professionals or technicians. Over the last decade there has been a resurgence in expectations of the irruption of that social sector, but its effective presence was exaggerated, ignoring how the tremendous inequality prevailing in Latin America obstructs this development. The expansion of the middle class would imply incorporating new education, health, and housing goods to current expenditures; it is not equivalent to an increase in credit or debt. That is why it is a mistake to present Brazil as a middle-class nation – the acquisition of large quantities of cell phones and computers does not change its ranking of 84th in the world on the Human Development Index.

The size of the middle class is not defined according to the number of recipients of some level of income, but by assessing the dimension of that sector in relation to the richest and poorest social groups (Adamovsky, 2012). Its narrow scale perpetuates the dualized pattern of consumption that Marini ascribed to the dependent cycle.

3   Effects of Extractivism

The technification and capitalization of agriculture has introduced important changes in the Latin American economy. Agribusiness reinforces the importance of crops oriented by foreign demand, to the detriment of local supply. The same specialization is found in mining, as in the open pit mining promoted by transnational corporations. They obtain large profits, pay low taxes, and generalize environmental calamities. That model of export extractivism reinforces the predominance of primary activities, at the expense of industrial production aimed at the domestic market. The rent derived from property in natural resources has greater relevance than the profits from industrial investment. The large firms prioritize the appropriation of a surplus that they send out of the country, recreating the tendency of the dependent cycle. This drainage, combined with the growing trade opening, multiplies the tensions envisaged by the early dependency theorists.

The current model accentuates the way that all the economies are tied to international movements in the prices of raw materials, making the level of activity more volatile. Argentina's GDP, for example, contracted and expanded significantly on 12 occasions over the last 35 years. The same price fluctuations had a lesser intensity in Brazil. Those oscillations obstructed the continuity of accumulation in both countries, generating little investment, high financial costs, and frequent crises (Arriazu, 2015).

In periods of high export prices, hard currency flows inward, currencies tend to appreciate, and spending expands. In the opposite phases, capitals emigrate, consumption decreases, and fiscal accounts deteriorate. At the height of that adversity, devaluations and adjustments burst forth. The renewed weight of primary export activities intensifies the effects of the trade cycle. Those fluctuations also magnify indebtedness. In the boom phases, capital enters in order to profit from high-yield financial operations. In the opposite phases, the risk of impending convulsions grows and capital flight is generalized. Compulsive refinancing, moratoriums, and suspension of payments – the legacies of indebtedness – lead to deeper crises than those discussed by Marini.

Those turbulences intensify the structural deficit of hard currency that plagues industry, and the same sequence observed in the 1960s appears with a greater magnitude. Industrial activity depends on a rentier sector that is reluctant to supply the dollars that the manufacturing sector needs for its imports. Competition from foreign products accentuates that vulnerability. The two types of crisis that Marini conceptualized reemerge with greater virulence. The lack of hard currency widens disproportionalities, and the loss of purchasing power aggravates the stifling of consumption. These tensions are frequently counteracted with indebtedness, fiscal policy, and monetary management, but industrial regression and extractivism reduce the margins for those sorts of state intervention. The dependentist diagnosis is corroborated in a more turbulent context.

4   Cycle and Crisis

Marini analyzed what had happened in the import substitution period (1935–1970), during which production expanded into heavy industry without resolving its periodic external strangulation. That model fell apart in the 1980s under the impact of a 'lost decade' of indebtedness and hyperinflation. The fiscal adjustment to contain this disaster led to prolonged stagnation, and the regional GDP only recovered its 1980 level in 1994. The same thing happened with poverty averages (Salama, 2017a). Debt payments absorbed between two and seven percent of the product, recreating the acute disaccumulation crisis of the dependent cycle.

In the 1990s, neoliberalism appeared with economic policies of convertibility, dollarization, and high interest rates. Privatization, productive restructuring, and the selling of strategic sectors of the economy to foreign actors followed. These measures deepened the vulnerability described by Marini. The free movement of capital opened the gates to an unprecedented scale of financial speculation, and the reduction of tariffs worsened the trade deficit of industry. Social inequality and impoverishment crowned this regression, accentuating the periodic contraction of consumption. These neoliberal experiences culminated in the fall of several governments and the beginning of the so-called 'progressive cycle' in South America.

At the start of the new century, neo-developmentalism reappeared with strategies for overcoming economic backwardness based on state aid, low interest rates, and competitive exchange rates. Unlike the policies of the past, these did not attempt to eradicate the agro-mining export model. It sought alliances with the protagonists of that model, partially rejected protectionism, and strengthened ties with transnational corporations. With this conservative profile, it prioritized macroeconomic policy and omitted structural transformations (Katz, 2016: 139–157).

But that effort once again depended on the international conjuncture, and there were only booms when high raw material prices prevailed. In the favorable phase, indebtedness was reduced, some level of trade surplus emerged, and industry was partially recomposed; growth was sustained with the inflow of dollars. Since the foundations of underdevelopment remained intact, the end of the booms recreated the crisis. In the principal neo-developmentalist experiment (Argentina), the state's incentive to consumption stopped functioning when high inflation and the budget deficit reappeared. The same decline occurred in Brazil. Dependent reproduction tied to the inflows and outflows of hard currency again blocked sustained growth, but with lesser margins for the reindustrializing effort. Industrial regression, extractivism, and the predominance of rentier sectors narrowed that space. The same limitations affected the ability of states to reverse social exclusion.

The current conservative restoration in Argentina and Brazil and neoliberal continuity in Mexico fully renew the dependent cycle. The same balance of payments imbalances and stifling of consumption reemerge on a higher scale. Marini's thesis is verified as dramatically as in the past. But this affirmation is only the starting point for reassessing his approach.

5   The Contrast with Korea

It is relatively simple to demonstrate that Marxist dependency theory is corroborated in Latin America, but extending that corroboration to other latitudes is more complex. Neoliberal globalization does not simply recreate the old disparities between center and periphery. It introduces new bifurcations at both poles. That type of cleavage especially separates Latin America from Southeast Asia – two regions that shared the same relegated status have followed opposite trajectories. The stagnation of the former contrasts with the growth of the latter.

The contrast with South Korea is particularly notable, both for its industrial productivity and for its industrial density (weight of the manufacturing sector in GDP). On both planes, a huge difference is found from Brazil and Argentina. The contrast with the *maquilas* is also evident in value added to products. That difference shows the reduced competitiveness of the Mexican model, which combines formal surpluses with the United States with enormous imbalances in its transactions with the East (Salama, 2012b). The differentiated exploitation of labor power is the main explanation for the gap that separates Southeast Asia and Latin America. The first Marxist characterizations underscored that factor, contrasting the Korean industrial nightmare of the 1960s–1970s with the conquests obtained by Latin American workers (Tissier, 1981). That combativeness explains the persistence of lack of investor confidence by the transnationals when in the following decade the average wage in the two regions converged.

The preference of capitalists for South Korea also had a geopolitical root in the role played by the dictatorships of that country in the containment of the Chinese revolution. The high level of financing from the United States was also strengthened during the Vietnam War. The imperial response to the Cuban revolution was very different in Latin America. In the new century, the disparities on wage costs changed. After a prolonged process of accumulation, the productivity difference between South Korea and its Latin American peers are more significant than their wage differences. That change illustrates the development gap; while real investment per worker in Brazil in 2010 was slightly below it 1980 level, in South Korea it was 3.6 times higher (Salama, 2012a). The same contrast is found in the coefficients that measure the share of each economy in global value chains.

But the old comparisons are not enough in today's world. South Korea is now integrated into the upper link of a vast Asian web of productive globalization. That conglomeration renews itself as a bloc, recreating the comparative advantage of a cheap labor force. Successive waves of industrial expansion have diversified that incentive to capitalists through the extension of brutal forms of subjugation of the workers of new countries (Thailand, Philippines, Bangladesh, etc.). Exploitation of that worker contingent includes growing modalities of flexibilization. Asian firms especially outpace their Latin

American counterparts in subcontracting, combining digital technologies, cheap transportation, and extensive communications with precarization, segmentation, and outsourcing of labor processes.

Latin America was functional to the old import substitution model, while Southeast Asia optimizes the current internationalization of production. The preexistence of a certain level of domestic market was advantageous for postwar industrialization, but is inconvenient for an industrial model oriented toward export. The paucity of local consumption has become an asset for these models.

The role of the United States has also changed. In the past, its industrial dominance complemented the takeoff of Latin American industry. Today, on the contrary, transnational firms compensate for the industrial decline of the metropolis with the installation of plants in Asia. In this new context, the conjunctural reduction of Latin American wages is no longer sufficient to reinitiate investment. The recipe once applied in Brazil does not work. Since the preceding model continues to have some weight in South America, protectionism there surpasses Asian averages, but elimination of those safeguards would completely destroy the industrial structure. Neoliberal capitalism imposes that dramatic dilemma on Argentina and Brazil.

Latin America cannot join the club of economies that South Korea belongs to. That group includes about 20 countries, of which eight contain the bulk of wage-workers. Since the 1980s, this new map of the proletariat has doubled the labor force connected to the global economy (Smith, 2010: 111–113). Argentina, Brazil, and Mexico do not fit into this circuit. The disparity is also deepened by Asia's retention of significant portions of surplus value. In Latin America, on the contrary, the drainage of value toward the metropolis only grows larger. The limited expansion of Korean domestic consumption also contrasts with the sharp deterioration of purchasing power in the New World. In sum, the full-fledged continuity of the dependent cycle does not extend, in Marini's strict terms, to the Asia-Pacific world.

6   Other Interpretations

Our characterization of the dependency model has advantages over other rival explanations for the contrast between Latin America and Southeast Asia. The neoliberal view attributes that bifurcation to the trade opening carried out by the East and rejected by Latin America, claiming that this shift allowed the Asian economies to improve their allocation of resources and make use of their comparative advantages. But in both cases, there was a reduction in tariffs. The difference lies in the goods imported in each case – the flood of consumer products to Latin America contrasts with the acquisition of equipment on the part of South Korea. The existence of conditions for the exploitation of labor that were more favorable to capital underpinned that productive path. The orthodoxy explains that asymmetry by claiming the existence of 'global wage arbitrage', which rewards the regions with lower labor costs for the same tasks. But those activities are not carried out by inanimate objects; 'arbitrage' selects different levels of employee subjugation.

Heterodox economists dispute the neoliberal interpretation of Eastern growth. They demonstrate the fallacy of trade opening, illustrating the bundle of tariffs, financial regulations, and export subsidies that prevail in South Korea (Gereffi, 1989), but they exalt that model while opposing it to the passive adaptation of Latin America to the world market. They maintain that this passivity keeps it from benefitting from the opportunities of globalization (Bresser Pereira, 2010: 119–143). With this logic, they locate all the obstacles to Latin American development in the domestic sphere, forgetting that the international division of labor impedes the free choice of a country's destiny. If countries could decide their own future, all would choose to be like Switzerland and none like Mozambique.

Capitalism is not an open field for the prosperity of the brightest, but a stratified order that inhibits collective welfare. Since there is not room for all, the development of some economies is realized at the expense of others. At each stage of the system, there are regions that are favored and others that are penalized by the dynamics of accumulation. That choice is not a menu at the disposition of the different countries. For Southeast Asia, imitating Latin America was not feasible in the 1960s, and the same impossibility is now reproduced in the opposite direction. The New Continent lacks the labor base of the East and does not conform to the needs of the transnational corporations. South Korea achieved its insertion into globalization without carrying the burden of obsolete industry.

The heterodoxy assumes that the progress of any emerging economy depends on its capture of complex activities in the value chain (Milberg, 2014: 164–168). It asserts that manufacture should follow assembly, until reaching an original production (Gereffi, 2001). It recognizes that firms located at the head of this process take the bulk of the surplus, and they call for a change in this distribution. However, they neglect that the increasing capture of value requires greater extraction of surplus value. That omission can be seen in the equivalence they draw between wages, productivity, and exchange rate policy in the determination of development strategies, failing to recognize that these three dimensions are not comparable. The subjection of the worker to a given rate of remuneration is an assumption of any investment decision. Dependentist Marxism highlights this fact that is ignored by the heterodoxy.

7   Other Comparisons

South Korea did not have to deal with the problems of exchange rate appreciation that plague the natural resource exporting economies. It adapted to the new stage of capitalism without confronting that old adversary of the intermediate countries of Latin America, where the preeminence of agro-export rents dissuades industrial investment. Since the mid-20th century, Argentina, Brazil, and Mexico have tried to channel that surplus toward industrial activity, but the conflicts generated by that strategy blocked its implementation.

Many debates of the 1960s–1970s assessed the productive use of rents. Dependency theorists proposed capturing that surplus with punitive state measures against the privileges of the oligarchy. Those initiatives were presented with greater detail and precision by the endogenist Marxist currents. Marini emphasized the external drain much more than the domestic squandering of the resources needed for development, and paid more attention to the surplus value expropriated from the wage-workers than to the rents of the latifundistas.

In that era, the first debates were being launched about the financial internationalization of rent. The main debate revolved around the character of OPEC. The suggestion that the members of that cartel could escape from dependency (Semo, 1975: 92–100) was objected to by a keen exponent of dependentism (Bambirra, 1978: 39–45). The later evolution of the oil-exporting economies verified that critique. Underdevelopment continued to rule in the Arab, African, and Asian countries that made up that organization.

Nevertheless, that outcome did not dispel the enigmas created by the economies that drew on rents for their development. That question has stimulated growing interest in recent years. Some studies highlight what has occurred in Norway or Australia, and contrast their evolution with Argentina. With some precautions, that comparison could be extended to Brazil or Mexico.

Norway and Australia specialized in the export of raw materials, at the same time expanding certain services and intensive industries (Schorr, 2017: 29–31). Unlike the liberal Latin American governments (who squandered the rents) or the developmentalist governments (who failed to transform them into accumulation), they channeled that resource toward some degree of development. A combination of objective conditions and ruling class behaviors determined that course. Norway's and Australia's abundant resources are concentrated in energy and minerals, and their per capita endowment of those resources are far higher than their potential peers in Latin America.

Norway is a typical case of very high rents with a sparse population. It benefits from a pattern of rent similar to those of the banking havens (Switzerland) or the tourist havens (small Caribbean islands). With five million inhabitants, Norway occupies first place in the Human Development Index. In addition, it has a peculiar history of limited political conflicts and high social spending. When it began to exploit its oil resources in the 1960s, it was already a productively-differentiated country with some level of industrialization. That trajectory explains how it offset the exchange rate appreciation effect of exports through state regulation of rents. It achieved that productive reinvestment from an economic status already integrated into the major metropolises of the Old Continent.

Australia is also unique in some notable ways. It has a lower demographic density and a higher percentage of natural resources per inhabitant than Argentina. It went through an import substitution process, but it specialized in primary exports and products of low technological content. The proximity to Southeast Asia was key to that reconversion. Moreover, its economy was always outside of the agricultural complementarity (and hence rivalry) that Argentina maintained with the United States (Schteingart, 2016). In the domestic sphere, Australia has preserved a relatively egalitarian structure, and never faced the social tensions of any South American countries. It received a large level of external financing because of its participation in the Cold War, and its privileged relationship with England evolved toward a close imperial association with the United States (DSP, 2001). The same sorts of comparisons could be extended to Canada. The differences between those countries and Latin America do not invalidate the comparison. That counterpoint opens an important area of study for Marxist dependency theory. It is critical that the impact of rent management on development be analyzed.

8   Relation with China

The great leap in Latin America's commercial exchange with China illustrates another contemporary dimension of dependency. Total transactions passed from 10 billion dollars in 2000 to 240 billion dollars in 2015, under a relation of total asymmetry. The region exports simple raw materials in exchange for manufactures (Emmerich, 2015). China not only provides industrial goods; it also snatches markets for those products from Latin America. The weight of the trade flow between the two regions is completely unequal. While Mexico and

Brazil are among the 25 main importers of Chinese merchandise, their sales only represent one percent of the new power's acquisitions (Salama, 2012b).

The new colossus also expands its investments at a frenzied pace, without any consideration in the opposite direction toward the *multilatina* companies. All its ventures are concentrated on capturing natural resources. It provides funds for oil exploration, mine drilling, and agricultural projects; it improves ports and the routes that guarantee the transportation of primary goods. But is always imposes strict clauses of input provision, and never contemplates technology transfers.

China also promotes free trade agreements to ensure its dominance. Having achieved the status of 'market economy', it blocks any local protection from the entry of its products. It safeguards its expansion with loans, which now surpass the amount granted by the IMF and the World Bank, the two traditional financiers of the Latin American economies. Only Africa can compete in subordination to the new economic power.

That subjection crowns an astonishing disparity of trajectories, which can be clearly seen in comparing Brazil with China. The per capita incomes of the two countries in 1980 were 4,809 dollars and 306 dollars, respectively. In 2015 those figures were 15,614 and 14,107. This dramatic comparison illustrates the paltry progress of Brazil (3.25 times as high) in the same period as the spectacular leap of China (46 times) (Salama, 2017a). The same disparity can be seen in the world rankings of exports. The Asian giant currently occupies first place, after appearing in the group of 50 top participants in that activity. In contrast, Brazil has moved back to the 25th spot after having earlier reached 16th (Salama, 2012b). The disparity in the impact of the two economies in the global value chain is much more significant. All the data confirm the dominant economic place of China in Latin America. Its presence is not comparable to any of the countries typically compared to Brazil, Mexico, or Argentina; it is on a very different level than South Korea, Australia, or Norway. It has begun to develop a relationship with the region that is more comparable with the old European metropolises or with the United States.

Certainly, China's presence challenges the domination of the United States. But so far, it is more of an economic than a geopolitical threat. It does not project its impressive commercial expansion to the military sphere. China advanced cautiously on the diplomatic plane, displaying 'soft power' with discourses of cooperation far from a hegemonic message and utilizing a rhetoric of reciprocity and mutual benefit in its 'South-South' relations. Its policies are based on the great mutation generated by productive globalization. The old bipolar relation (center-periphery) now takes on certain triangular features; there is competition between the metropolitan economies and the new industrialized powers for the subjection of the periphery. China and the United States are rivals for harnessing the benefits of Latin America's export primarization (Salama, 2012c).

The outcome of that confrontation between the two powers is uncertain, but the subordination of Latin America is a given in any outcome. A drastic reversion of that subordination is the condition for engaging in a relation of association with China that contributes to liberation from U.S. domination (Katz, 2016: 299–311).

9   Geopolitics, Classes, Governments

Marxist dependency theorists have always underscored the political dimension of that subjection (Dos Santos, 1998). They argued that the subordination of Latin American governments to imperialism was in harmony with bourgeoisies closely associated with foreign capital. That logic was inspired by an international stage marked by tensions between central powers, peripheral countries, and members of the so-called socialist bloc. Marini also highlighted distinctions within the periphery and differences between countries with a subimperial or purely subordinate profile.

This map has changed, but his observations on the geopolitical meaning of global stratification are still valid. Those arguments clarify the forces that complement the insertion of each economy in the international division of labor. Military might, diplomatic weight, and cultural influence reinforce, temper, or counteract the dominant or subordinate status of different countries. In the present period, neoliberal globalization reformulates the rises and falls of countries in the global pyramid.

It is evident that the major capitalist empire (United States) and its rival empire in formation (China) dispute positions at the top of the system. The resources of Latin America, Africa, and a large portion of Asia are the booty of that competition. However, the tradition begun by Marini calls for taking into account the roles of intermediate formations as well. On these grounds, the reversal of Brazil's subimperial status is very significant. This retreat is consistent with the country's industrial regression and its shift toward primary exports. Argentina and Mexico never reached that category, and they have moved even further away from it. In the former case this is due to its devastating loss of economic positions, and in the latter to its growing subordination to the United States.

The subempires of other regions have, in contrast, reinforced their military interventionism, with uncertain results for the development of their economies. Turkey has consolidated a more significant industrial base amidst its conflicts. India managed to stabilize a cycle of continual growth, and accentuated its specialization in certain segments of subcontracting. However, it maintains a vulnerable industrial structure that is far from the Chinese model.

The close partnership of Australia with U.S. imperialism widens its margins of autonomy for ensuring the reinvestment of mining rents, although that did not stop its regression relative to its Asian competitors. In South Korea, militarization under the direct control of the Pentagon provides guarantees for investment, but submission to the United States obstructs more ambitious projects for the eventual reunification with North Korea. Changes in geopolitical status have very contradictory effects on the performance of the intermediate countries. The feedback that clearly exists between imperial power and economic supremacy (or between political dependency and underdevelopment) does not extend to equivalent parameters in the semi-periphery.

All the transformations in process likewise affect the profiles of the ruling classes. In the Latin American case, the conversion of the old national bourgeoisies into local bourgeoisies who no longer support inward-looking development has been consolidated. They prioritize exports and prefer cost reduction to the broadening of consumption. Their tightening of ties to foreign capital does not imply the disappearance of the Latin American bourgeoisie, as the country of origin continues to be their base of operations, source of profits, and decision-making center. That sector has not become a purely transnational class; nor has it become a satellite manipulated by the metropolises or a 'lumpen-bourgeoisie' dedicated to plunder. However, the autonomy that the nascent industrial bourgeoisie exhibited in the postwar era for promoting the region's industrialization is reduced. Transnational corporations now define their strategies with the approval of their local partners. This subordination reinforces the influence of international finance and agro-mining capitalists over Latin American states.

Thus, the developmentalist hope of reversing economic regression has shifted toward the state bureaucrats. The clear lack of interest of the bourgeoisie in sustained growth has led to the glorification of public officials. They are seen as a clear-headed, independent, or patriotic segment that takes the pending business of development in its hands. But the experience of the last decade disproves that belief; it confirms the close relationship between the bourgeoisie and its delegates in the state. Both groups have been formed in the same environments, sharing the same behaviors. The parasitical bourgeoisies create ineffective bureaucracies. Very few exceptions violate this norm.

In the end, the different governments tend to express this succession of conditions that determine the level of dependency of each country. The further entrenchment of underdevelopment and political subordination is the rule for right-wing presidents and their neoliberal ministers, while progressive presidents and their neo-developmentalist teams have unsuccessfully attempted to reverse both of these afflictions. They all act within a framework that severely limits their actions. In Latin America, dependency relations precede and put boundaries on the policies of any government.

10   Determinants of Dependency

A variety of processes defines the current status of different countries in the global hierarchy. A country's place in the division of labor is the key historical factor of a location closely connected to the value of labor power, the dynamics of transfers, the allocation of rents, geopolitical-military weight, and the roles of the ruling classes, bureaucracies, and governments. Those factors determine the distances that separate the advanced centers (United States) and the new centers (China) from the rising (South Korea, Norway) or stagnating (Australia) semi-peripheries, or those of an uncertain evolution (India). The same elements affect the status of the descending semi-peripheries (Brazil, Mexico), the new peripheries integrated into productive globalization (Bangladesh), or the basic product exporters (Guatemala).

The changes found in that structure are currently very much influenced by the investments of transnational corporations, which place their capitals following the barometer of profitability. That parameter particularly takes into account the modes of exploitation and super-exploitation existing in each economy, and the predominance of high, medium, or low values of labor power (Katz, 2017). With that strategic criterion, they seek to cheapen labor costs in accordance with the complexity of different activities.

International transfers of value decisively affect the mutations of that global hierarchy. They are placements of capital that recreate polarities and bifurcations, following the movements of surplus value imposed by the metamorphosis of capital in its distinct financial, commercial, and productive phases. Transfers can be absorbed (+), drained (–), or retained (=) by countries. On a world scale, mobile surplus value is absorbed by the central economies, retained by the rising semi-peripheries, and drained from the declining semi-peripheries and the peripheries. One gains what the other loses within a structure marked by relative stability of the global hierarchy.

Rents are generated only by the countries with significant natural resources. They can be captured (+), reinvested (=), or lost (–). Rent is a surplus that moves internationally like surplus value, but coming from a different origin.

Because rent is qualitatively different from the portion of surplus value appropriated as profit, it must be treated in a differentiated form. Some world powers have their own rents and recycle them internally (United States), while others lack that form of surplus and depend on its capture (China). There are semi-peripheries that do not have those resources (South Korea), others that have and retain them (Australia, Norway); while on the opposite side are the nations that lose their rents partially (Brazil) or completely (Guatemala).

International geopolitical status determines another hierarchy with some level of autonomy from the productive, commercial, or financial weight of each country. That classification defines the places of the established empires (United States) and their partners or appendages (Australia), and also locates the empires in formation (China), subempires (India), and the countries that face different levels of dependency. Cases of greater autonomy (Brazil) differ from those of subordination (South Korea) or total subjugation (Guatemala). The ability of the imperial states to bolster their development at the expense of the dependent formations is indisputable, but the in the remaining spectrum there are different types of variations.

Finally, the realm of ruling classes, bureaucracies, and governments generates an enormous diversity of impacts on development. Undoubtedly, the metropolitan ruling classes with efficient bureaucracies and stable governments have a favorable impact on accumulation. The inverse phenomenon can also be observed in countries with peripheral bourgeoisies, parasitical public officials, and inconsistent governments. But in a field shaped so much by the actions of social subjects, many types of combinations can be found.

11   Reasons for Reconsideration

Our view of the global polarizations and bifurcations prevailing under neo-liberal capitalism is inspired by Marxist dependency theory, but it broadens, complements, and corrects several assumptions of that conception. In accordance with the Marxist pillar, we highlight the preeminence of an economic-social system based on competition for profits arising from exploitation, which is why we put the value of labor power in the front row of our interpretation. It is the central determinant of the changes that have occurred in contemporary capitalism.

The dependency thesis adds to this assessment a diagnosis of global stratification around central, peripheral, and semi-peripheral segments. The three strata operate in differentiated forms, determined by a great variety of situations of development and underdevelopment. The main mechanism of change is the international transfer of surplus value, which in the last two centuries has taken different directions, volumes, and recipients. Marxist dependency theorists have always emphasized that unequal distribution of value, explaining how the surpluses created in the periphery were captured by the central economies. Our proposal retakes this idea, incorporating analysis of movements of rent that were omitted, or little mentioned, by that tradition.

We also take up the geopolitical dimension underscored by the dependency theorists. However, we reformulate the categories in this sphere in order to integrate the complex variants assumed by contemporary imperialism. In addition, we stress that different outcomes of the class struggle define the roles of the ruling classes and their functionaries or governments. Our synthesis is supported by an interpretation of capitalism that is critical rather than merely descriptive. We emphasize how that system deepens inequality and the privileges of minorities at the expense of popular suffering. We also highlight the importance of periodic crises that erode the continuity of that social regime. This perspective is the polar opposite of neoliberalism, which idealizes capitalism and denies its intrinsic imbalances. The orthodoxy assumes that globalization brings society close to the idyllic state of perfect markets, optimal distribution of resources, and convergence between advanced and backward economies. The unreality of this view is apparent.

Our proposal also objects to the heterodox view that recognizes the conflicts of capitalism but plays down its scale and intensity. It minimizes global stratification, imagines wide margins for modifying the status of the disadvantaged, and ignores the weight of imperial domination. Thus, it proposes developmentalist strategies that assume a potentially friendly functioning of capitalism. It calls for overcoming the backwardness of the periphery with accumulation policies guided by the state.

Our perspective draws on various arguments of the system theorists who refute the assumptions of the heterodoxy. Those observations illustrate how global capitalism operates around a zero-sum principle by which the expansion of some economies is achieved at the expense of the regression suffered by others. National accumulation processes unfold in competition for the same niche, and the progress achieved by some participants does not provide blueprints for the rest. It is important to view this dispute in terms of different pieces of the same global pyramid in order to escape from the fantasy of 'imitating Southeast Asia', which neglects that the options available to each economy are not an open course to any outcome they choose. They are shaped by their place in the global division of labor, and they do not provide unobstructed paths that depend purely on economic policy. There is no formula that allows Haiti to copy the path of the United States.

Our characterization draws on the traditions that preceded Marini and on his contemporaries who converged with his work. This broadening and reformulation of dependency theory allows us to treat problems that cannot be resolved with the formulas conceived in the 1960s and 1970s. With this perspective, we replace the traditional acceptance of super-exploitation with three scales of the value of labor power. This approach facilitates research into the enormous variety of situations generated by productive globalization. Analysis of these novel forms of globalizing the extraction of surplus value, together with the interpretation of value transfers and rent, clarify the new map of dependency.

These realities are incomprehensible with merely economic readings. The updating of dependency theory in the political sphere is particularly urgent. That school of thought was able to preserve a rich legacy of studies on capitalism, but it did not extend that tradition to the analysis of imperialism, systems of government, and popular resistance. These shortcomings explain the difficulty in explaining processes that challenge the center-periphery model (South Korea), and also cause the omission of decisive problems (such as the role of China) or the simplification of Latin American political divisions (equating neoliberalism with progressivism).

The renewal of Marxist dependency theory requires a joint treatment of economics and politics. Rereadings of *Capital* and *Dialectic of Dependency* are useful, in close connection with the current dilemmas of socialist strategies. From this synthesis will emerge a new flowering of Latin American Marxism.

Dependency and the Theory of Value

Marxist dependency theory posited an explanation for underdevelopment based on the dynamics of value. With this foundation, it explained the unequal exchange and industrial cycles of Latin America in a period preceding the current predominance of extractivism and *maquilas*. Which concepts of that characterization are valid for the present period? How should its omissions or insufficiencies be assessed?

1   Causes of Unequal Exchange

In the 1970s, Marini analyzed the imbalances of industry that kept Brazil, Mexico, and Argentina from repeating the development of the central economies. He described how the preeminence of foreign capital incentivized transfers of value abroad, while foreign provision of obsolete machinery increased the loss of hard currency. He underscored that the large companies paid workers below the average prevailing in the metropolises, and argued that their local counterparts compensated for their competitive weaknesses with greater extraction of surplus value (Marini, 1973: 16–66).

His analysis shared many similarities with the unequal exchange theories of that era, whose arguments involved situations of transfers of value from the backward to the advanced economies, attributed to differential international remuneration for the labor incorporated in the goods produced at the two poles. These views extended Marx's model to the global context in order to illustrate the way in which prices of production alter the values of commodities in accordance with the productivities prevailing in the different branches of the economy. They took into account transactions with products of differing complexities, produced in countries with large disparities in levels of development.

The debate began with Emmanuel's thesis that explained inequality in exchange by wage differences. He postulated that the globalization of prices of production and profit rates did not include labor power. This separation determined the perpetuation of the gaps between the two types of economies (Emmanuel, 1972: Chapter 3). As this characterization highlighted the centrality of exploitation and anticipated descriptions of the *maquilas*, some analysts saw similarities with Marini's model (Rodrigues, 2017), but in fact Marini had greater affinities with Emmanuel's Marxist critics who ascribed unequal exchange to differences in productivities rather than wages. They maintained that the wage gaps were explained by disparities in the development of the productive forces rather than vice versa (Bettelheim, 1972a). This perspective held that the wage is a result rather than a determinant of accumulation, arguing that wage levels in each country depend on productivity, cycles, capital stock, and the intensity of the class struggle (Mandel, 1978: Chapter XI). Those objections also cautioned against magnifying the international wage gap, arguing that analysis of that cleavage should take into account the higher productivity of the skilled activities that were predominant in the central economies (Bettelheim, 1972b).

None of those characterizations calls into question the existence of unequal exchange, but they indicate that asymmetry in trade represents only one cause of underdevelopment, with dissimilar effects at each stage of global capitalism (Arrighi, 1990). The debate also led to other propositions that posited the presence of unequal exchange when the disparities in wages are greater than the disparities in productivities (Amin, 1976: 159–161). This perspective argues that the separation is based on the growing international mobility of capital and commodities while the immobility of labor power remains unchanged (Amin, 2003: Chapter 4).

Marini's perspective was in tune with these corrective approaches. In his explanation of the dependent cycle, he emphasized that transfers of surplus value to the advanced economies were a consequence of the large disparities in levels of development, recognizing the big differences in wages without seeing them as determinants of the center-periphery cleavage. This perspective not only coincided with the synthesis between participants in the debate at its more mature stage, but also confirmed that, unlike many heterodox economists, Marini attributed underdevelopment to the polarizing dynamics of world capitalism rather than the lag in Latin American wages.

2 The Extent of Globalization

The debates on globalization also included attempts to clarify the level of internationalization capitalism had reached. All the participants recalled that in Marx's models he conceived of national situations, which were his points of reference at the distinct levels of abstraction of his model, such as in the formation of the individual and social values of commodities, in the definitive modal techniques of sectoral productivity, in the formation of average profits, and in production, market, or monopoly prices. These analytical pillars were radically modified in Emmanuel's sketch of internationalized variables, which replaced Marx's British scale of reference with a global equivalent. That reconsideration was logical a century after the publication of *Capital* – but was it appropriate to analyze unequal exchange in a framework of completely globalized economies?

A distinguished theorist objected to that assumption, stressing the continued relevance of national variables. He observed how prices of production and average profits were still established at that scale, resulting in a variety of situations that were juxtaposed on the world level, and highlighting how the absence of global state institutions determined the continuity of nationally differentiated currencies, tariffs, exchange rates, and prices (Mandel, 1978: Chapter XI). From that perspective, he deduced unequal exchange from transactions between commodities with different quantities of hours worked for their production. He understood that transfers of surplus value were related to the higher international remuneration of more industrialized labor. That thesis was consistent with the postwar Keynesian framework and the import substitution models in the semi-peripheries. Integrated national production prevailed at both poles – the country on a product's label represented production completely within that country.

However, that approach was countered by another interpretation that underscored the presence of a new framework of internationalized variables. It explained the centrality of unequal exchange by the new divide between capitals circulating across the entire planet and labor forces tied to national locations. This perspective challenged the portrayal of the world economy as a conglomeration of juxtaposed units and underscored the preeminence of internationalized mechanisms, arguing that 'world value' represented a new ordering principle for all the categories of capitalism (Amin, 1973: 12–87). Other authors extended this characterization, explicitly contrasting Marx's era with the new age of multinational corporations. They argued that companies, branches, and processes of production now operated in an internationalized form at the intra- and inter-sectoral scales (Carchedi, 1991: Chapters 3, 7). In his writings in the 1960s and 1970s, Marini did not specify his preference for one or the other approach, but later he would emphasize the overwhelming primacy of the globalizing tendency (Marini, 2007b: 231–252). That tendency has since gone further, and therefore requires another conceptualization.

3   Productive Globalization

The qualitative advance of globalization modifies the terms of the debate that developed several decades ago. The globalized character of many activities that were not so in the 1970s stands out, as it consolidates the tendency of a large segment of the economy to operate with internationalized prices and profit rates. The new global division of labor that emerged in the early stages of neoliberalism has been consolidated with the current relocation of industry. The displacement of transnational corporations that emigrate to the periphery to profit from the cheapness, discipline, or subservience of the workers has been generalized. That change was even perceived by the authors who, in the 1970s, rejected the accuracy of an advanced stage of globalization; in the following decade, they recognized the new presence of fields of valorization governed by international barometers (Mandel, 1996).

The current preeminence of that global segment is well known. Traditional limits to the mobility of capital and commodities were overcome through financial globalization and free trade agreements, while the obstruction to international patterns of prices and profits imposed by the multiplicity of exchange rates were weakened. Some economies joined together with common currencies (Europe) and others dollarized their movements or enacted regional forms of exchange rate coordination. The absence of a state system on a planetary scale still makes the full globalization of variables impossible, but transnational corporations operate at that scale and the organizations that undergird their activities (World Bank, IMF, WTO) administer arrangements that reinforce that trend.

The mechanisms of greater internationalization have appeared especially in global value chains, which include very advanced forms of diversifying the locations of production processes as companies take advantage of the differences in profitability made possible by the variety of forms of exploitation. Value chains ensure the capture of extraordinary profits by the companies located at the top of the network. In the clothing industry, for example, super-profits remain in the hands of the large buyers (brands) at the expense of textile producers (automated plants) and labor-intensive firms (Starosta and Caligaris, 2017: 237–276). The same principle of redistribution of surplus value operates in the territorial operations of the satellite companies. Subcontracting is the key device for value transfers; the leading company obtains higher profits by setting the conditions for the acquisition of the inputs supplied by its providers.

A unified circuit of internationalized prices and average profit rates now operates in the chains. Marini only observed, in the *maquilas*, the beginnings of a mechanism that would remodel the dynamics of unequal exchange. In the current stage, the creation of surplus value diverges significantly from its geographical distribution. The process of transformation of values into prices occurs on an international scale with the split between commodities produced in one country and consumed in another. Surplus value generated in Asian factories with low costs is realized in markets in the United States and Europe under the management of transnational corporations (Smith, 2010: 246–249). In this new sequence, international transfers of value assume an unprecedented scale.

4   The Meaning of Intensified Labor

The global movements of surplus value that underpin the dynamics of unequal exchange have provoked major controversies. Some authors deny their validity, arguing that the differences between developed and backward economies derive from the existence of dissimilar productivities. They assert that their labor times cannot be simply compared, as the level of complexity of labor in the center, and consequently the higher expense of formation of the labor force, must be considered (Astarita, 2010a: 140–145).

That inequality is summed up in the idea of intensified labor (or multiplied simple labor), which Marx used to characterize advanced labor modalities. The periphery, where those skills are scarce, trades from a different status, without generating transfers in the exchange of commodities (Astarita, 2011). Capital from the center does not extract value from the relegated economies; rather, they produce more valorized commodities with better techniques and less hours of labor (Astarita, 2013b).

In the 1970s, debates on this same problem were posed in different terms. Bettelheim argued that it was incorrect to compare the wages of different economies without taking account of productivity differences, but he made that observation only to review the extent of unequal exchange. He sought to amend this thesis, not to invalidate it. He connected the magnitude of wages to their different productivities, but never questioned the existence of international transfers of value as the foundation of global capitalism. His argument shows that intensified labor does not disprove the existence of international movements of surplus value, but simply incorporates different complexities of labor into a structure of global operations, modifying the magnitudes in play.

Intensified labor is a relevant concept in relation to the socially necessary labor time that governs each branch of production; analysis of the category is on the level of the determination of the values of commodities. However, goods do not exchange at those magnitudes, but as a function of the prices of production of products after a process of adjustment to the average profit rate. That process involves transfers of value between different branches in processes of circulation mediated by money. Through this link, the commodities produced with different levels of skill and diverse productivities become inter-changeable units.

The analysis of unequal exchange is on this second level of surplus value transfers. At that scale, of the world market and the totality of commodities, there is no incompatibility with the parameters of intensified labor that pre-viously define the values of commodities in each sector. This difference in analytical levels has been underscored by authors who recall why the idea of intensified labor was introduced in the first volume of *Capital*, which is where the formation of values is analyzed.

In his observations on the world market, Marx added another concept to highlight the differences between products made with dissimilar levels of accumulation. His concept of differential international remuneration of more productive labor refers to this gap (Machado, 2011). This second category, on a more concrete-empirical plane, was the starting point for the debates over unequal exchange.

Using a contemporary example of these distinctions, it could be argued that intensified labor was corroborated when Microsoft displaced IBM, setting a new parameter for value in the sphere of information technology. The dynam-ics of surplus value transfers were, on the other hand, on another level and another scale when the same company absorbed value in the form of tech-nological rent from multiple firms in different sectors. Its rise on the NASDAQ Index on Wall Street illustrates that capture. The question initially analyzed as unequal exchange is located on this second dimension and in the international sphere. It began with conceptualizations of international flows of surplus value coming from the backward economies. Those countries export basic goods and participate in basic tasks in the internationalized production of commodities. Intensified labor is a component, not a refutation, of that process.

5   Monopoly and the Duality of Value

Challenges to the concept of international value transfers postulated by depen-dency theory are based, as well, on the relevance ascribed to monopolies. The critics claim that the importance that approach attaches to large companies in the determination of prices detaches those prices from the objective logic of the law of value (Astarita, 2014). However, the impact of monopolies is only conceived over temporary periods, in favor of the firms with relative power over the market. Since they will sooner or later face competition from other com-panies of similar weight, their control cannot be made eternal. Recognizing the ability of monopolies to multiply profits in differentiated sectors does not imply nonrecognition of the law of value, but only treats this principle on another level of its operation.

Marini was always closer to the Marxist thinkers like Mandel who highlighted this dynamic of differentiated competition among monopolies. He maintained greater distance from theorists like Sweezy who stressed the unrestrained ability of large firms to manage prices. Those who, on the contrary, accurately criticized the magnification of monopolies (such as Shaikh) are now at the opposite extreme – they deny the clear existence of gigantic corporations that obtain extraordinary profits in certain markets at the expense of smaller companies.

Monopolies achieve extraordinary profits because of their dominant weight, but in the long run they cannot withdraw from the principles that govern price formation under the combined impact of productivity and social needs. The former factor affects valorization through the types of companies that dominate supply in each sector; the latter influences prices through the role of demand (Rosdolsky, 1979: 101–125). For example, if a branch (such as sports shoes) is rising, there will be room for lower and higher productivity firms, while in the opposite case (such as hats), only the most efficient will tend to survive. The intersection of the two processes generates the rewards and punishments of the market to companies that economize or squander social labor (Katz, 2009: 31–60).

The large companies tend to obtain higher than average profits because of their primacy in innovation (technological rents) or their control over the supply of a scarce good (natural rent), but they only preserve those super-profits during the period in which competition in the hegemonized sector is limited, and they take advantage of social needs related to the demand for their products. Both of these determinants shape the final prices of all commodities (Mandel, 1985: 209–216), This characterization of the dual dimension of value not only clarifies the singularities and limits of monopolies, but also highlights the importance of the market in the *ex post* recognition of the labor incorporated in commodities. This last dimension clarifies the existence of crises specifically related to the realization of value.

Marini studied these types of problems deriving from the double aspect of commodities, analyzing the pyramid of monopolies, demand imbalances, and crises caused by the tightness of consumption in the periphery (Marini, 1979: 18–39). He belonged to a tradition in Marxist economics that disagreed with the approaches centered exclusively on the analysis of value in the sphere of production. That approach quantifies value only in the initial phase of surplus value creation, insistently pointing to the weight Marx put on the logic of exploitation and deducing all the contradictions of capitalism from this sphere. From that perspective, it dismisses all the imbalances located in the sphere of demand.

The critique of dependentism is rooted in this old 'technological' interpretation of value, which some analysts have recently objected to (Solorza and Deytha, 2014). With this conceptual foundation, it is very difficult to grasp the particularities of the peripheral economies studied by Marini.

6   Misunderstanding Underdevelopment

Transfers of value provide the theoretical support needed to assess how surplus value is channeled between the different sectors of the bourgeoisie. It is impossible to understand the forms of distributive conflict that appear in the countries affected by them without recognizing this dimension. The dispute in Argentina with the soy growers in 2008 is an example of that type. It has been asserted that this approach obscures the central contradiction between capital and labor (Astarita, 2009b), but in practice it is quite the contrary. It clarifies the reality of that social antagonism by situating it in the framework of tensions on the side of the oppressors. No political action by workers is effective if it ignores conflicts at the higher levels.

The importance of conflicts among the dominators is dismissed as a distraction from the primary attention that should be given to the proletariat. In this view, it is a distortion associated with 'national and popular Marxism' that posits paths to convergence of anti-imperialism with socialism (Astarita, 2014). Marxist dependency theory is visualized as a supreme expression of that mistake. However, that attitude shuts off all possibilities for participation in the popular struggles of Latin America and for promoting strategies of radicalization to advance toward the achievement of anti-capitalist goals, and reflects its theoretical difficulties for explaining underdevelopment. By rejecting the idea of value transfers from the periphery to the center, it obstructs any understanding of global stratification. The relative historical stability of this cleavage becomes an unsolvable enigma.

The simple acknowledgment of greater productivity in the advanced economies does not explain the reproduction of that gap in a system governed by competition. The anti-dependency thesis evades these dilemmas. At best, it assesses the historical origin of the asymmetries of development, indicating the place each country occupies in the international division of labor (Astarita, 2013c). It also takes note of the legacy inherited from pre-capitalist systems and the roles played by different bourgeoisies (Astarita, 2004: Chapter 8). However, these observations are limited to describing the polarization of accumulation on a world scale, without clarifying the mechanisms of that cleavage.

The answer is not to be found in what happened during the rise of capitalism, but in what happened afterward. The contemporary process of underdevelopment and its continuation require some explanation. In the face of the silence of its critics, Marxist dependency theory offers an interpretation based on transfers of surplus value.

7   Raw Material Cycles

Marini's scarce participation in debates on unequal exchange was probably due to his peculiar use of the concept. He used it as a simple foundation of the structural disadvantage of the Latin American economy, identifying that asymmetry with the deterioration of the terms of trade (Marini, 1973: 24–38). That principle was the undisputed foundation for many approaches of the era. The persistent devaluation of primary exports was attributed by the Economic Commission for Latin America and the Caribbean (ECLAC) to the socioeconomic structure of the periphery. In that view, profits and wages in the metropolises grew at a level above productivity (maintaining high industrial prices), while an opposite process prevailed in the agro-export countries (Prebisch, 1986).

Marini shared that conclusion, but not its institutionalist interpretation. He explained the depreciation of primary goods by the objective dynamics of accumulation on an international scale. He described how foreign investment facilitated the appropriation of resources from the periphery, and attributed that exaction to the subordination of the backward countries. However, this accurate diagnosis did not clarify the mechanisms that devalued raw materials. An influential clue to resolving that enigma was provided by the first studies of surplus value transfers between advanced and backward regions of Europe (Howard and King, 1992: 189–200). This characterization contrasted with the simple developmentalist identification of disadvantages in exchange with the implementation of erroneous economic policies.

Just when these perspectives were at the height of their influence, the first challenge to the principle of the inexorable depreciation of primary exports appeared. This critique was provoked by the rise in the price of oil with the emergence of OPEC, along with the amassing of hard currency on the part of the backward economies of the Middle East. This episode involved a very peculiar raw material and enriched only a small number of countries, but the conceptual objection to deterioration of the terms of trade was strengthened with empirical challenges to the Prebisch thesis. The critics used the case of the United States to exemplify the absence of a completely automatic relationship between agro-export and underdevelopment (Bairoch, 1999: 234–236).

A reconsideration of the specificity of basic products also began among Marxists. Given their dependence on nature, those inputs differ from their industrial counterparts in terms of their lesser flexibility for technological innovation and therefore for productivity growth. Thus, their prices tend to increase, giving rise to reactive processes of industrialization of raw materials (Grossman, 1979: 269–290). Those waves of investment create substitutes, as happened, for example, with synthetic rubber when demand from the automobile sector appreciated the price of its natural precursor.

While the deterioration of prices is corroborated for a large number of basic products, the prevailing dynamics in the sector depend on a cyclical price pattern. That fluctuation subjects the prices of those goods to the double process of upward pressures and downward reactions. Applying this criterion, some studies depicted the historical cycles of raw materials. The initial appreciation (1820–73) was followed by two upward spikes in the first half of the 20th century and a third caused by the oil shocks (1970–80). Waves of investment in primary activity to reverse those increases were found in all those cases (Mandel, 1978: Chapter 3). This clarification of the specificity of basic inputs led to the revision of another key idea about the peripheral economies.

8   The Reintroduction of Rent

The modalities of agro-mining rents drew little attention from dependency theory. In contrast, they were analyzed by endogenist Marxism as a way to understand Latin American backwardness. Most of those analyses portrayed that surplus as a 'feudal relic'. Marini rejected that characterization, objecting to the notion of the survival of pre-capitalist forms of exaction. The backdrop to the controversy was political – the Brazilian theorist promoted an uninterrupted socialist process counterposed to a project for eradicating 'feudal impediments' with some variety of 'progressive capitalism'.

These necessary debates still obscured the enormous importance of a completely capitalist rent. That category had drawn less interest in most of the world since the early 20th century because of its decreasing weight in the advanced economies. The share of rent in the national income of England fell from 30 percent in 1688 to 20 percent in 1801, and then from 14 percent in 1855 to 12 percent in 1900 and 6 percent in 1963 (Baptista, 2010: 16–20). Because of that waning influence, it was assumed that rents did not have significant effects on prices, an impression that was reinforced by the postwar mechanization of agriculture.

However, there was renewed interest in rent beginning in the 1980s, leading to corroboration of the fact that nature-dependent activities never become ordinary industrial sectors. That revival of interest was sparked by the oil shock, followed by the appreciation of certain metals. The recent 'supercycle of raw materials' reinforced curiosity about rent. Chinese demand in recent decades revalorized all basic products and caused record-breaking prices for food, energy, and mineral inputs.

The debate over the peculiarities of payment for property in natural resources has fully reemerged. The classical economists in the 19th century had grasped the mechanisms of that rent, but without understanding its social content. Marx clarified its foundations in surplus value, and argued that the surplus did not arise spontaneously from nature, but feeds on the unpaid labor of workers and is captured by landowners when they are able to exercise their territorial monopoly (Marx, 1973: Vol. 3, 209–216). But the basis of the rent in surplus value represents only a generic beginning that does not specify how it is sustained by the exploitation of workers. Some approaches identify that basis with the extraordinary surplus value created by wage-workers engaged in primary sector activity, while others situate the origin of those profits in portions of the surplus value extracted from industrial workers and transferred to landowners.

Both characterizations agree on the need to update the criteria established by Marx for assessing the amount and the duration of rent. The prices of agricultural goods are set by their cost of production plus the average profits on the land (or the investment) of lowest yield. The owners of the other lands obtain an increasing rent in accordance with the fertility or location of their properties. The magnitude of the profit depends on the prices of primary products, given that the advantages of the owners of the best lands grow with increases in those prices.

Rent is set according to those singularities and oscillates with the desire or disinterest around each use-value. Some commodities have a stable demand over prolonged periods because of their food (wheat) or energy (uranium) function; others suffer abrupt declines owing to the appearance of substitutes (sugar). Certain products show recurring price swings (oil), and others sudden upswings (lithium). Replacements produced in laboratories expand rapidly but can never break the peculiar connection of those products to nature. Like most economists of their era, dependency theorists did not analyze those peculiarities of rent. The continuation of that omission is very problematic in the stage of neoliberal capitalism, centered to such a great extent on the devastating exploitation of natural resources.

9   Imperialist Rents

The priority of usufruct rights to nature for large corporations can be seen in the new concept of extractivism. That term highlights how the rules of contemporary capitalism impose destruction on the environment, which is striking in the mining activities that dynamite mountains, dissolve rocks with chemical compounds, and squander the water needed for agriculture. The effect of this calamity is the disappearance of the Andean glaciers, the deforestation of the Amazon Basin, and coastal flooding.

The very high profitability of raw materials has brought this into the sophisticated world of financial transactions, while multiplying intense disputes over the capture of the profits in play. The advantages obtained by each competitor do not depend solely on its technological capacity or commercial astuteness – the geopolitical weight of the world powers has become decisive for exercising effective control over the desired territories.

The flags of the major developed economies wave on the map of oil, metals, water, and pastures. Some theorists have used the accurate concept of imperialist rent to chart the form now taken by the appropriation of that wealth, as the large companies operate under the strategic protection of their states (Amin, 2011a: 119–126). Imperialist rent is a term that confronts the widespread denigration of the 'rentier states' of the periphery, a term neoliberals use to discredit the underdeveloped countries, justifying the plunder perpetrated by the transnational corporations with hypocritical critiques of the corruption that prevails in those regions.

The scandalous pillage in process in Africa and Latin America shows certain similarities with the precedents described by Lenin in the early 20th century. The ruling classes of the center and the periphery seek rents in a framework of social struggles that determine whether they will eventually be captured by the popular sectors. Analyzing that surplus in these terms allows us to overcome the narrow economism that tends to neglect the peculiar dependence of those resources on the political power of its captors. Marx stressed that specificity in his treatment of agrarian rent. After describing its varying economic forms, he attributed the direction of that income to the unfolding of political conflicts, explaining in those terms the clashes of the bourgeoisie with the landlords that ended with the importation of wheat. He analyzed a similar crisis in

France with the same logic. In both cases, his explanations were situated in the arena of the class struggle (Amin, 2011a: 81–82).

This treatment illustrates the weight of the political dimension in any reflection about rent. Because of the strategic importance of the desired resources, the battle over their appropriation includes major confrontations. For the same reason, states can play leading roles as administrators, managers, or owners of that income, allowing them to retain, drain, or absorb the rent. Each state's arbitration can define which social sectors are favored by its distribution. The idea of imperialist rent is compatible with Marxist dependency theory and underscores the specificity of that concept relative to profit, facilitating the separation of the two categories. Its incorporation into dependentist thought contributes to the updating of that paradigm.

10   International Rent

One interpretation of the Argentine economy posits that the country has been a beneficiary of differential rent on an international scale. That idea emerged in the 1960s, asserting that the prices of exported grains were set at the international level, with the profits captured by the landowners representing a transfer of surplus value created in the countries that imported those grains.

This perspective underlined the specificity of rent based on exceptional fertilities rather than the exploitation of labor power, as had been the case in tropical plantations (Flichman, 1977: 15–80). The theoretical significance of this new concept was not developed very far by its creators and was disconnected from the question of dependency. It was used only to clarify the causes of Argentine agrarian stagnation, and it inspired interpretations of the conservative behavior of the *latifundista* landowners.

The same thesis was later improved upon to explain the enormous incomes received by Argentina since the late 19th century. Since most of its agrarian production was exported with lower costs than the rest of the world, the country absorbed extraordinary profits originating outside its national space. The sale of food products that cheapened the reproduction of European labor power generated those high rents for the landowners (Iñigo Carrera, 2015: 710–740).

However, this approach also argued that local capture of that surplus was tempered by its recapture at the hands of foreign firms. Rents flowed back into the English storage plants, banks, and railroads that controlled and financed the foreign sales of wheat and beef (Iñigo Carrera, 2017). The surplus value appropriated by the Argentine ruling class was reappropriated by its British competitors. That same circuit was later recreated by the U.S. capitalists who replaced the declining British empire.

The same interpretation has been applied in the current context, emphasizing that the huge transformations since the 1960s have not altered the old dynamics of international rents that flow in and out at the same speed. In this view, that mechanism survived the great mutation of agriculture. The soy boom replaced the stagnated meat and cereal sectors, the landowners became entrepreneurs, and the farmworkers became contractors. The activities of the sector capitalized on sophisticated forms of direct planting and transgenic seeds.

But the international rent theorists stressed that this modernization did not change the old mechanism of neutralization of the surplus. The favorable balance of agro-export was countered by the trade deficit of a more concentrated, foreign-owned, and subsidized industry. Indebtedness continued to absorb the lion's share of hard currency in an economy that had been dollarized because of inflation, frequent crises, and the wealthy keeping much of its wealth outside the country.

This portrayal of repeating sequences of inflows and outflows of international rents has provoked controversies about the consistency of this thesis with Marx's thought (Astarita, 2009a; Mercatante, 2010), but from a dependency view it could be interpreted as a variant of the cycle analyzed by Marini. As the initial capture of hard currency by the agricultural sector then vanishes in industry and finance, Argentina faces a structural loss of resources. The status underscored by dependency theory is corroborated without the initial deterioration of the terms of trade.

The international rent theorists reject this eventual convergence and explicitly counterpose their thesis to dependentism. They question all the terms used by the dependency tradition to characterize the country's backwardness, and object to the depiction of a 'deformed economy' with a 'drain of resources' and to the use of ideas like 'unequal exchange' and 'imperialism' (Iñigo Carrera, 2015: 739–740). Is this counterpoint valid?

11   Forced Incompatibilities

The proponents of international rent close their eyes to the clear similarity of their descriptions to the approach they dismiss. Both theses highlight the centrality of global movements of surplus value and describe how those movements obstruct the development of the productive forces. It is true that dependency theory neglected rent in the 1970s, but no theory begins without some omissions. What matters is to determine whether this omission disproves or is compatible with Marini's conception.

The compatibility between the two approaches has been shown in a recent comparison (Lastra, 2018), which underlines the relevance both theories ascribe to value transfers. The dependency approach analyzes movements of surplus value while international rent theory focuses on movements of rent. Other scholars in the tradition of Marini's work have also incorporated rent into his conception (Carrizalez and Sauer, 2017).

In contrast, the forced counterpoint ((Iñigo Carrera, 2017: xi–xviii) challenges the authors (Laclau, 1973) who take dependentist views of international rent that support the later Marxist synthesis between endogenist Marxism and dependency theory. Rather than deepening this convergence, it posits an opposition that separates rent from similar obstructions to Latin American development. It fails to recognize that the forms of those obstructions are secondary to the core of the problem, which is underdevelopment. By itself, international rent theory contributes little as a simple description of a dependent cycle or a flow of financial payments.

Those processes are of interest to the extent that they help to clarify regional backwardness. If they do not generate different effects in Argentina, Colombia, or Bolivia than they do in Switzerland, the United States, or Japan, they should be seen simply as features of the economy; but if, on the contrary, they reinforce the perpetuation of the distances of the former group of countries from the latter, they must be integrated into some theory of dependency.

Refusal to acknowledge that convergence leads to an ambiguous view of the final effect of those rents, stressing how it obstructs the sustained accumulation of capital but denying its impact on underdevelopment. It describes the inflows and outflows of hard currency but objects to the existence of a structural drainage. This type of vagueness has been noted by several authors (Anino and Mercatante, 2009); it is a consequence of absolutizing rent at the expense of other processes that have the same effects on the structural regression of the Argentine economy. If we only look at the movement of rent, we can't see the forest for the tree, as the exception obscures the final outcome. This view forgets that in the very thesis of international rent, the initial absorption of value by primary exporters is neutralized by the subsequent dynamics of dependent capitalism. Marini neglected rent, but his critics disconnect it from the contradictions he uncovered about center-periphery inequalities.

The consequence of this form of reasoning is an anti-dependentist political position. Proponents of international rent reject any convergence of anti-imperialism with socialism, instead promoting analytical treatments based on the 'global unity of capitalism' that are contrary to all variants of nationalism

(Kornblihtt, 2017). That approach only seeks affinities with proletarian internationalism (Iñigo Carrera, 2008: 27), ignoring all the precedents in Latin
American history of convergence between the two traditions. However, it is
clear that in any interpretation, those controversies can only be processed
through political action. Thus, Marxist dependency theorists very early on
connected their conception with the socialist strategy of the Cuban revolution. Their critics prefer to adopt abstract logic, purely economic reflections,
and philosophical assessments anchored in dialectical language. With this distance from the class struggle, it is impossible to understand and act upon Latin
American reality.

12   The Contrast with Venezuela

Studies of oil or mining rents are currently of great importance, and probably
more decisive for updating dependency theory than those focused on the agricultural sphere. They differ in several ways. Oil rents operate with limited reserves
and with estimated dates of depletion. They benefit from a type of extraction of
great importance for the functioning of capitalism, and have barriers to entry
and much higher costs than those prevailing in agriculture. In the energy sector, the differential element is determined by the quality, location, and conditions of extraction of each source. The dominant presence of the state is also
much higher – private property no longer obstructs investment, as was the case
with agriculture. Absolute rent, which landowners received from their territorial
monopolies, does not have much impact on the extraction of energy sources.

Oil falls under the overall management of the state in all the Latin American
countries. In the important case of Venezuela, rents that in the early 20th century were disputed between foreign companies and landowners were gradually nationalized through tax policies. The nationalization in 1976 reinforced
this tendency, which included the creation of a state enterprise (PDVSA) operating at all levels of the activity (Mommer, 1999).

Estimations of oil rents do not face the difficulties of its agrarian counterparts. U.S. contracts, taken as references for global transactions, distinguish this
concept from taxes and profits, facilitating the calculation of the surplus when
the dominant companies (the 'seven sisters') lost control over the market and
setting off the dispute for rents between the producers' cartel (OPEC), its import-
side adversary (International Energy Agency), and the intermediary firms.

Like their Argentine colleagues, Venezuelan Marxists dissented in the conceptualization of that surplus. Those who characterized it as an international
rent described the magnitude of the inflows of hard currency and how they

were then channeled toward paying for imports. They argued that the favorable initial exchange was completely neutralized in a country lacking significant production of its own (Mommer, 1998: 305–310). The squandering of hard currency consolidated a more vulnerable rentier capitalism in Venezuela than in the Argentine model. Unproductive consumerism and the inefficiency of public administration have obstructed the creation of even the tenuous industry that arose in the Southern Cone. Unlike Argentina, however, this analysis of international rent was not counterposed to dependency theory. On the contrary, it conceived of rentier capitalism as a variety of dependent capitalism (Trompiz Vallés, 2013). With these foundations, it analyzed indebtedness and periodic crises (Mora Contreras, 1987).

This perspective, combining international rent with dependentism, was carried over into the political sphere. It allowed the establishment of an area of convergence with *Chavismo* that supported the linking of anti-imperialism with socialism, in contrast with Argentina, and demonstrated the practical ramifications of a dependentist approach.

13   Totalizing Visions

Marini posited a comprehensive interpretation of the causes of underdevelopment that enriched the tradition forged by various anti-capitalist thinkers. He also absorbed innovative ideas from other currents, distancing himself from the conventional theses that involved liberal proposals while maintaining debates with kindred approaches that led to agreements. That trajectory indicates a path to the renewal of the dependency theses, which requires an understanding of the new stage of neoliberal globalized capitalism and modification of insufficient concepts while incorporating missing ideas.

Value theory is the organizing principle of that reformulation. It explains how productive globalization based on the exploitation of workers remodels the cleavages between center and periphery through transfers of surplus value. The omission of that mechanism prevents the critics of dependentism from understanding the logic of underdevelopment. Reintegrating the theory of value into the explanation of dependency is also vital for uncovering the hidden skeleton of present-day capitalism. There is no invisible hand guiding markets, nor is there a wise state institution steering the economy. The foundation of the system is competition for profits arising from exploitation, multiplying the wealth of minorities and the suffering of the majorities. The same indignation and rebelliousness that drove the study of underdevelopment in the past orients that inquiry in the present.

Epilogue

Dependency theory has been making a comeback in recent years along with the progressive cycle of the last decade, above all of *Chavismo*. Dependency theory was very much present in Chávez's conceptual universe and in some of Evo Morales's ideas. It has not been the viewpoint of Lula in Brazil or of Cristina Kirchner in Argentina, who are tolerant of, but not allied to, that perspective. Chávez reclaimed the dependentist legacy with the same emphasis he put on the rediscovery of communism and the current relevance of socialism.

The renewed influence of that perspective can also be seen in its implicit presence in several theoretical proposals of recent years. There are elements of dependentism in '21st century socialism' and in '*buen vivir*' (good living). For the same reason, tributes to the major figures of that tradition have multiplied, and there are many initiatives for republication of their books.

The intellectual climate of the 1970s has not returned, but there are indications of a resurgence of dependency thought. This can be seen in a core of research groups that are emerging in Brazil, while in Mexico there continue to appear works by authors who were disciples of Marini, and there are initiatives of this type in countries without a strong dependentist tradition. The current debates between the theory's defenders and its critics from various anti-dependency perspectives is also notable. They return to the questions that appeared in the 1980s, and in Argentina have sparked some level of renewed interest in academia.

The dependency perspective currently has influence in assessments of the progressive cycle, which was unable to deal with overcoming underdevelopment. This characterization is valid not only for Argentina or Brazil, but also for Venezuela. Partial redistribution of income was insufficient for transforming agrarian or oil rent into a source of egalitarian development, though those processes are not over and their outcomes are still being debated in a framework of inconclusive disputes.

The dependency perspective is very useful for assessing the limits of the conservative restoration, as right-wing governments face similar limits. In the economic sphere, they attempt to deepen primarization and extractivism in an adverse international context, implementing a passive adaptation to free trade while Trump and Macron revise all tariffs, and they are disoriented with their pro-U.S. ideological primitivism in a context of Chinese preponderance in the acquisition of raw materials. In the political sphere, the conservative governments lose legitimacy as they eliminate constitutional guarantees and resort to increasingly repressive abuses to create more authoritarian systems.

The capacity of those regimes for implementing neoliberal reorganization is very much in doubt, as they all face great popular resistance, while on a continental level the right has not been able to remove the bastions of Venezuela, Bolivia, and Cuba.

Dependency theory is also renewing its influence outside the region. Its ideas are welcomed by activists from the European periphery who confront very similar problems to those of Latin America. For example, comparisons to Argentina spread widely in Greece during the debt crisis. These views adopted a dependency perspective. The similarities are evident, even though the role of the United States in Latin America is taken by Germany in Europe, and the European Commission complements the oversight of the IMF.

Some economists on the Old Continent have done interesting work with a dependentist theoretical foundation to clarify the question of the Euro. They have explained how the monetary association of European countries with different wages generates transfers of value from the periphery to the center. That mechanism has many similarities with Marini's thesis – the Euro confers trade imbalances in favor of Germany that culminate in debt and dependency. However, the future vitality of dependency theory depends on its capacity to comprehend the current stage of capitalism. Work is already being done in that direction to analyze the globalization of production, highlighting especially the new global arbitrage of labor and the ways in which value created at one part of the planet is realized at another.

There is no doubt that the neoliberal period that is still in force is significantly distinct from the late Keynesian era that was still present at the birth of dependency theory. To carry out its aggression against workers, 21st century capitalism operates with different mechanisms in support of a model based on the dominance of transnational corporations. Forty years ago, capitalism was already global but did not function with value chains, financial globalization, and assembly for trade. In this new context, the distinction between exploitation in the center and super-exploitation in the periphery does not define dividing lines. There are modalities of both types at both poles of the world economy, with strong differences in the status of formal and informal labor.

The hierarchical world structure and the networks of value transfers have also changed. Those mutations explain the unprecedented contemporary dynamics of employment cuts. Not only are more jobs destroyed than created, but that destruction occurs at an unprecedented speed. Four decades ago, the digital revolution was only imagined in science fiction. Geopolitical transformations have been equally dramatic. The Soviet Union disappeared, China emerged, and there is an unresolved debate over the decline of the United States, all in a context of a great reshaping of imperial arrangements. The old national configurations have changed substantially without generating the full globalization described by some analysts. A hybrid mode of globalization of production has been created, without an equivalent correlate in social classes and states.

In this context, intermediate formations occupy a significant place that breaks the strict parallel between subimperial powers and economic semi-peripheries, as the geopolitical weight of some countries differs from the integration into globalized production achieved by others. Dependency theory is very useful for understanding that variety of situations. It explains the logic of the underdevelopment and marginalization of the periphery without limiting its analysis to global polarities, and also analyzes the bifurcations and differences between distinct intermediate formations.

This type of treatment must be enriched in order to broaden our understanding of contemporary reality. The updating of dependency theory continues to develop with a commitment to resistance to imperial aggressiveness and to all the nightmares that capitalism causes. The same roots that nourish dependency theory also orient the search for new paths to building a society where no one is an exploiter or exploited.

References

Adamovsky, Ezequiel. (2012). "El mito del aumento de la clase media global," *Clarín*, 26–12. https://www.clarin.com/opinion/mito-aumento-clase-media-global_o_S1d8 VvnsvXg.html.

Aguirre Rojas, Carlos Antonio. (2007). "Immanuel Wallerstein y la perspectiva crítica del Análisis de los Sistemas-Mundo," *Textos de Economía*, vol. 10, no. 2 (jul./ dez.): 11–57.

Albo, Gregory. (2004). "Paul Sweezy and American Marxism," Department of Political Science York University Toronto, Ontario, April, www.nodo50.org. América Latina, dependencia y globalización. Bogotá: CLACSO.

Amin, Samir. (1973). *¿Cómo funciona el capitalismo?* Buenos Aires: Siglo XXI.

Amin, Samir. (1976). *Imperialismo y desarrollo desigual*. Barcelona: Fontanella.

Amin, Samir. (1988). *La desconexión*. Buenos Aires: Pensamiento Nacional.

Amin, Samir. (2001a). "Capitalismo, imperialismo, mundialización," *Resistencias Mundiales*, pp. 15–29. Buenos Aires: CLACSO.

Amin, Samir. (2001b). *Crítica de nuestro tiempo: Los ciento cincuenta años del Manifiesto comunista*. México: Siglo XXI.

Amin, Samir. (2003). *Más allá del capitalismo senil*. Buenos Aires: Paidós.

Amin, Samir. (2004). "Geopolítica del imperialismo colectivo," *Nueva Hegemonía Mundial*, pp. 37–58. Buenos Aires: CLACSO.

Amin, Samir. (2005). "He sido y sigo siendo un comunista," *La teoría del sistema capitalista mundial: Una aproximación al pensamiento de Samir Amin*, ed. by Roffinelli Gabriela, Panamá: Ruth Casa Editorial.

Amin, Samir. (2006). "La historia comprendida como ciclo eterno," *Revista Mundo Siglo XXI*, número 5: 5–22. México: verano.

Amin, Samir. (2008). *Modernité, religion et démocratie: Critique de l'eurocentrisme*. Lyon: Parangon.

Amin, Samir. (2011a). *La ley del valor mundializada Por un Marx sin fronteras*. Madrid: El Viejo Topo.

Amin, Samir. (2011b). *El mundo árabe: raíces y complejidades de la crisis*. La habana: Ruth Ediciones.

Amin, Samir. (2013a). "El imperialismo colectivo: Desafíos para el Tercer Mundo," 19/8, http://www.fisyp.org.ar/article/entrevista-a-samir-amin-el-imperialismo-colectivo-.

Amin, Samir. (2013b). Transnational capitalism or collective imperialism?, 23–03.

Anderson, Benedict. (1993). *Comunidades imaginadas. Reflexiones sobre el origen y la difusión del nacionalismo*. México: F.C.E.

Anderson, Kevin B. (2010). *Marx at the Margins*. Chicago, IL: University of Chicago Press.

Anderson, Perry. (1985). *Teoría, política e historia. Un debate con E.P. Thompson.* Madrid: Siglo XXI.

Anderson, Perry. (2002). "Internacionalismo: un breviario," *New Left Review,* no. 14 (mayo–junio): 5–24.

Anderson, Perry. (2016). "A crise no Brasil," http://www.pambazuka.org/pt/democrac ygovernance/crise-no-brasil-uma-an%C3%A1lise-profunda-de-perry-anderson.

Angotti, Thomas. (1981). "The political implications of Dependency Theory," *Latin American Perspectives,* vol. 8, nos. 3–4: 124–137.

Anino, Pablo, and Mercatante, Esteban. (2010). "Informe sobre ciegos. Razón y Revolución y su "mirada" del capitalismo argentino," www.ips.org.ar.

Anino, Pablo, and Mercatante, Esteban. (2009). "Renta diferencial y producción agraria en Argentina Una respuesta a Rolando Astarita," www.ips.org.ar, agosto.

Annis, Roger. (2014). "The Russia as "Imperialist" Thesis Is Wrong and a Barrier to Solidarity With the Ukrainian and Russian People," *Truthout,* 18–06, https://truth out.org/articles/the-russia-as-imperialist-thesis-is-wrong-and-a-barrier-to-solidar ity-with-the-ukrainian-and-russian-people/.

Arcary, Valerio. (2016). "Uma nota sobre o lugar do Brasil no mundo em perspectiva histórica," 20–12, http://blog.esquerdaonline.com/?p=7760.

Aricó, José. (2012). *Nueve lecciones sobre economía y política en el marxismo.* México: El Colegio.

Armanian, Nazanín. (2016). "La rivalidad entre Rusia e Irán remodela el mercado del gas en Eurasia," http://blogs.publico.es/puntoyseguido/3144/la-rivalidadentre-rusia -e-iran-remodela-el-mercado-del-gas-en-eurasia/.

Arriazu, Ricardo. (2015). "Las razones de la nueva crisis de Brasil," *Clarín,* 19–9.

Arrighi, Giovanni. (1990). "The developmentalist illusion: a reconceptualization of semiperiphery," in W.G. Martin (ed.), *Semiperipheral states in the world economy,* pp. 11–42. Westport: Greenwood Press.

Arrighi, Giovanni. (2005). "Hegemony Unravelling, Part I," *New Left Review,* no. 32 (March/April).

Arrighi, Giovanni. (2006). "El mundo según André Gunder Frank," *Revista Mundo Siglo XXI,* no. 6 (otoño): 5–18.

Arrighi, Giovanni (2007). *Adam Smith en Pekín.* Madrid: Akal.

Arrighi, Giovanni, Silver, Beverly J., and Brewer, Benjamin D. (2003). "Industrial Convergence, Globalization, and the Persistence of the North-South Divide," *Studies in Comparative International Development,* Vol. 38, no. 1 (Spring): 3–31.

Ashman, Sam, and Callinicos, Alex. (2006). "Capital Accumulation and the State System," *Historical Materialism,* vol. 14.4: 107–131.

Assadourian, Carlos Sempat. (1973). *Modos de producción, capitalismo y subdesarrollo en América Latina, Modos de Producción en América Latina.* Buenos Aires: Siglo XXI.

Astarita, Rolando. (2004). *Valor, mercado y globalización*. Buenos Aires: Ediciones cooperativas.

Astarita, Rolando. (2009a). "Respuesta al profesor Juan Iñigo Carrera," www.rolando astarita.com, septiembre.

Astarita, Rolando. (2009b). "Renta agraria, ganancia del capital y tipo de cambio," www.rolandoastarita.com/ntRenta, junio.

Astarita, Rolando. (2010a). Subdesarrollo y dependencia, Universidad de Quilmes.

Astarita, Rolando. (2010b). "La teoría de la dependencia y la teoría de Marx," *Globalización, dependencia y crisis económica*. Málaga: FIM.

Astarita, Rolando. (2011). "Discusiones sobre intercambio desigual," 25–6, https://rola ndoastarita.blog/2011/06/25/discusiones-sobre-intercambio-desigual.

Astarita, Rolando. (2013a). "Mandel sobre la plusvalía extraordinaria," 9–9, rolando astarita.wordpress.com.

Astarita, Rolando. (2013b). "Marx sobre trabajo potenciado," 21–9, https://rolandoastar ita.wordpress.com.

Astarita, Rolando. (2013c). "Renta petrolera y capitalismo de estado (1)," 19–5, https:// rolandoastarita.wordpress.com.

Astarita, Rolando. (2014). "Plusvalía extraordinaria y renta agraria (1)," 9–4, rolando astarita.wordpress.

Bagu, Sergio. (1977). *Feudalismo, capitalismo, subdesarrollo*. Madrid: Akal.

Bairoch, Paul. (1973). *El tercer mundo en la encrucijada: el despegue económico desde el siglo*. Barcelona: Alianza.

Bairoch, Paul. (1999). *Mythes et paradoxes de l'histoire economique*. Paris: La Découverte.

Bambirra, Vania. (1978). *Teoría de la dependencia: una anti-critica*. México: Era.

Bambirra, Vania. (1986). *El capitalismo dependiente latinoamericano*. México: Siglo XXI.

Baptista, Asdrúbal. (2010). *Teoría económica del capitalismo rentístico*. Caracas: BCV.

Baran, Paul. (1959). *Economía política del crecimiento*. México: Fondo de Cultura Económica.

Barker, Colin. (2006). "Beyond Trotsky: extending combined and uneven development," *Permanent Revolution: Results and Prospects 100 Years*. London; Ann Arbor, MI: Pluto Press.

Barker, Colin. (2010). "Review: Marx at the margins," *Socialist Review*, July–August.

Barkin, David. (1981). "Internationalization of Capital: An Alternative Approach," *Latin American Perspectives*, Vol. 8, No. 3–4 (Summer–Autumn): 156–161.

Barreto, Helena Marroig. (2013). "Marini ontem e hoje: Pontuações sobre a teoria Marxista da dependência e novas perspectiva." Novembro, Universidad Federal do Rio de Janeiro, http://pantheon.ufrj.br/handle/11422/1488.

Batou, Jean. (2015). "Cien años después, lo que plantea el reconocimiento del genocidio armenio," *Viento Sur*, 23–04, https://vientosur.info/cien-anos-despues-lo-que-plantea-el-reconocimiento-del-genocidio-armenio/.

Behrouz, Farahany. (2017). "El papel de Irán en la tragedia siria," *Viento Sur*, http://vientosur.info/spip.php?article12116.

Bernstein, Eduard. (1982). *Las premisas del socialismo y las tareas de la socialdemocracia*. México: Siglo XXI.

Bettelheim, Charles. (1972a). "Intercambio internacional y desarrollo regional," *Imperialismo y comercio internacional*. Córdoba: Cuadernos de Pasado y Presente n 24.

Bettelheim, Charles. (1972b). "Los trabajadores de los países ricos y pobres tienen intereses solidarios," *Imperialismo y comercio internacional*. Córdoba: Cuadernos de Pasado y Presente n 24.

Bianchi, Alvaro. (2013). "Determinação e tendências históricas no pensamento de Trotsky," 5–2, https://esquerdaonline.com.br/2013/02/05/determinacao-e-tendenc ias-historicas-no-pensamento-de-trotsky/.

Blaut, J.M. (1994). "Robert Brenner in the tunnel of time," *Antipode: A radical journal of Geography*, 26.4: 351–374.

Blomstrom, Magnus, and Hettne Bjorn. (1990). *La teoría del desarrollo económico en transición*. México: Fondo de Cultura Económica.

Bond, Patrick. (2005). *El imperio norteamericano y el subimperialismo sudafricano. El Imperio Recargado*. Buenos Aires: CLACSO.

Bond, Patrick. (2015). "BRICS and the sub-imperial location," *BRICS: An Anti-Capitalist Critique*. Chicago: Haymarket.

Bond, Patrick. (2016). "BRICS banking and the debate over sub-imperialism," 15–11, http://www.cadtm.org/spip.php?page=imprimer&id_article=13946.

Boron, Atilio. (2008). "Teorías de la dependencia," *Realidad Económica*, n. 238 (agosto–septiembre), Buenos Aires.

Bourguignon, François, and Morrisson, Christian. (2002). "Inequality among World Citizens: 1820–1992," *American Economic Review*, 92(4): 727–744.

Bourguignon, François, and Châteauneuf-Malclès, Anne. (2016). "L'évolution des inégalités mondiales de 1870 à 2010," 20–06, http://ses.ens-lyon.fr/ressources/stats -a-la-une/levolution-des-inegalites-mondiales-de-1870-a-2010.

Brenner, Robert. (1977)." The Origins of Capitalist Development, A Critique of NeoSmithian Marxism," *New Left Review*, I/104 (July–August).

Brenner, Robert. (1988). *Estructura de clases agraria y desarrollo económico en Europa Preindustrial, El debate Brenner*. Barcelona: Crítica.

Brenner, Robert. (2006). "What Is, and What Is Not, Imperialism?," *Historical Materialism*, vol. 14.4: 79–105.

Bresser Pereira, Luiz Carlos. (2010). *Globalización y competencia*. Buenos Aires: Siglo XXI.

Bueno, Fabio Marvulle. (2016). "A Superexploracao so trabalho and polemicas em torno do conceito na obra de Ruy Mauro Marini e a vigencia na década de 2000," Tesis de Doutorado, Brasilia, março repositorio.unb.br/bitstream/10482/22734/1/2016.

Bueno, Fabio, and Seabra, Raphael. (2010). "A teoría do subimperialismo brasileño: notas para uma (re) discussao contempoánea," 26–11, www.buenastareas.com.

Bugarelli, Luiz. (2011). "Dependência e Revolução na América Latina: uma introdução ao debate de Agustín Cueva e Ruy Mauro Marini," www.uff.br/niepmarxmarxismo/ .../AMC333F.pdf.

Çağlı, Elif. (2009). "On Sub-imperialism: Regional Power Turkey, Marksist," Tutummarxist.cloudaccess.net, August.

Callinicos, Alex. (2001). *Imperialismo Hoy*, Montevideo: Ediciones Mundo Al revés.

Callinicos, Alex. (2009). "How to solve the many-state problem: a reply to the debate," *Cambridge Review of International Affairs*, vol. 22, no. 1 (March): 89–105.

Carcanholo, Marcelo Dias. (2013). "(Im)precisiones acerca de la categoría superexplotación de la fuerza de trabajo," *Razón y Revolución*, nº 25, Buenos Aires.

Carchedi, Gugliemo. (1991). *Frontiers of political economy*. London: Verso.

Cardoso, Fernando Henrique. (1972). "Notas sobre el estado actual de los estudios sobre dependencia," *Revista Latinoamericana de Ciencias Sociales*, no. 4, Santiago.

Cardoso, Fernando Henrique. (1973)."Contradicciones del desarrollo asociado," *Cuadernos de la Sociedad Venezolana de Planificación*, número 113–115, Caracas.

Cardoso, Fernando Henrique. (1977a). "La originalidad y la copia." Revista de la CEPAL, 2.

Cardoso, Fernando Henrique. (1977b). "Las clases sociales y la crisis política," *Clases sociales y crisis política en América Latina*. México: Siglo XXI-UNAM.

Cardoso, Fernando Henrique. (1978). "Estados Unidos y la teoría de la dependencia," *América Latina: 50 años de industrialización*. México: Col. La Red de Jonás, Premiá.

Cardoso, Fernando Henrique. (1980). "El desarrollo en el banquillo," *Revista de Comercio Exterior*, agosto, México.

Cardoso, Fernando Henrique. (2012). *A Suma e o resto*. Rio de Janeiro: Editorial Civilización Brasileira.

Cardoso, Fernando Henrique, and Faletto, Enzo. (1969). *Desarrollo y dependencia en América Latina. Ensayo de interpretación sociológica*. Buenos Aires: Siglo XXI.

Cardoso, Fernando Henrique, and Faletto, Enzo. (1977). "Post Scriptum a dependencia y desarrollo en América Latina," *Desarrollo Económico*, vol. 17, no. 66 (julio-septiembre), Buenos Aires.

Cardoso, Fernando Henrique, and Serra José. (1978). *Las desventuras de la dialéctica de la dependencia*. México: Revista Mexicana de sociología.

Cardoso, Ciro F.S. (1973). *Sobre los modos de producción coloniales den América, Assadourian, C. S. Modos de Producción en América Latina*. Buenos Aires: Siglo XXI.

Cardoso, Ciro F.S, and Pérez Brignoli, Héctor. (1979). *Historia económica de América Latina*, T I y II. Barcelona: Crítica.

Carrizalez Nava, Pablo, and Sauer, Ildo Luis. (2017). "Intercambio desigual y renta petrolera: una aproximación teórica necesaria," *Cadernos CERU*, serie 2, vol. 28, no. 2 (dezembro).

Carroll, William K. (2012). "Global corporate power and a new transnational capitalist class?" Presentation to the Centre for Civil Society, Durban, January 17.

Carroll, William K., and Carson, Colin. (2003). "Forging a New Hegemony? The Role of Transnational Policy Groups in the Network and Discourses of Global Corporate Governance," *Journal of World-Systems Research*, IX, 1 (Winter).

Castañeda, Jorge, and Hett, Enrique. (1991). *El economicismo dependentista*. México: siglo XXI.

Castañeda, Jorge, and Morales, Marco. (2010). *Lo que queda de la izquierda*. México: Taurus.

Chase-Dunn, Christopher. (1999). "Globalization: A World systems perspective," *Journal of World-Systems Research*, Vol. V, 2.

Chase Dunn, Christopher. (2012). "The Emergence of Predominant Capitalism: The Long Sixteenth Century," *Contemporary Sociology* 41.1: 9–12. ASA, January 18.

Chavolla, Arturo. (2005). *La imagen de América en el marxismo*. Buenos Aires: Prometeo Libros.

Chen, Kathy. (2010). "Wallerstein's World Economic System Theory," February 1, https://www.slideshare.net/expattam/wallersteins-world-systems-analysis-14644076.

Chilcote, Ronald. (1981). "Issues of Theory in Dependency and Marxism," *Latin American Perspectives*, vol. 8, nos. 3–4 (Jan.): 3–16.

Chilcote, Ronald. (1983). "Teorías reformistas e revolucionarias de desenvolvimento e subdesenvolvimento," *Revista Economía Política*, Vol. 3, N. 3 (julo–setembro).

Chilcote, Ronald. (1990). "Post-Marxism: The Retreat from Class in Latin America," *Latin American Perspectives*, vol. 17, n° 2.

Chilcote, Ronald. (2009). "Influencias trostkistas sobre a teoria do desenvolvimento da America Latina," *Revista de Ciencias Socias*, vol. 40, no. 1.

Chinchilla, Norma Stoltz, and Dietz, James Lowell. (1981). "Toward a new understanding of development and underdevelopment," *Latin American Perspectives*, vol. 8, nos. 3–4 (Jan.): 138–147.

Chingo, Juan. (2012). "El fin de las "soluciones milagrosas" de 2008/9 y el aumento de las rivalidades en el sistema mundial," 28–9, www.fti.org/IMG/pdf/EI28_Economia_y_geopolitica.pdf.

CLACSO. (2016). Carta Abierta al Congreso de la Latin American Studies Association (LASA) Nueva York, 27, 28, 29 y 30 de mayo.

Claudín, Fernando. (1970). *La crisis del movimiento comunista*. Madrid: Ruedo Ibérico.

Cordova, Armando. (1974). "Rosa Luxemburgo y el mundo subdesarrollado," *Problemas del Desarrollo*, vol. 5, no. 18.

Correa Prado, Fernando, and Rodrigo, Castelo. (2013). "O início do fim? Notas sobre a teoria marxista da dependência no Brasil Contemporáneo," *Revista Pensata*, vol. 3, no. 1 (novembro).

Cri, Adrian and Robles Marcos. (2014). "Los tiempos del imperio," *Ideas de Izquierda* no. 13, septiembre, Buenos Aires.

Cueva, Agustín. (1973). *El desarrollo del capitalismo en América Latina*. México: Siglo XXI.

Cueva, Agustín. (1976). "Problems and Perspectives of Dependency Theory," *Latin American Perspectives*, Vol. 3, No. 4 (Autumn): 12–16.

Cueva, Agustín. (1977). *Comentario, Clases sociales y crisis política en América Latina*. México: Siglo XXI.

Cueva, Agustín. (1978). *El uso del concepto de modo de producción en América Latina: algunos problemas teóricos*. México: Ediciones de Cultura Popular.

Cueva, Agustín. (1979a). *Teoría social y procesos políticos en América Latina (Línea Crítica)*. México: Edicol.

Cueva, Agustín. (1979b). "¿Vigencia de la "anticrítica" o necesidad de autocrítica? respuesta a Theotonio Dos Santos y Vania Bambirra," *Teoría social y procesos políticos en América Latina*. México: UNAM.

Cueva, Agustín. (1982). *Cultura, Clase y Nación: Cuadernos Políticos*, no. 20, México: ERA.

Cueva, Agustín. (1986). "Entrevista: Ciencias sociales y marxismo hoy," *Sociológica*, UAM, vol. 1, no. 1, México.

Cueva, Agustín. (1988). "Prólogo a la edición ecuatoriana," *Teoría social y procesos políticos en América Latina (Línea Crítica)*.

Cueva, Agustín. (2007). *El marxismo latinoamericano: historia y problemas actuales*. Buenos Aires: Entre la ira y la esperanza CLACSO- Prometeo.

Cueva, Agustín. (2007). *Problemas y perspectivas de la teoría de la dependencia*. Buenos Aires: Entre la ira y la esperanza CLACSO-Prometeo.

Cueva, Agustín. (2012). "Las interpretaciones de la democracia en América Latina," *Algunos problemas, Ensayos Sociológicos y Políticos*. Quito: Ministerio de Coordinación.

Davidson, Neil. (2006). *From uneven to combined development in Permanent Revolution: Results and Prospects 100 Years*. London: Pluto Press.

Davidson, Neil. (2010). "From deflected permanente revolution to the law of uneven and combined development," *International Socialist*, no. 128 (autumn).

Day, Richard B., and Gaido, Daniel. (2011). *Discovering Imperialism: Social Democracy to World War I*. Leiden: Brill Academic Publishers.

Demier, Felipe. (2013). "Ainda sobre a lei do desenvolvimento desigual e combinado: Trotsky e Novack," 3–3, https://esquerdaonline.com.br/2013/03/03/ainda-sobre-a-lei-do-desenvolvimento-desigual-e-combinado-trotsky-e-novack/.

Democratic Socialist Party. (2001). "The role of Australian imperialism in the AsiaPacific region," 3–7, http://links.org.au/node/116.

Di Meglio, Mauro, and Masina, Pietro. (2013). "Marx And Underdevelopment," in Saad Filho, Alfredo and Fine, Ben (eds.), *The Elgar Companion to Marxist Economics*. Aldershot: Edward Elgar.

Dobb, Maurice. (1969). *Capitalismo, crecimiento económico y subdesarrollo*. Barcelona: Oikos.

Dobb, Maurice. (1974). "Prefacio, Respuesta, Nuevo Comentario," *La transición del feudalismo al capitalismo*. Buenos Aires: Ediciones La Cruz del Sur.

Dockès, Pierre. (2013). "Mondialisation et impérialisme à l'envers," *La mondialisation, stade supreme du capitalisme*, pp. 129–151. Nanterre: Presses universitaires de Paris Quest.

Domingues, José Mauricio. (2012). *Desarrollo, periferia y semiperiferia en la tercera fase de la modernidad global*. Buenos Aires: CLACSO.

Dore, Elizabeth, and Weeks, John. (1979). "International Exchange and the causes of backwardness," *Latin American Perspectives*, vol. 6, no. 2: 66–87.

Doronenko, M. (2005). "Boris Kagarlitsky's plagiarism," 14/10/2005, india.indymedia .org/en.

Dos Santos, Theotonio. (1978). *Imperialismo y dependencia*. México: ERA.

Dos Santos, Theotonio. (1983). *Revolucao cientifico-técnica e capitalismo contemporaneo*. Río: Voces.

Dos Santos, Theotonio. (1998). "La teoría de la dependencia un balance histórico y teórico," *Los retos de la globalización*. Caracas: UNESCO.

Dos Santos, Theotonio. (2000). "World Economic System: On the Genesis of a Concept," *Journal of World-Systems Research*, Vol. XI, no. 2 (Summer/Fall).

Dos Santos, Theotonio. (2003). *La teoría de la dependencia: balance y perspectivas*. Buenos Aires: Plaza Janés.

Dos Santos, Theotonio. (2011). *Marxismo y ciencias sociales*. Luxemburg; Buenos Aires: Una revisión crítica.

Dos Santos, Theotonio. (2009a). *Bendita Crisis, socialismo y democracia en el Chile de Allende*. Caracas: El Perro y la Rana.

Dos Santos, Theotonio. (2009b). "Rui Mauro Marini: un pensador latino-americano," *A América Latina e os desafíos da globalizacao*. Rio: Boitempo.

Dos Santos, Theotonio, and Bambirra, Vania. (1980). *La estrategia y la táctica socialistas de Marx y Engels a Lenin*. México: ERA.

DSP (Democratic Socialist Party). (2001). "The role of Australian imperialism in the Asia-Pacific region," 3–7, http://links.org.au/node/116.

Duarte, Daniel. (2013). "Reseña de Bajo el Imperio del capital," *Hic Rhodus. Crisis capitalista, polémica y controversias*, no. 3(2).

Dussel, Enrique. (1988). *Hacia un Marx desconocido. Un comentario de los Manuscritos del 61–63*. Iztapalapa: Siglo XXI.

Dzarasov, Rusian. (2015). "Modern Russia as semi-peripheral, dependent capitalism," *BRICS: An Anti-Capitalist Critique*. Chicago: Haymarket.

Edelstein, Joel C. (1981). "Dependency: a special theory within marxian analysis," *Latin American Perspectives July*, vol. 8, nos. 3–4. Buenos Aires: Ediciones.

Emmanuel, Arrighi. (1971). "El intercambio desigual, Imperialismo y comercio internacional," *Pasado y Presente*, no. 24. Buenos Aires.

Emmanuel, Arrighi. (1972). *El intercambio desigual*. México: Siglo XXI.

Emmerich, Norberto. (2015). "China y América Latina: ¿cooperación sur-sur o estatus semicolonial," 12–3, http://www.pensamientocritico.org/noremmo415.htm.

Escobar, Pepe. (2014). "¿Pueden China y Rusia echar a Washington a empujones de Eurasia?," 9–10, rebelion.org/noticia.php?id=190582.

Escobar, Pepe. (2015). "¿Año de la Cabra, Siglo del dragón?," 4–3, www.ojosparalapaz.com/ano-de-la-cabra-siglo-del-dragon/.

Feres Júnior, João. (2016). "FHC: Embaixador do golpe no Brasil," http://cartamaior.com.br/?/Editoria/Politica/FHC-Embaixador-do-golpe-noBrasil/4/36175.

Ferguson, Philip. (1999). "Paul Cockshott, Bill Warren and anti-Irish nationalism," *Marxism Mailing List*, January.

Fernández, Raúl A. and Ocampo, José F. (1974). "The Latin American Revolution: A theory of imperialism, not dependence," *Latin American Perspectives*, vol. 1, no. 1, Spring.

Figueroa, Víctor. (1986). *Reinterpretando el subdesarrollo*. México: Siglo XXI.

Flichman, Guillermo. (1977). *La renta del suelo y el desarrollo agrario argentino*. México: Siglo XXI.

Foster, John Bellamy. (2011). "Samir Amin al 80: An Introduction and tribute," 1–10, http://monthlyreview.org/2011/10/01/samir-amin-at-80-an-introduction-and-tribute/.

Foster, John Bellamy. (2015). "The New Imperialism of Globalized Monopoly-Finance Capital," *Monthly Review*, vol. 67, issue 3, July–August.

Frank, André Gunder. (1965). *¿Con qué modos de producción convierte la gallina maíz en huevos de oro?* México: Gallo Ilustrado-El Día.

Frank, André Gunder. (1970). *Capitalismo y subdesarrollo en América Latina*. Buenos Aires: Siglo XXI.

Frank, André Gunder. (1973). "De la dependencia a la acumulación," *Problemas del Desarrollo* no. 13, enero, México.

Frank, André Gunder. (1979). *Lumpenburguesía y lumpendesarrollo*. Barcelona: Laia.

Frank, André Gunder. (1979). *La crisis mundial*. Barcelona: Burguesa.

Frank, André Gunder. (1991). *El subdesarrollo del desarrollo*. Caracas: Nueva Sociedad.

Frank André Gunder. (2005a). "Celso Furtado y la teoría de la dependencia," *Revista Memoria*, enero.

Frank, André Gunder. (2005b). "Responses to ReOrient Reviews," www.rrojasdatabank.info.

Frank, André Gunder. (2009). "ReOriente Economía global en la Era Asiática," *C y E*, Año I N° 2, Primer Semestre 2009, bibliotecavirtual.clacso.org.ar/ar/libros/secret/.

Galba de Paula, Patrick. (2014). *Duas teses sobre Marx e o desenvolvimento: considerações sobre a noção de desenvolvimento em Marx.* Universidade Federal do Rio de Janeiro.

Gandásegui, Marco A. (2009). "Vigencia e debate en torno da teoría da dependencia," *A América Latina e os desafíos da globalizacao.* Rio: Boitempo.

Garcia, Ana. (2015). "Building BRICS from below?," *BRICS: An Anti-Capitalist Critique.* Chicago: Haymarket.

Gellner, Ernest. (1991). *Naciones y nacionalismo.* Madrid: Alianza.

Gereffi, Gary. (1989). "Los nuevos desafíos de la industrialización. Observaciones sobre el Sudeste Asiático y Latinoamérica," *Pensamiento Iberoamericano,* no. 16, Madrid, julio–diciembre.

Gereffi, Gary. (2001). "Las cadenas productivas como marco analítico," *Problemas del Desarrollo,* vol. 32, no. 125.

Goda, Thomas. (2013). "Changes in income inequality from a global perspective: an overview," April, *Post Keynesian Economics Study Group Working Paper* 1303.

Goldfrank, Walter L. (2000). "Paradigm Regained? The Rules Of Wallerstein's WorldSystem Method," *Journal of World-Systems Research,* Vol. XI, No. 2, Summer/Fall.

Grossman, Henryk. (1979). *La ley de la acumulación y el derrumbe del sistema capitalista.* México: Siglo XXI.

Guillén Romo, Héctor. (1978). "La teoría del imperialismo de Ernest Mandel," *Criticas de la Economía Política,* no. 9, octubre–diciembre, México.

Harman, Chris. (1992). "The return of the national question," *International Socialism,* 2, no. 56, autumn, London.

Harman, Chris. (2003). "Analysing Imperialism," *International Socialism,* 99, Summer.

Harris, Nigel. (1987). *The end of the Third World.* New York: The Meredith Press.

Harvey, David. (1982). *Los límites del capitalismo y la teoría marxista.* México: Fondo de Cultura Económica.

Harvey, David. (2003). *The New Imperialism.* Oxford University Press.

Harvey, David. (2006). "Comment on Commentaries," *Historical Materialism,* vol. 14, no. 4.

Healy, Barry. (2010). "Was Karl Marx Eurocentric?," *Links International Journal of Social Renewal,* October 22.

Henfrey, Colin. (1981). "Dependency, modes of production and class analysis of Latin America," *Latin American Perspectives,* vol. 8, nos. 3–4, Jan.

Herrera, Remy. (2001). *Les theories du systeme mundial capitaliste, Dictionnaire Marx Contemporain.* Paris: PUF.

Higginbottom, Andy. (2012). "Structure and Essence in Capital I: Extra Surplus-Value and the Stages of Capitalism," *Journal of Australian Political Economy,* 70, Australia.

Hilferding, Rudolf. (2011). "German Imperialism and Domestic Politics (October 1907)," *Discovering Imperialism: Social Democracy to World War I*. Leiden: Brill Academic Publishers.

Hilton, Rodney. (1974). *Comentario, La transición del feudalismo al capitalismo*. Buenos Aires: Ediciones La Cruz el Sur.

Hobsbawm, Eric. (1983). "Marxismo, nacionalismo e independentismo," en *Marxismo e historia social*, Universidad Autónoma de Puebla.

Hobsbawm, Eric. (2000). *Naciones y nacionalismo desde 1780*. Barcelona: Crítica.

Howard, M.C. and King, J.E. (1989). *A History of Marxian Economics*, vol. 1. New Jersey: Princeton University Press.

Howard, M.C. and King, J.E. (1992). *A History of Marxian Economics*, vol. 2. New Jersey: Princeton University Press.

Hung, Ho-fung. (2015). "China and the lingering Pax Americana," *BRICS: An Anti-Capitalist Critique*. Chicago: Haymarket.

Husson, Michel. (1999). "Apres l'age d'or: sur Le Troisieme Age du Capitalisme," *Le Marxisme d'Ernest Mandel*. Paris: Actuel Marx-PUF.

Husson, Michel. (2001). "L'ecole de la Regulation de Marx a la fondation Saint Simon: un aller sans retour?," Bidet Jacques and Kouvélakis Eustache (eds.), *Dictionnaire Marx contemporaine*. Paris: PUF.

Iñigo Carrera, Juan. (2008). "La unidad mundial de la acumulación de capital en su forma nacional históricamente dominante en América Latina." *Crítica de las teorías del desarrollo, de la dependencia y del imperialismo*, www.cicpint.org/Investigación/JIC/.../Iñigo%20Carrera_SEPLA_2008.

Iñigo Carrera, Juan. (2009). *Renta diferencial y producción agraria en Argentina: respuesta a Pablo Anino y Esteban Mercatante*, agosto.

Iñigo Carrera, Juan. (2015). *La especificidad nacional de la acumulación de capital en la Argentina: Desde sus manifestaciones originarias hasta la evidencia de su contenido en las primeras décadas del siglo XX*. Buenos Aires, noviembre, http://repositorio .filo.uba.ar/jspui/bitstream/filodigital/3004/1/uba_ffyl_t_2015_893711.

Iñigo Carrera, Juan. (2017). *La renta de la tierra formas, fuentes y apropiación*. Buenos Aires: Imago Mundi.

Jahanpour, Farhang. (2014). http://www.ipsnoticias.net/2014/11/las-raices-profunda sde-la-rivalidad-entre-sunies-y-chiies/.

Johnson, Dale L. (1981). "Economism and determinism in Dependency Theory," *Latin American Perspectives*, vol. 8, nos. 3–4, Jan.

Kagarlisky, Boris. (2015). "The new cold war: Ukraine and beyond," www.newcoldwar .org/interview-with-boris-kagarlitsky-on-ukraine-march.

Katz, Claudio. (1989). "Intercambio desigual en América Latina," en *Problemas del Desarrollo*, no. 79, octubre–diciembre, México.

Katz, Claudio. (1999). "Discutiendo la mundialización," *Razón y Revolución*, no. 5, otoño, Buenos Aires.

Katz, Claudio. (2001). "Sweezy: los problemas del estancacionismo. Taller." *Revista de sociedad, cultura y política*, vol. 5, np. 15, abril, Buenos Aires.

Katz, Claudio. (2007). "Argumentos pela palestina," *Revista Outubro*, no. 15, junio, Sao Paulo.

Katz, Claudio. (2008). "Ernest Mandel y la teoría de las ondas largas," *Mundo Siglo XX*, no. 14, otoño, México.

Katz, Claudio. (2009). *La economía Marx hoy seis debates teóricos*. Madrid: Maia Ediciones.

Katz, Claudio. (2011). "Bajo el imperio del capital," diciembre, Luxemburg, Buenos Aires.

Katz, Claudio. (2015). *Neoliberalismo, Neodesarrollismo, Socialismo*. Buenos Aires: Batalla de Ideas.

Katz, Claudio. (2017). "El tormentoso debut de Trump," 2–2, www.lahaine.org/katz.

Kautsky, Karl. (1978). *El camino al poder*. México: Siglo XXI.

Kautsky, Karl. (2011a). "Germany, England and world-policy (May 1900)," "The war in South Africa (November 1899)," *Discovering Imperialism: Social Democracy to World War I*. Leiden: Brill Academic Publishers.

Kautsky, Karl. (2011b). "Imperialism (September 1914)," *Discovering Imperialism: Social Democracy to World War I*. Leiden: Brill Academic Publishers.

Kaye, Harvey J. (1989). "Los historiadores marxistas británicos," Universidad de Zaragoza.

Kohan, Néstor. (1998). *Marx en su (Tercer) Mundo: hacia un socialismo no colonizado*. Buenos Aires: Biblos.

Kohan, Néstor. (2011). *Nuestro Marx*. Caracas.

Kornblihtt, Juan. (2012). "Del socialismo al estatismo capitalista." Debate sobre la teoría de la dependencia con Ruy Mauro Marini, 11–9.

Kornblihtt, Juan. (2017). "La unidad mundial en El Capital de Marx y la apariencia de la superación del capitalismo a nivel nacional," Colóquio Internacional Marx e o marxismo 2017: De O capital à Revolução de Outubro.

Kowalewski, Zbigniew Marcin. (2014). "Impérialisme russe," *Inprecor* nos. 609–610, octubre–décembre.

Krätke, Michael R. (2007a). "Rosa Luxemburg: Her analysis of Imperialism and her contribution to the critique of political economy," March 2007, http://www2.chuou.ac.jp/houbun/sympo/rosa_confe2007/pdf/papers/Kratke.pdf.

Kratke, Michel. (2007b). "On the history and logic of Modern capitalism: the legacy or Ernest Mandel," *Historical Materialism* 15.

Laclau, Ernesto. (1973). "Feudalismo y capitalismo en América Latina, Modos de Producción en América Latina," *Cuadernos de Pasado y Presente* no. 40, Buenos Aires.

Lastra, Facundo. (2018). "La teoría marxista de la dependencia y el planteo de la unidad mundial." Contribución a un debate en construcción. Cuadernos de Economía Crítica.

Lenin, Vladimir. (1973). *Obras Escogidas*. Moscú: Editorial Progreso.

Lenin, Vladimir. (1974a). *El derecho de las naciones a la autodeterminación (julio 1914)*. Buenos Aires: Anteo.

Lenin, Vladimir. (1974b). *Balance de una discusión sobre el derecho de las naciones a la autodeterminación (julio 1916)*. Buenos Aires: Anteo.

Lenin, Vladimir. (2006). *El imperialismo, fase superior del capitalismo*. Buenos Aires: Quadrata.

Lipietz, Alain. (1992). *Espejismos y milagros: problemas de la industrialización en el Tercer Mundo*. Bogotá: Editores Tercer Mundo.

López Hernández, Roberto. (2005). "La dependencia a debate," *Latinoamérica*, 40, enero, México.

López Segrera, Francisco. (2009). "A revolucao cubana e a teoría da dependencia: Ruy Mauro Marini como fundador," *A América Latina e os desafíos da globalizacao*. Rio: Boitempo.

Lowy, Michael. (1998). *¿Patrias o planeta?* Rosario: Homo Sapiens.

Lowy, Michael, and Traverso, Enzo. (1990). "The Marxist Approach to the National Question: An Interpretation," *Science and Society*, vol. 54, no. 2.

Luce, Mathias Seibel. (2011). "A economía política do subimperialismo em Ruy Mauro Marini: uma historia conceitual," *Anais do XXVI Simposio Nacional do Historia*, Sao Paulo, julio.

Luce, Mathias Seibel. (2015). "Sub-imperialism, the highest stage of dependent capitalism," *BRICS: An Anti-Capitalist Critique*. Chicago: Haymarket.

Luxemburg, Rosa. (1968). *La acumulación del capital*. Buenos Aires: Editoral sin especificación.

Luxemburg, Rosa. (1977). *Textos sobre la cuestión nacional*. Madrid: Ediciones de la Torre.

Luxemburg, Rosa. (2008). "Obras escogidas," Ediciones digitales Izquierda Revolucionaria, abril.

Luxemburg, Rosa. (2011). "Morocco (August 1911)," *Discovering Imperialism: Social Democracy to World War I*, Leiden: Brill Academic Publishers.

Lvovich, Daniel. (1997). "De la determinación a la imaginación: las teorías marxistas del nacionalismo. Una interpretación." Buenos Aires: FLACSO.

Machado Borges Neto, Joao. (2011). "Ruy Mauro Marini: dependência e intercâmbio desigual," *Crítica Marxista*, no. 33.

Magdoff, Harry. (1971). "La obra de Paul Baran," *Paul Baran el hombre y su obra*. Madrid: Siglo XXI.

Magdoff, Harry. (1972). *La era del imperialismo*. Montevideo: Serie del Ciclo Básico.

Mandel, Ernest. (1969a). *Traite d'Economie marxiste*, T II, Paris: Maspero.

Mandel, Ernest. (1969b). "Las leyes del desarrollo desigual," *Ensayos sobre el neocapitalismo*. México: ERA.

Mandel, Ernest. (1971a). *Ensayos sobre el neocapitalismo*. México: ERA.

Mandel, Ernest. (1971b). *La acumulación originaria y la industrialización del tercer mundo, Ensayos sobre el neocapitalismo*. México: ERA.

Mandel, Ernest. (1977). *Comentario, Clases sociales y crisis política en América Latina*. México: Siglo XXI.

Mandel, Ernest. (1978). *El capitalismo tardío*. México: ERA.

Mandel, Ernest. (1980). *El pensamiento de León Trotsky*. Bercelona: Fontamara.

Mandel, Ernest. (1985). *El capital. Cien años de controversias*. México: Siglo XXI.

Mandel, Ernest. (1986). *Semicolonial countries and semiindustrialized dependent countries*. New York: New International.

Mandel, Ernest. (1995). *Trotsky como alternativa*. Sao Paolo: Xamá editora.

Mandel, Ernest. (1996). "Capitalismo internacional en crisis. Qué sigue?," *Hojas Económicas*, no. 5, febrero.

Mandel, Ernest. (1983). *Trotsky: teoría y práctica de la revolución permanente*. México: Siglo XXI.

Mandel, Ernest. (1986). *Semicolonial countries and semiindustrialized dependent countries*. New York: New International.

Mandel, Ernest, and Jaber, A. (1978). "Sobre el nuevo capital financiero árabe e iraní," *Colección Cuadernos de Coyoacán* no. 2. México: El Caballito.

Manzanera Salavert, Miguel. (2013). "Sobre plusvalía relativa y ganancias extraordinarias. Contestación a Rolando Astarita," 18–9, https://rolandoastarita.wordpress.com.

Mariátegui, José Carlos. (1984). *Siete ensayos de interpretación de la realidad peruana*. Lima: Biblioteca Amauta.

Marini, Ruy Mauro. (1973). *Dialéctica de la dependencia*. México: ERA.

Marini, Ruy Mauro. (1976a). "La pequeña-burguesía y el problema del poder," *El reformismo y la contrarrevolución. Estudios sobre Chile*. México: ERA.

Marini, Ruy Mauro. (1976b). "Dos estrategias en el proceso chileno," *El reformismo y la contrarrevolución. Estudios sobre Chile*. México: ERA.

Marini, Ruy Mauro. (1978). Razones del neo-desarrollismo, Revista Mexicana de Sociología, vol. XL, México.210.

Marini, Ruy Mauro. (1979). "Plusvalía extraordinaria y acumulación de capital," *Cuadernos Políticos*, no. 20, México, abril–junio.

Marini, Ruy Mauro. (1982). "Sobre el patrón de reproducción de capital en Chile," *Cuadernos CIDAMO*, número 7, México.

Marini, Ruy Mauro. (1985). "La dialéctica del desarrollo capitalista en Brasil," *Subdesarrollo y revolución*. México: Siglo XXI.

Marini, Ruy Mauro. (1991). "Memoria," www.marini-escritos.unam.mx/001.

Marini, Ruy Mauro. (1993). "La crisis teórica," *América Latina: integración y democracia*. Caracas: Editorial Nueva Sociedad.

Marini, Ruy Mauro. (1994). "La crisis del desarrollismo," *Archivo de Ruy Mauro Marini*, www.marini-escritos.unam.mx.

Marini, Ruy Mauro. (1996). *Procesos y tendencias de la globalización capitalista*. Buenos Aires: Prometeo.

Marini, Ruy Mauro. (2005). "En torno a Dialéctica de la dependencia," *Proceso y tendencias de la globalización capitalista*. Buenos Aires: CLACSO.

Marini, Ruy Mauro. (2007a). "La dialéctica del desarrollo capitalista en Brasil," *Proceso y tendencias de la globalización capitalista*. Buenos Aires: CLACSO.

Marini, Ruy Mauro. (2007b). "La sociología latinoamericana: origen y perspectivas," *Proceso y tendencias de la globalización capitalista*. Buenos Aires: CLACSO-Prometeo.

Marini, Ruy Mauro. (2012). "O ciclo do capital na economía dependente," *Padrão de reprodução do capital*. Sao Paulo: Boitempo.

Marini, Ruy Mauro. (2013). "En torno a la dialéctica de la dependencia," Post-Scriptum, *Revista Argumentos*, vol. 26, no. 72, may–ago, México.

Martínez Peinado, Javier. (2012). "La estructura teórica Centro/Periferia y el análisis del Sistema Económico Global: ¿obsoleta o necesaria?," *Revista de Economía Mundial*, enero.

Martins, Carlos Eduardo. (2001). "O pensamento social e atualidade da obra de Ruy Mauro Marini," www.ifch.unicamp.br/criticamarxista/arquivos_biblioteca/artigo236artigo6.pdf.

Martins, Carlos Eduardo. (2009). "André Gunder Frank: el intelectual insurgente," *C y E*, Año I N° 2, Primer Semestre, bibliotecavirtual.clacso.org.ar/ar/libros/secret/.

Martins, Carlos Eduardo. (2011a). *Globalizacao, Dependencia e Neoliberalismo na América Latina*. Sao Paulo: Boitempo.

Martins, Carlos Eduardo. (2011b). "O pensamento social de Ruy Maurio Marini e sua actualidade: reflexoes parea o seculo XXI," *Crítica Marxista*, no. 32.

Martins, Carlos Eduardo. (2013). "El pensamiento de Ruy Mauro Marini y su actualidad para las ciencias sociales," *Revista Argumentos*, vol. 26, no. 72, México.

Marx, Carlos [Karl]. (1964). *Sobre el sistema colonial del capitalismo*. Buenos Aires: Ediciones Estudio.

Marx, Carlos [Karl]. (1967). *El Manifiesto Comunista*. Buenos Aires: Claridad.

Marx, Carlos [Karl]. (1973). *El Capital*. México: Fondo de Cultura Económica.

Marx, Carlos [Karl], and Engels, Federico [Friedrich]. (1972). "Materiales para la historia de América Latina," *Cuadernos de Pasado y Presente* 30, Córdoba.

Marx, Carlos [Karl], and Engels, Federico [Friedrich]. (1973). *La guerra civil en los Estados Unidos*. Buenos Aires: La Rosa Blindada.

Marx, Carlos [Karl], and Engels, Federico [Friedrich]. (1979). "Imperio y colonia. Escritos sobre Irlanda," *Pasado y Presente*, no. 72, México.

Marx, Carlos [Karl], and Engels, Federico [Friedrich]. (1980). "El porvenir de la comuna rural rusa," *Cuadernos de Pasado y Presente* 90, México.

Massa, Andrei Chikhani. (2013). Superexploração da força de trabalho, uma categoria em disputa, Guarulhos: Universidade Federal de São Paulo, UNIFESP.

Matos, Daniel. (2009). La falacia del nuevo subimperialismo brasileño, Estrategia Internacional, no. 25, enero.

Mendonça, José Carlos. (2011). "Notas sobre o Estado no pensamento político de Ruy Mauro Marini," *Revista Historia e Luta de Classes*, año 5, no. 7.

Mercatante, Esteban. (2010). "Los efectos de su apropiación parcial vía retenciones (2002–2008)," diciembre, http://www.ips.org.ar/?p=1559.

Mercatante, Esteban. (2016). "Las venas abiertas del Sur," laizquierdadiario.com/ ideasdeizquierda/ wp-content/uploads /2016/05/32_34.

Meiksins Wood, Ellen. (2002). *The origin of capitalism*. London: Verso.

Meiksins Wood, Ellen. (2007). "A reply to critics," *Historical Materialism*, vol. 15, issue 3.

Milanovic, Branko. (2014). "Las cifras de la desigualdad mundial en las rentas Historia y presente," *Globalización y desarrollo*, no. 880, Septiembre–Octubre.

Milberg, William, Jiang Xiao, and Gereffi, Gary. (2014). "Industrial policy in the era 5 of vertically specialized industrialization," http://www.ilo.org/wcmsp5/groups/public/.

Milelli, Christian. (2013). "L'émergence des firmes multinationales en provenance du « Sud »," *La mondialisation, stade supreme du capitalisme? Hommage a Charles Albert Michalet*, Nanterre: Presses Universitaires de Paris Ouest.

Mommer, Bernard. (1998). *La cuestión petrolera*. Caracas: Universidad Central de Venezuela y Trópikos.

Mommer, Bernard. (1999). "Venezuela Política y petroleros. El ingreso fiscal y la pobreza," https://www.ucab.edu.ve/.../INV-IIES-REV-024- enero.

Mora Contreras, Jesús Alberto. (1989). "Renta de la tierra, renta petrolera y renta petr-olera en Venezuela: su cuantía y significación," *Revista BCV*, vol. 4, issue 2: 165–195.

Morales Ruvalcaba, Daniel Efrén. (2013). *En las entrañas de los BRCIS Revista Brasileira de Estratégia e Relações Internacionais*, vol. 2, no. 4, Jul.–Dez.

Moreano, Alejandro. (2007). "Agustín Cueva hoy," *Entre la ira y la esperanza*. Buenos Aires: CLACSO-Prometeo.

Moyo, Sam, and Yeros, Paris. (2015). "Scramble, resistance and a new non-alignment strategy," *BRICS: An Anti-Capitalist Critique*. Chicago: Haymarket.

Munck, Ronaldo. (1981). "Imperialism and dependency: recent debates and old dead ends," *Latin American Perspectives*, vol. 8, nos. 3–4, Jan.

Munck, Ronaldo. (2010). "Marxism and nationalism in the era of globalization," *Capital and Class*, vol. 34, no. 1, February.

Murua, Gabriela. (2013). "Apresentação," *Revista Pensata*, vol. 3, no. 1, novembro.

Nascimento, Carlos Alves do, Dillenburg, Fernando Frota, and Sobral, Fábio Maia. (2013). "Exploração e superexploração da força de trabalho em Marx e Marini," Almeida Filho, N. (ed.), *Desenvolvimento e Dependência: cátedra Ruy Mauro Marini*. Brasilia: IPEA.

Nepomuceno, Eric. (2016). "El canciller del oportunismo," *Página 12*, 25–5.

Niemeyer, Almeida Filho. (2005). "O debate atual sobre a dependencia," *Revista da Sociedade Brasileira de Economía Política*, no. 16, junho.

Nimni, Ephraim. (1989). "Marx, Engels and the National Question," *Science and Society*, vol. 53, no. 3.

Novack, George. (1974). *La ley del desurrollo desigual y combinado de la sociedad*. Bogotá: Editorial Pluma.

O'Brien, Patrick. (2007). "Global economic history as the accumulation of capital through of combine and uneven development," *Historical Materialism*, 15.

Osorio, Jaime. (2007). "América Latina, entre la explotación y la actualidad de revolución," *Herramienta*, 35.

Osorio, Jaime. (2009a). "Dependencia e superexplotacao," *A América Latina e os desafíos da globalizacao*. Rio: Boitempo.

Osorio, Jaime. (2009b). *Explotación redoblada y actualidad de la revolución*. México: ITACAUAM.

Osorio, Jaime. (2012). "Padrão de reprodução do capital: una proposta teórica," *Padrão de reprodução do capital*. Sao Paulo: Boitempo.

Osorio, Jaime. (2013a). "Fundamentos de la superexplotación," *Razón y Revolución*, no. 25, Buenos Aires.

Osorio, Jaime. (2013b). "Sobre dialéctica, superexplotación y dependencia," *Revista Argumentos*, vol. 26, no. 72, may–ago, México.

Osorio, Jaime. (2017). "La teoría marxista de la dependencia revisitada," 22–3, vientosur.info/spip.php?article12379.

Ouriques, Nildo. (2005). "André G Frank: A genial trajectoria de um intellectual anti-académico," *Instituto de Estudos Latinoamericanos*, UFSC, 7–6, www.iela.ufsc.br.

Panitch, Leo, and Gindin, Sam. (2014). "American empire or empire of global capitalism?," *Studies in Political Economy*, 93, Spring.

Panitch, Leo. (2015). "BRICS, the G20 and the American Empire," *BRICS: An Anti-Capitalist Critique*. Chicago: Haymarket.

Penston, Kilembe, and Busekese, Matthews. (2010). "Re-visioning marxism in world politics," elitepdf.com/re-visioning-marxism-in-world-politics.

Peña, Miliciades. (2012). *Historia del pueblo argentino*. Buenos Aires: Emecé.

Petras, James. (2014). "The foundation of the US Empire: Axes of Evil," July, http://pet
    ras.lahaine.org/?p=1995.

Piketty, Thomas. (2013). *Le capital au XXIe siècle*. Seuil.

Portes, Alejandro. (2004). *El desarrollo futuro de América Latina: neoliberalismo, clases
    sociales y transnacionalismo*. Bogotá: Antropos.

Post, Charles. (2011). *The American Road to Capitalism*. Boston/Leiden: Brill.

Pozo-Martin, Gonzalo. (2015). "Russia's neoliberal imperialism and the Eurasian chal-
    lenge," *BRICS: An Anti-Capitalist Critique*. Chicago: Haymarket.

Prado, Maria Lígia Coelho. (1992). "A trajetória de Agustin Cueva," *Estudos Avancados*,
    vol. 6 no. 16, Sept.–Dec., São Paulo.

Prebisch, Raúl. (1986). "Notas sobre el intercambio desigual desde el punto de vista
    periférico," *Revista de la CEPAL*, no. 28, abril, Santiago de Chile.

Presumey, Vincent. (2014). "Les impérialismes au miroir de la crise ukrainienne,"
    Inprecor, no. 611.

Pritchett, Lant. (1997). "Divergence," *Big Time Journal of Economic Perspectives*, 11(3):
    3–17.

Proyect, Louis. (2008). "Bill Warren's folly," 18–11, louisproyect.wordpress.com.

Puiggrós, Rodolfo. (1965). *Los modos de producción en Iberoamérica*. México: Gallo
    IlustradoEl Día.

Radice, Hugo. (2009). "Halfway to Paradise? Making Sense of the Semiperiphery,"
    Globalization and the New Semi-Peripheries. Palgrave Macmillan.

Rao, Nagesh. (2010). "When Marx Looked Outside Europe," *International Socialist
    Review*, Sept.–Oct.

Robinson, William I. (2011). "Globalization and the sociology of Immanuel Wallerstein: A
    critical appraisal," *International Sociology*, 1-23.

Robinson William I. (2014). "The fetishism of empire: a critical review of Panitch and
    Gindins's making of global capitalism," *Studies in Political Economy*, 93, Spring.

Rodrigues, Lucas. (2017). "Transferência de Valor e Desenvolvimento Desigual: uma
    Análise Comparada," *Análise Econômica, Porto Alegre*, ano 35, jul.

Rodrik, Dani. (2013). "The Past, Present, and Future of Economic Growth," Working
    Paper 1, June, Global Citizen Foundation.

Rosdolsky, Román. (1979). *Génesis y estructura de El Capital*. México: Siglo XXI.

Rosdolsky, Román. (1981). *El problema de de los pueblos sin historia*. Barcelona: Fontamara.

Rosenberg, Justin. (2009). "Basic problems in the theory of uneven and combined
    development: a reply to the CRIA forum," *Cambridge Review of International Affairs*,
    vol. 22, no. 1, march.

Rousset, Pierre. (2014). "China: Un imperialismo en construcción," *Viento Sur*, 15–7.

Rozhin, Boris. (2015). "Un año después: la izquierda y Maidán," 24–04, www.rebelion.org.

Ruiz Acosta, Miguel A. (2013). "Devastación y superexplotación de la fuerza de tra-
    bajo en el capitalismo periférico: una reflexión desde América Latina," *Razón y
    Revolución*, no. 25, 1er. semestre, Buenos Aires.

Sader, Emir. (2009). "Ruy Mauro Marini, intelectual revolucionario," *A América Latina e os desafíos da globalizacao*. Rio: Boitempo.

Sader, Emir. (2012). "América Latina y la economía global. En diálogo con "Dialéctica de la dependencia", de Ruy Mauro Marini," *Nueva Sociedad*, 238, marzo–abril.

Salama, Pierre. (1976). *El proceso de subdesarrollo*. México: ERA.

Salama, Pierre. (2012a). "Globalización comercial: desindustrialización prematura en América Latina e industrialización en Asia," *Comercio Exterior*, Vol. 62, Núm. 6, Noviembre–Diciembre.

Salama, Pierre. (2012b). "Amérique Latine, Asie: une globalisation commerciale accompagnée d'une redistribution des cartes," *Problèmes d'Amérique latine*, No. 85, Été.

Salama, Pierre. (2012c). "Una globalización comercial acompañada de una nueva distribución cartográfica," *Revista de Economía Institucional*, vol. 14, no. 27, segundo semestre.

Salama, Pierre. (2017a). "Mutaciones, apogeo y nuevas dependencias en América latina," *Realidad Económica*, no. 308, año 46, 30–6.

Salama, Pierre. (2017b). "Menos globalización: ¿marginación u oportunidad para América Latina?," *Nueva Sociedad*, 271, septiembre–octubre.

Saludjian, Alexis, Dias Carcanholo, Marcelo, Figueira Corrêa, Hugo, and Ferreira de Miranda, Flávio. (2013). "Marx's theory of history and the question of colonies and noncapitalist world." Discussion Paper 015.

Santana, Pedro Marques. (2012). "Um estudo sobre o conceito de superexploração do trabalho na obra de Ruy Mauro Marini," Dissertação de Mestrado em Economia, Universidade Federal da Bahia.

Savran, Sungur. (2016). "Turkey: Atlanticism versus Rabiism," http://socialistproject.ca/bullet/1286.php.

Schorr, Martín, Cassini, Lorenzo, and Zanotti García, Gustavo. (2017). "Los caminos al desarrollo. Trayectorias nacionales divergentes en tiempos de globalización." *Documento de Investigación*, no. 29.

Schteingart, Daniel. (2016). "Comparación problemática," *Pagina 12*, 3–10.

Schwartzman, Kathleen. (2006). "Globalization from a World-System Perspective," *Journal of world-system research*, XII, II.

Sebreli, Juan José. (1992). *El asedio a la modernidad*. Buenos Aires: Sudamericana.

Semo, Emrique. (1975). *La crisis actual del capitalismo*. México: Cultura Popular.

Sender, John (ed.). (1980). "Introduction," Warren Bill, *Imperialism, pioneer of capitalism*. London: NLB/Verso.

Serfati, Claude. (2005). "La economía de la globalización y el ascenso del militarismo," *Coloquio Internacional Imperio y Resistencias*. México: Universidad Autónoma Metropolitana, Unidad Xochimilco.

Slee, Chris. (2014). "Are Russia and China imperialist powers?," 7–04, http://links.org.au/node/3795.

Smith, Ashley. (2014). "Global empire or imperialism?," *International Socialist Review*, Issue 92, Spring.

Smith, John. (2010). *Imperialism & the Globalisation of Production*. Sheffield: University of Sheffield.

Smith, Tony. (1979). "The underdevelopment of development literature: the case of dependency theory," *World Politics*, Vol. 31, no. 2, January.

Solorza, Hdez A. Sebastián, and Deytha, Mon Alan A. (2014). "Crítica a la interpretación que hace Rolando Astarita de la plusvalía extraordinaria," *Revista de Economía Crítica*, no. 18, segundo semestre.

Sotelo Valencia, Adrián. (2005). "Dependencia y sistema mundial: ¿convergencia o divergencia?," *Rebelión*, 4–9, www.rebelion.org/noticia.

Sotelo Valencia, Adrián. (2012). *Los rumbos del trabajo: Superexplotación y precariedad social en el siglo XXI*. México: Porrúa.

Sotelo Valencia, Adrián. (2013). "Capitalismo contemporáneo en el horizonte de la Teoría de la Dependencia," *Revista Argumentos*, vol. 26, no. 72, may–ago, México.

Sotelo Valencia, Adrián. (2015a). "La Crisis de los Paradigmas y la Teoría de la Dependencia en América Latina," http://www.rebelion.org/docs/15161.pdf.

Sotelo Valencia, Adrián. (2015b). *Sub-Imperialism Revisited: Dependency Theory in the Thought of Ruy Mauro Marini*. Leiden: Brill.

Sousa Santos, Boaventura. (2014). "¿Una tercera guerra mundial?," *Pagina 12*, 30–12, https://www.pagina12.com.ar/diario/elmundo/4-262898-2014-12-30.html.

Starosta, Guido and Caligaris, Gastón. (2017). *Trabajo, valor y capital*. Universidad de Quilmes.

Stutje, Jan Wilem. (2007). "Concerning Der Spätkapitalismus: Mandel's Quest for a Synthesis of Late Capitalism," *Historical Materialism*, vol. 15, no. 1: 167–198.

Sutcliffe, Bob. (2008). "Marxism and development," *International Handbook of Development Economics*, Volumes 1 & 2. Edward Elgar Publishing.

Sweezy, Paul. (1973a). "Sobre la teoría del capitalismo monopolista," *El capitalismo moderno y otros ensayos*. México: Nuestro Tiempo.

Sweezy, Paul. (1973b). *Teoría del desarrollo capitalista*. México: Fondo de Cultura Económica.

Sweezy, Paul. (1974). Comentario crítico, Contra-réplica, *La transición del feudalismo al capitalismo*. Buenos Aires: Ediciones La Cruz del Sur.

Sweezy, Paul and Baran, Paul. (1974). *El capital monopolista*. Buenos Aires: Siglo XXI.

Sweezy, Paul, and Magdoff, Harry. (1981). "The deepening crisis of U.S. Capitalism," *Monthly Review Press*, vol. 33, no. 5.

Szentes, Tamás. (1984). *La economía política del subdesarrollo*. La Habana: Editorial de Ciencias Sociales.

Thalheimer, August. (1946). "Linhas e conceitos básicos da política internacional apos a II guerra mundial," www.centrovictormeyer.org.br/.

Therborn, Göran. (2000). "Time, space, and their knowledge," *Journal of World-Systems Research*, Vol. XI, no. 2 (Summer/Fall).

Tinajero, Fernando. (2012). "Agustín Cueva, o la lucidez apasionada," in Agustín Cueva (ed.), *Ensayos Sociológicos y Políticos*. Quito: Ministerio de Coordinación de la Política y Gobiernos Autónomos Descentralizados.

Tissier, P.L. (1981). "L'industrialisation dans huit pays asiatiques depuis la fin de la Seconde Guerre Mondiale," *Critiques de l'Economie Politique*, vol. 14: 78–118.

Traspadini, Roberta. (2013). "Ruy Mauro Marini e a Teoria Marxista da Dependência," *Pensata*, Vol. 3, no. 1 (novembro).

Trimberger, Ellen Kay. (1979). "World systems analysis, the problem of unequal development," *Theory and Society*, Vol. 8, no. 1: 127–137.

Trompíz Vallés, Humberto. (2013). "Bernard Mommer y la cuestión petrolera," 9-4, https://www.aporrea.org/energia/a163048.htm.

Trotsky, León. (1972). *Historia de la Revolución Rusa, Tomo 1*. México: Juan Pablo Editor.

Trotsky, León. (1975). *Tres concepciones de la revolución rusa. Resultados y perspectivas*. Buenos Aires: El Yunque.

Trotsky, León. (2000). *La teoría de la revolución permanente*. Buenos Aires: CEIP.

Valenzuela, Feijoo J. (1997). "Sobreexplotación y dependencia," *Investigación Económica*, no. 221 (julio-sept), México.

Van der Linden, Marcel. (2007). "The "law" of uneven and combined development," *Historical Materialism*, vol. 15: 145–165.

Vitale, Luis. (1981). "Los períodos de transición en la historia económica y social de América Latina," *Seminario de Historia de Latino américa*, http://mazinger.sisib.uch ile.cl/repositorio/lb/filosofia_y_humanidades/vitale/obras/sys/d th/d.pdf.

Vitale, Luis. (1984). "Modos de producción y formaciones sociales en América Latina," www.mazinger.sisib.uchile.cl/repositorio.

Vitale, Luis. (1992). *Introducción a una teoría de la historia para América Latina*. Buenos Aires: Planeta.

Vitale, Luis. (2000). "Hacia El Enriquecimiento de la teoría del desarrollo desigual," *Estrategia Internacional*, no. 16, invierno, Buenos Aires.

VVAA. (1973). *Los cuatro primeros congresos de la Internacional Comunista, Primera Parte*. Buenos Aires: Siglo XXI.

Wallerstein, Immanuel. (1979). *El moderno sistema mundial, tomo I*. México: Siglo XXI.

Wallerstein, Immanuel. (1984). *El moderno sistema mundial, Volumen II: El mercantilismo y la consolidación de la economía-mundo europea, 1600–1750*. México: Siglo XXI.

Wallerstein, Immanuel. (1986). "Marx y el subdesarrollo," *Zona Abierta*, no. 38: 19–40.

Wallerstein, Immanuel. (1988). *El capitalismo histórico*. México: Siglo XXI.

Wallerstein, Immanuel. (1989). *Marx, Marxism-Leninism, and Socialist experiences in Modern World System*. Binghamton, NY: Fernand Braudel Center.

Wallerstein, Immanuel. (1992). *Revolution as strategy and tactics of transformation.* Binghamtom, NY: Fernand Braudel Center.

Wallerstein, Immanuel. (1999a). *El moderno sistema mundial, Volumen III.* Madrid: Siglo XXI.

Wallerstein, Immanuel. (1999b). *Chiapas y la historia de los movimientos antisistémicos.* Madrid: El Viejo Topo.

Wallerstein, Immanuel. (2002). *Los intelectuales en una era de transición: Un mundo incierto.* Buenos Aires: Del Zorzal.

Wallerstein, Immanuel. (2004). *Capitalismo histórico y movimientos anti-sistémicos: Un análisis de sistemas-mundo.* Madrid: Akal.

Wallerstein, Inmanuel. (2005). *Análisis de sistemas-mundo: Una introducción.* México: Siglo XXI de España Editores, S.A.

Wallerstein, Immanuel. (2006–7). "Frank demuestra el milagro europeo," *Revista Mundo Siglo XXI,* no. 7: 5–14.

Wallerstein, Immanuel. (2008). "Remembering Andre Gunder Frank While Thinking About the Future," *Monthly Review,* vol. 60, no. 2.

Wallerstein, Immanuel. (2011). *The Modern World-System, Vol. I: Capitalist Agriculture and the Origins of the European World-Economy in the Sixteenth Century.* Berkeley: University of California Press.

Wallerstein, Immanuel. (2012a). "Nehnhum sistema e para sempre," www.outraspalavras .net, 12/11.

Wallerstein, Immanuel. (2012b). "Reflections on an Intellectual Adventure," *Contemporary Sociology* 41(1): 6–9. ASA, January 18.

Wallerstein, Immanuel. (2012c). "E se nao houver saida alguma?," www.outraspalavras .net, 17/08.

Wallerstein, Immanuel. (2013). "Retrospective on the Origins of World-Systems Analysis," Interview, *American Sociological Association,* vol. 19, no. 2: 202–210.

Wallerstein, Immanuel. (2016). "Estancamiento secular," *La Jornada,* www.jornada .unam.mx/2016/09/25.

Warren, Bill. (1980). *Imperialism, pioneer of capitalism.* London: NLB/Verso.

Wolf, Eric. (1993). *Europa y la gente sin historia.* Buenos Aires: Fondo de Cultura Económica.

Worsley, Peter. (1980). "One world or three? A Critique of the World-System Theory of Immanuel Wallerstein," *The Socialist Register 1980,* vol. 17.

Yu, Au Loong. (2015). "China's Rise: Strength and Fragility," www.internationalviewpoint .org/spip.php?article3936.

Zibechi, Raúl. (2014). "China y Rusia: Las locomotoras del nuevo orden mundial," 28–1, http://www.alainet.org/es/active/79077.

Zibechi, Raúl. (2015). "Brasil. ¿El nuevo imperialismo?," 04–11, http://www.lavaca.org/ libros/brasil-el-nuevo-imperialismo.

Index

abolitionism   5–6
accumulation   9, 11, 12, 21, 27, 31, 32, 33, 34,
    37, 38, 39, 40, 45, 47, 50, 51, 53, 54, 61,
    63, 65, 71, 76, 83, 86, 87, 90, 91, 93, 94,
    100, 102, 111, 117, 118, 119, 120, 121, 122, 124,
    127, 128, 130, 132, 136, 139, 151, 156, 158,
    178, 181, 185, 188, 189, 190, 192, 196, 198,
    199, 201, 202, 204, 205, 211, 212, 214, 215,
    218, 220, 222, 223, 229, 230, 233, 237,
    240, 246
  autonomous   65
  capital   22, 34, 63, 76, 77, 114, 139, 246
  dis-accumulation   12, 218
  European   115
  global   61, 62, 67, 185
  industrial   63
  national   230
  primitive   xiii, 5, 10, 12, 32, 33, 34, 49, 65,
    119, 188, 201
  primitive de-accumulation   78, 114, 182
  primitive dis-accumulation   11
  world   97, 98
Africa   xiv, 11, 15, 16, 23, 28, 31, 35, 41, 54, 62,
    66, 95, 97, 100, 106, 139, 140, 156, 173, 176,
    178, 201, 202, 204, 212, 223, 225, 226, 243
agricultural   9, 10, 11, 60, 72, 115, 136, 224, 225,
    242, 245, 247
agriculture   7, 28, 94, 112, 113, 117, 118, 119, 120,
    134, 136, 217, 242, 243, 245, 247
agro-mining economies   38, 46, 50, 51, 60,
    69, 130, 136, 153, 159, 219, 227, 241
Algeria   7, 32, 52, 135
Althusser, Louis   8, 79, 86
Amin, Samir   xiv, 38, 42–49, 51, 53, 54, 55, 61,
    62, 63, 64, 65, 87, 97, 106, 121, 122, 123,
    124, 150, 186, 191
anarchism   7
Andean region   66
Anderson, Kevin   8
anti-imperialism. *See* imperialism
Argentina   28, 52, 62, 70, 71, 76, 128, 129, 131,
    135–137, 139, 152, 153, 155, 156, 157, 159,
    174, 176, 177, 184, 187, 210, 214, 216, 217,
    219, 220, 221, 223, 224, 225, 226, 232, 239,
    244, 245, 246, 248, 249, 250

Arrighi, Giovanni   52, 121, 124, 125
Asia   xiv, 4, 9, 11, 12, 15, 16, 26, 31, 35, 41, 54,
    62, 66, 97, 110, 111, 121, 122, 125, 126, 129,
    130, 156, 157, 169, 172, 173, 174, 178, 193,
    194, 197, 198, 199, 200, 201, 203, 204, 206,
    207, 210, 211, 212, 220, 221, 223, 225, 226,
    227, 236
Astarita, Rolando   127, 128, 131, 132, 133, 135,
    139, 140, 141, 144, 158, 190, 191, 236, 237,
    239, 245
Australia   23, 130, 167–169, 179, 223–224, 225,
    227, 228, 229
Austria   6, 7, 11
Austro-Hungarian Empire   21, 24, 25

Bambirra, Vania   xi, 59, 61, 62, 65, 66, 68, 69,
    70, 71, 72, 73, 76, 81, 82, 87, 88, 89, 97,
    99, 103, 105, 129, 134, 138, 150, 153, 181,
    209, 223
Banco del Sur   175
Baran, Paul   38, 39, 40, 41, 42, 44, 49, 53, 54,
    55, 65, 87
Belgium   11, 22, 151
Bernstein, Eduard   22, 24, 27, 29
Bettelheim, Charles   46, 53, 62, 236
Bolivia   xiv, 79, 136, 139, 153, 158, 177, 184, 210,
    246, 250
Brazil   xi, xiv, xv, 49, 52, 59, 62, 63, 64, 66, 67,
    68, 69, 70, 71, 72, 73, 74, 75, 76, 77, 79,
    85, 116, 129, 131, 132, 149, 150, 151, 152, 153,
    156, 158, 159, 160, 174–176, 177–178, 179,
    180, 189, 192, 193, 194, 195, 209, 210, 211,
    214, 216, 217, 218, 219, 220, 221, 223, 225,
    226, 228, 229, 232, 249
Brenner, Robert   117, 120, 121
BRICS   xv, 153–154, 170, 174–175, 203

Canada   130, 136, 167–168, 169, 179, 224
capital   3, 4, 30, 31, 33, 34, 41, 42, 43, 45, 46,
    48, 49, 50, 52, 61, 64, 71, 83, 123, 128,
    129, 135, 136, 139, 141, 149, 150, 160, 161,
    169, 172, 185, 186, 191, 192, 198, 201, 207,
    211, 215, 218, 219, 222, 228, 233, 234, 235,
    236, 239
  accumulation. *See* accumulation

capital   (*cont.*)
  commercial   34, 114
  commodity   214
  financial   54
  foreign   10, 27, 54, 62, 65, 69, 73, 74, 127,
    128, 214, 226, 227, 232
  metropolitan   32, 49, 50, 53, 63
  money   214
  monopoly   127, 131, 132
  multinational   73
  national   138
  productive   214
Capital. See Marx, Karl
capitalism   xiii, xv, 3, 4, 8, 9, 10, 12, 13, 19, 22,
    23, 24, 27, 29, 30, 31, 32, 33, 35, 37, 39, 42,
    43, 44, 45, 46, 47, 50, 51, 52, 53, 54, 60,
    61, 66, 67, 69, 71, 73, 78, 79, 80, 81, 83, 84,
    86, 87, 88, 90, 91, 93, 95, 96, 97, 98, 99,
    100, 101, 102, 103, 104, 105, 108, 110, 111,
    112, 113, 114, 117, 118, 119, 120, 123, 124, 125,
    126, 127, 128, 129, 131, 132, 133, 134, 138,
    139, 143, 144, 158, 161, 162, 169, 171, 172,
    173, 178, 181, 182, 188, 189, 195, 198, 200,
    201, 202, 203, 204, 205, 207, 211, 222, 223,
    230, 231, 233, 234, 238, 246, 247, 250, 251
  21st century   152, 250
  advanced   68
  anti-capitalism   xii, 13, 36, 41, 55, 59, 71,
    84, 102, 105, 106, 128, 137, 138, 142, 144,
    239, 248
  central   11, 20, 36, 50, 52, 97
  colonial   xiv
  commercial   78, 111, 113, 115, 116, 117
  competitive   132
  contemporary   33, 43, 44, 48, 51, 91, 98,
    158, 161, 178, 199, 229, 243
  current   30, 49, 109, 162, 212, 248, 250
  dependent   xvi, 28, 60, 63, 65, 89, 90, 98,
    113, 159, 196, 215, 246, 248
  early   208
  elective   87
  European   10, 14, 122
  expansion of   4, 5, 8, 10, 12, 24, 38, 91, 96,
    143, 144
  German   21, 36
  global   31, 52, 93, 110, 127, 130, 136, 208,
    230, 233, 236
  globalized   24, 87, 93, 248
  historical   97, 116
  immature   36
  international   89
  internationalized   34
  Iranian   166
  late   36, 51, 53, 204
  Latin American   98, 121, 197
  laws of   8
  metropolitan   39, 214
  millennial   xiii, 124
  nascent   32, 113
  national   41, 59, 65, 71, 82, 86, 97, 106,
    138, 208
  native   156
  neo-capitalism   53
  neoliberal   221, 229, 243, 248
  origin of   xiv, 10, 11, 29, 32, 114, 117, 118,
    119, 121
  pan-capitalism   78, 79, 113
  post-capitalism   6, 7, 17, 25, 47, 106, 150
  postwar   61, 68, 152, 204
  progressive   241
  redistributive   86
  rentier   248
  rise of   114, 119, 120, 122, 204, 240
  rural   120
  Russian   28
  self-correcting   86
  semi-capitalism   119, 181
  U.S.   39
  Western   13
  world   3, 31, 32, 40, 51, 67, 95, 104, 136, 158,
    208, 233
capitalist
  adversity   63
  agriculture   112, 120
  character   28, 111
  class   205
  colonization   79, 89, 115, 116
  continuity   114
  determinant   133
  development   7, 13, 33, 41, 52, 60, 89, 121,
    125, 132, 189
  economy   48, 105, 116, 203
  empire   226
  eternity   123
  formation   171
  foundation   137
  framework   36
  functioning   133

history 11
imbalances 141
logic 76
maturation 143
modality 78
modernization 141
nature 115
non-capitalist regime 171
non-capitalist system 170
oppression 173
order 154, 158, 175, 203
parameters 173
property 113
protection 64, 161
reality 133
regime 117, 172, 203
rent 241
restoration 170
roots 115
rule 91
rules 183
sector 68, 151
subject 71
world 35, 125
capitalists 5, 11, 30, 40, 42, 50, 53, 63, 69, 71,
81, 102, 118, 136, 138, 152, 158, 171, 180, 185,
186, 187, 190, 212, 215, 220, 227, 245
Cardoso, Fernando Henrique xi, xiii, 59, 70–
75, 76–77, 80, 81, 85, 87, 88, 90, 112, 127,
132, 134, 135, 138, 150, 180
Caribbean xi, 66, 70, 224
CELAC 175
center-periphery gap 10, 46, 47, 50, 53,
61, 156
center-periphery relation 18, 19, 24, 29, 35,
37, 38, 41, 42, 44, 47, 49, 50, 51, 54, 67, 87,
90, 97, 109, 110, 119, 126, 135, 206
Central America 66, 70, 76
Chavismo 128, 248, 249
Chile xii, 59, 67, 68, 69, 77, 81–82, 116,
136, 155
China xiii, 3, 4, 5, 7, 8, 9, 10, 15, 26, 28, 35, 48,
54, 66, 93, 104, 105, 111, 121, 122, 123, 124,
125, 131, 138, 142, 154, 161, 169, 172, 173,
174, 178, 179, 194, 197, 199, 202, 203–204,
205, 206, 207, 208, 212, 214, 220, 224–
226, 227, 228, 229, 231, 242, 249, 250
circulationism 78, 91, 123
Civil War, United States 5, 6, 13, 16

class 4, 17, 18, 26, 71, 77, 79, 84, 90, 101, 108,
117, 128, 137, 138, 140, 143, 157, 160, 190,
205, 208, 211, 226, 227
dominant 27, 28, 53, 61, 63, 77, 80, 137,
139, 143, 155
industrialist 64
middle 63, 70, 72, 77, 104, 128, 142, 217
multi- 18, 82
reductionism 13
relations 13
ruling xiv, 22, 48, 53, 64, 67, 69, 73, 138,
150, 151, 154, 159, 160, 169, 170, 174, 175,
176, 180, 187, 203, 206, 207, 208, 212, 223,
227, 228, 229, 230, 243, 244
social 13, 19, 68, 251
struggle 14, 30, 36, 46, 76, 89, 103, 114, 120,
121, 183, 187, 230, 233, 244, 247
working 6, 25, 36, 128, 141, 142, 145
classical Marxists xiii, 21, 64, 159, 204
collective imperialism. *See* imperialism
Colombia 77, 155, 176, 246
colonialism xiii, xiv, 3, 4, 6, 8, 9, 10, 11, 12, 13,
14, 15, 18, 19, 21, 22–23, 24, 26, 27, 28, 30,
31, 33, 34, 35, 37, 41, 59, 66, 67, 77, 78, 79,
89, 91, 106, 110, 111, 113, 114, 115, 116, 119, 122,
140, 157, 159, 167, 168, 173, 175, 176, 182
colonization 12, 23, 37, 38, 79, 89, 107,
110, 111, 112, 113, 114, 115, 116, 117, 118, 119,
171, 205
colonizer 6, 21, 167
colony 4, 10, 11, 12, 22, 23, 26, 27, 28, 31,
51, 53, 76, 94, 99, 120, 149, 158, 159, 160,
177, 178, 188
communism 7, 26, 82, 83, 142, 249
communist parties 24, 41, 59, 76, 82, 105,
106, 115, 125
competition 21, 29, 30, 33, 36, 39, 40, 44, 45,
53, 69, 78, 105, 112, 116, 119, 123, 132, 164,
179, 196, 198, 207, 218, 225, 226, 229, 230,
237, 238, 239, 248
Congo 22, 177
consumption 38, 39, 61, 63, 72, 102, 104, 177,
183, 184, 189, 190, 200, 201, 215–217, 218,
219, 221, 227, 238
crisis 9, 21, 29, 32, 40, 50, 51, 52, 61, 68, 72, 86,
93, 102, 103, 104, 112, 133, 136, 139, 143,
150, 152, 159, 161, 162, 170, 174, 176, 177,
190, 199, 200, 201, 202, 203, 212, 214, 215,
218, 219, 230, 238, 243, 245, 248, 250

Cuba   54, 59, 69, 138, 142, 250

Cuban revolution   xii, 59, 66, 69, 83, 105, 116,
    128, 138, 142, 150, 187, 220, 247

Cueva, Agustín   xiii–xiv, 76–79, 80–81, 82,
    83, 84, 85, 86, 87, 88, 89, 90, 91, 121, 150,
    181, 182, 185

debt   6, 62, 120, 139, 209, 217, 218, 250
    foreign   36, 85, 139, 202
    public   33

deindustrialization   10, 38, 216

dependency theorists   59, 61, 64, 65, 70, 82,
    83, 97, 99, 100, 105, 122, 128, 133, 137,
    149, 152, 192, 204, 211, 214, 215, 217, 223,
    230, 242
    Latin American   100, 103, 104
    Marxist   60, 69, 77, 116, 130, 137, 138, 174,
        226, 230, 247

dependency theory   xi, xii, xiii, xiv, xv, 55, 59,
    62, 65, 66, 72, 76, 78, 80, 82, 83, 84, 85,
    86, 87, 89, 92, 96, 97, 99, 106, 109, 110,
    116, 125, 127, 128, 129, 130, 131, 132, 137,
    138, 141, 149, 153, 180, 186, 187, 190, 196,
    204, 206, 213, 231, 237, 241, 245, 246, 247,
    248, 249, 250, 251
    Marxist   xiii, 59, 66, 79, 81, 89, 90, 93, 105,
        109, 110, 125, 130, 143, 144, 156, 182, 185,
        187, 191, 193, 197, 214, 219, 224, 229, 231,
        232, 239, 240, 244

dependent cycle   xv, 63, 68, 99, 135, 151, 187,
    214, 215, 217, 218, 219, 221, 233, 246

developmentalism   xi, xiv, 43, 60, 65, 67, 72,
    74, 86, 96, 106, 130, 138, 178, 214, 219, 223,
    227, 228, 230, 240

dispossession   3, 26, 33, 37, 91

Dos Santos, Theotônio   xi, xii, xiii, xiv, 59,
    60, 61, 62, 65, 66, 68, 69, 70, 71, 72, 73,
    76, 81, 82, 85, 87, 89, 90, 97, 98, 103, 105,
    129, 132, 134, 138, 150, 151, 187, 200, 226

Dussel, Enrique   185, 186

ECLAC   xi, 60, 61, 63, 71, 74, 77, 125, 130, 240

Ecuador   xiv, 76, 79, 80, 139, 177

Egypt   27, 41, 52, 66, 95, 156, 157, 163, 166, 168

Emmanuel, Arghiri   45, 46, 62, 138, 232, 233

endogenism   xiii, 10, 11, 28, 35, 39, 77, 78, 82,
    83, 86, 87, 88, 89, 90, 91, 92, 112, 115, 123,
    128, 133, 134, 135, 209, 223, 241, 246

endogenous. See endogenism

Engels, Friedrich   14, 15, 131

England   4, 5, 7, 8, 9, 10, 11, 12, 17, 21, 22, 23,
    26, 32, 35, 41, 49, 64, 66, 67, 94, 95, 111,
    112, 120, 121, 122, 134, 140, 142, 155, 161,
    163, 165, 167, 173, 181, 188, 203, 204, 224,
    241, 244, See also Great Britain

Eurocentrism   13–14, 15–16, 107, 124, 125,
    142, 168

Europe   xiv, 4, 5, 6, 7, 8, 10, 11, 12, 14, 15, 16,
    28, 34, 41, 48, 66, 67, 79, 93, 100, 103, 111,
    112, 113, 114, 115, 116, 119, 121, 122, 123, 124,
    134, 135, 136, 149, 157, 172, 178, 179, 201,
    202, 203, 205, 207, 225, 235, 236, 240,
    244, 250
    eastern   15, 24, 26, 94, 95, 105, 117, 120
    European Union   139
    non-European   16, 19
    northern   124
    southern   164
    western   9, 16, 24, 25, 32, 42

exogenism   xiii, 10, 11, 28, 35, 39, 77, 83, 87,
    89, 90, 91, 92, 115

exogenous. See exogenism

exploitation   11, 12, 13, 17, 18, 33, 34, 37, 42,
    43, 46, 63, 69, 76, 79, 86, 96, 97, 104, 111,
    112, 128, 133, 137, 157, 158, 170, 183, 185,
    188, 190, 191, 192, 193, 195, 196, 199, 201,
    212, 214, 220, 228, 229, 232, 235, 238, 243,
    248, 250
    labor   xii, 43, 61, 71, 72, 79, 95, 97, 100, 113,
        119, 123, 140, 186, 200, 209, 213, 220, 222,
        242, 244, 248
    redoubled   189
    super-   xv, 63, 68, 72, 87, 104, 180, 181, 182,
        183, 184, 185, 186, 187, 188, 189, 190, 191,
        193, 195, 196, 197, 214, 228, 231, 250

extractivism   170, 217–218, 219, 232, 243, 249

falling rate of profit tendency   9, 40, 61, 67,
    72, 143, 188, 190, 215

fascism   84, 150

feudalism   xiv, 11, 17, 34, 35, 37, 78, 79, 80, 83,
    89, 93, 100, 103, 111, 112, 113, 114, 115, 116,
    117, 119, 120, 122, 133, 134, 171, 241

First International   4, 6, 22

Ford Foundation   74

Fordism   63, 189–190, 198, 216

France   6, 9, 10, 11, 16, 17, 21, 26, 32, 35, 36, 54, 64, 66, 73, 76, 86, 94, 95, 120, 131, 155, 160, 161, 163, 165, 167, 169, 177, 210, 244
Frank, André Gunder   xiii, xiv, 59, 60, 66, 67, 68, 69, 70, 71, 73, 77, 78, 79, 81, 82, 83, 87, 88, 90, 110, 111, 112, 113, 114, 115, 116, 117, 118, 119, 121, 122, 123, 124, 125, 126, 131, 158
free trade   4, 9, 13, 22, 23, 50, 51, 249
free trade agreements   202, 225, 235
French Revolution   4, 108
Furtado, Celso   60, 70, 72, 87, 131

geopolitics   213, 226
   geopolitical   xv, 35, 40, 48, 49, 64, 123, 149, 151, 153, 154, 158, 160, 169, 170, 173, 174, 175, 177, 178, 179, 206, 207, 211, 220, 225, 226, 227, 229, 230, 243, 250, 251
   geopolitical-military. See military
Germany   6, 10, 11, 15, 17, 18, 21, 22, 23, 25, 26, 32, 35, 36, 45, 49, 64, 94, 99, 142, 153, 155, 157, 161, 167, 169, 173, 191, 193, 194, 203, 207, 250
global manufacturing networks   xv
globalization   xv, 4, 9, 44, 68, 87, 91, 130, 144, 173, 195, 198, 199, 200, 201, 202, 204, 206, 207, 208, 209, 211, 212, 213, 222, 230, 232, 233, 234, 235, 250, 251
   capitalist   xv
   economic   49, 235, 250
   neoliberal   143, 144, 153, 154, 155, 191, 193, 195, 197, 200, 205, 211, 220, 226
   present-day   201, 208
   productive   192, 194, 198, 199, 202, 206, 207, 211, 213, 220, 225, 228, 231, 234, 248
globalized
   business   154
   capitalism. See capitalism
   character   234
   class   160
   economies   234
   economy   48
   finance   152
   firms   212
   functioning   45
   institutions   210
   management   44
   manufacturing   198

production   208, 209, 251
   structures   44
Great Britain   3, 4, 5, 9, 11, 12, 16, 23, 31, 67, 94, 107, 110, 127, 142, 157, 169, 234, 245, See also England
Greece   139, 157, 250

Haiti   62, 129, 159, 175, 230
Harvey, David   33, 52
Hegel, Georg   14, 19
heterodox theory   xii, 36, 41, 47, 86, 131, 134, 189, 212, 215, 222, 223, 230, 233
heterogeneity   52, 154
   structural   35, 60, 63, 70
Hilferding, Rudolf   29, 31, 32, 34
Holland. See Netherlands, the
Honduras   134, 159, 160, 175

imperialism   xv, 22, 29, 30, 31, 32, 40, 42, 47, 54, 64, 65, 66, 105, 138, 150, 156, 158, 160, 170, 171, 173, 178, 179, 202, 226, 231, 245
   anti-   19, 26, 55, 84, 85, 86, 105, 106, 141, 142, 171, 205, 239, 246, 248
   central   151, 167, 172
   classical   50, 51, 91, 157, 161, 202
   collective   xv, 48, 49, 64, 150, 154, 157, 167
   contemporary   40, 49, 170, 230
   French   177
   postwar   151
   present-day   162
   secondary   167
   traditional   xv, 169
   U.S.   26, 59, 151, 210, 227
   Western   179
   See also subimperial, subimperialism
imperialist   xi, 29, 34, 37, 75, 149, 151, 159, 165, 171, 172, 243, 244
   anti-   26, 27, 28, 47, 54, 80, 82, 85, 91, 99, 106, 137, 139, 142, 144, 156, 162
   co-   168
   inter-   24, 151, 154, 156, 157, 160, 161
   pro-   83, 142
   super-   40
   ultra-   162
imperialists   83
import substitution   51, 181, 195, 200, 218, 221, 224, 234

India   xv, 3, 4, 5, 7, 8, 10, 12, 18, 19, 22, 23, 26,
    27, 32, 35, 41, 52, 66, 94, 95, 105, 111, 122,
    140, 153, 154, 156, 157, 169, 170, 172, 176,
    204, 205, 209, 211, 227, 228, 229
industrial development   37, 50, 51, 52, 53, 71,
    88, 129, 153, 209, 214
industrialization   xii, xiv, 3, 4, 5, 9, 10, 28, 32,
    34, 35, 36, 38, 41, 47, 51, 52, 53, 54, 60, 62,
    64, 68, 72, 73, 74, 76, 95, 98, 115, 120, 127,
    128, 130, 131, 132, 135, 136, 140, 151, 169,
    171, 180, 181, 193, 195, 197, 201, 203, 209,
    214, 221, 224, 227, 241
industrialized peripheral economies   47, 63
industrialized periphery   181, 183, 191,
    205, 215
inflation   62, 218, 219, 245
informal labor   91, 129, 192, 193, 194, 196, 199,
    201, 216, 250
intensified labor   236–237
intermediate economies   xv, 35, 50, 52, 62,
    63, 98, 152, 153, 164, 174, 180, 193, 195, 210
international division of labor   47, 61, 86, 88,
    95, 96, 99, 106, 134, 135, 138, 179, 183, 192,
    210, 222, 226, 239
international rent   244–248
internationalism   13, 22, 25, 141
    proletarian   4, 140, 247
Iran   135, 152, 156, 157, 163, 164, 165, 166–167,
    168, 179
Ireland   4, 5, 7, 8, 9, 10, 12, 13, 15, 16, 17, 19,
    140, 142
Israel   49, 152, 157, 163, 166, 167–168, 169, 179
Italy   6, 11, 17, 28, 35, 50, 53, 95, 124, 140, 210

Japan   9, 18, 21, 26, 32, 35, 41, 48, 50, 73, 94,
    134, 153, 155, 157, 160, 161, 167, 169, 172,
    173, 178, 184, 191, 194, 202, 203, 206, 246
Juárez, Benito   6

Kautsky, Karl   16, 22, 23, 24, 27, 29, 145, 162
Keynesian theory   39, 47, 86, 96, 132, 152, 180,
    192, 195, 205, 234, 250
Kohan, Néstor   8, 22
Kondratieff cycles   94, 103

labor. See informal labor, intensified labor,
    international division of labor,
    outsourcing of labor, value of labor
    power, wage-labor

Latin America   xi, xii, xiii, xiv, 9, 11, 16, 31, 34,
    35, 54, 55, 59, 60, 61, 62, 63, 65, 66, 67,
    68, 69, 70, 74, 76, 77, 78, 79, 80, 81, 83,
    84, 85, 86, 87, 88, 89, 90, 91, 92, 97, 98,
    99, 100, 103, 104, 105, 106, 107, 108, 110,
    111, 112, 113, 114, 115, 116, 118, 119, 121, 126,
    127, 128, 129, 130, 135, 138, 141, 142, 144,
    149, 153, 156, 164, 175, 180, 182, 184, 186,
    187, 196, 197, 201, 204, 207, 208, 209, 210,
    211, 212, 214, 215, 216, 217, 219, 220, 221,
    222, 223, 224, 225, 226, 227, 228, 231, 232,
    233, 239, 240, 241, 243, 246, 247, 250
law of value. See value, law of
Lenin, Vladimir   xiii, xiv, 21, 23, 24–30, 31, 32,
    33, 34, 37, 41, 42, 51, 61, 65, 131, 132, 139–
    141, 150, 160, 161, 162, 171, 202, 243
liberalism   xi, xiv, 40–41, 59–60, 71, 130
Lincoln, Abraham   6
Lipietz, Alain   86–87
Luxemburg, Rosa   21, 22, 23, 24, 25, 26, 29,
    30–33, 34, 37, 63, 64, 65, 131, 139, 140, 149

Magdoff, Harry   39, 40, 150
Mandel, Ernest   xiii, 38, 49–55, 61, 62, 63, 65,
    73, 87, 103, 119, 121, 132, 150, 185, 238
Maoism   48
maquilas   xv, 46, 129, 196, 216, 220, 232, 235
Marini, Ruy Mauro   xi, xii, xiii, xiv, xv, 59, 60,
    61, 62, 63, 64, 65, 66, 67, 68, 69, 70, 71,
    72, 73, 74, 75, 76, 80, 81, 82, 84, 85, 87, 88,
    89, 90, 97, 98, 99, 103, 104, 105, 127, 129,
    132, 134, 135, 138, 149, 150, 151, 152, 153,
    154, 155, 156, 158, 160, 162, 166, 167, 169,
    174, 175, 176, 177, 178, 180, 181, 182, 185,
    186, 187, 188, 189, 190, 191, 192, 193, 195,
    196, 197, 198, 199, 200, 201, 202, 203, 204,
    205, 206, 207, 208, 209, 210, 211, 213, 214,
    215, 216, 217, 218, 219, 221, 223, 226, 231,
    232, 233, 234, 235, 238, 239, 240, 241,
    245, 246, 248, 249, 250
Marx, Karl   xiii, 3–20, 23, 25, 28, 29, 31, 33, 35,
    45, 79, 91, 100, 123, 127, 131, 132, 133, 139,
    140, 181, 183, 184, 188, 189, 214, 232, 233,
    234, 236, 237, 238, 242, 243, 245
    Capital   xiii, xiv, 3, 5, 8, 9, 14, 19, 31, 63, 133,
    139, 181, 188, 189, 214, 231, 234, 237
Marxism   xi, 29, 60, 65, 79, 86, 100, 101, 125,
    131, 144, 150
    Althusserian   86

classical   138
dependentist   131, 142, 144, 223
deterministic   xii
endogenist   35, 209, 241, 246
historicist   108
Latin American   xiv, 86, 231
national and popular   239
orthodox   150, 187
post-   84, 86
postwar   38
revolutionary   21
Marxist   14, 87, 100, 127, 134, 137
    analysts   47
    authors   xiii, 14, 132
    characterizations   201, 220
    circles   75
    conception   42, 59
    concepts   76, 183
    critics   76, 232
    currents   16, 223
    debates   67, 143
    dependency theory. See dependency
        theory
    economics   238
    economists   38, 40, 61, 68, 185
    endogenism   86
    historians   11
    ideas   100
    intellectuals   84, 86
    interpretation   38
    interpretations   86
    pillars   229
    principle   43
    synthesis   246
    terms   63, 215
    theories   103, 189
    theorists   15, 35, 42, 45, 46, 48, 51, 53, 72,
        74, 80, 88, 97, 127, 133, 150, 159, 180, 208
    thesis   158
    thinkers   238
    thought   29, 37, See also Marxism
    tradition   xii
    traditions   62, 71
    variant   xi
    views   101, 103
Marxists   3, 24, 33, 41, 52, 102, 203, 211, 241
    Argentine   247
    Austro-   25
    Brazilian   66

classical. See classical Marxists
    Latin American   64, 97, 98, 105
    orthodox   118
    postwar   xiii, 55, 87, 96, 207
    Venezuelan   247
MERCOSUR   175
metropolis-satellite perspective   xiii, 59,
    66–68, 76, 77, 78, 89, 110, 111, 114, 117, 119,
    126, 158
Mexico   6, 7, 15, 27, 52, 62, 63, 76, 77, 79, 91,
    129, 152, 153, 155, 159, 174, 196, 214, 216,
    219, 220, 221, 223, 224, 225, 226, 228,
    232, 249
military   9, 17, 24, 27, 29, 30, 36, 48, 49, 59, 64,
    84, 90, 93, 94, 96, 123, 150, 153, 154, 155,
    157, 161, 162, 164, 165, 166, 167, 169, 170,
    173, 175, 176, 177, 178, 202, 203, 225, 226
    action   xv, 38, 155, 169, 176, 177, 179,
        202, 211
    foreign   169, 176, 177
    geopolitical-   149, 155, 156, 158, 173,
        211, 228
    political-   155
mode of production   12, 35, 79, 80, 86, 89, 90,
    91, 97, 100, 101, 112, 114, 118, 123
modernization   xi, 8, 12, 21, 36, 40, 60, 85, 96,
    141, 165, 167, 173, 180, 245
monopoly   29, 30, 33, 39, 40, 44, 45, 53, 127,
    131, 132–133, 168, 233, 237, 242, 247
Monthly Review   39, 40, 41, 45
multilatina   153, 225
multinational corporations   42, 44, 68, 74,
    149, 151, 158, 160, 177, 209, 214, 234

national struggle   xiii, 5, 15, 18, 19, 27, 106
nationalism   xiv, 16–18, 22, 25, 26, 80, 85, 106,
    128, 138, 141, 247
NATO   139, 161, 162, 164, 167, 168, 172, 176, 179
neoclassical theory   xii, 41, 60, 123, 129, 130,
    132, 134
neoliberal   xiv, 3, 74, 75, 84, 91, 135, 143, 144,
    152, 153, 154, 155, 169, 191, 193, 195, 197,
    200, 202, 203, 205, 207, 211, 212, 219, 220,
    221, 222, 226, 228, 229, 243, 248, 250
neoliberalism   xi, xii, 74, 127, 130, 154, 170,
    176, 187, 195, 218, 230, 231, 235
Netherlands, the   11, 94, 95, 121, 151, 159, 167
Nicaragua   xii, 59, 84, 160
Norway   25, 140, 223–224, 225, 228, 229

oil   41, 54, 62, 135, 136, 137, 163, 165, 166, 168,
       224, 225, 240, 241, 242, 243, 247, 249
oil-exporting countries   54, 223
OPEC   53, 137, 165, 223, 240, 247
Osorio, Jaime   89, 90, 98, 101, 151, 153, 189, 191
Ottoman Empire   7, 95, 105, 122
outsourcing of labor   192, 199, 221

Pakistan   156, 157, 169
Paraguay   62, 175, 177
pattern of reproduction   90, 151, 215
Pentagon   40, 49, 64, 75, 139, 149, 150, 155,
       156, 161, 162, 164, 165, 166, 167, 169, 172,
       175, 176, 177, 179, 202, 203, 204, 227
Peru   xiv, 62, 67, 77, 182
Poland   7, 13, 15, 16, 17, 18, 26, 31, 172
polarization   10, 19, 28, 33, 34, 37, 39, 40, 42,
       43–45, 46–47, 48, 51, 52, 53, 65, 67, 68,
       69, 86, 98, 134, 144, 186, 193, 204, 205,
       229, 240
Popular Unity government   xii, 59, 81–82
Portugal   11, 59, 67, 68, 110, 115, 121, 167,
       169, 210
poverty   32, 85, 183, 184, 189, 196, 216, 218
Prebisch, Raúl   45, 60, 63, 70, 99, 240, 241
pre-capitalist
       agricultures   113
       areas   32
       components   119
       features   115
       formations   50
       forms   35, 89, 119, 241
       foundations   79
       hindrances   11
       impediments   133
       institutions   67
       period   122
       processes   37
       profits   188
       regimes   79
       relations   113
       relics   91
       remnants   88
       states   91
       structures   10, 115, 117, 134
       systems   42, 239
productivity   5, 40, 43, 45, 46, 51, 63, 72, 115,
       118, 120, 121, 122, 136, 180, 182, 184, 191,

       196, 200, 207, 216, 220, 222, 233, 236,
       238, 239, 240, 241
   gap   42, 46, 159, 183, 186, 191
protectionism   9, 23, 29, 30, 32, 34, 130, 199,
       202, 219, 221
Prussia   7, 28, 36, 120, 149, 176, 210

raw materials   11, 21, 27, 38, 40, 41, 46, 51, 53,
       54, 61, 94, 99, 102, 170, 180, 214, 223, 224,
       240–241, 242, 243, 249
   prices   53, 54, 217, 219
reformism   24, 27, 59, 143, 166
rent   xv, 9, 11, 28, 54, 62, 69, 77, 83, 112, 113,
       120, 122, 136, 137, 165, 214, 217, 223, 224,
       227, 228, 229, 230, 231, 237, 238, 241–245,
       246, 247, 249
   rentier   11, 39, 53, 218, 219, 243, 248
   rentism   30, 135, 159
Russia   6, 7, 8, 9, 15, 17, 19, 21, 26, 28, 32, 34,
       35, 36, 50, 95, 132, 140, 152, 154, 161, 163,
       164, 165, 166, 170, 171, 172, 173, 178, 179,
       203, See also USSR, Soviet Union
Russian Revolution   24, 30, 35

Sandinistas   xii
Saudi Arabia   135, 136, 163, 164, 165, 166, 168,
       170, 179
Second International   19, 22
semi-industrialized economies   35, 51, 52, 88
semi-peripheral   35, 95, 96, 99, 130, 153, 156,
       169, 208, 209, 210, 229
semi-periphery   xiii, 10, 48, 52, 99, 151, 152,
       183, 193, 194, 194t.1, 209, 210, 211, 227,
       228, 229, 234, 251
Serfati, Claude   33
serfdom   9, 11, 96, 112, 113, 114, 118, 120
Serra, José   72, 75, 180
slavery   5–6, 11, 13, 16, 21, 32, 35, 79, 95, 96,
       100, 106, 107, 113, 118, 140, 182, 188
Slavs   15
Smith, Adam   19, 78
socialism   xii, xiv, 3–4, 7, 8, 14, 17, 18, 22, 24,
       30, 36, 46, 54, 59, 67, 82, 84, 85, 91, 97,
       104, 105, 106, 115, 128, 135, 141, 142, 143–
       145, 150, 211, 239, 246, 248, 249
socialist   3, 6, 12, 15, 17, 18, 19, 21, 22, 23, 24,
       25, 27, 28, 30, 31, 35, 37, 41, 42, 47, 48, 54,
       55, 59, 65, 71, 80, 81, 83, 84, 86, 103, 104,

105, 106, 107, 109, 115, 116, 127, 138, 139,
  142, 143, 144, 145, 187, 203, 205, 226, 231,
  241, 247
Socialist Party   82
Sotelo Valencia, Adrián   60, 98, 178, 196
South Africa   xv, 32, 49, 52, 152, 156, 176–177,
  179, 211
South Korea   xv, 52, 130, 131, 152, 155, 178, 193,
  194, 197, 199, 203, 206, 209, 210, 212, 220,
  221, 222, 223, 225, 227, 228, 229, 231
Southeast Asia   xii, 121, 125, 127, 129, 131, 214,
  220, 221, 222, 224, 230
Southern Cone   66, 248
sovereignty   17, 18, 22, 23, 24, 25, 26, 27, 114,
  120, 138, 141, 157
Soviet Union   24, 25, 26, 28, 41, 48, 54, 55, 59,
  64, 76, 83, 84, 104–105, 131, 138, 142, 143,
  165, 166, 169, 170, 171, 203–204, 205, 250
Spain   11, 35, 59, 67, 94, 99, 110, 111, 113, 115,
  120, 152, 167, 210
stagnation   xii, 30, 39, 45, 53, 60, 70, 78, 83,
  89, 103, 104, 110, 112, 115, 121, 131, 170, 190,
  196, 210, 218, 220, 244
stagnationism   35, 72, 73, 87, 104, 127, 131,
  132, 181
subcontracting   199, 221, 227, 235
subimperial   130, 150, 151, 152, 153, 154, 155,
  156, 157, 160, 162, 163, 164, 165, 166,
  167, 169, 170, 172, 174, 175, 176, 177, 179,
  226, 251
subimperialism   xv, 35, 64, 149–162, 163–179,
  210, 211
surplus profits   11, 50
surplus value   xv, 9, 31, 33, 40, 43, 45, 46, 53,
  63, 66, 69, 72, 79, 98, 117, 118, 123, 158,
  180, 181, 185, 186, 187, 188, 189, 190, 191,
  192, 193, 194, 195, 197, 198, 199, 212, 213,
  215, 221, 222, 228, 229, 230, 231, 232, 233,
  234, 235, 236, 237, 238, 239, 240, 242,
  244, 245, 246
Sweden   25, 140, 210
Sweezy, Paul   xiii, 38, 39–40, 41, 42, 44–45,
  49, 53, 54–55, 61, 65, 73, 87, 112, 117,
  150, 238

Taiping Rebellion   4
Taiwan   52, 130, 131, 173, 199, 203, 212
technological change   39

terms of trade   45, 46, 60, 62, 70, 72, 77, 180,
  240, 245
theory of value. See value, theory of
Third International   24, 26, 27
Third World   xiv, 41, 46, 61, 66, 97, 127, 155, 204
  Third-Worldism   138, 141, 196
traditional imperialism. See imperialism
transnational corporations   xi, 127, 152, 155,
  173, 192, 193, 197, 200, 209, 212, 217, 219,
  222, 228, 235, 236, 243, 250
Transnational corporations   198, 199, 227
Trotsky, Leon   xiii, 21, 23, 24, 34–35, 36, 37, 51,
  53, 54, 65, 100, 131
Turkey   xv, 22, 27, 28, 35, 49, 156, 157, 163–
  164, 166, 167, 168, 169, 170, 172, 176, 179,
  211, 227

UNASUR   175
underconsumption   9, 29, 32, 63, 67, 143,
  149, 190
underconsumptionism   32, 39, 40, 190
underdevelopment   xi, xiii, xv, 9, 11, 18, 19, 21,
  28, 32, 34, 35, 39, 40, 41, 45, 47, 51, 52, 54,
  59, 60, 61, 62, 66, 67, 70, 71, 72, 73, 74, 75,
  76, 77, 78, 79, 83, 85, 86, 87, 88, 90, 91,
  95, 98, 99, 110, 111, 113, 114, 115, 119, 125,
  126, 127, 128, 130, 131, 133–134, 135, 137,
  144, 180, 181, 185, 195, 197, 209, 219, 223,
  227, 228, 229, 232, 233, 239, 240, 241,
  246, 248, 249, 251
unemployment   60, 72, 152, 184, 195, 201
unequal and combined development   xiii,
  51, 65, 83, 119, 211, See also uneven and
  combined development
unequal exchange   xv, 10, 45–46, 53, 62, 95,
  97, 185, 186, 204, 214, 232–233, 234, 235,
  236, 237, 240, 245
uneven and combined development   34–35,
  36, See also unequal and combined
  development
United Nations Economic Commission for
  Latin America and the Caribbean.
  See ECLAC
United States   5, 6, 9, 10, 21, 23, 26, 32, 35, 39,
  40, 41, 48, 49, 53, 59, 60, 61, 64, 66, 68,
  73, 75, 93, 94, 95, 99, 103, 104, 105, 107,
  120, 129, 131, 134, 135, 136, 138, 150, 151,
  152, 153, 154, 155, 156, 157, 158, 159, 160,

United States (*cont.*)
  161, 162, 163, 164, 165, 166, 167, 168, 169,
  170, 171, 172, 173, 175, 176, 178, 179, 184,
  189, 191, 193, 194, 195, 196, 200, 202, 203,
  204, 205, 207, 208, 210, 211, 212, 214, 216,
  220, 221, 224, 225, 226, 227, 228, 229,
  230, 236, 241, 245, 246, 247, 249, 250
USSR. *See* Soviet Union

value chain   xv, 153, 209, 210, 211, 222, 235, 250
  global   192, 193, 194, 195, 197, 200, 216, 220,
  225, 235
value of labor power   9, 46, 182, 183, 184, 186,
  187, 190, 192, 193, 194, 194t.1, 228, 229, 231
value, law of   30, 40, 43, 44, 45, 48, 61, 62, 98,
  127, 132, 133, 185, 189, 237, 238
value, theory of   xv, 9, 43, 44, 189, 232, 248
Venezuela   62, 75, 135, 139, 176, 177, 247–248,
  249, 250
Vietnam   54, 138, 142, 156, 169, 220

wage-labor   xii, 5, 6, 11, 42, 72, 79, 95, 112, 113,
  117, 118, 119, 120, 123, 124, 137, 140, 141, 181,

  182, 183, 186, 188, 190, 191, 192, 193, 196,
  209, 223, 242
wages   6, 9, 42, 45, 46, 53, 60, 61, 63, 72, 97,
  139, 152, 180, 181, 183, 184, 186, 188, 189,
  190, 191, 192, 194, 196, 197, 198, 199, 200,
  215, 220, 221, 222, 232, 233, 236, 240, 250
Wallerstein, Immanuel   xiii, 93–99, 100–101,
  102–106, 107–109, 110, 116–118, 119, 121,
  122, 123, 124
Warren, Bill   12, 127, 128–129, 130, 132, 138,
  140, 142, 143, 144
world market   9, 11, 34, 43, 47, 51, 63, 70, 77,
  79, 88, 89, 98, 110, 113, 114, 117, 119, 133,
  137, 144, 173, 178, 180, 185, 186, 188, 193,
  222, 237
World War
  First   21, 23, 24, 37, 161, 164
  Second   49, 161, 175
  Third   155
world-system theory   xiii, 93–109, 110, 116–
  117, 118, 121, 123, 124, 204, 206, 210

Yugoslavia   54, 138, 140

CPSIA information can be obtained
at www.ICGtesting.com
Printed in the USA
JSHW030036260123
36867JS00002B/3